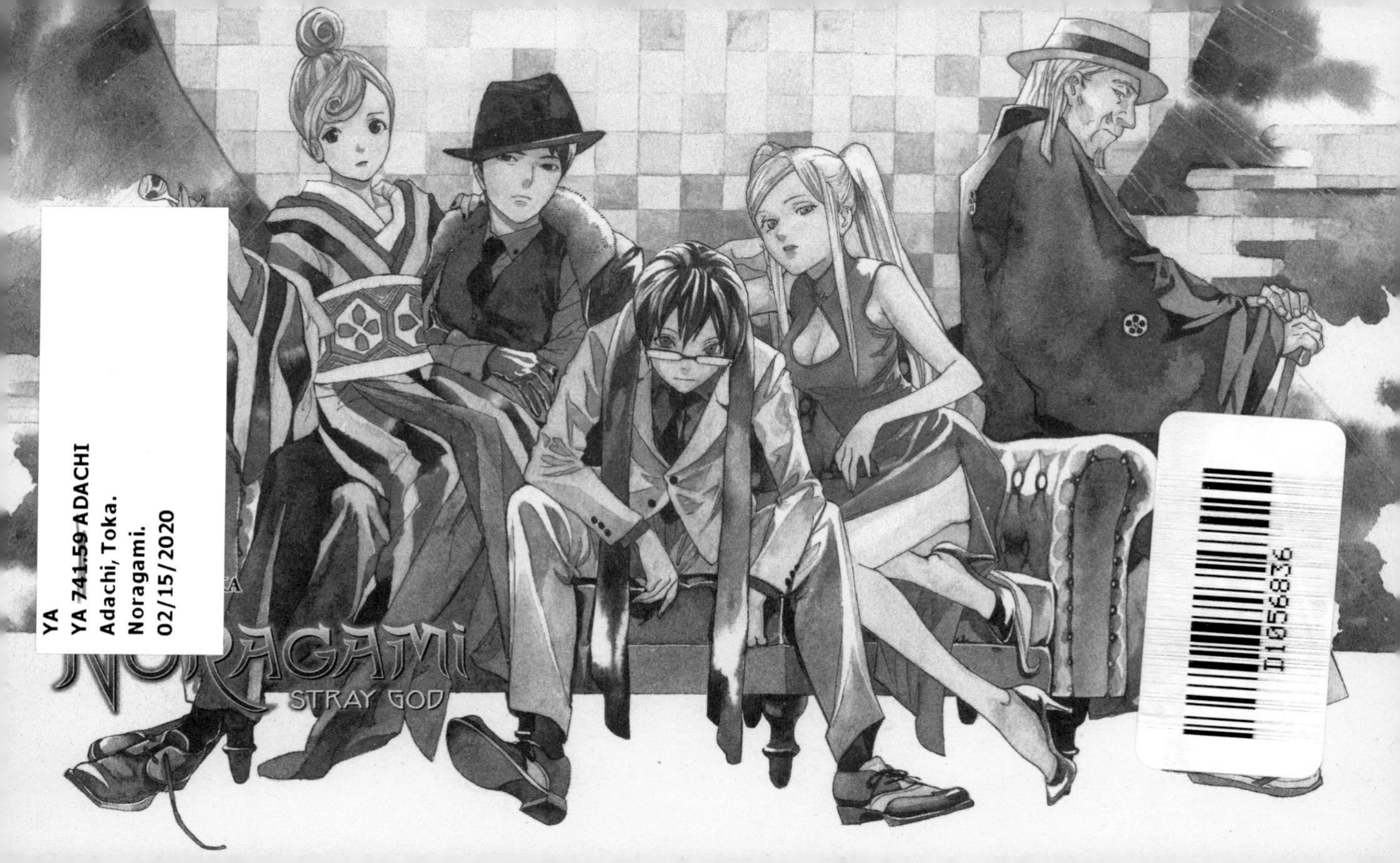
NORAGAMI
STRAY GOD

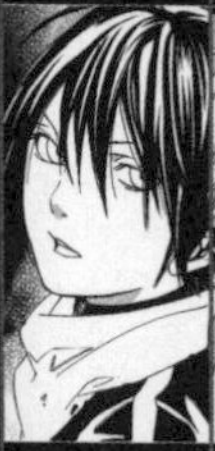

YATO

A minor deity who always wears a sweatsuit.

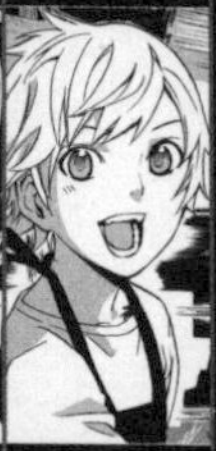

YUKINÉ

Yato's shinki who turns into swords.

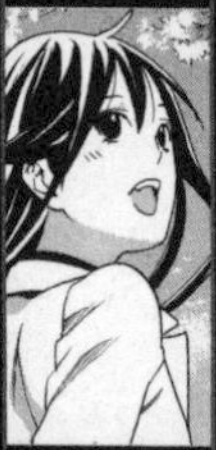

HIYORI IKI

A high school student who has become half ayakashi.

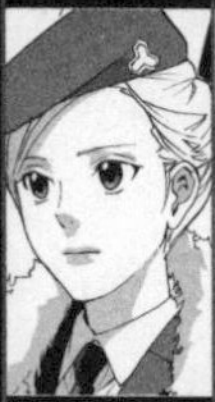

BISHAMONTEN

A powerful warrior god, one of the Seven Gods of Fortune.

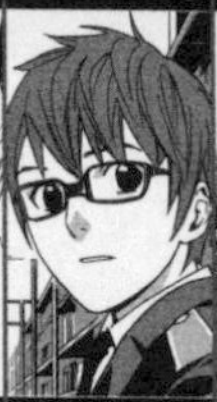

KAZUMA

A navigational shinki who serves as guide to Bishamon.

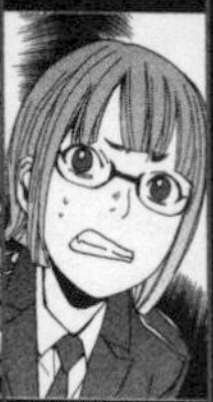

TSUGUHA

A shinki who turns into Bishamon's battledress.

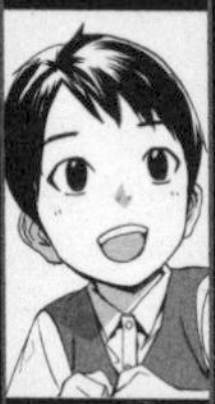

EBISU

A business-god in the making, one of the Seven Gods of Fortune.

characters

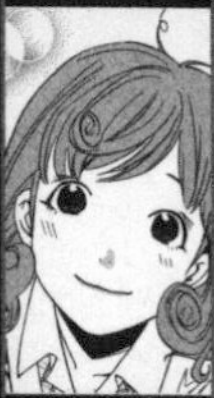

KOFUKU

A goddess of poverty who calls herself Ebisu, after the god of fortune.

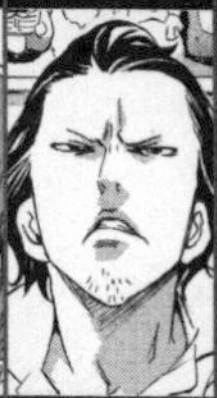

DAIKOKU

Kofuku's shinki who summons storms.

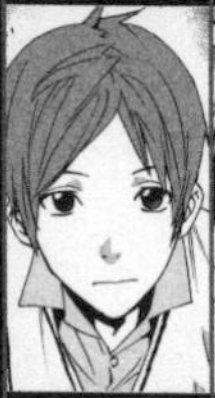

KÔTO FUJISAKI

Yato's "father."

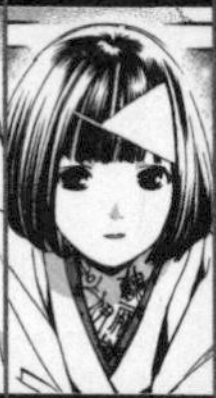

STRAY

A shinki who serves an unspecified number of deities.

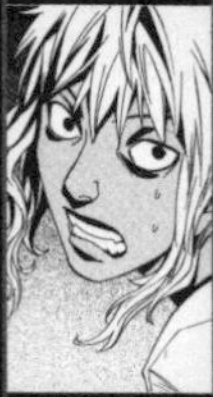

KUGAHA

A shinki who once deceived Bishamon.

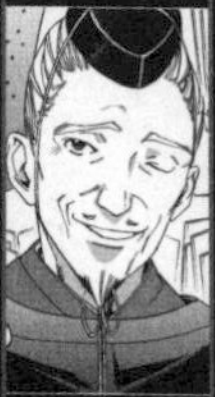

TENJIN

The god of learning, Sugawara no Michizane.

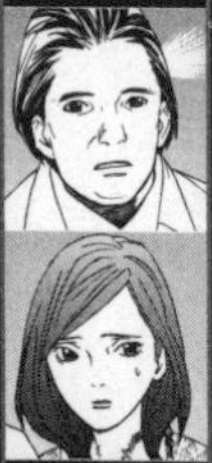

HIYORI'S PARENTS

They run a hospital.

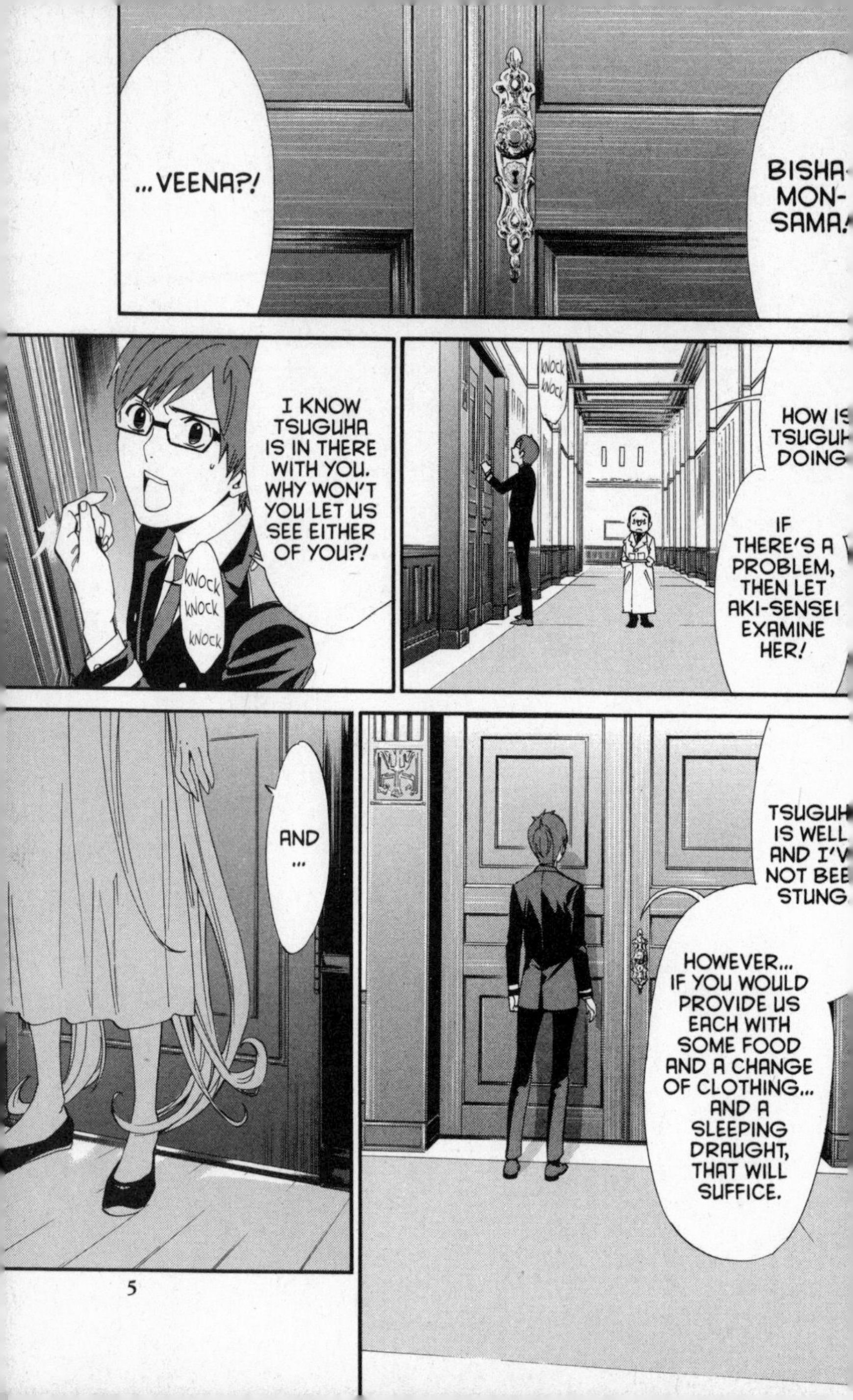
BISHA-MON-SAMA!
...VEENA?!
KNOCK KNOCK
HOW IS TSUGUH DOING
IF THERE'S A PROBLEM, THEN LET AKI-SENSEI EXAMINE HER!
I KNOW TSUGUHA IS IN THERE WITH YOU. WHY WON'T YOU LET US SEE EITHER OF YOU?!
KNOCK KNOCK KNOCK
TSUGUH IS WELL AND I'V NOT BEE STUNG.
HOWEVER... IF YOU WOULD PROVIDE US EACH WITH SOME FOOD AND A CHANGE OF CLOTHING... AND A SLEEPING DRAUGHT, THAT WILL SUFFICE.
AND ...

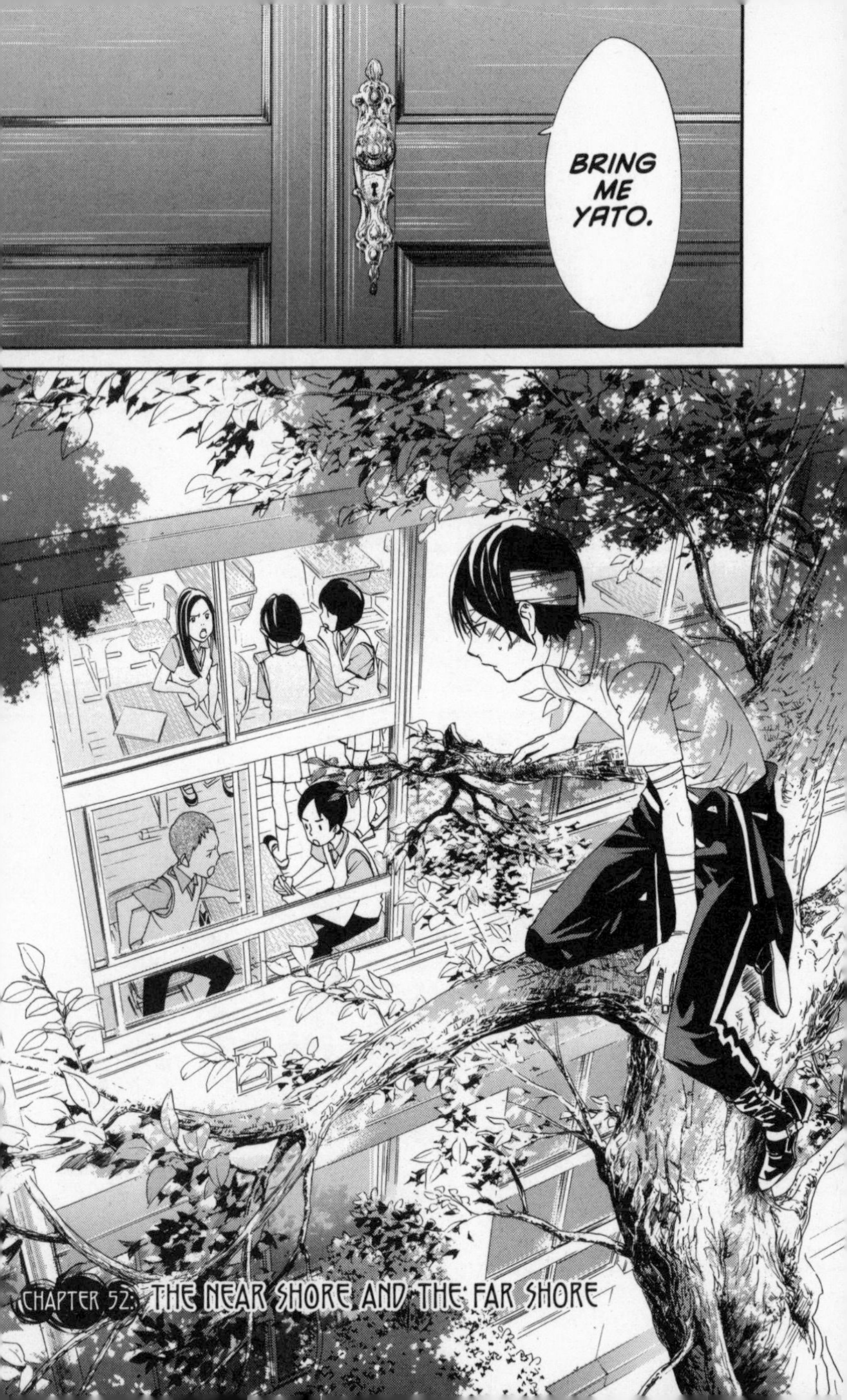
BRING ME YATO.
CHAPTER 52: THE NEAR SHORE AND THE FAR SHORE

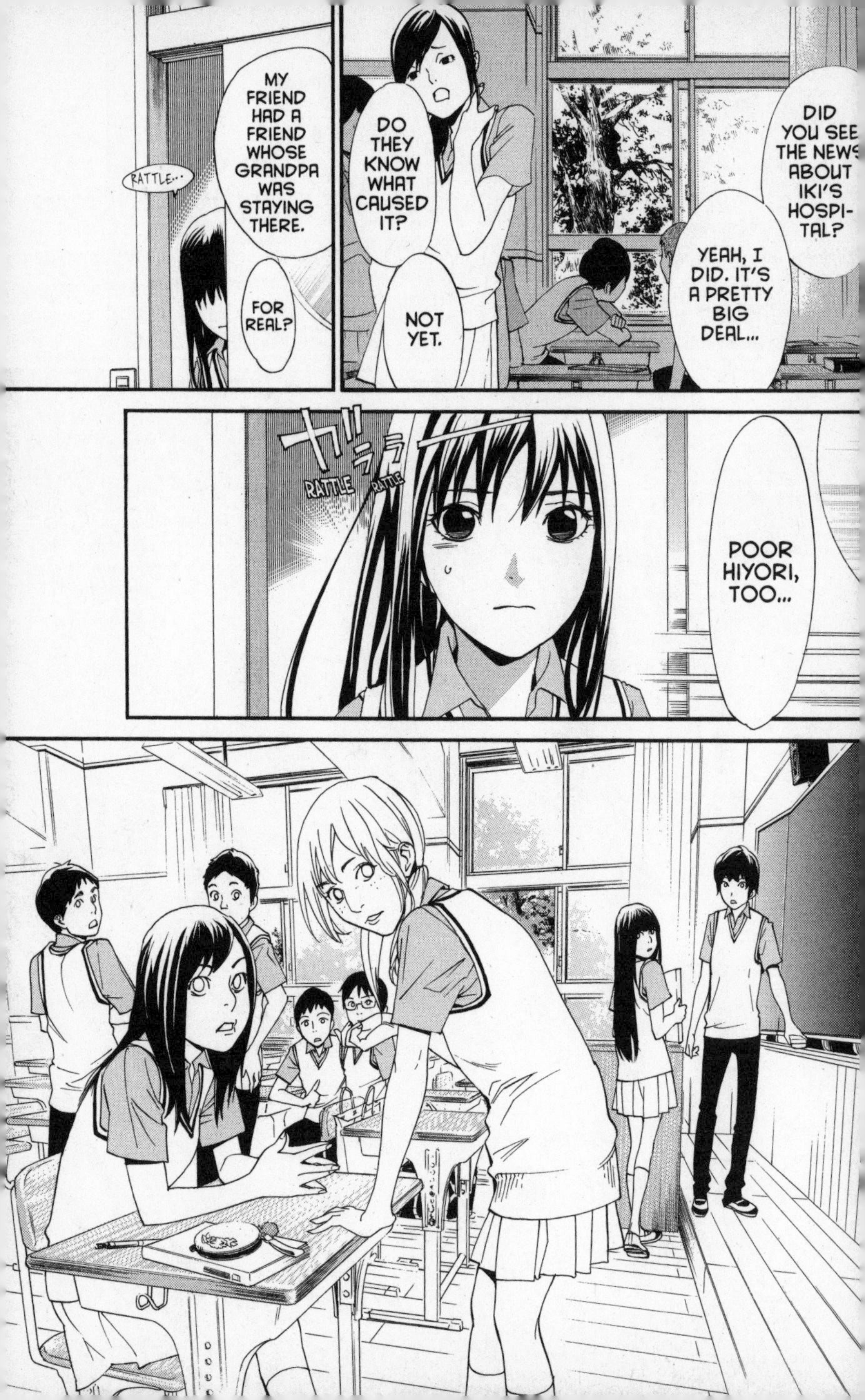
DID YOU SEE THE NEWS ABOUT IKI'S HOSPI-TAL?
YEAH, I DID. IT'S A PRETTY BIG DEAL...
DO THEY KNOW WHAT CAUSED IT?
NOT YET.
MY FRIEND HAD A FRIEND WHOSE GRANDPA WAS STAYING THERE.
FOR REAL?
RATTLE...
POOR HIYORI, TOO...
RATTLE RATTLE

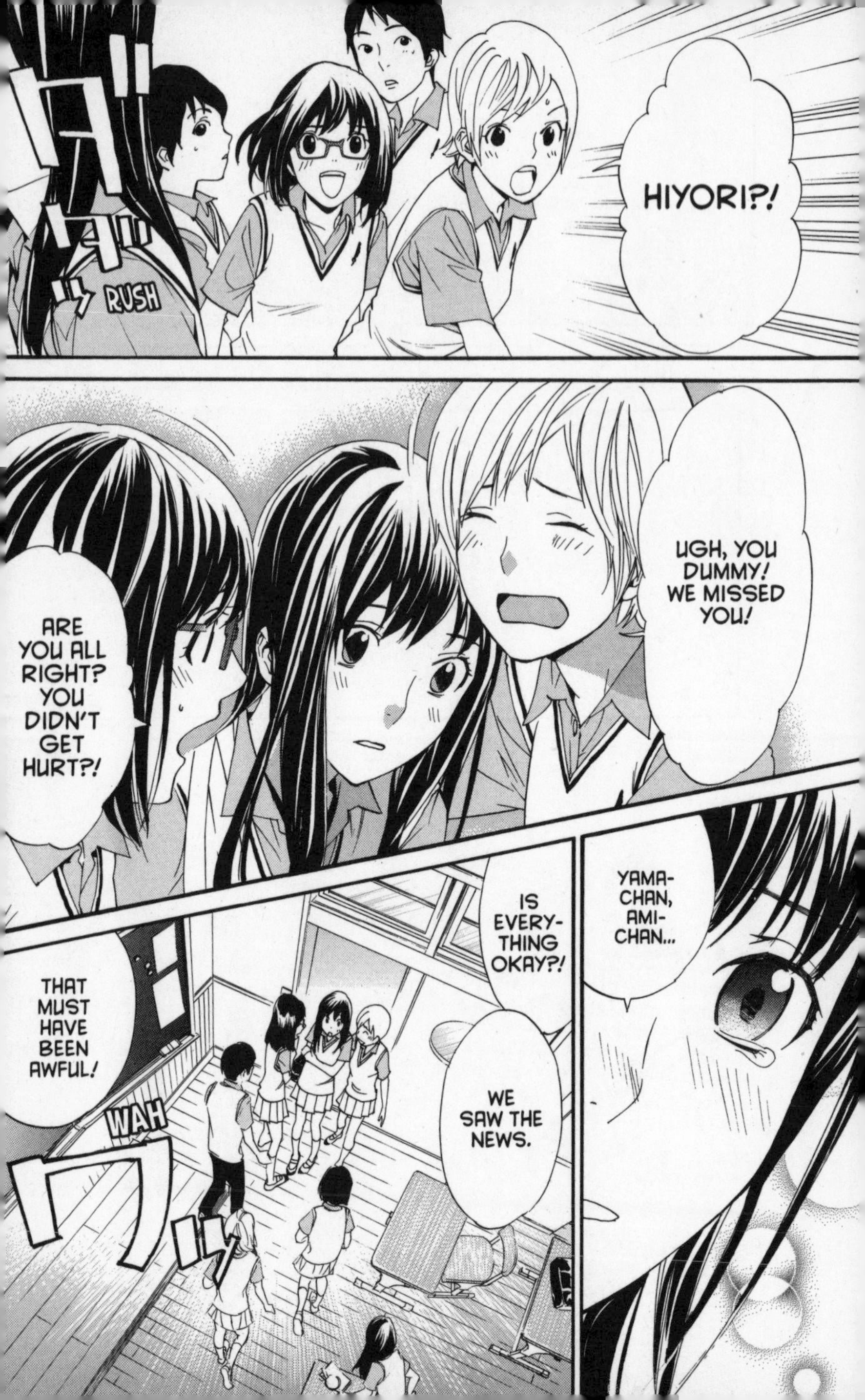
HIYORI?!
RUSH
UGH, YOU DUMMY! WE MISSED YOU!
ARE YOU ALL RIGHT? YOU DIDN'T GET HURT?!
YAMA-CHAN, AMI-CHAN...
IS EVERY-THING OKAY?!
WE SAW THE NEWS.
THAT MUST HAVE BEEN AWFUL!
WAH

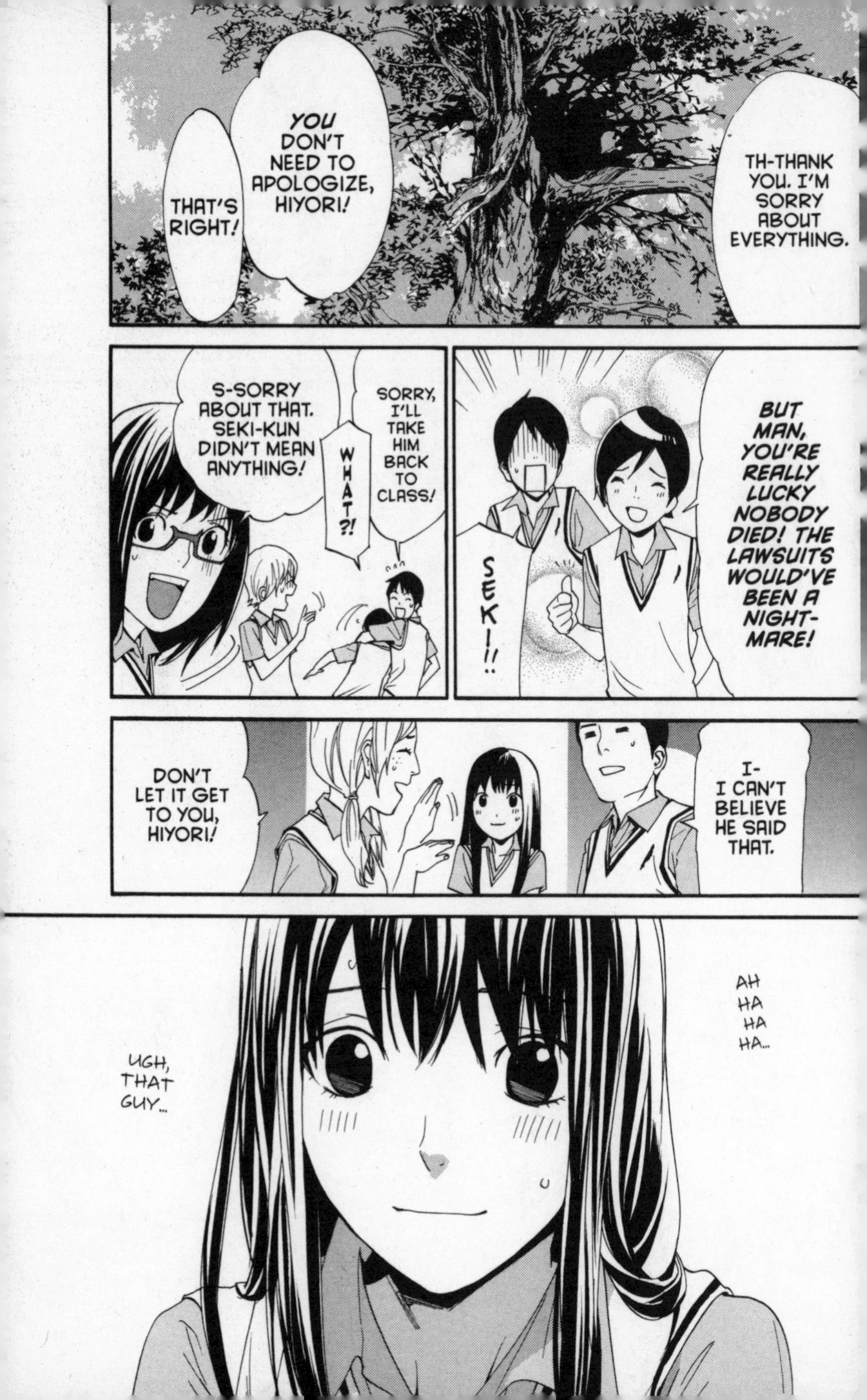
TH-THANK YOU. I'M SORRY ABOUT EVERYTHING.
YOU DON'T NEED TO APOLOGIZE, HIYORI!
THAT'S RIGHT!
BUT MAN, YOU'RE REALLY LUCKY NOBODY DIED! THE LAWSUITS WOULD'VE BEEN A NIGHT-MARE!
SEKI!!
SORRY, I'LL TAKE HIM BACK TO CLASS!
WHAT?!
S-SORRY ABOUT THAT. SEKI-KUN DIDN'T MEAN ANYTHING!
I- I CAN'T BELIEVE HE SAID THAT.
DON'T LET IT GET TO YOU, HIYORI!
AH HA HA HA...
UGH, THAT GUY...

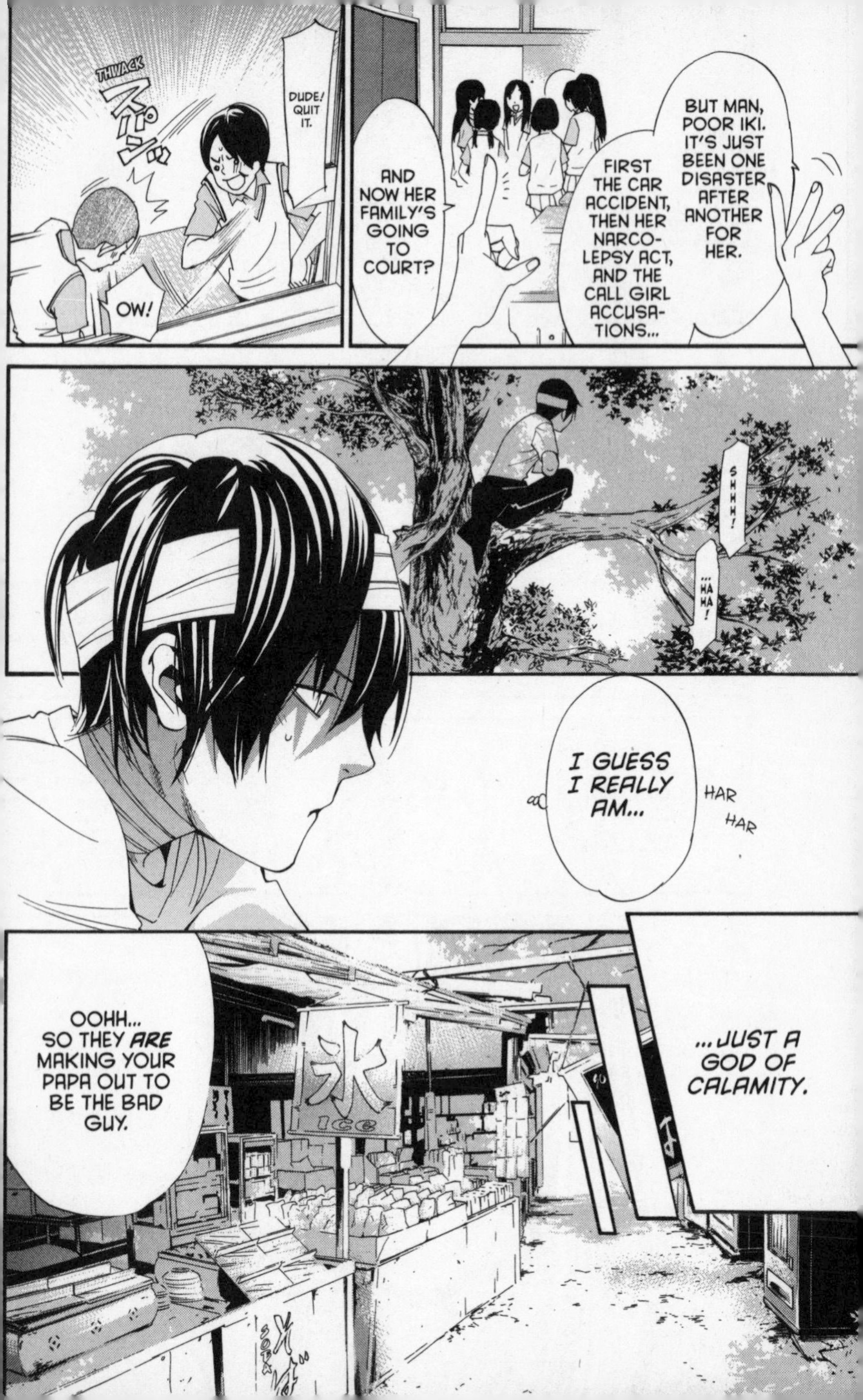
BUT MAN, POOR IKI. IT'S JUST BEEN ONE DISASTER AFTER ANOTHER FOR HER.
FIRST THE CAR ACCIDENT, THEN HER NARCOLEPSY ACT, AND THE CALL GIRL ACCUSATIONS...
AND NOW HER FAMILY'S GOING TO COURT?
THWACK
DUDE! QUIT IT.
OW!
SHHH!
...HA HA!
I GUESS I REALLY AM...
HAR HAR
...JUST A GOD OF CALAMITY.
氷
ICE
OOHH... SO THEY *ARE* MAKING YOUR PAPA OUT TO BE THE BAD GUY.

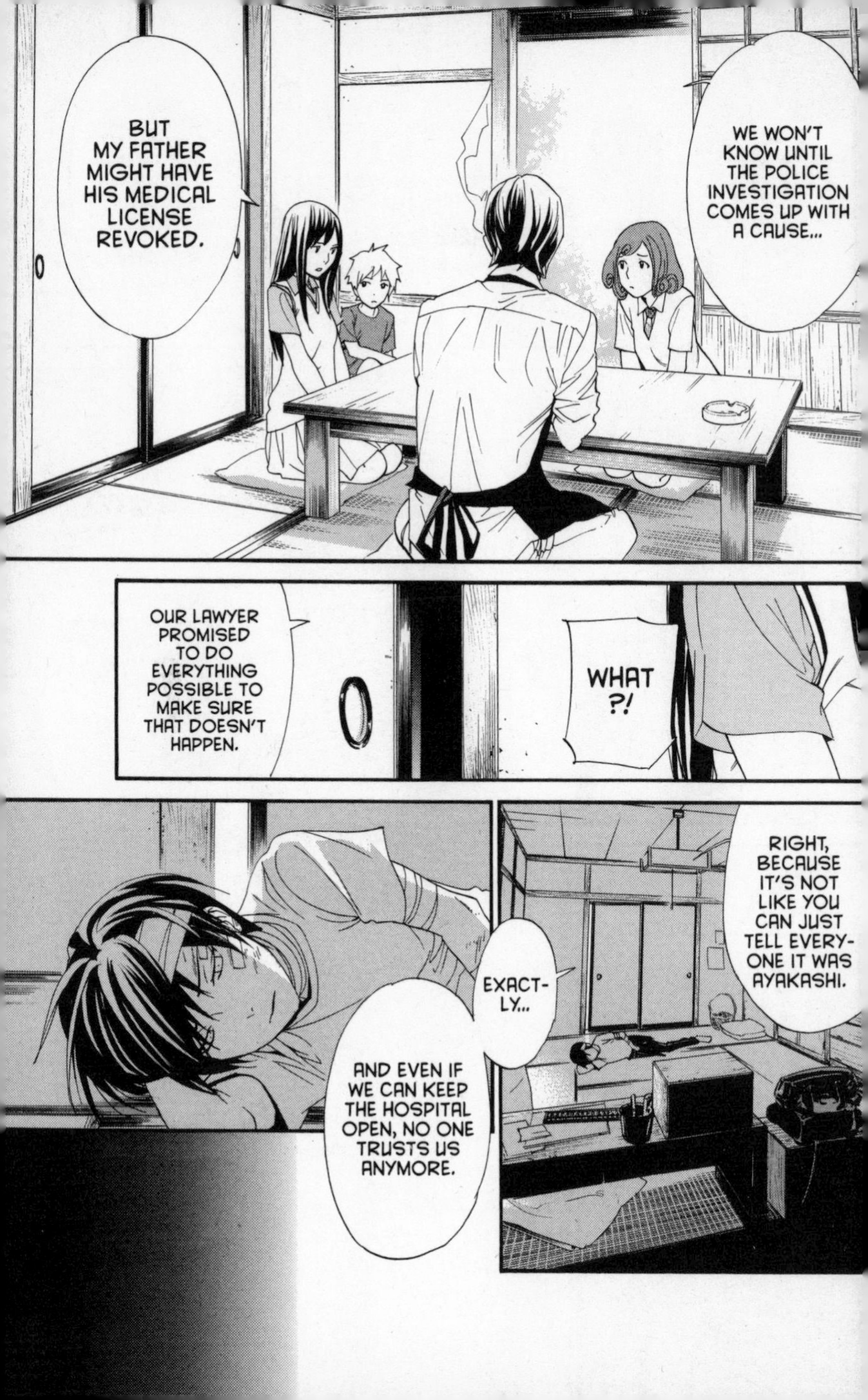
WE WON'T KNOW UNTIL THE POLICE INVESTIGATION COMES UP WITH A CAUSE...
BUT MY FATHER MIGHT HAVE HIS MEDICAL LICENSE REVOKED.
WHAT ?!
OUR LAWYER PROMISED TO DO EVERYTHING POSSIBLE TO MAKE SURE THAT DOESN'T HAPPEN.
RIGHT, BECAUSE IT'S NOT LIKE YOU CAN JUST TELL EVERY-ONE IT WAS AYAKASHI.
EXACT-LY...
AND EVEN IF WE CAN KEEP THE HOSPITAL OPEN, NO ONE TRUSTS US ANYMORE.

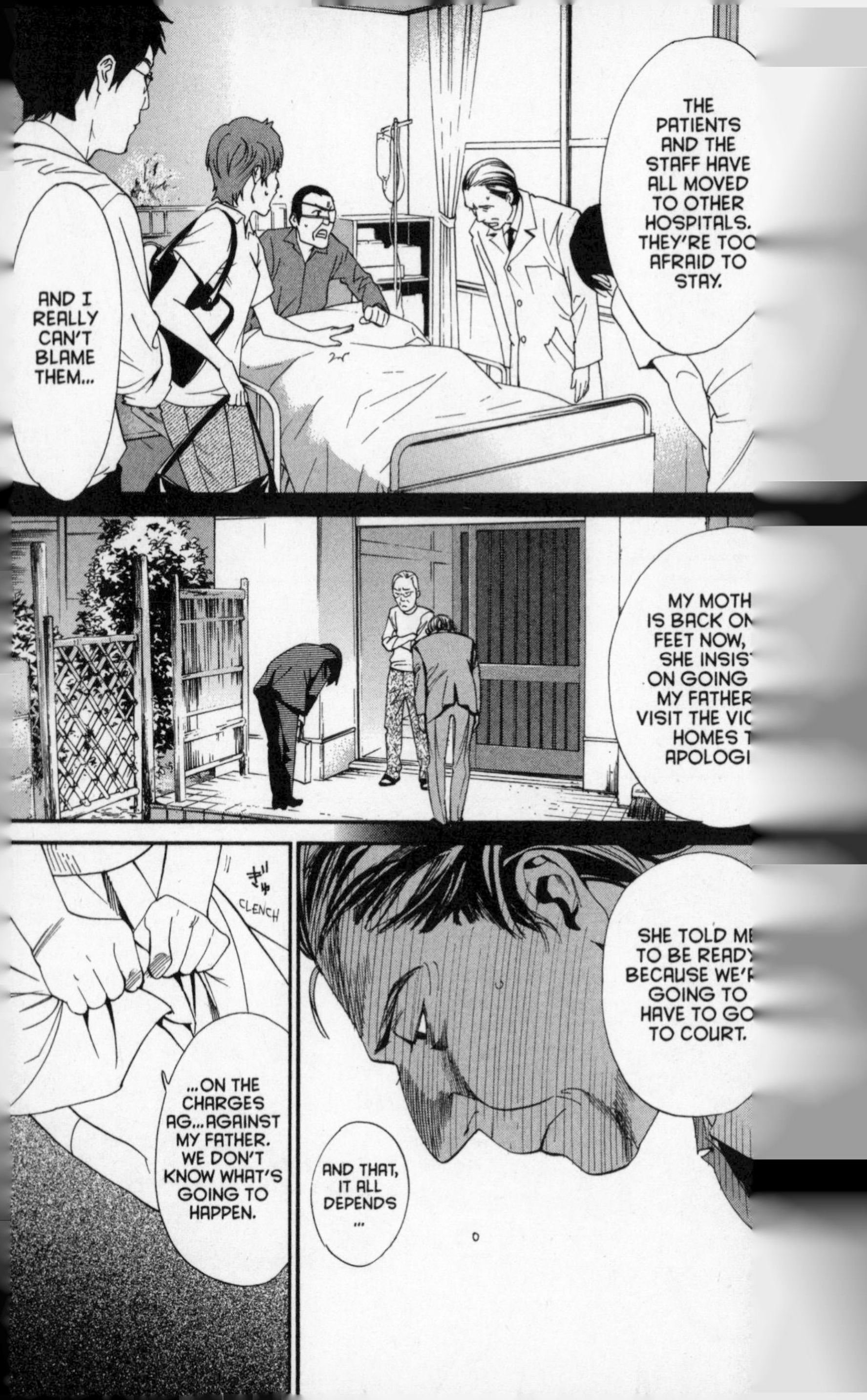
THE PATIENTS AND THE STAFF HAVE ALL MOVED TO OTHER HOSPITALS. THEY'RE TOO AFRAID TO STAY.
AND I REALLY CAN'T BLAME THEM...
MY MOTH IS BACK ON FEET NOW, SHE INSIS ON GOING MY FATHER VISIT THE VIC HOMES T APOLOGI
SHE TOLD ME TO BE READY BECAUSE WE'R GOING TO HAVE TO GO TO COURT.
AND THAT, IT ALL DEPENDS ...
ぎゅ
CLENCH
...ON THE CHARGES AG...AGAINST MY FATHER. WE DON'T KNOW WHAT'S GOING TO HAPPEN.

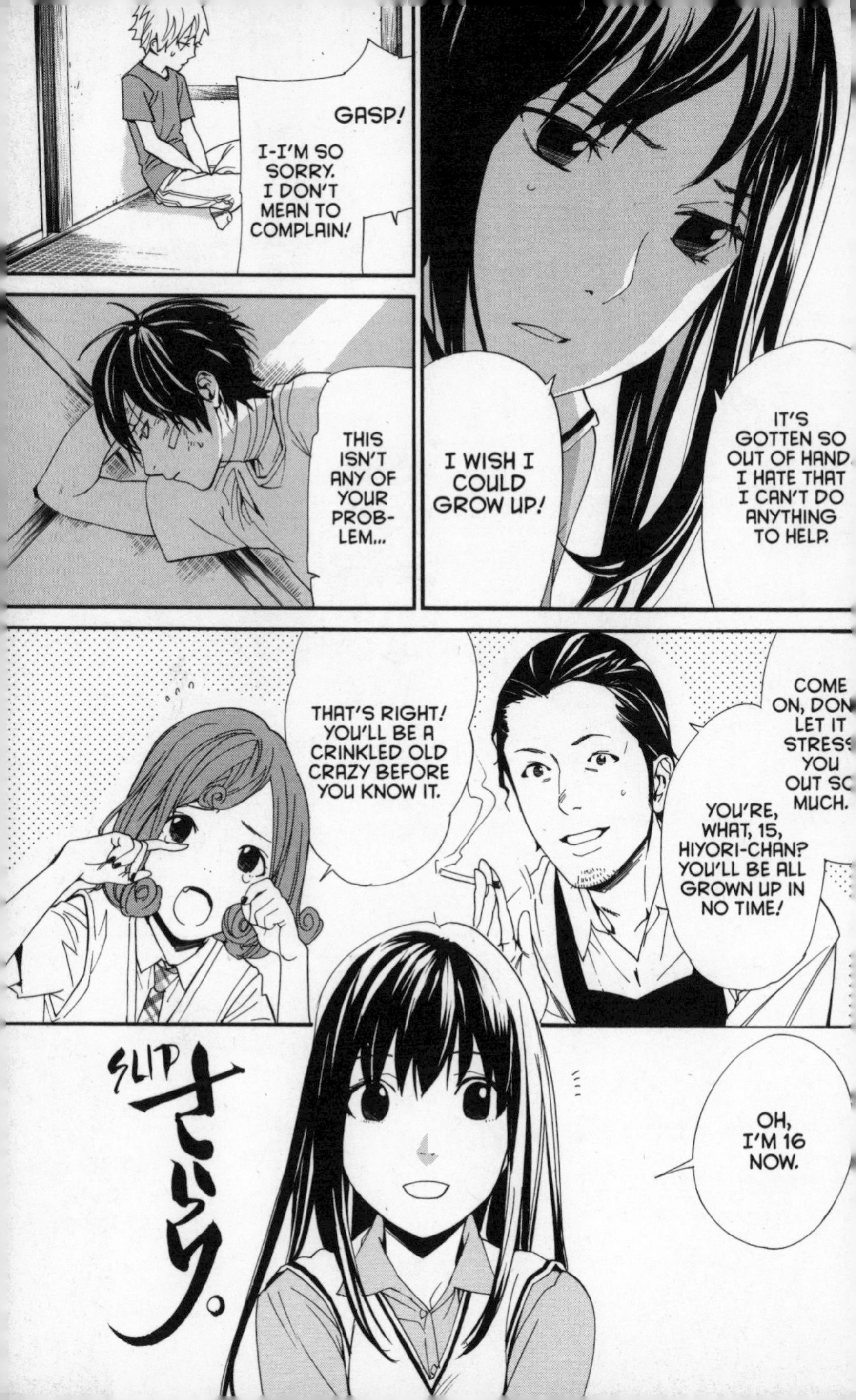
IT'S GOTTEN SO OUT OF HAND. I HATE THAT I CAN'T DO ANYTHING TO HELP.
I WISH I COULD GROW UP!
GASP!
I-I'M SO SORRY. I DON'T MEAN TO COMPLAIN!
THIS ISN'T ANY OF YOUR PROB-LEM...
COME ON, DON LET IT STRESS YOU OUT SO MUCH.
YOU'RE, WHAT, 15, HIYORI-CHAN? YOU'LL BE ALL GROWN UP IN NO TIME!
THAT'S RIGHT! YOU'LL BE A CRINKLED OLD CRAZY BEFORE YOU KNOW IT.
OH, I'M 16 NOW.
SLIP

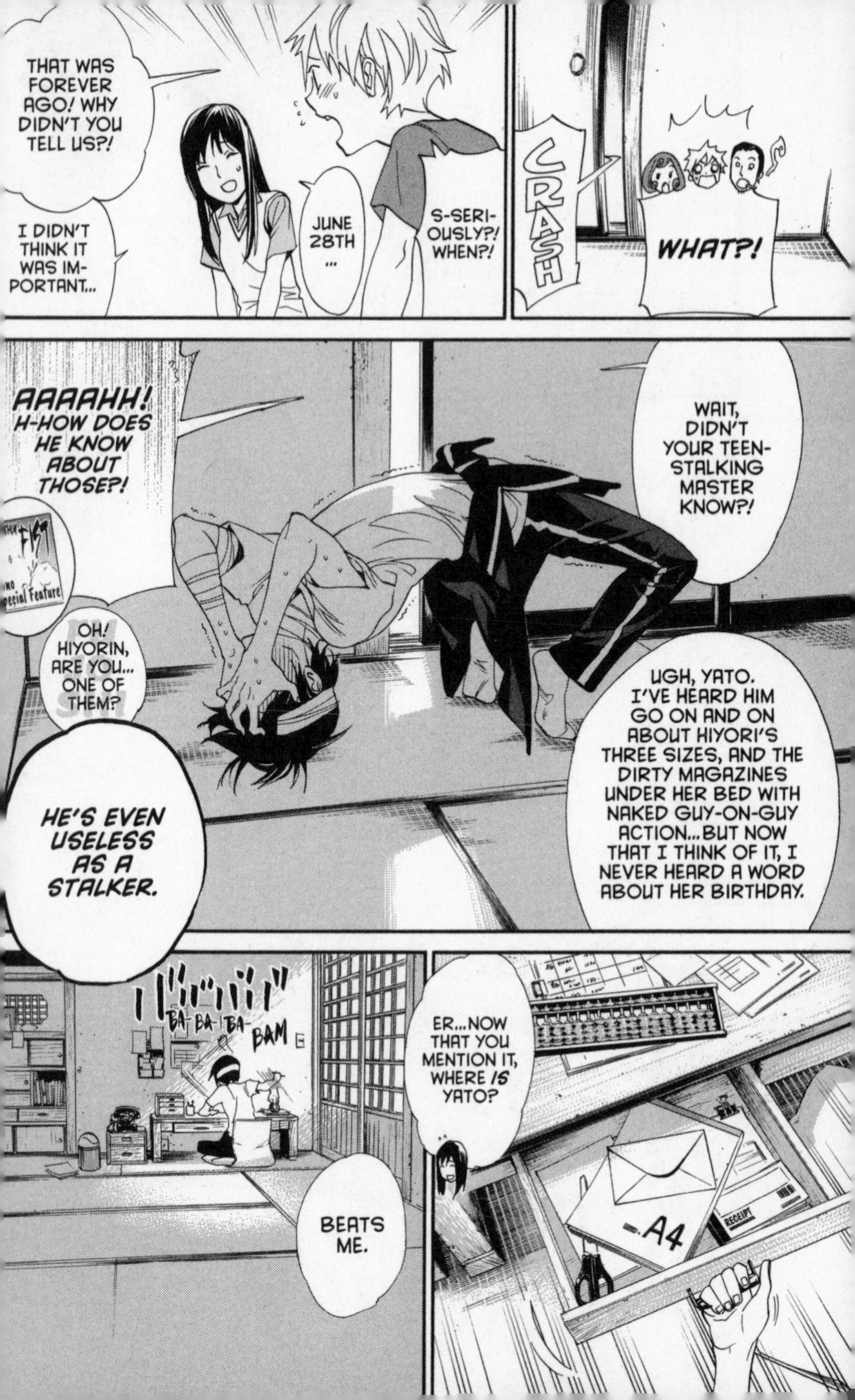
CRASH
WHAT?!
S-SERIOUSLY?! WHEN?!
JUNE 28TH ...
THAT WAS FOREVER AGO! WHY DIDN'T YOU TELL US?!
I DIDN'T THINK IT WAS IMPORTANT...
WAIT, DIDN'T YOUR TEEN-STALKING MASTER KNOW?!
AAAAHH! H-HOW DOES HE KNOW ABOUT THOSE?!
UGH, YATO. I'VE HEARD HIM GO ON AND ON ABOUT HIYORI'S THREE SIZES, AND THE DIRTY MAGAZINES UNDER HER BED WITH NAKED GUY-ON-GUY ACTION...BUT NOW THAT I THINK OF IT, I NEVER HEARD A WORD ABOUT HER BIRTHDAY.
Special Feature
OH! HIYORIN, ARE YOU... ONE OF THEM?
HE'S EVEN USELESS AS A STALKER.
ER...NOW THAT YOU MENTION IT, WHERE IS YATO?
A4
RECEIPT
BA-BA-BA-BAM
BEATS ME.

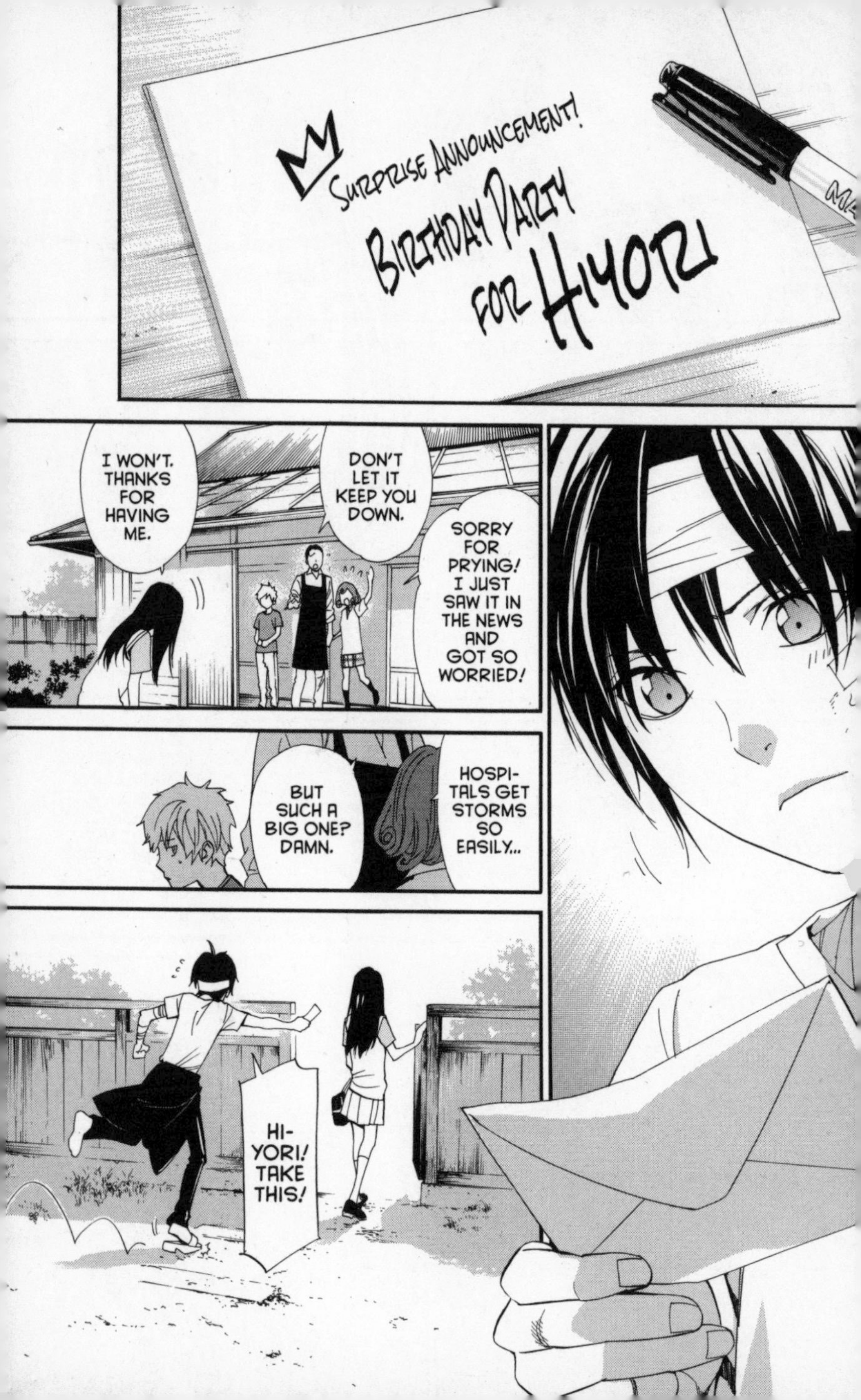
SURPRISE ANNOUNCEMENT!
BIRTHDAY PARTY FOR HIYORI
SORRY FOR PRYING! I JUST SAW IT IN THE NEWS AND GOT SO WORRIED!
DON'T LET IT KEEP YOU DOWN.
I WON'T. THANKS FOR HAVING ME.
HOSPI-TALS GET STORMS SO EASILY...
BUT SUCH A BIG ONE? DAMN.
HI-YORI! TAKE THIS!

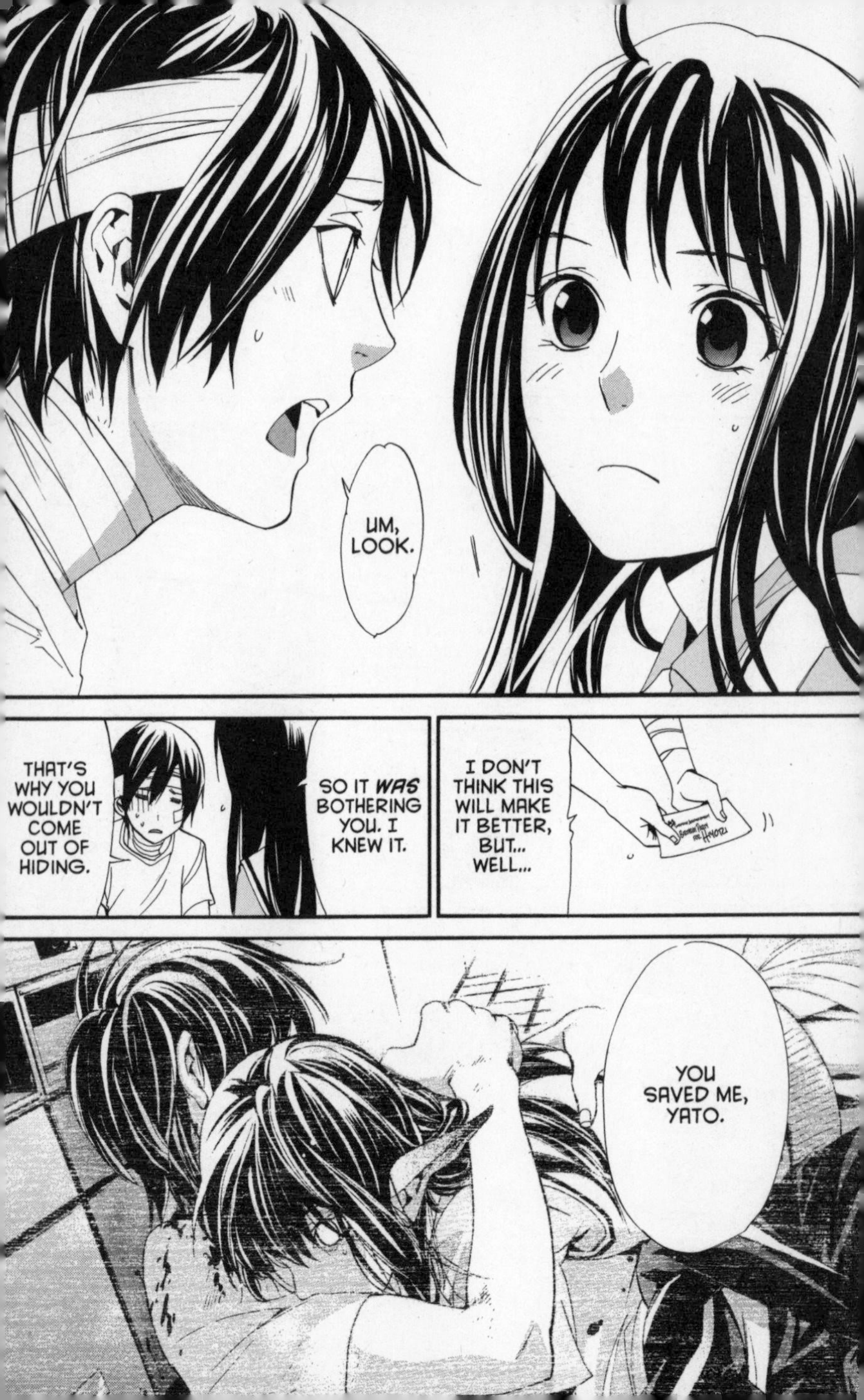
UM, LOOK.
I DON'T THINK THIS WILL MAKE IT BETTER, BUT... WELL...
SO IT *WAS* BOTHERING YOU. I KNEW IT.
THAT'S WHY YOU WOULDN'T COME OUT OF HIDING.
YOU SAVED ME, YATO.

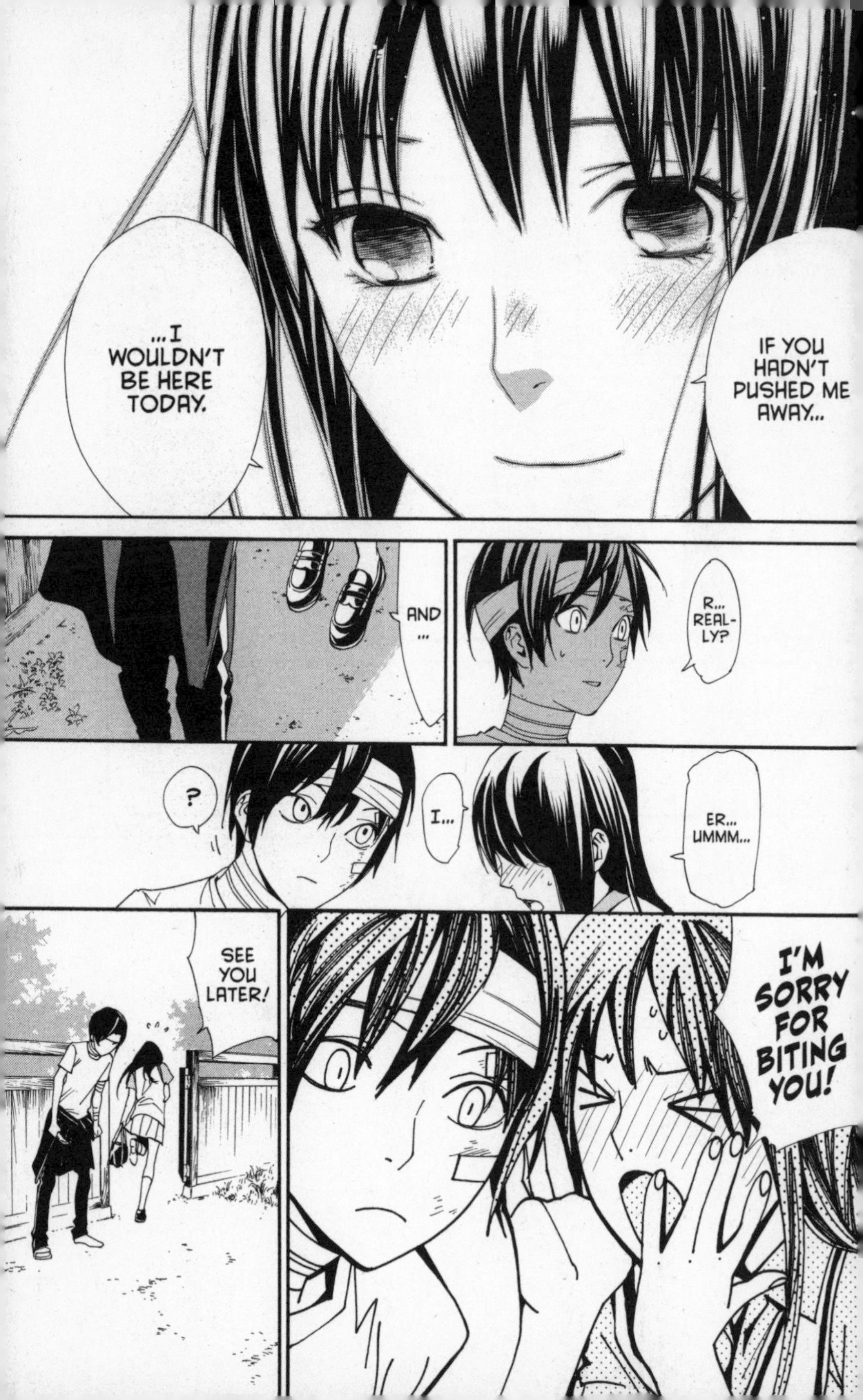
IF YOU HADN'T PUSHED ME AWAY...
...I WOULDN'T BE HERE TODAY.
R... REAL-LY?
AND ...
ER... UMMM...
I...
?
I'M SORRY FOR BITING YOU!
SEE YOU LATER!

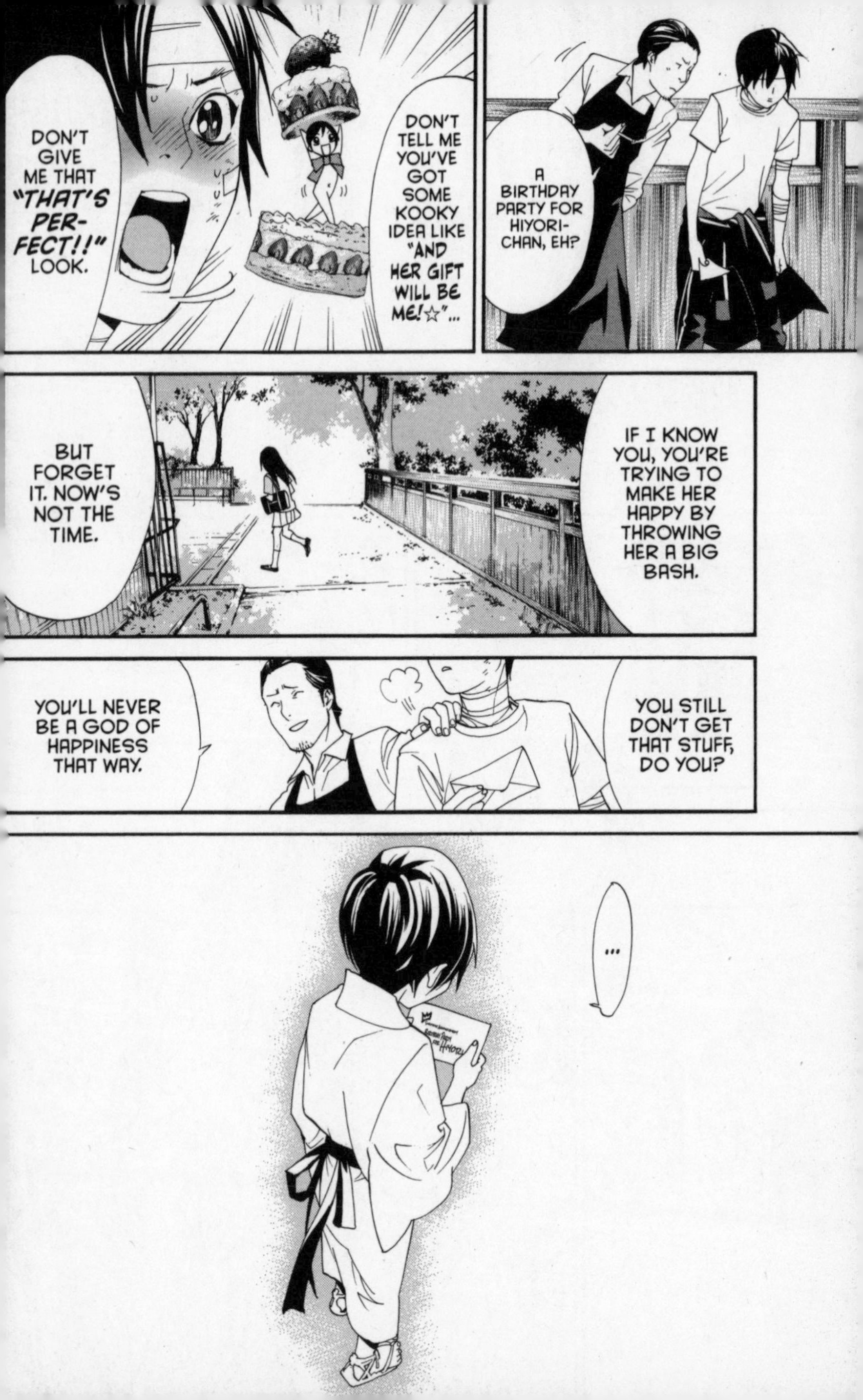
A BIRTHDAY PARTY FOR HIYORI-CHAN, EH?
DON'T TELL ME YOU'VE GOT SOME KOOKY IDEA LIKE "AND HER GIFT WILL BE ME!☆"...
DON'T GIVE ME THAT "THAT'S PERFECT!!" LOOK.
IF I KNOW YOU, YOU'RE TRYING TO MAKE HER HAPPY BY THROWING HER A BIG BASH.
BUT FORGET IT. NOW'S NOT THE TIME.
YOU STILL DON'T GET THAT STUFF, DO YOU?
YOU'LL NEVER BE A GOD OF HAPPINESS THAT WAY.
...

Uni

Career Path Survey

Grade: 1st yr Class: 1 Name: Hiyori Iki

First choice	National University, medical school
choice	

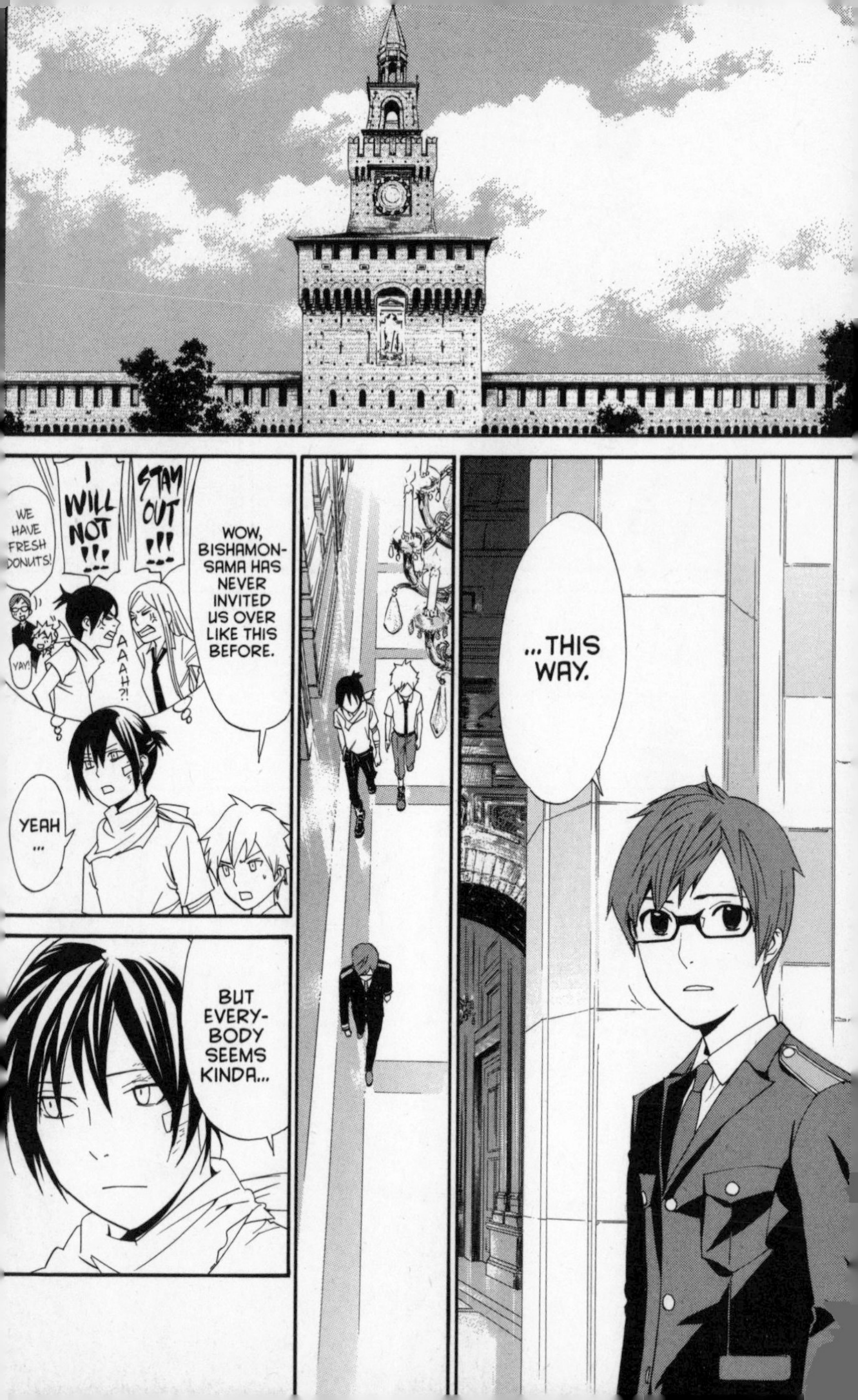
...THIS WAY.
WOW, BISHAMON-SAMA HAS NEVER INVITED US OVER LIKE THIS BEFORE.
STAY OUT!!! ...
I WILL NOT!!! ...
WE HAVE FRESH DONUTS!
AAAH?!
YAY!
YEAH ...
BUT EVERY-BODY SEEMS KINDA...

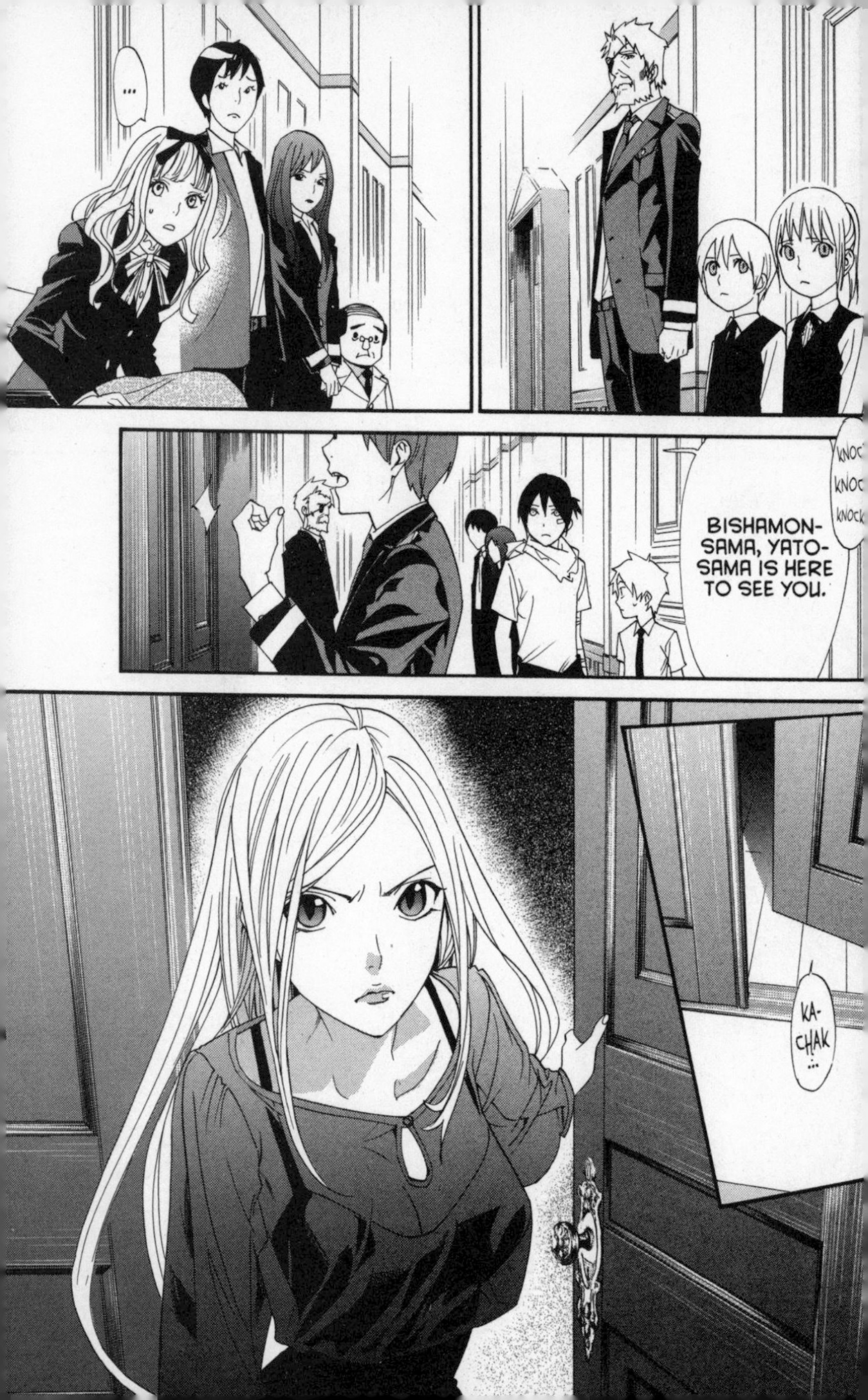
...
KNOCK KNOCK KNOCK
BISHAMON-SAMA, YATO-SAMA IS HERE TO SEE YOU.
KA-CHAK...

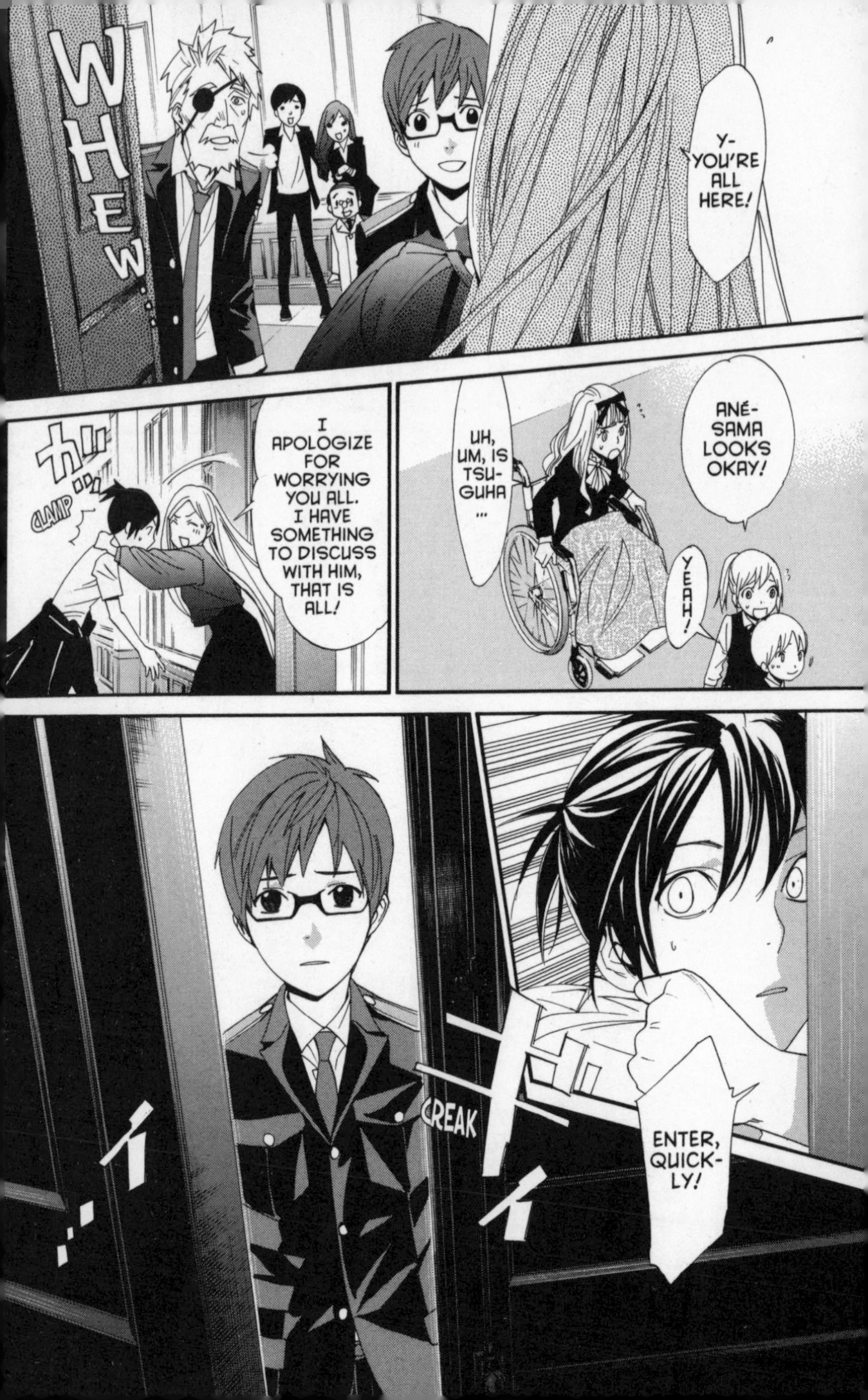
Y-YOU'RE ALL HERE!
WHEW
ANÉ-SAMA LOOKS OKAY!
UH, UM, IS TSUGUHA...
YEAH!
I APOLOGIZE FOR WORRYING YOU ALL. I HAVE SOMETHING TO DISCUSS WITH HIM, THAT IS ALL!
CLAMP
ENTER, QUICKLY!
CREAK

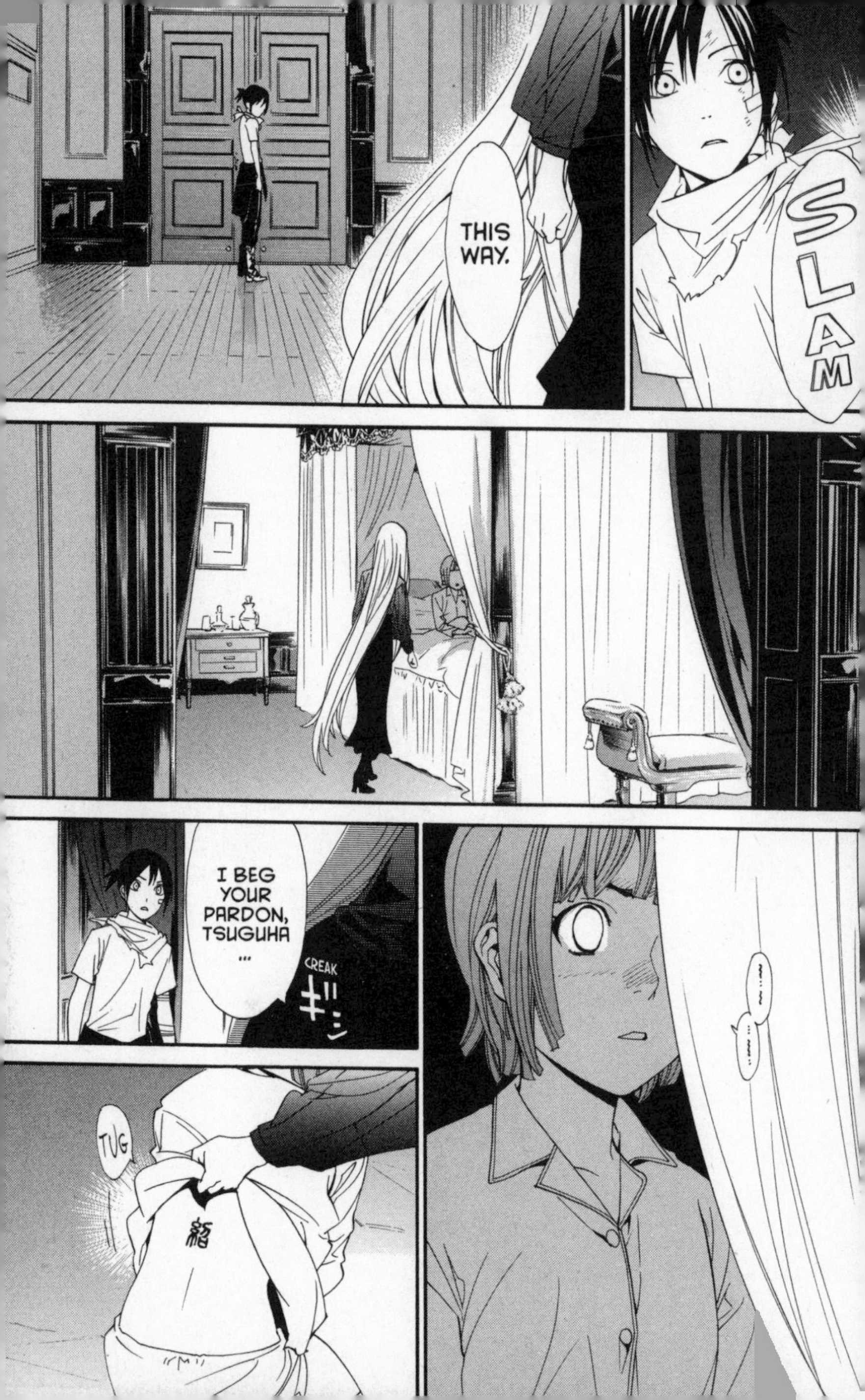
SLAM
THIS WAY.
I BEG YOUR PARDON, TSUGUHA ...
CREAK
ギッ
TUG
紹

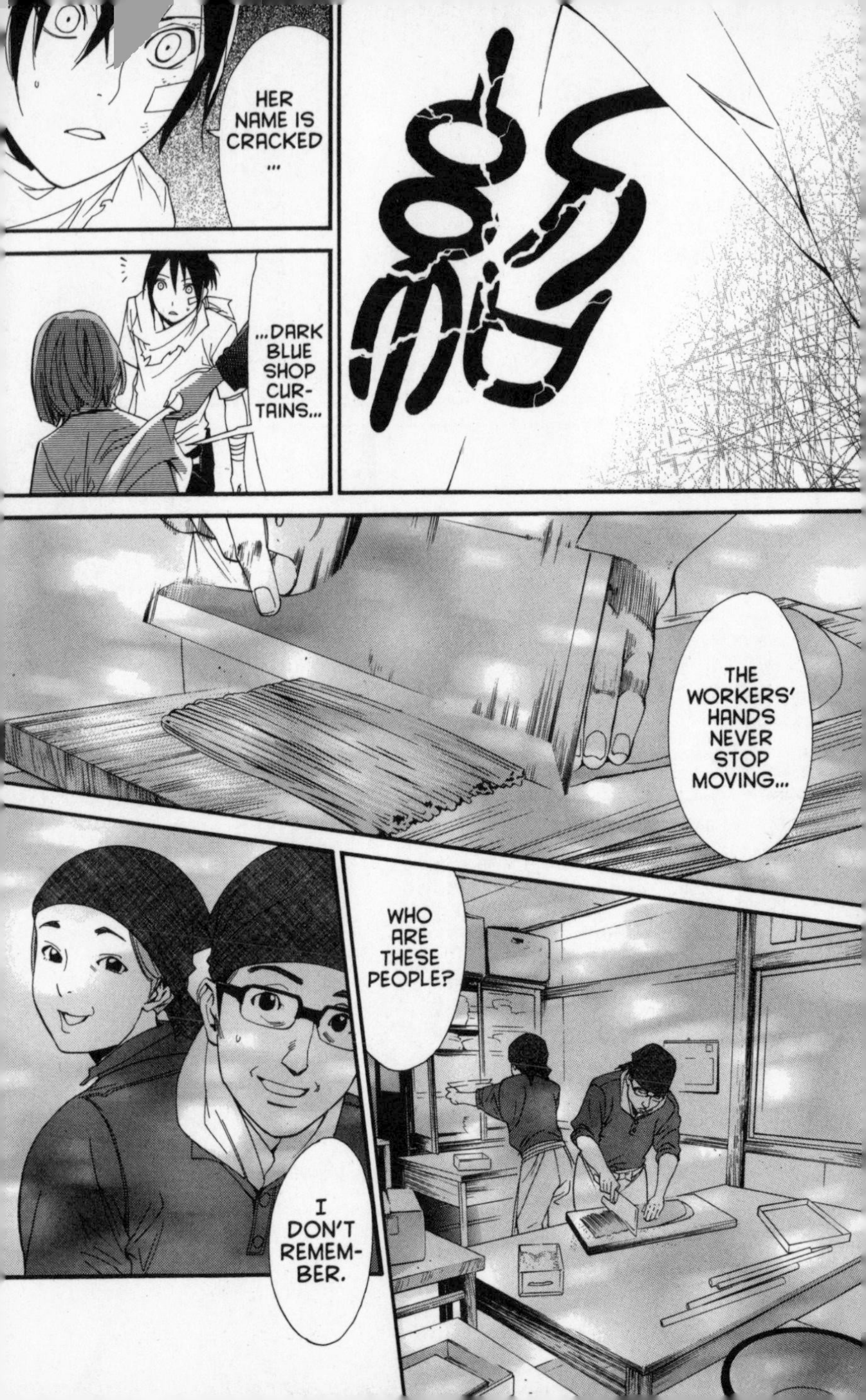
HER NAME IS CRACKED ...
...DARK BLUE SHOP CUR-TAINS...
THE WORKERS' HANDS NEVER STOP MOVING...
WHO ARE THESE PEOPLE?
I DON'T REMEM-BER.

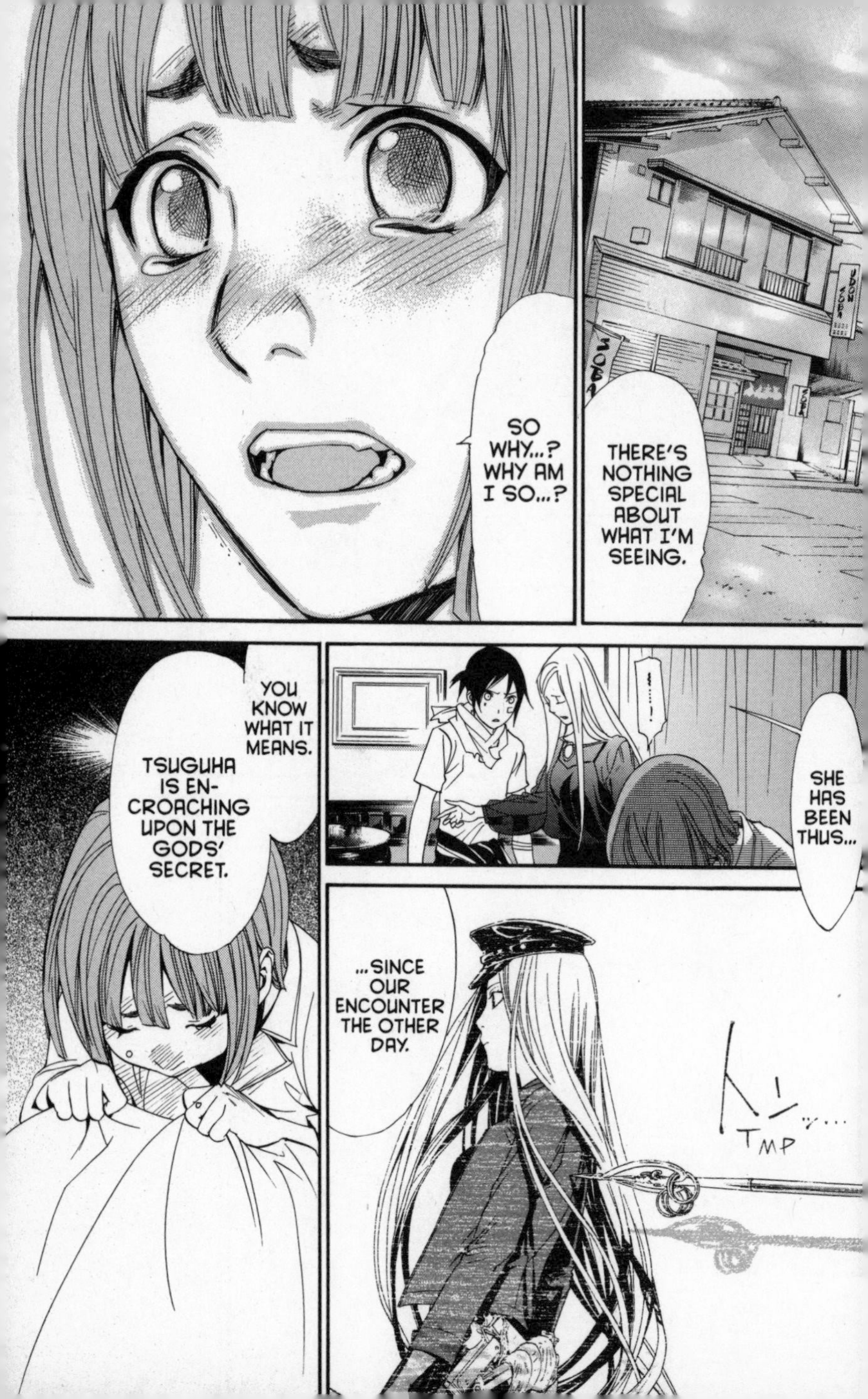
THERE'S NOTHING SPECIAL ABOUT WHAT I'M SEEING.
SO WHY...? WHY AM I SO...?
...!
SHE HAS BEEN THUS...
...SINCE OUR ENCOUNTER THE OTHER DAY.
TMP
YOU KNOW WHAT IT MEANS.
TSUGUHA IS EN-CROACHING UPON THE GODS' SECRET.

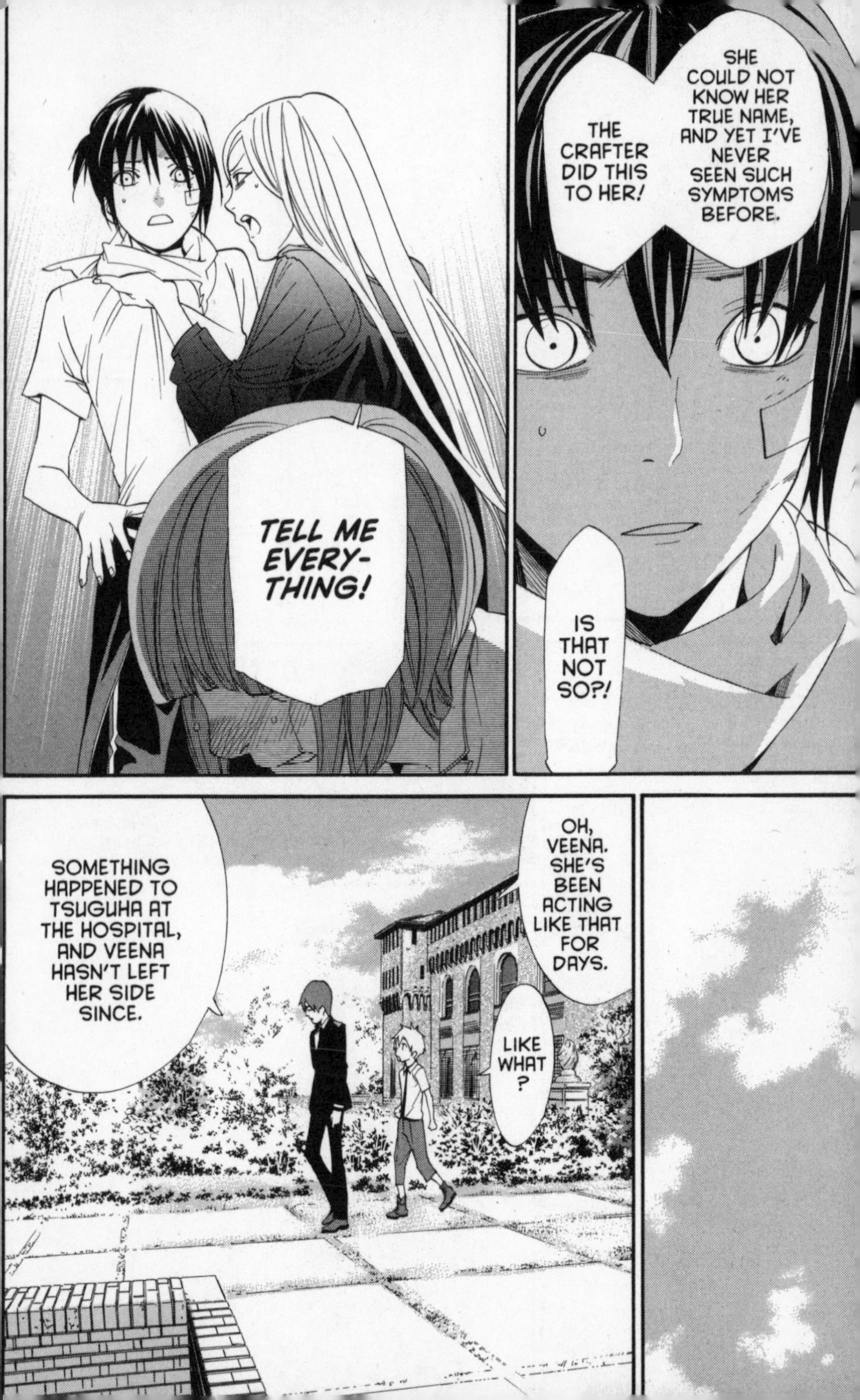
SHE COULD NOT KNOW HER TRUE NAME, AND YET I'VE NEVER SEEN SUCH SYMPTOMS BEFORE.
THE CRAFTER DID THIS TO HER!
IS THAT NOT SO?!
TELL ME EVERY-THING!
OH, VEENA. SHE'S BEEN ACTING LIKE THAT FOR DAYS.
LIKE WHAT?
SOMETHING HAPPENED TO TSUGUHA AT THE HOSPITAL, AND VEENA HASN'T LEFT HER SIDE SINCE.

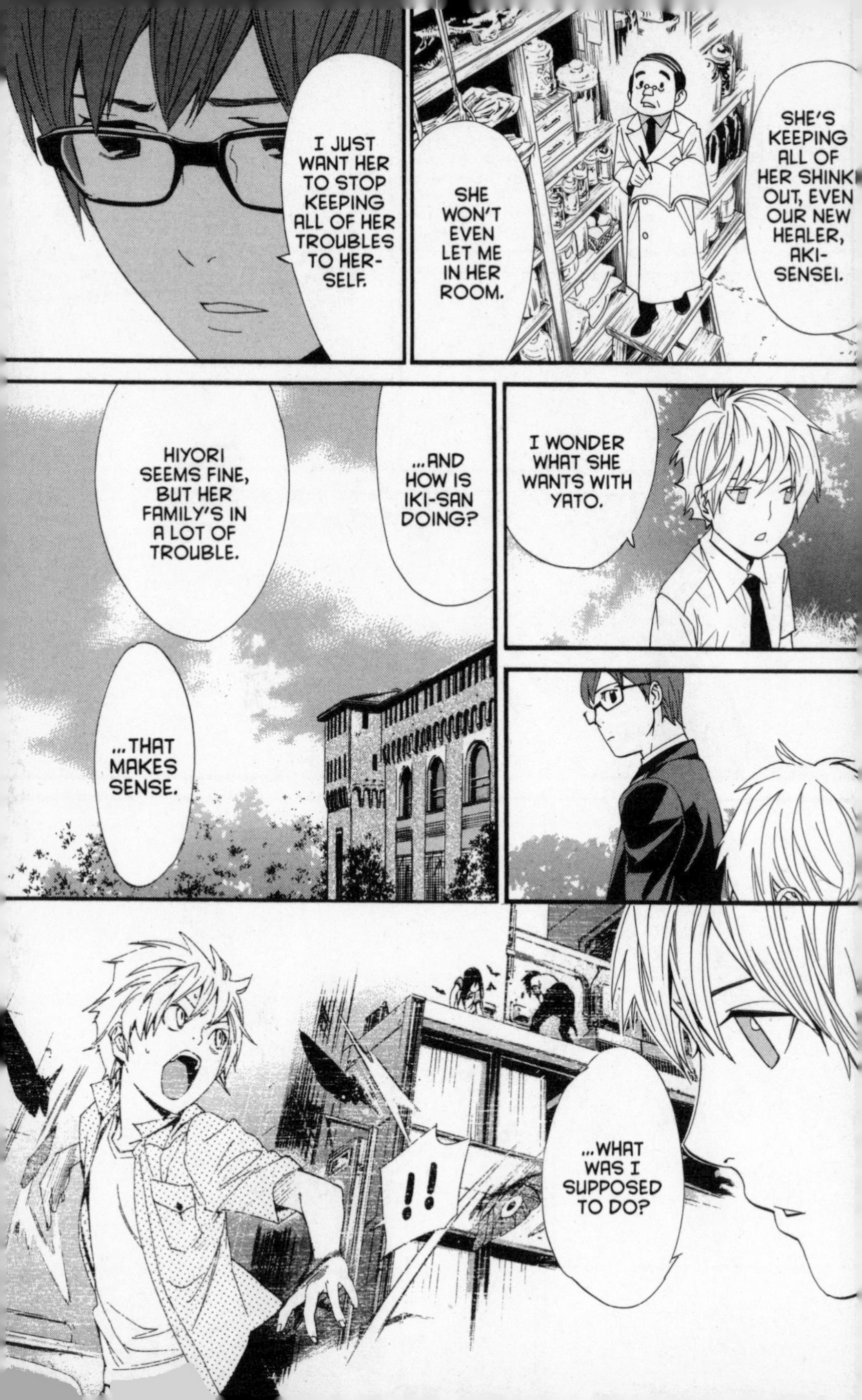
SHE'S KEEPING ALL OF HER SHINKI OUT, EVEN OUR NEW HEALER, AKI-SENSEI.
SHE WON'T EVEN LET ME IN HER ROOM.
I JUST WANT HER TO STOP KEEPING ALL OF HER TROUBLES TO HER-SELF.
I WONDER WHAT SHE WANTS WITH YATO.
...AND HOW IS IKI-SAN DOING?
HIYORI SEEMS FINE, BUT HER FAMILY'S IN A LOT OF TROUBLE.
...THAT MAKES SENSE.
...WHAT WAS I SUPPOSED TO DO?
!!

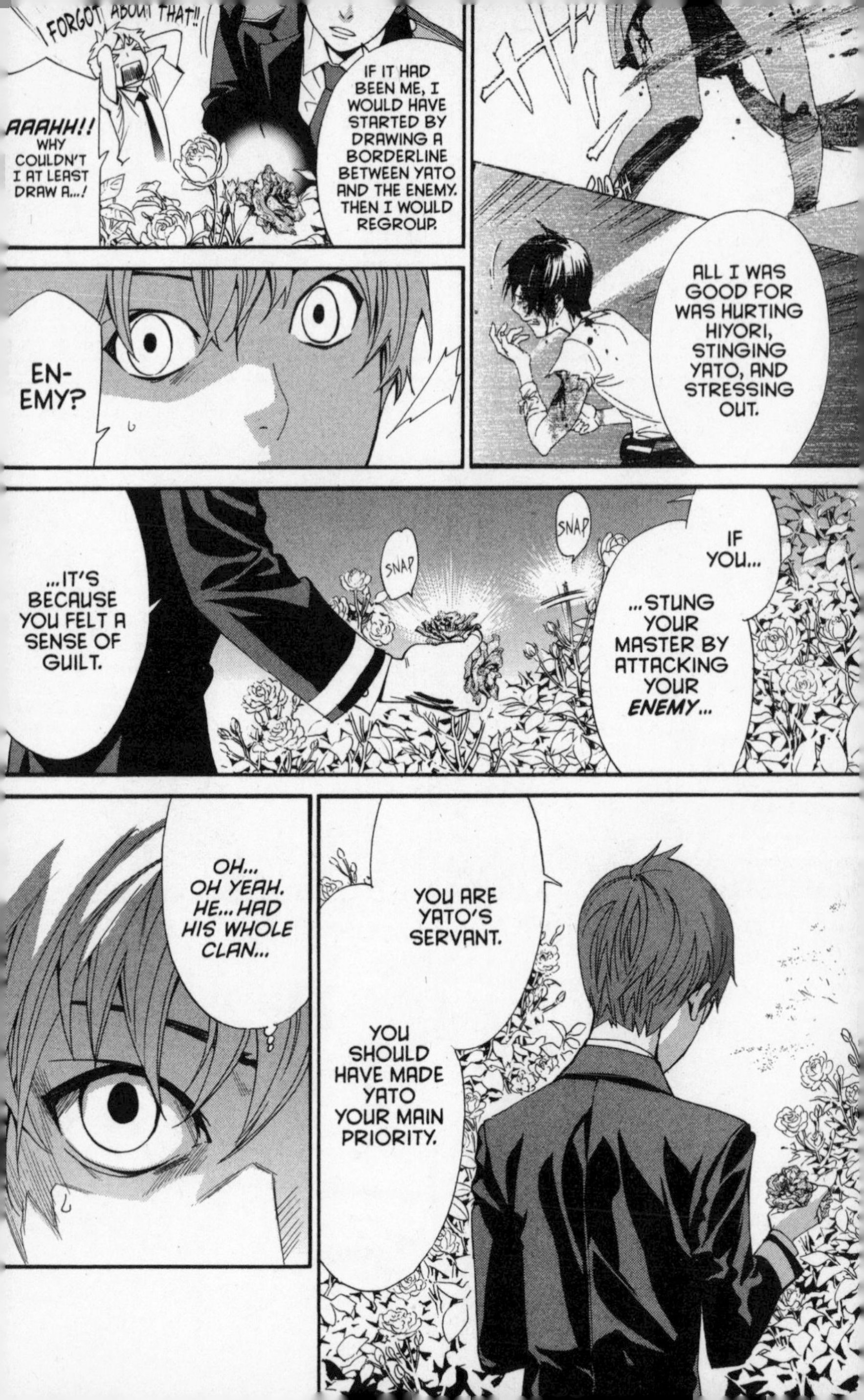
ALL I WAS GOOD FOR WAS HURTING HIYORI, STINGING YATO, AND STRESSING OUT.
IF IT HAD BEEN ME, I WOULD HAVE STARTED BY DRAWING A BORDERLINE BETWEEN YATO AND THE ENEMY. THEN I WOULD REGROUP.
I FORGOT ABOUT THAT!!
AAAHH!! WHY COULDN'T I AT LEAST DRAW A...!
EN-EMY?
IF YOU...
...STUNG YOUR MASTER BY ATTACKING YOUR *ENEMY*...
SNAP
SNAP
...IT'S BECAUSE YOU FELT A SENSE OF GUILT.
YOU ARE YATO'S SERVANT.
YOU SHOULD HAVE MADE YATO YOUR MAIN PRIORITY.
OH... OH YEAH. HE...HAD HIS WHOLE CLAN...

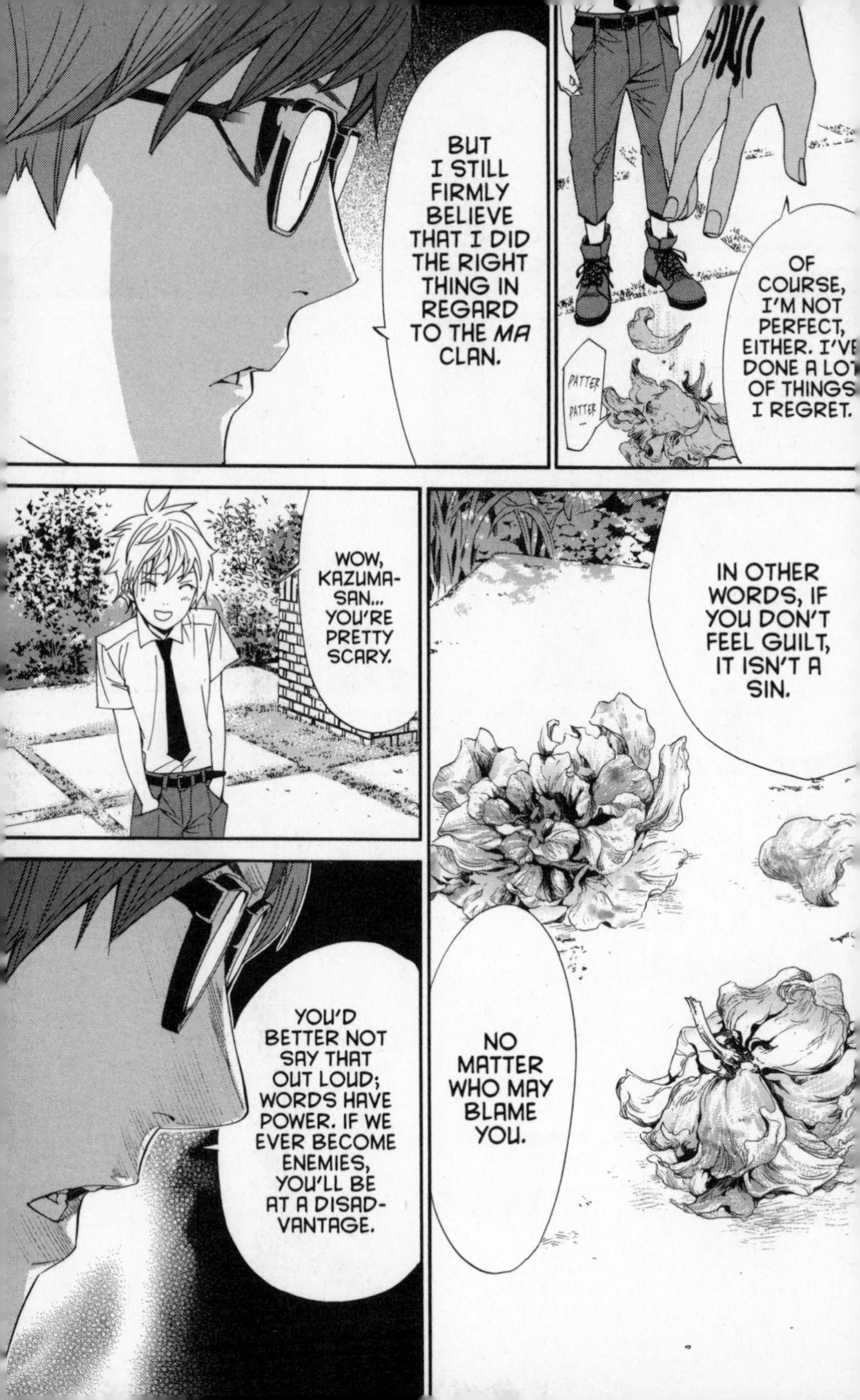
OF COURSE, I'M NOT PERFECT, EITHER. I'VE DONE A LOT OF THINGS I REGRET.
PATTER PATTER ...
BUT I STILL FIRMLY BELIEVE THAT I DID THE RIGHT THING IN REGARD TO THE *MA* CLAN.
IN OTHER WORDS, IF YOU DON'T FEEL GUILT, IT ISN'T A SIN.
NO MATTER WHO MAY BLAME YOU.
WOW, KAZUMA-SAN... YOU'RE PRETTY SCARY.
YOU'D BETTER NOT SAY THAT OUT LOUD; WORDS HAVE POWER. IF WE EVER BECOME ENEMIES, YOU'LL BE AT A DISAD-VANTAGE.

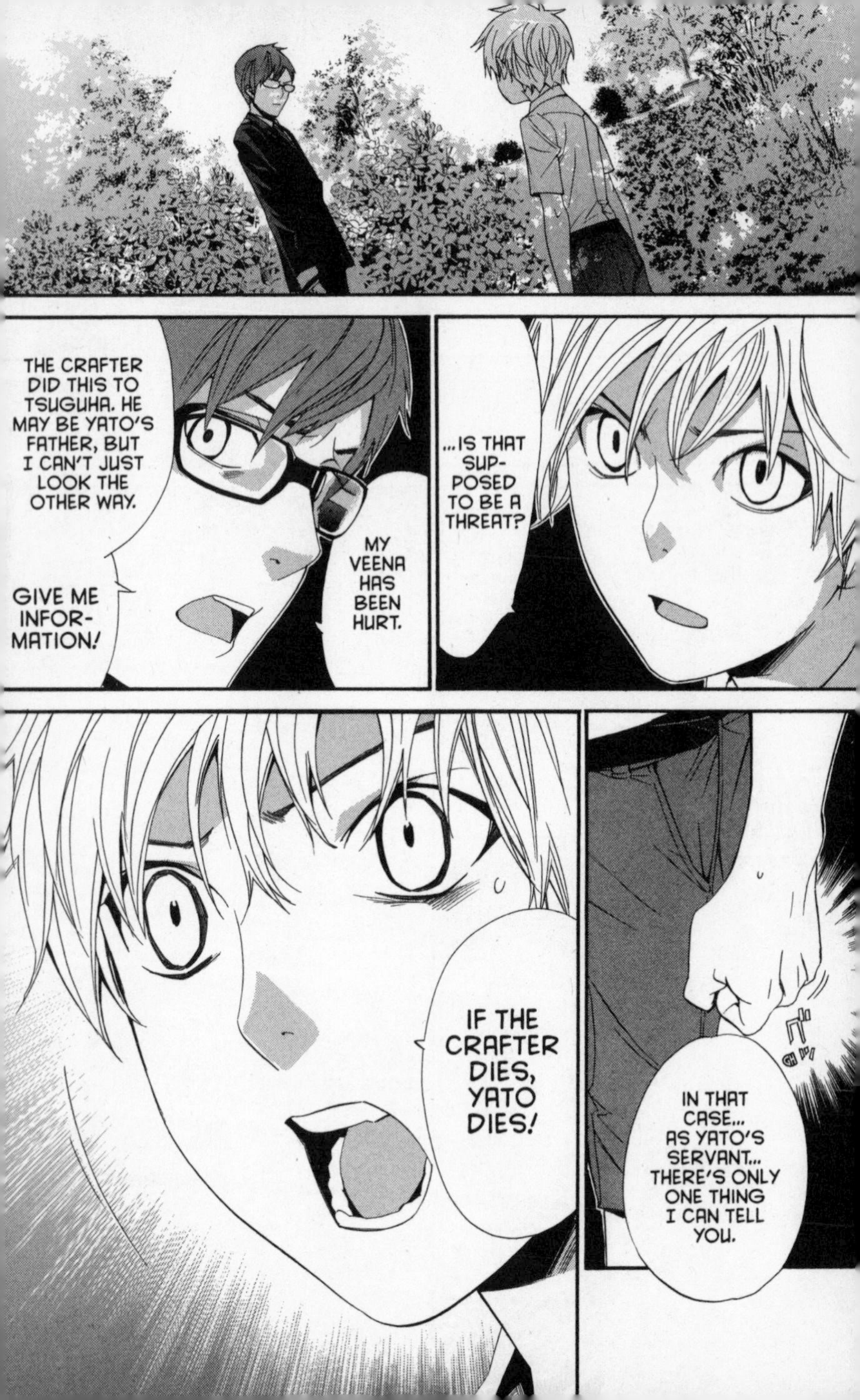
...IS THAT SUPPOSED TO BE A THREAT?
MY VEENA HAS BEEN HURT.
THE CRAFTER DID THIS TO TSUGUHA. HE MAY BE YATO'S FATHER, BUT I CAN'T JUST LOOK THE OTHER WAY.
GIVE ME INFORMATION!
GH
IN THAT CASE... AS YATO'S SERVANT... THERE'S ONLY ONE THING I CAN TELL YOU.
IF THE CRAFTER DIES, YATO DIES!

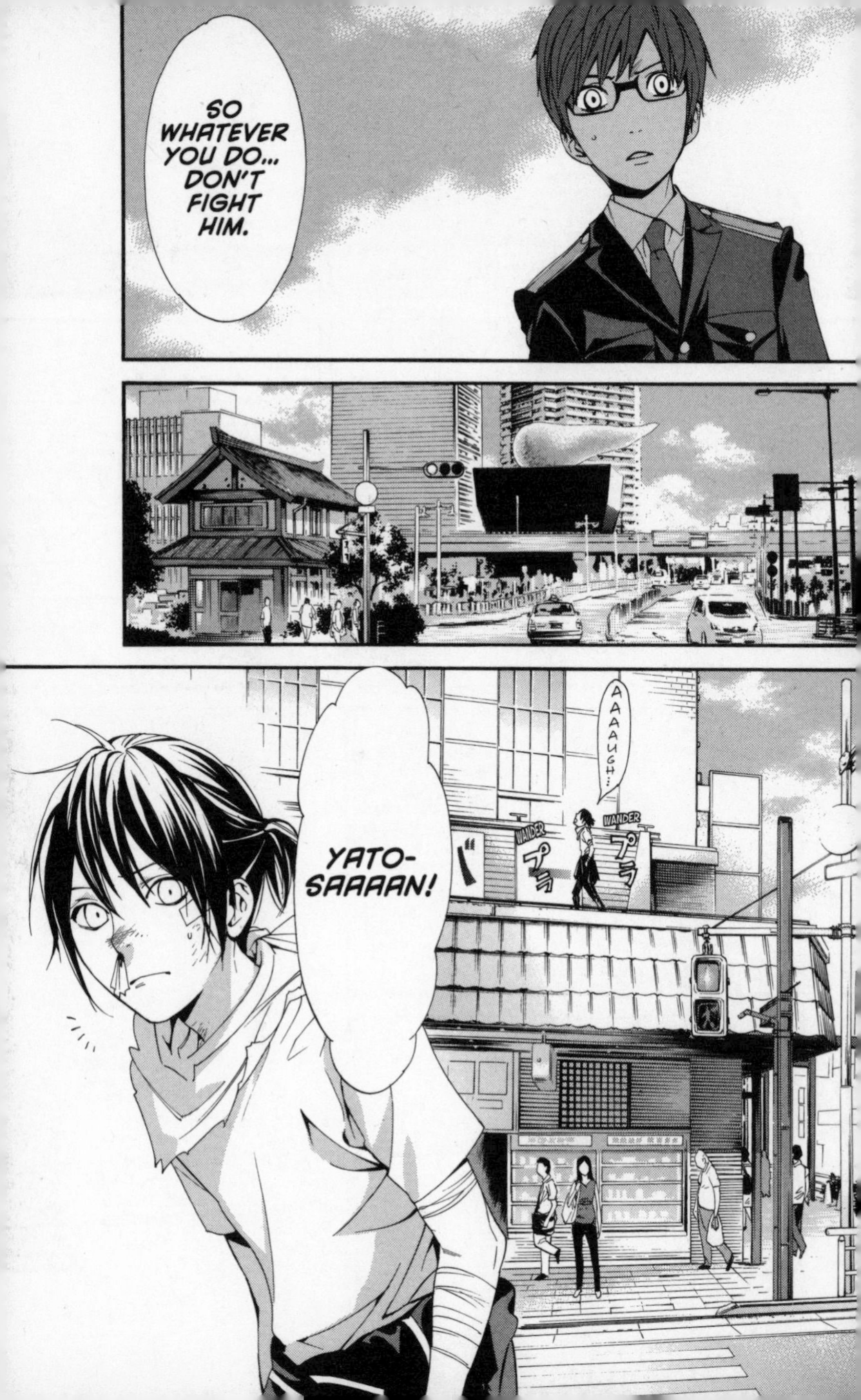
SO WHATEVER YOU DO... DON'T FIGHT HIM.
AAAAUGH...
WANDER
WANDER
YATO-SAAAAN!

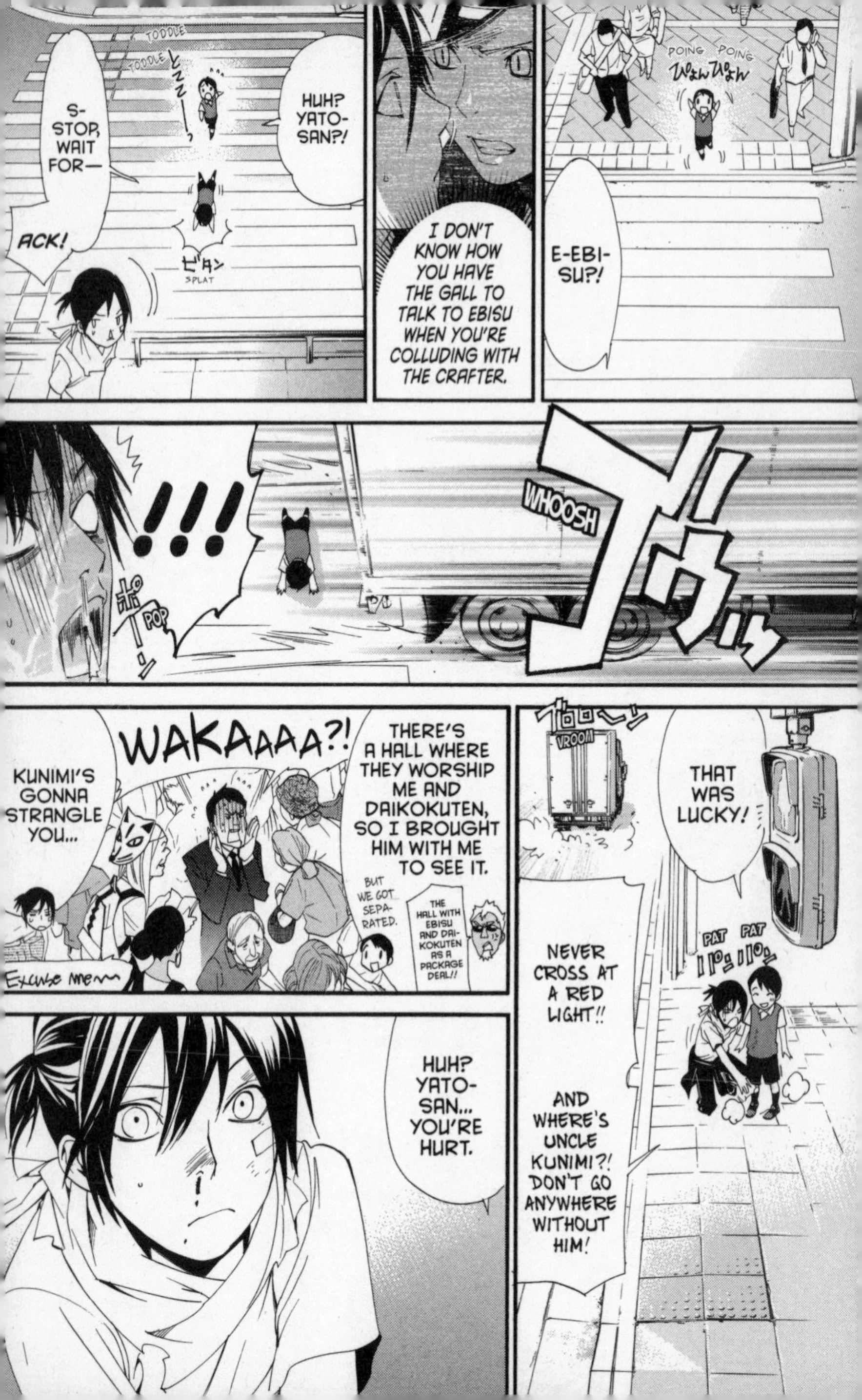
POING POING
ぴょんぴょん
E-EBI-SU?!
I DON'T KNOW HOW YOU HAVE THE GALL TO TALK TO EBISU WHEN YOU'RE COLLUDING WITH THE CRAFTER.
HUH? YATO-SAN?!
TODDLE TODDLE
S-STOP, WAIT FOR—
ACK!
ビタン
SPLAT
WHOOSH
!!!
POP
VROOM
THAT WAS LUCKY!
NEVER CROSS AT A RED LIGHT!!
PAT PAT
AND WHERE'S UNCLE KUNIMI?! DON'T GO ANYWHERE WITHOUT HIM!
THERE'S A HALL WHERE THEY WORSHIP ME AND DAIKOKUTEN, SO I BROUGHT HIM WITH ME TO SEE IT.
WAKAAAA?!
KUNIMI'S GONNA STRANGLE YOU...
THE HALL WITH EBISU AND DAIKOKUTEN AS A PACKAGE DEAL!!
BUT WE GOT SEPARATED.
Excuse me~
HUH? YATO-SAN... YOU'RE HURT.

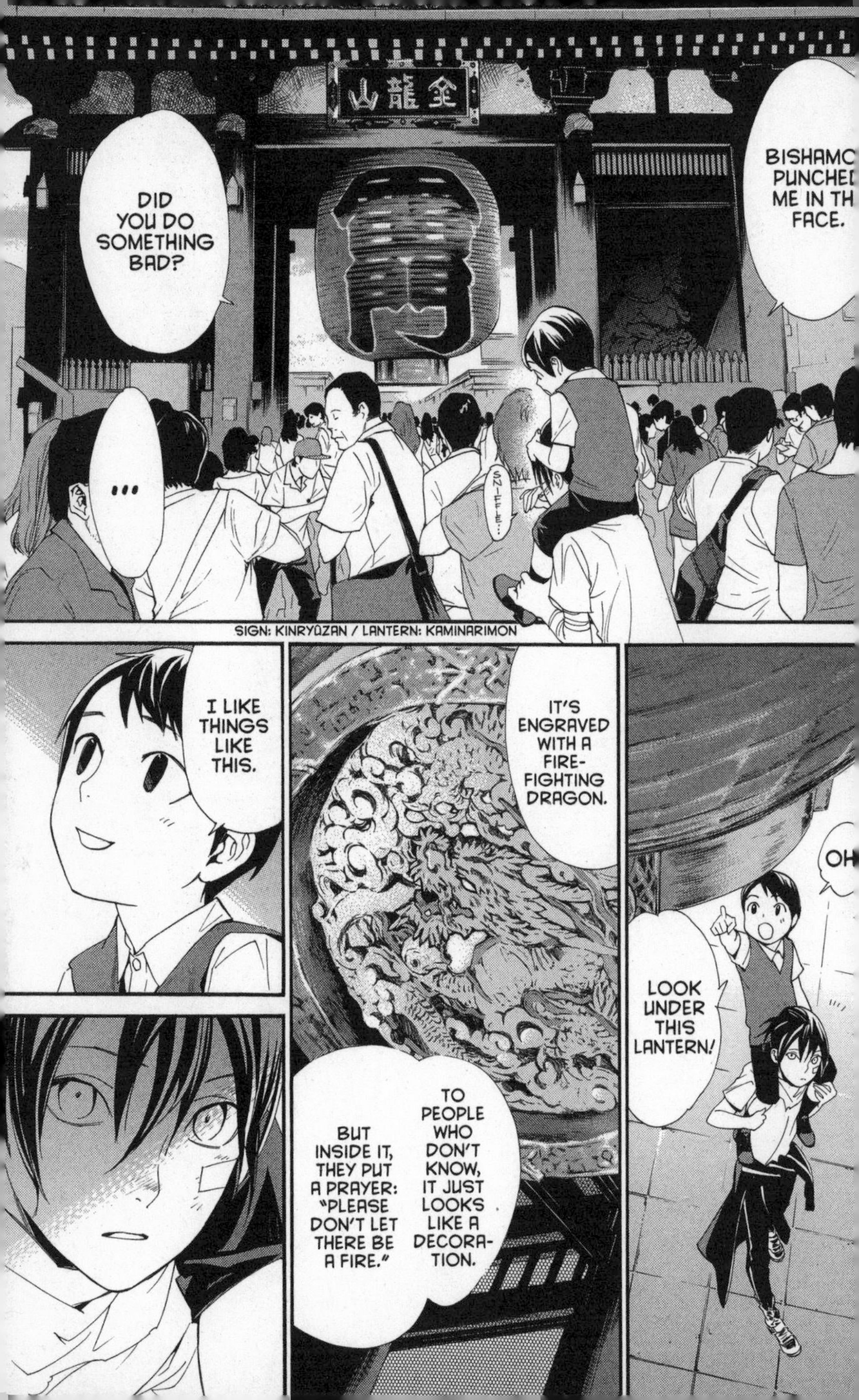
BISHAMO PUNCHEI ME IN TH FACE.
DID YOU DO SOMETHING BAD?
...
SNIFFLE...
SIGN: KINRYŪZAN / LANTERN: KAMINARIMON
OH
LOOK UNDER THIS LANTERN!
IT'S ENGRAVED WITH A FIRE-FIGHTING DRAGON.
TO PEOPLE WHO DON'T KNOW, IT JUST LOOKS LIKE A DECORATION.
BUT INSIDE IT, THEY PUT A PRAYER: "PLEASE DON'T LET THERE BE A FIRE."
I LIKE THINGS LIKE THIS.

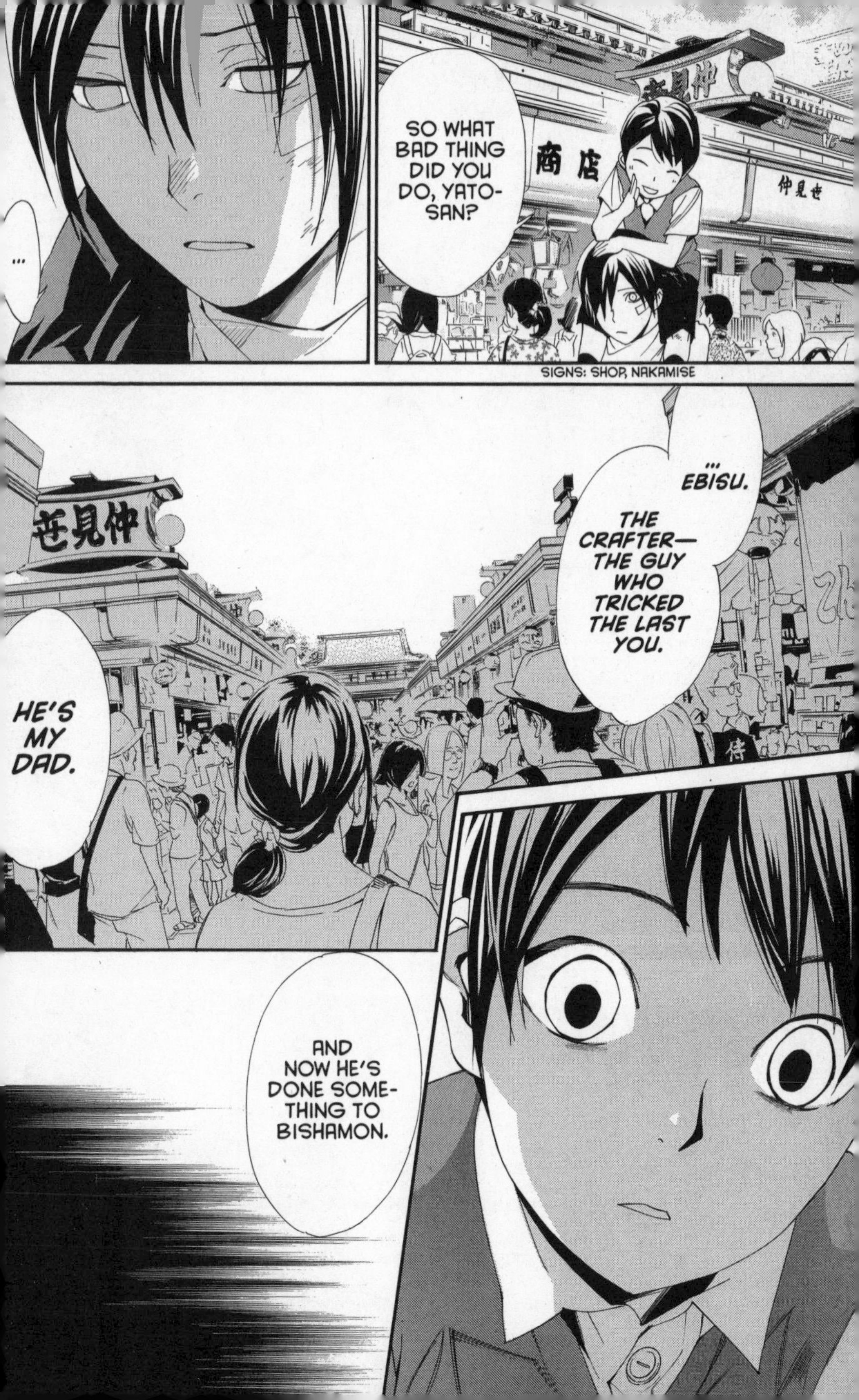
SO WHAT BAD THING DID YOU DO, YATO-SAN?
...
SIGNS: SHOP, NAKAMISE
... EBISU.
THE CRAFTER— THE GUY WHO TRICKED THE LAST YOU.
HE'S MY DAD.
AND NOW HE'S DONE SOME-THING TO BISHAMON.

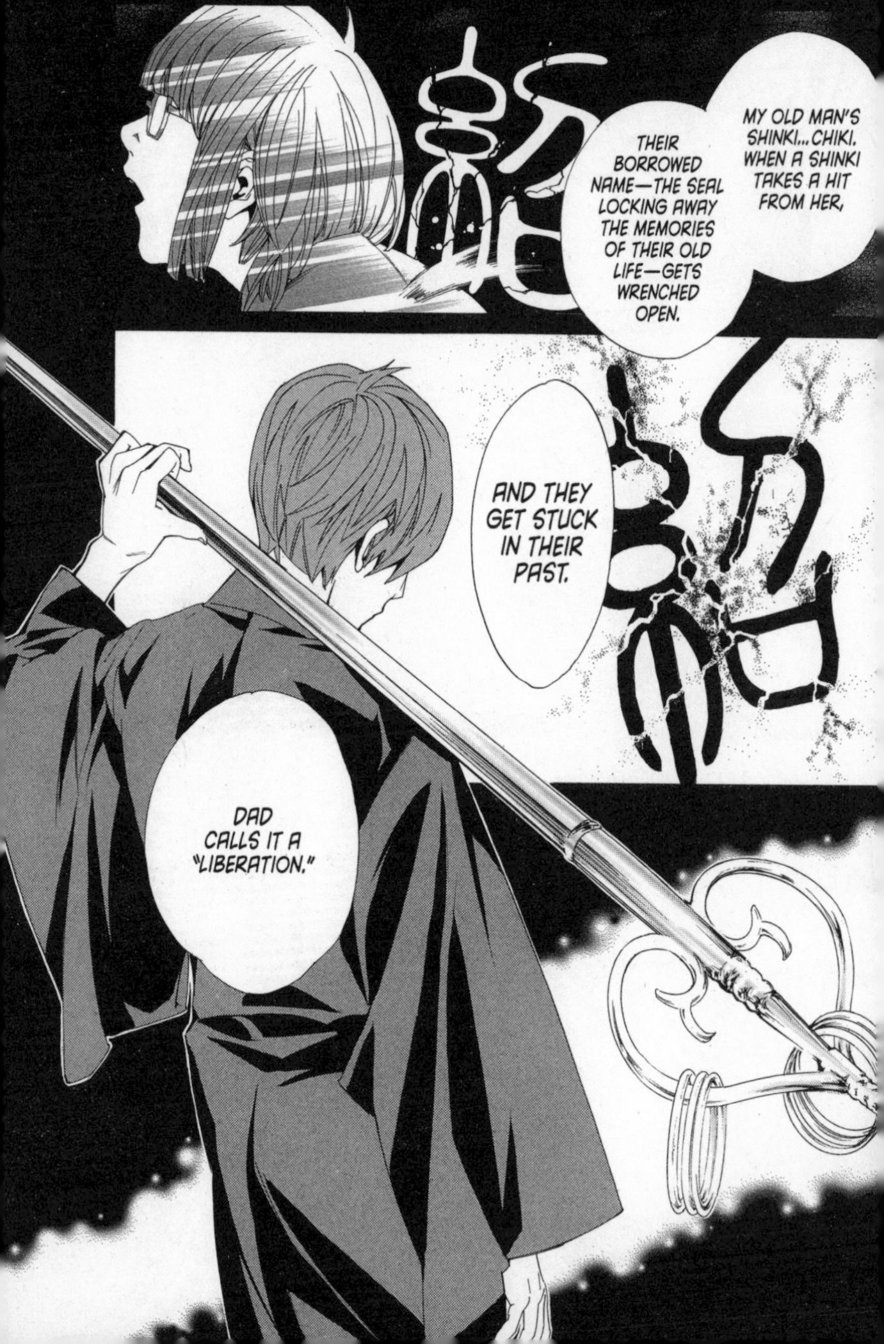
MY OLD MAN'S SHINKI...CHIKI. WHEN A SHINKI TAKES A HIT FROM HER,
THEIR BORROWED NAME—THE SEAL LOCKING AWAY THE MEMORIES OF THEIR OLD LIFE—GETS WRENCHED OPEN.
AND THEY GET STUCK IN THEIR PAST.
DAD CALLS IT A "LIBERATION."

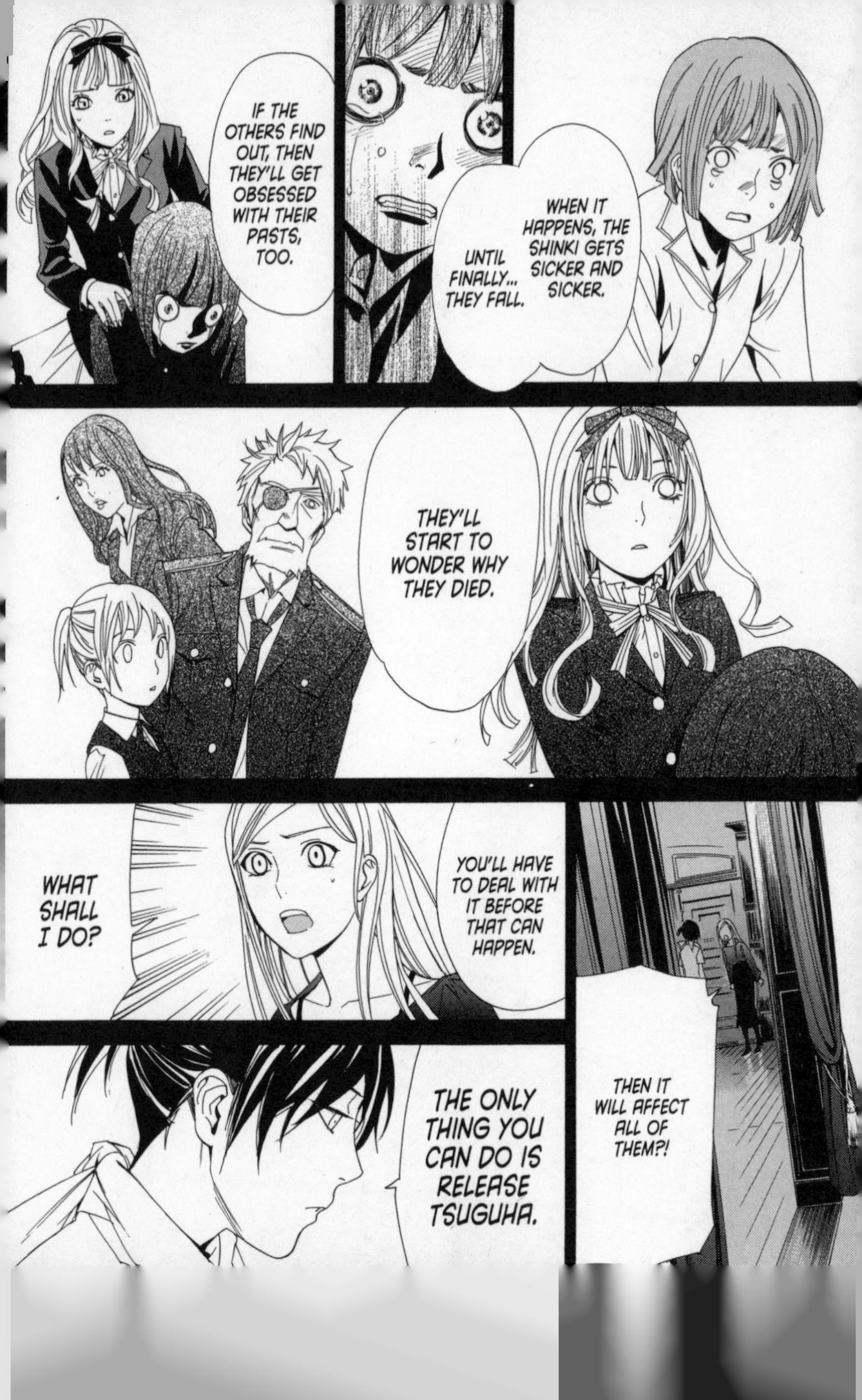
WHEN IT HAPPENS, THE SHINKI GETS SICKER AND SICKER.
UNTIL FINALLY... THEY FALL.
IF THE OTHERS FIND OUT, THEN THEY'LL GET OBSESSED WITH THEIR PASTS, TOO.
THEY'LL START TO WONDER WHY THEY DIED.
THEN IT WILL AFFECT ALL OF THEM?!
YOU'LL HAVE TO DEAL WITH IT BEFORE THAT CAN HAPPEN.
WHAT SHALL I DO?
THE ONLY THING YOU CAN DO IS RELEASE TSUGUHA.

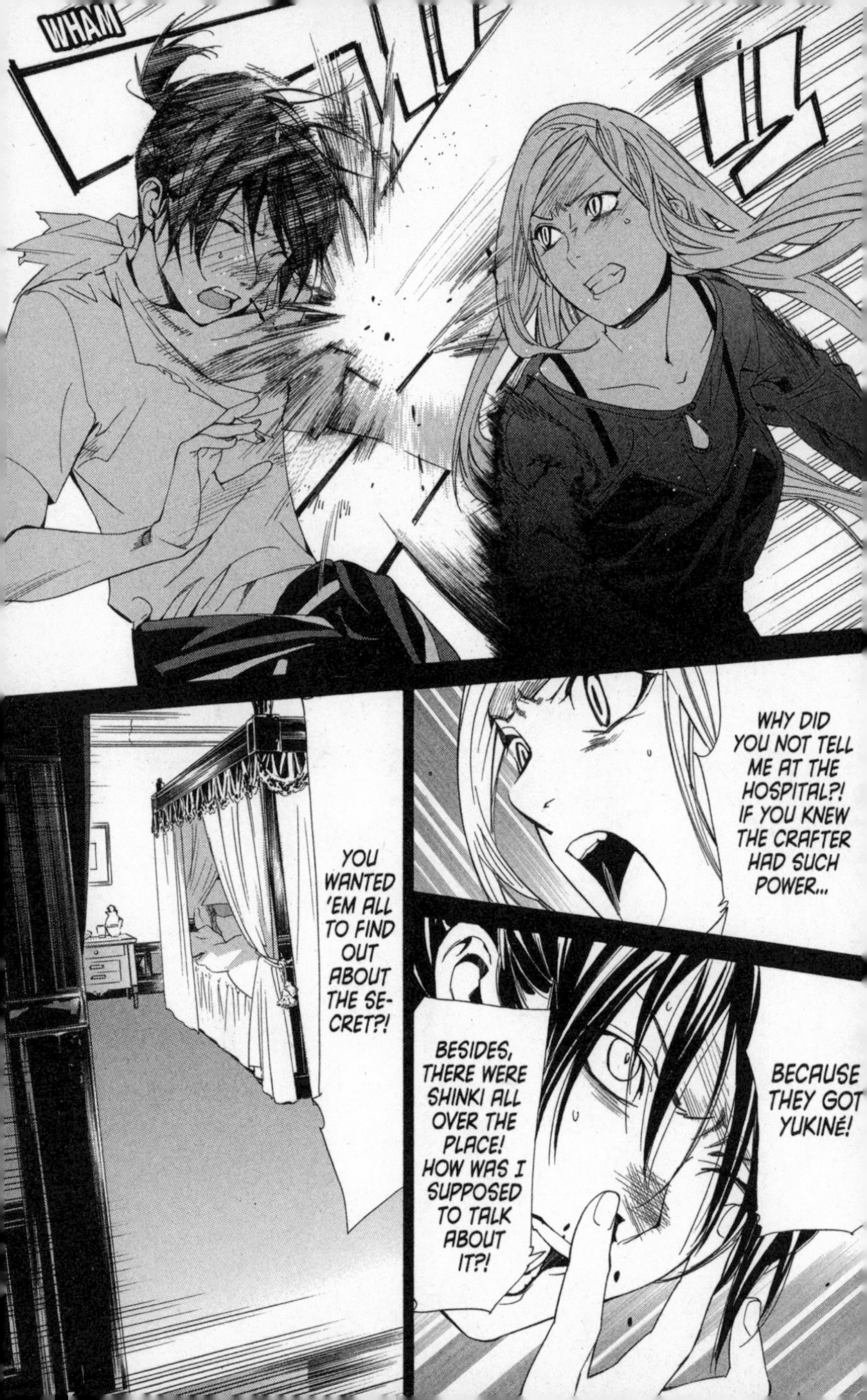
WHAM
WHY DID YOU NOT TELL ME AT THE HOSPITAL?! IF YOU KNEW THE CRAFTER HAD SUCH POWER...
BECAUSE THEY GOT YUKINÉ!
BESIDES, THERE WERE SHINKI ALL OVER THE PLACE! HOW WAS I SUPPOSED TO TALK ABOUT IT?!
YOU WANTED 'EM ALL TO FIND OUT ABOUT THE SE-CRET?!

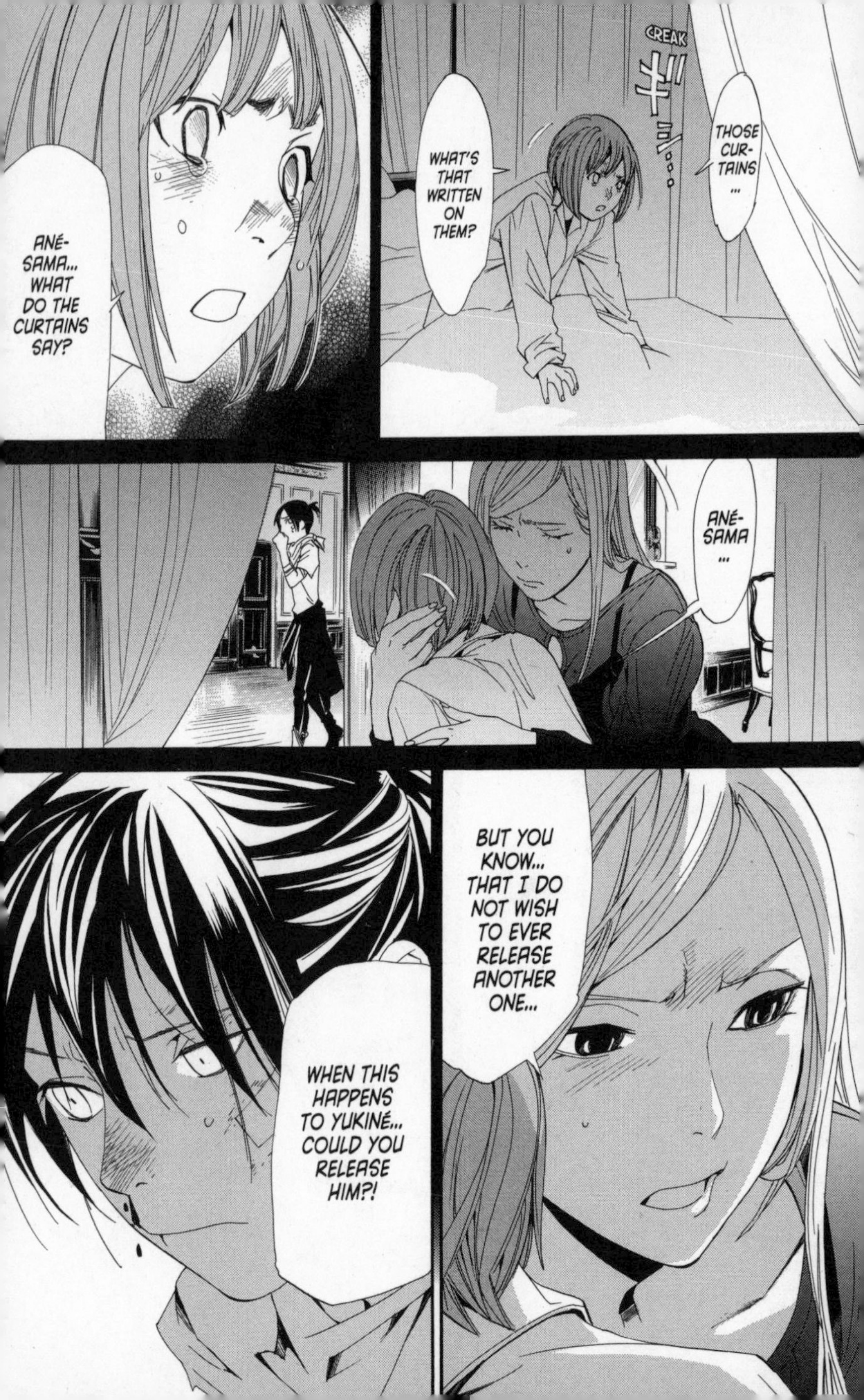
CREAK
THOSE CUR-TAINS ...
WHAT'S THAT WRITTEN ON THEM?
ANÉ-SAMA... WHAT DO THE CURTAINS SAY?
ANÉ-SAMA ...
BUT YOU KNOW... THAT I DO NOT WISH TO EVER RELEASE ANOTHER ONE...
WHEN THIS HAPPENS TO YUKINÉ... COULD YOU RELEASE HIM?!

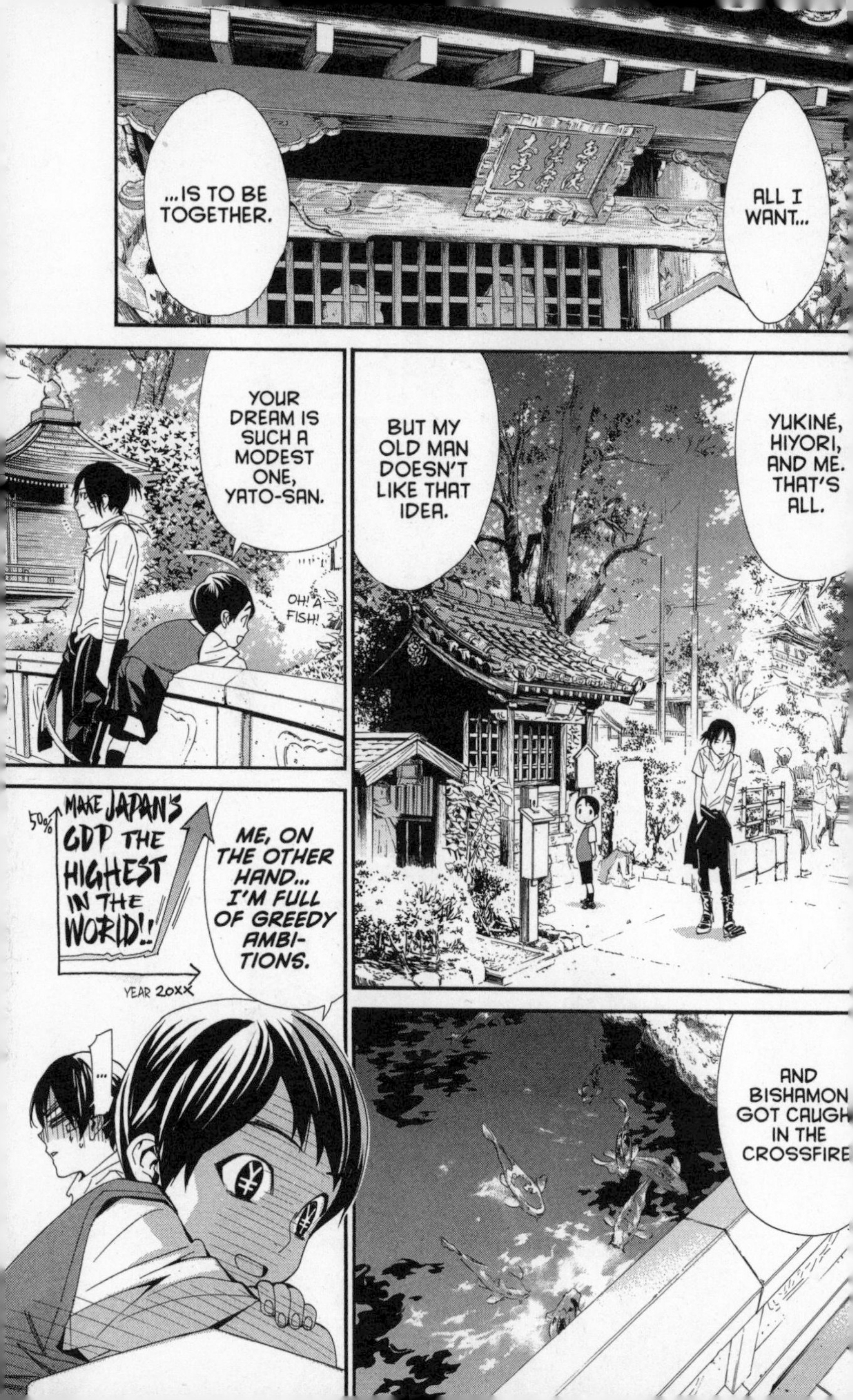
ALL I WANT...
...IS TO BE TOGETHER.
YUKINÉ, HIYORI, AND ME. THAT'S ALL.
BUT MY OLD MAN DOESN'T LIKE THAT IDEA.
AND BISHAMON GOT CAUGH IN THE CROSSFIRE
YOUR DREAM IS SUCH A MODEST ONE, YATO-SAN.
OH! A FISH!
ME, ON THE OTHER HAND... I'M FULL OF GREEDY AMBITIONS.
MAKE JAPAN'S GDP THE HIGHEST IN THE WORLD!!
50%
YEAR 20XX
...

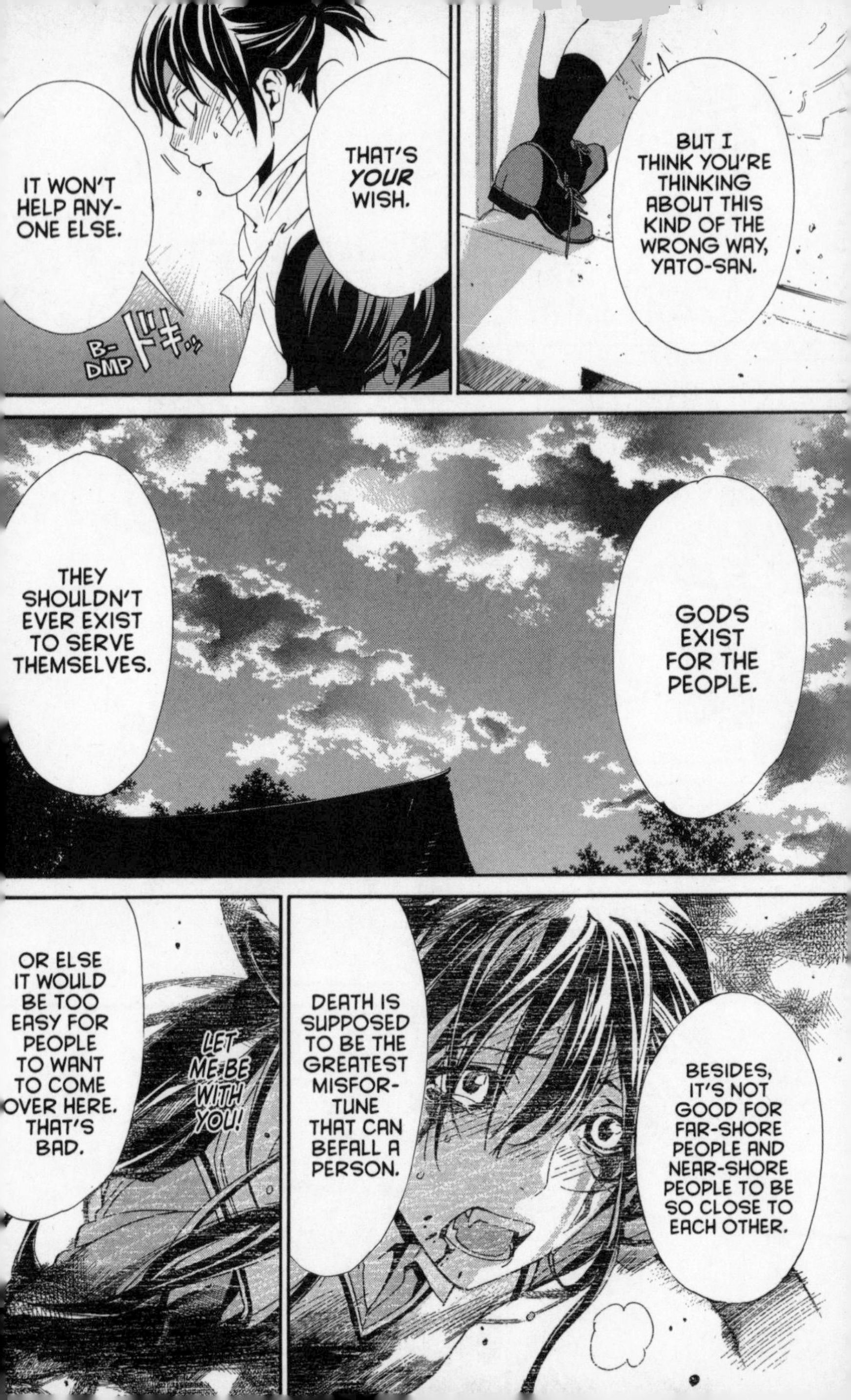

BUT I THINK YOU'RE THINKING ABOUT THIS KIND OF THE WRONG WAY, YATO-SAN.
THAT'S *YOUR* WISH.
IT WON'T HELP ANY-ONE ELSE.
B-DMP
GODS EXIST FOR THE PEOPLE.
THEY SHOULDN'T EVER EXIST TO SERVE THEMSELVES.
BESIDES, IT'S NOT GOOD FOR FAR-SHORE PEOPLE AND NEAR-SHORE PEOPLE TO BE SO CLOSE TO EACH OTHER.
DEATH IS SUPPOSED TO BE THE GREATEST MISFOR-TUNE THAT CAN BEFALL A PERSON.
OR ELSE IT WOULD BE TOO EASY FOR PEOPLE TO WANT TO COME OVER HERE. THAT'S BAD.
LET ME BE WITH YOU!

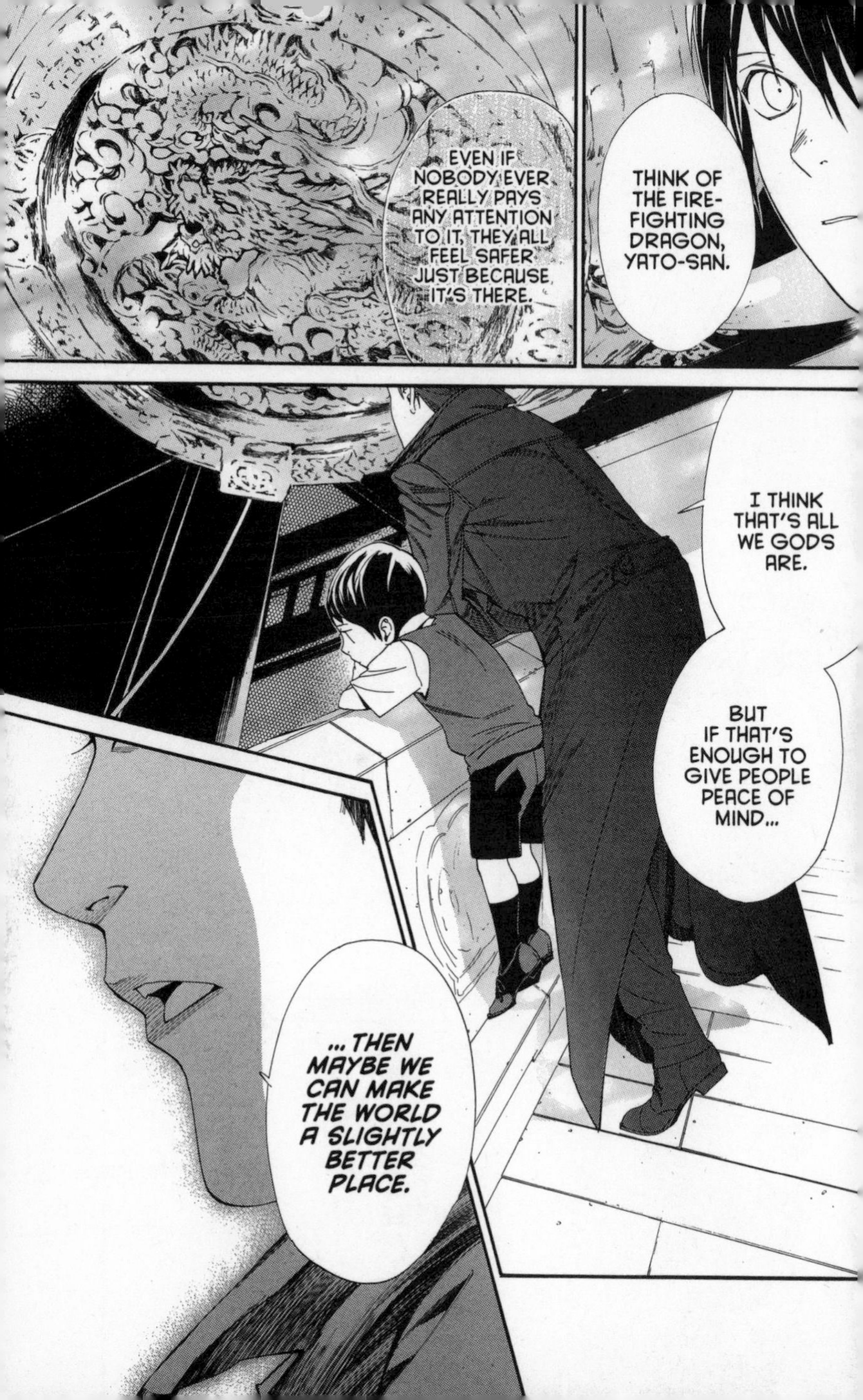
THINK OF THE FIRE-FIGHTING DRAGON, YATO-SAN.
EVEN IF NOBODY EVER REALLY PAYS ANY ATTENTION TO IT, THEY ALL FEEL SAFER JUST BECAUSE IT'S THERE.
I THINK THAT'S ALL WE GODS ARE.
BUT IF THAT'S ENOUGH TO GIVE PEOPLE PEACE OF MIND...
...THEN MAYBE WE CAN MAKE THE WORLD A SLIGHTLY BETTER PLACE.

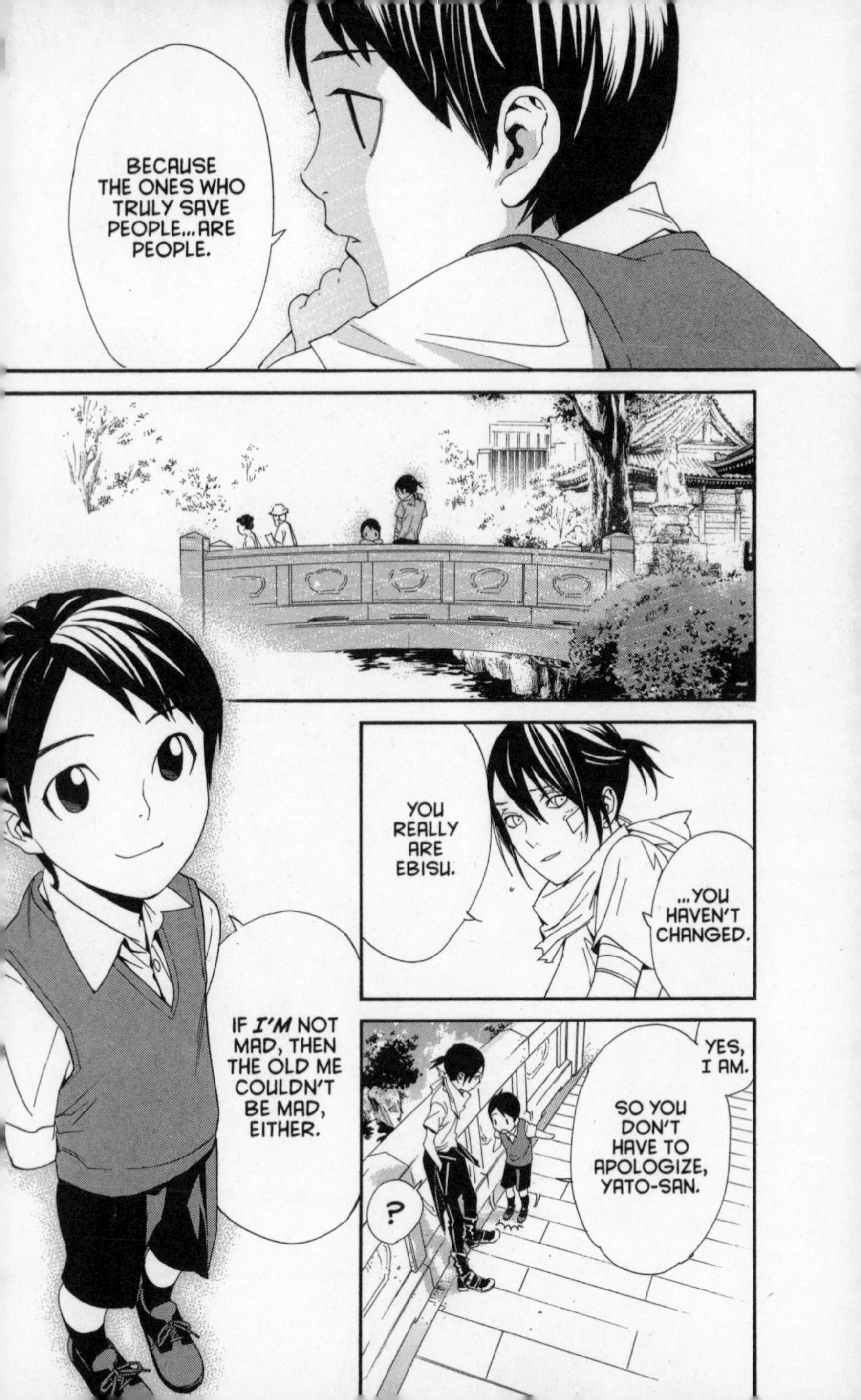
BECAUSE THE ONES WHO TRULY SAVE PEOPLE...ARE PEOPLE.
...YOU HAVEN'T CHANGED.
YOU REALLY ARE EBISU.
YES, I AM.
SO YOU DON'T HAVE TO APOLOGIZE, YATO-SAN.
?
IF *I'M* NOT MAD, THEN THE OLD ME COULDN'T BE MAD, EITHER.

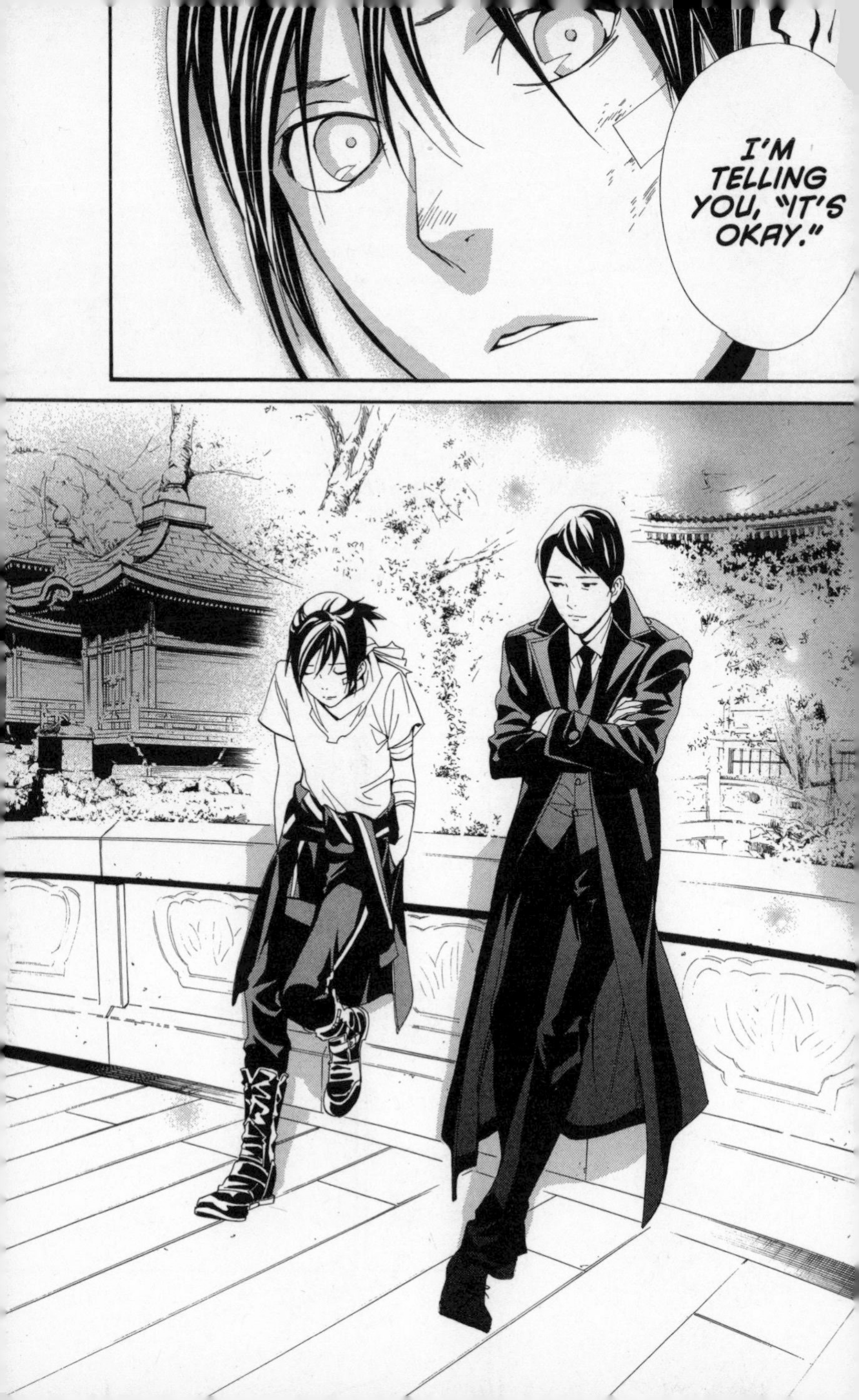
I'M TELLING YOU, "IT'S OKAY."

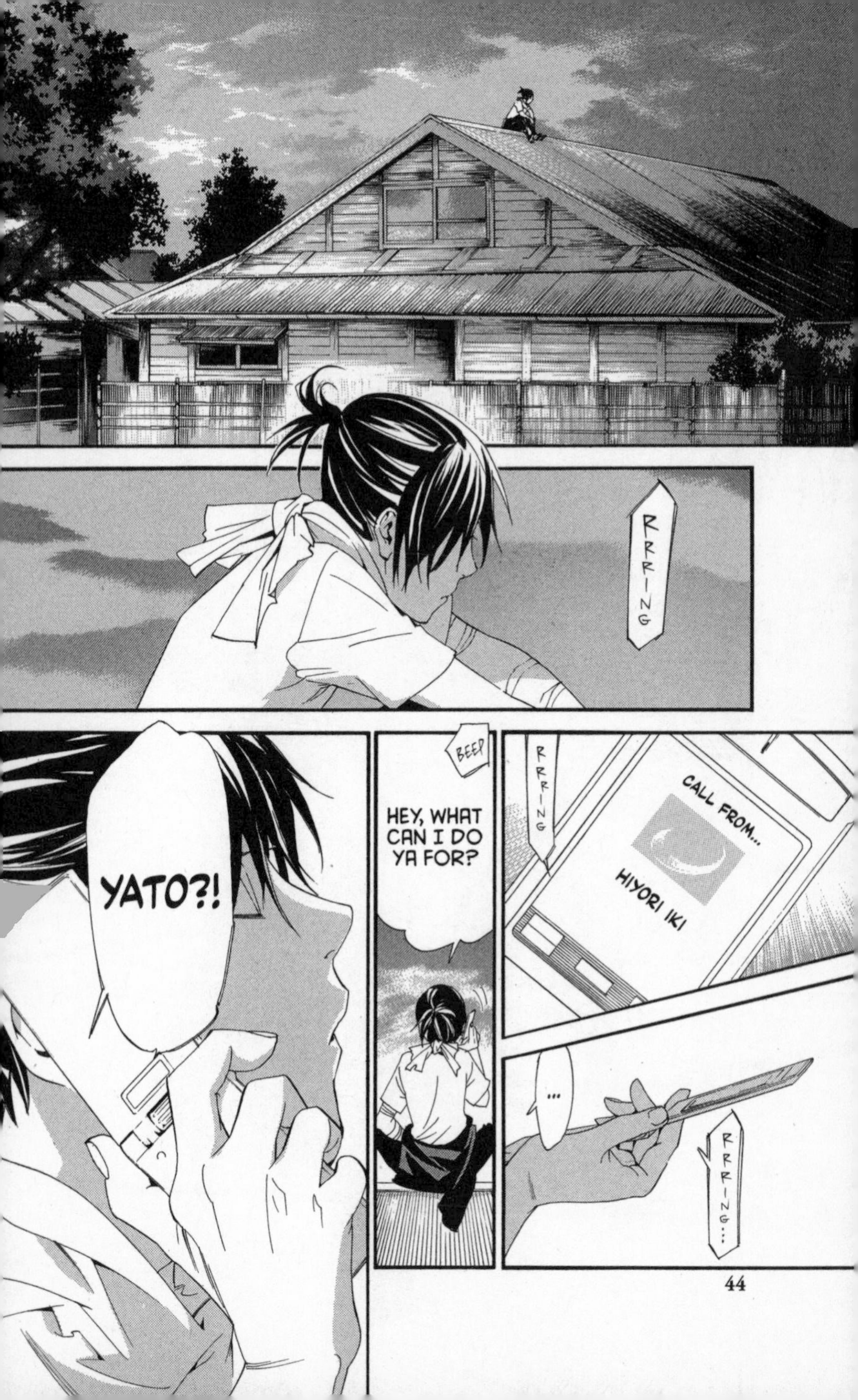
RRRING
RRRING
CALL FROM...
HIYORI IKI
...
RRRING...
BEEP
HEY, WHAT CAN I DO YA FOR?
YATO?!

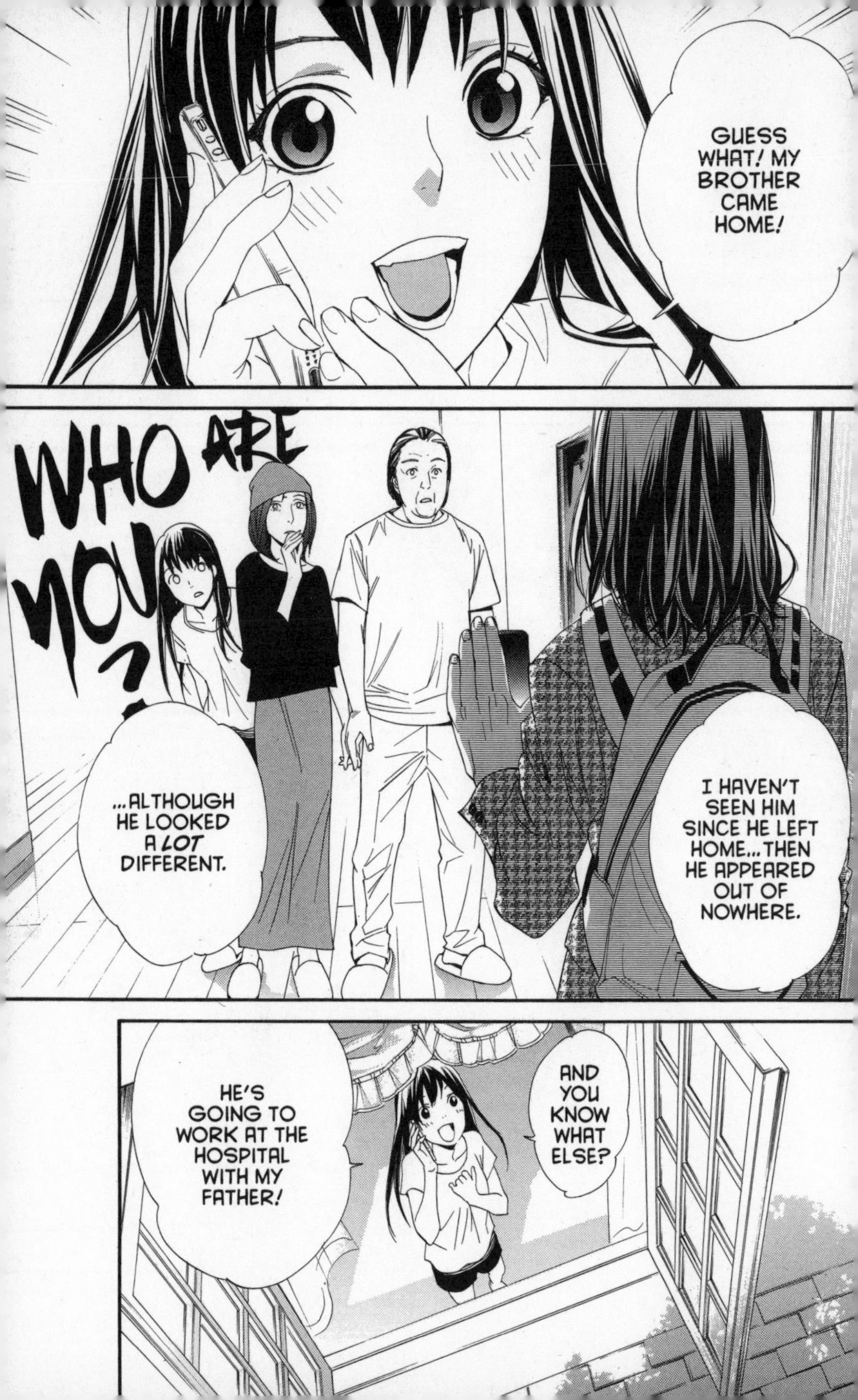
GUESS WHAT! MY BROTHER CAME HOME!
WHO ARE YOU?
I HAVEN'T SEEN HIM SINCE HE LEFT HOME...THEN HE APPEARED OUT OF NOWHERE.
...ALTHOUGH HE LOOKED A *LOT* DIFFERENT.
AND YOU KNOW WHAT ELSE?
HE'S GOING TO WORK AT THE HOSPITAL WITH MY FATHER!

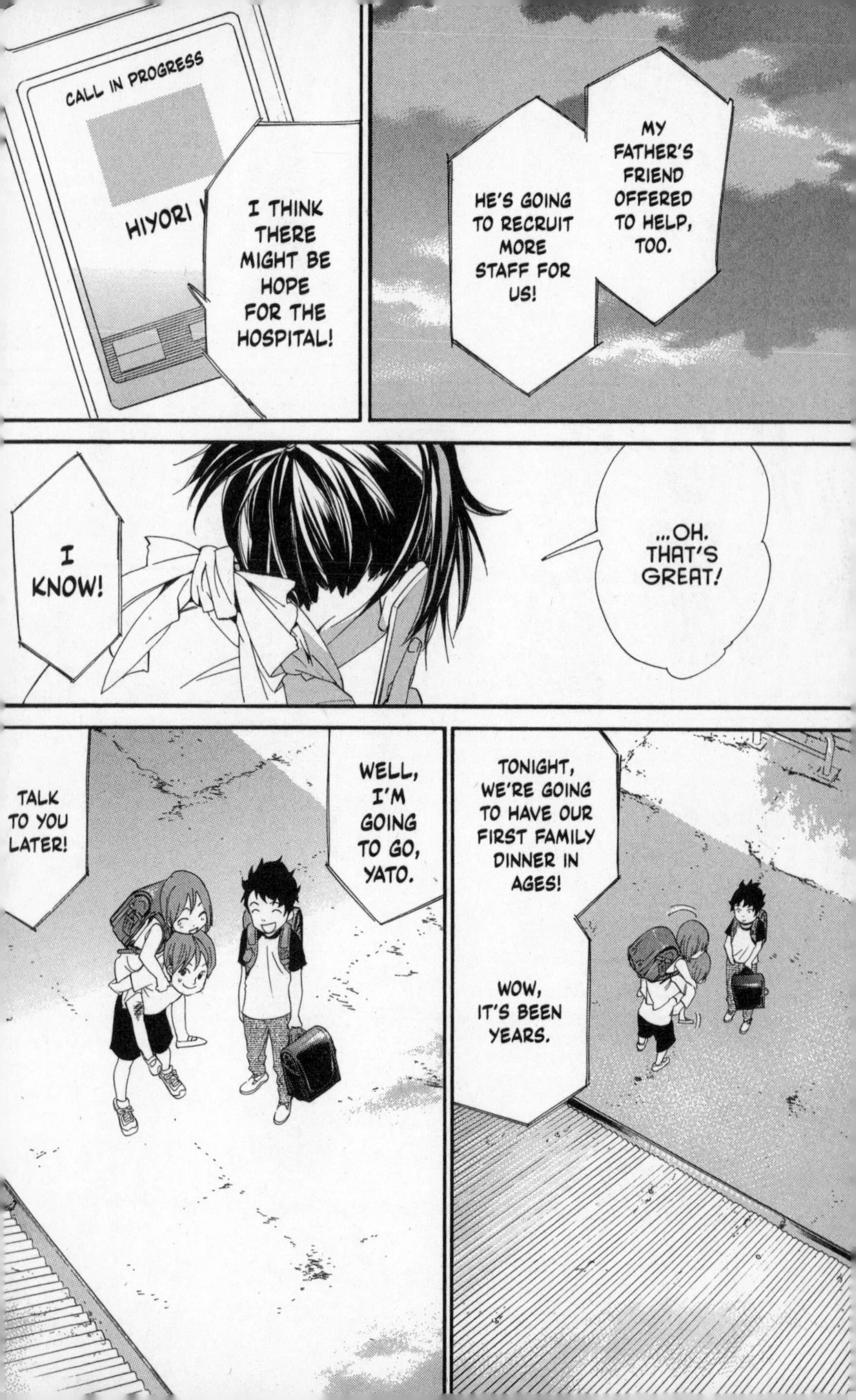
MY FATHER'S FRIEND OFFERED TO HELP, TOO.
HE'S GOING TO RECRUIT MORE STAFF FOR US!
CALL IN PROGRESS
HIYORI
I THINK THERE MIGHT BE HOPE FOR THE HOSPITAL!
...OH. THAT'S GREAT!
I KNOW!
TONIGHT, WE'RE GOING TO HAVE OUR FIRST FAMILY DINNER IN AGES!
WOW, IT'S BEEN YEARS.
WELL, I'M GOING TO GO, YATO.
TALK TO YOU LATER!

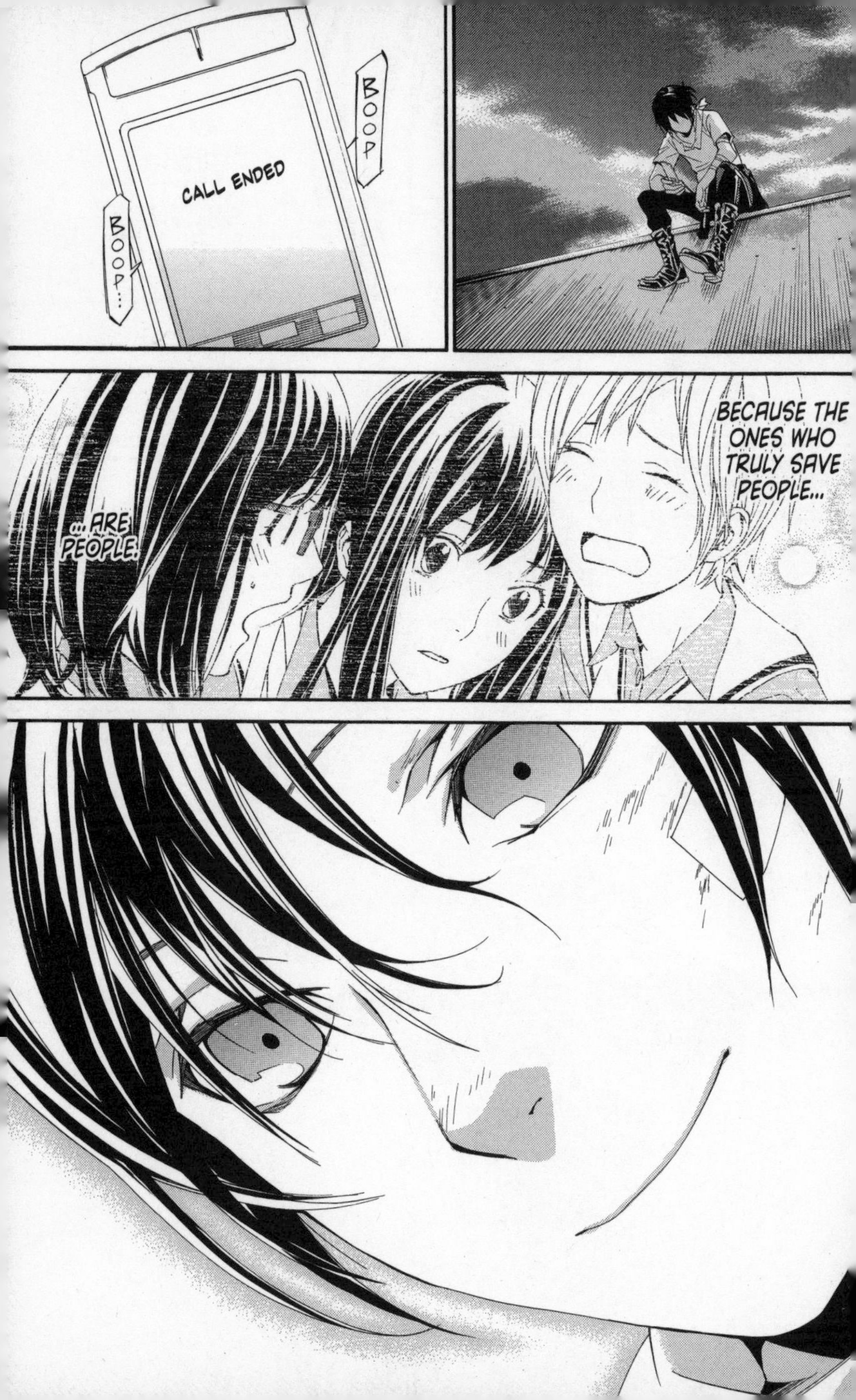
BOOP
CALL ENDED
BOOP...
BECAUSE THE ONES WHO TRULY SAVE PEOPLE...
...ARE PEOPLE.

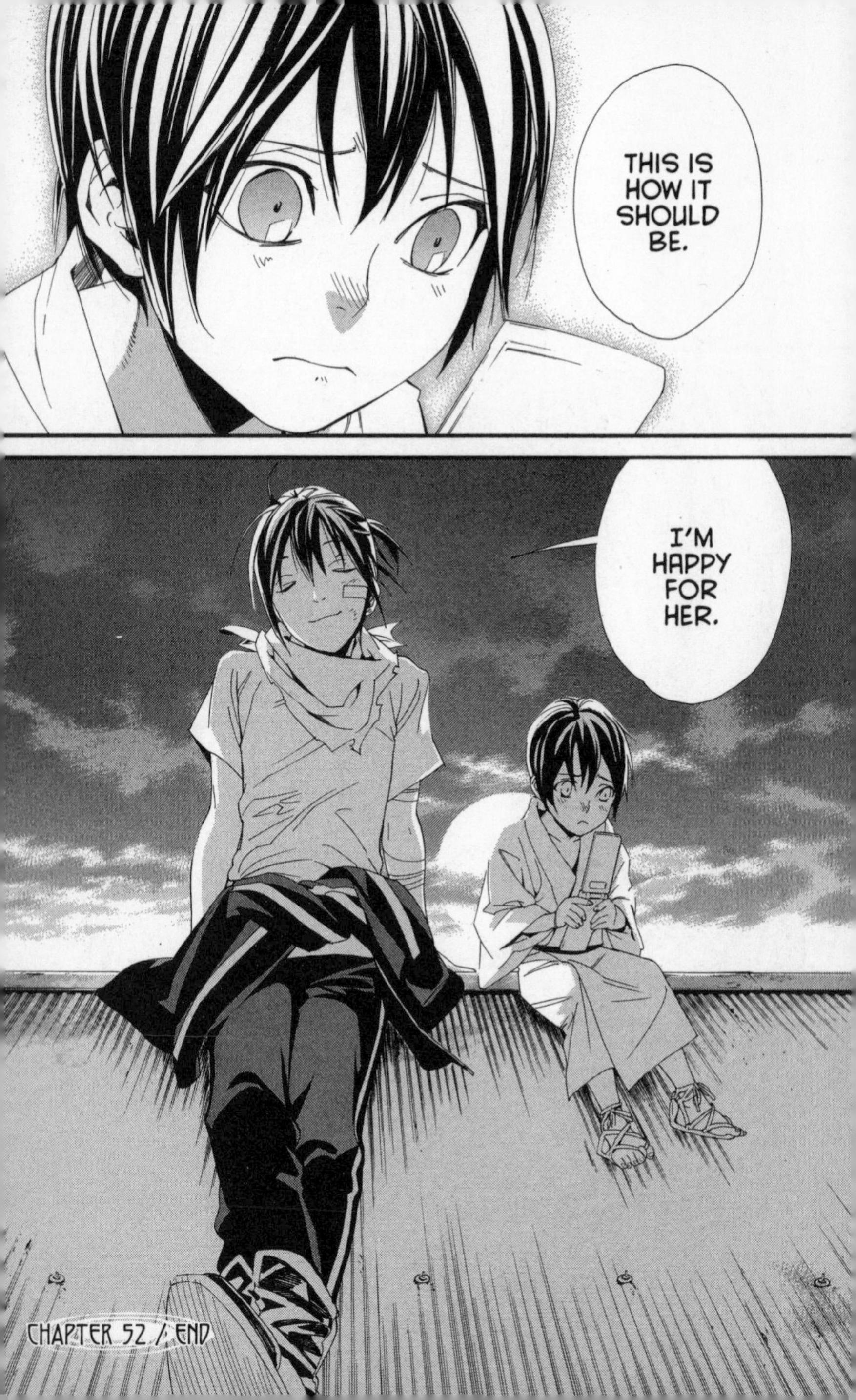
THIS IS HOW IT SHOULD BE.
I'M HAPPY FOR HER.
CHAPTER 52 / END

野

覺

禪

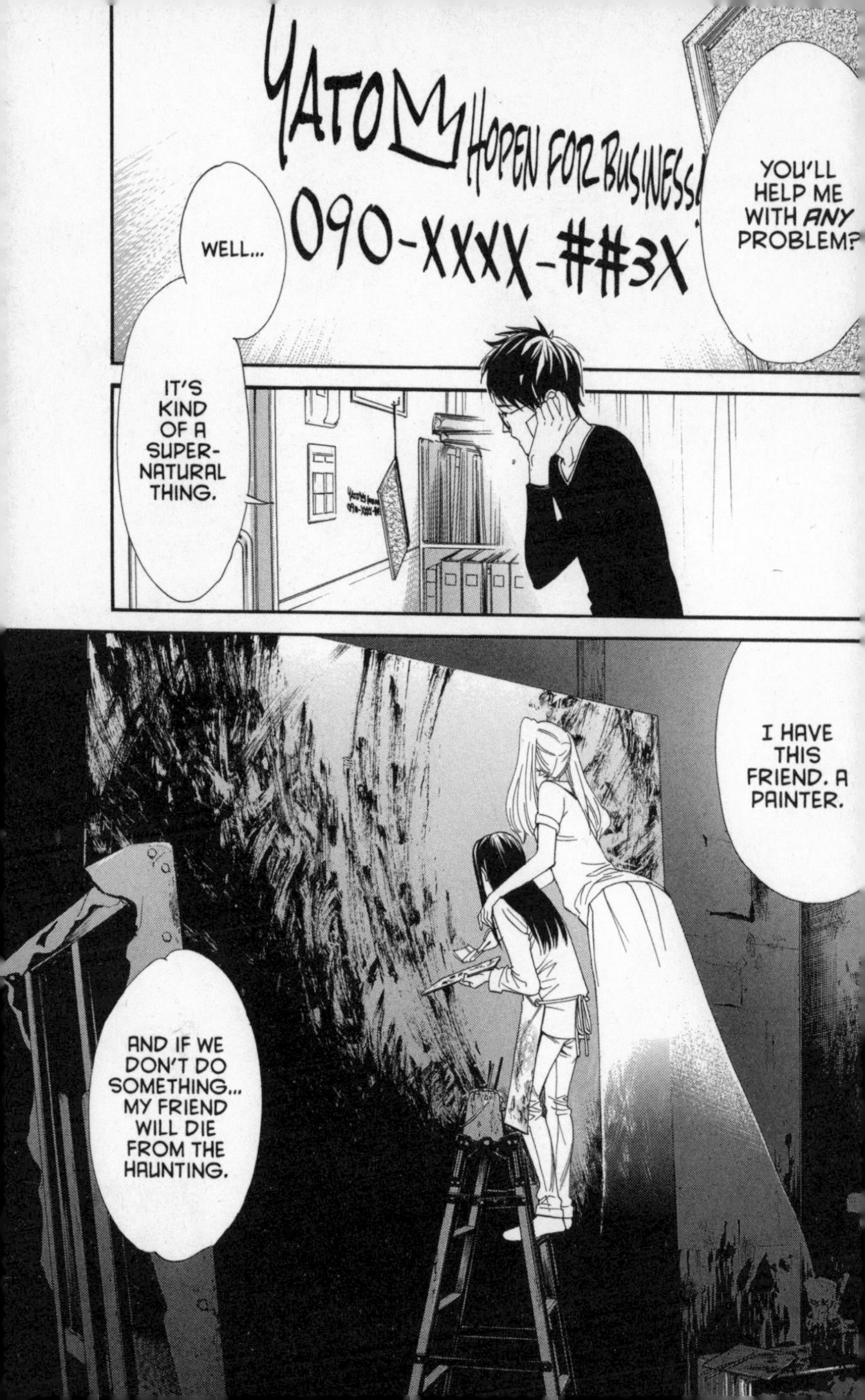
YOU'LL HELP ME WITH ANY PROBLEM?
YATO
OPEN FOR BUSINESS!
090-XXXX-##3X
WELL...
IT'S KIND OF A SUPER-NATURAL THING.
I HAVE THIS FRIEND. A PAINTER.
AND IF WE DON'T DO SOMETHING... MY FRIEND WILL DIE FROM THE HAUNTING.

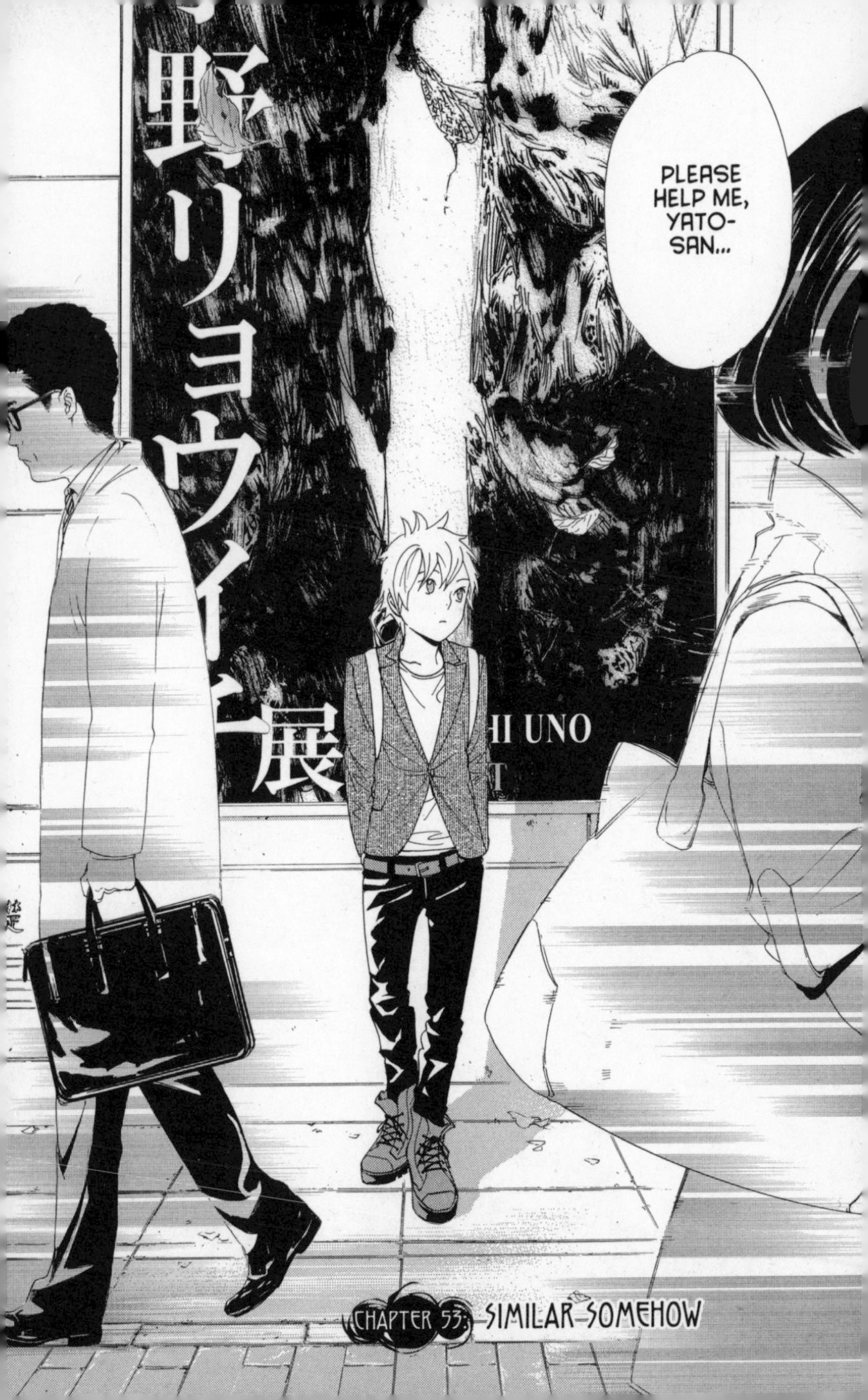
PLEASE HELP ME, YATO-SAN...
CHAPTER 53: SIMILAR SOMEHOW

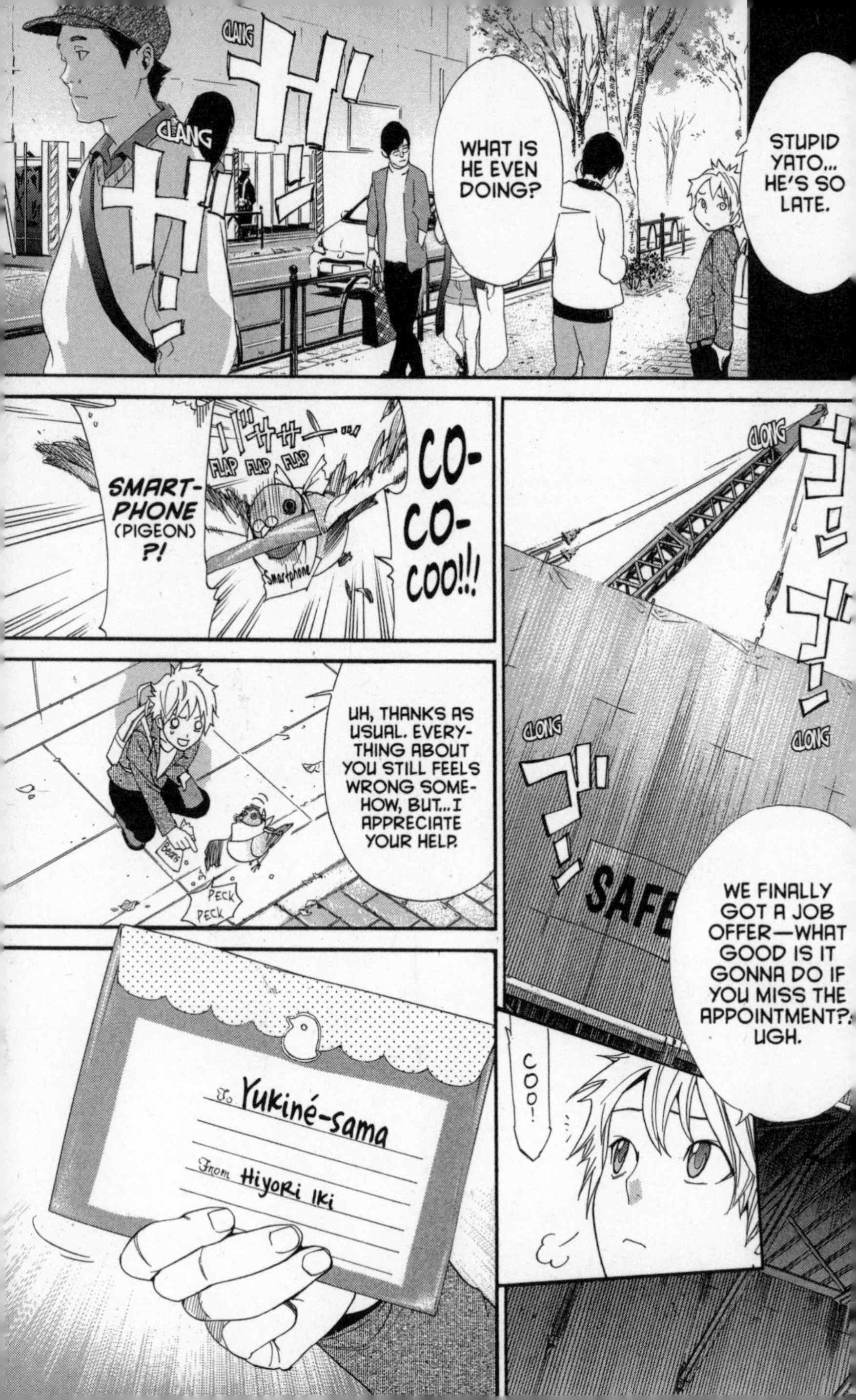
STUPID YATO... HE'S SO LATE.
WHAT IS HE EVEN DOING?
CLANG
CLANG
CLONG
CLONG
CLONG
SAFE
CO-CO-COO!!!
FLAP FLAP FLAP
Smartphone
SMART-PHONE (PIGEON) ?!
UH, THANKS AS USUAL. EVERY-THING ABOUT YOU STILL FEELS WRONG SOME-HOW, BUT...I APPRECIATE YOUR HELP.
PECK
PECK
Beans
WE FINALLY GOT A JOB OFFER—WHAT GOOD IS IT GONNA DO IF YOU MISS THE APPOINTMENT?. UGH.
COO!
To Yukiné-sama
From Hiyori Iki

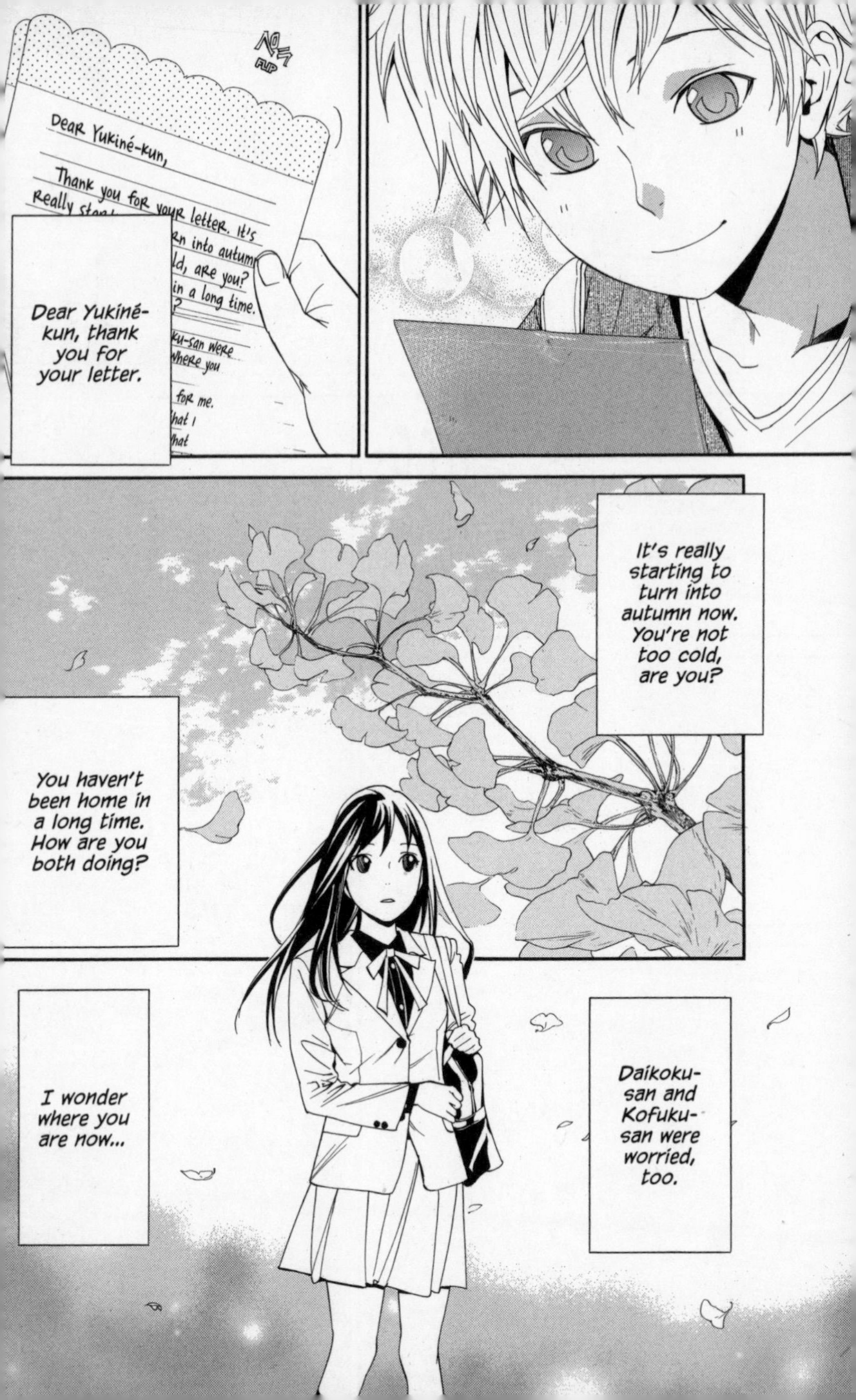
FLIP
Dear Yukiné-kun,
Thank you for your letter. It's
Dear Yukiné-kun, thank you for your letter.
It's really starting to turn into autumn now. You're not too cold, are you?
You haven't been home in a long time. How are you both doing?
Daikoku-san and Kofuku-san were worried, too.
I wonder where you are now...

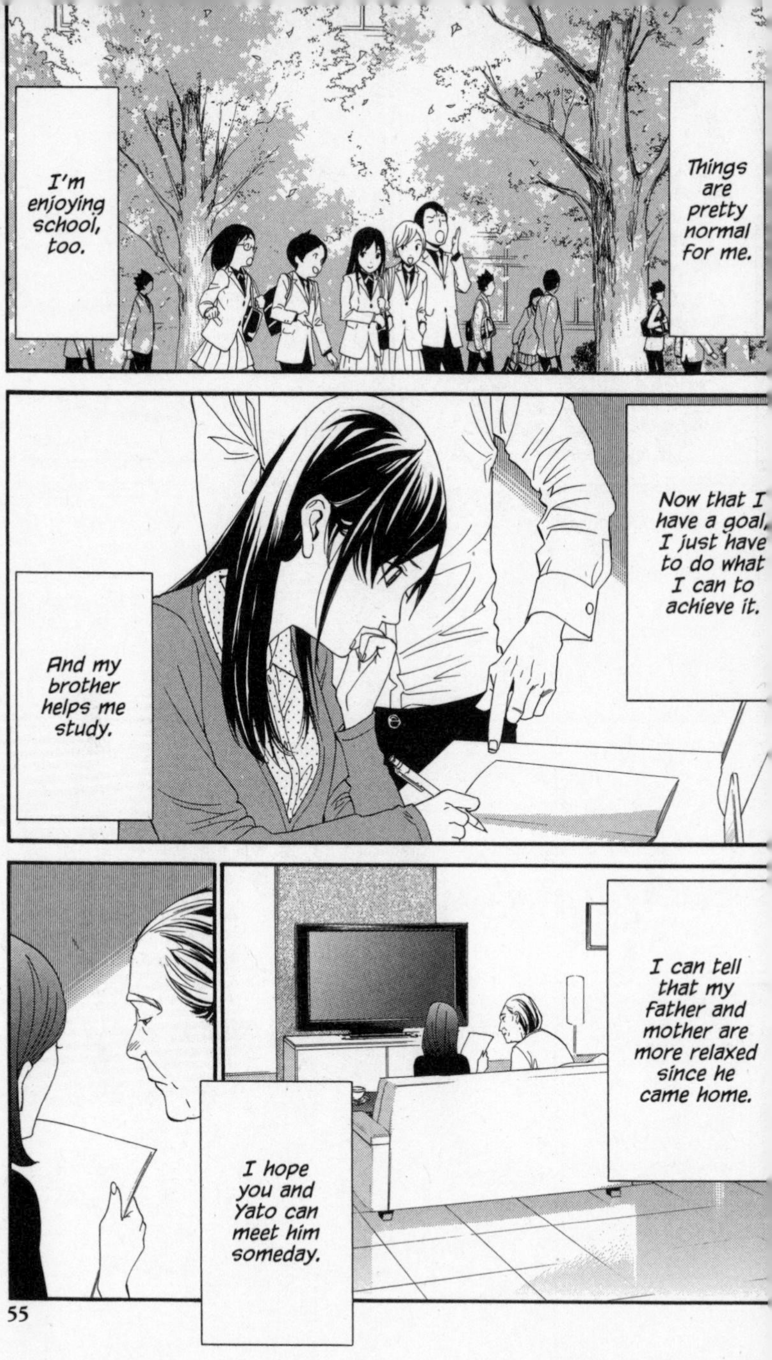
Things are pretty normal for me.
I'm enjoying school, too.
Now that I have a goal, I just have to do what I can to achieve it.
And my brother helps me study.
I can tell that my father and mother are more relaxed since he came home.
I hope you and Yato can meet him someday.

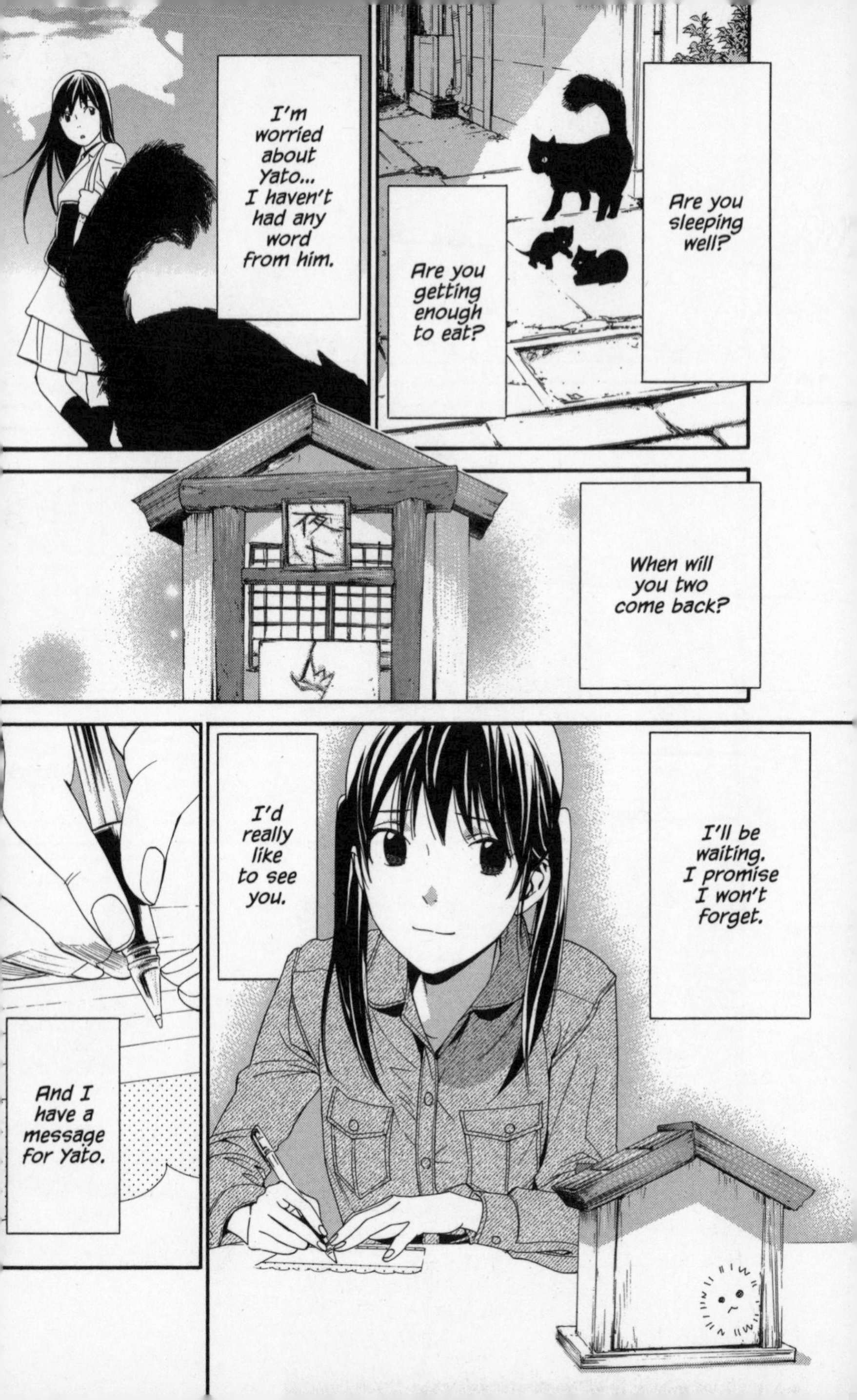
Are you sleeping well?
Are you getting enough to eat?
I'm worried about Yato... I haven't had any word from him.
When will you two come back?
I'll be waiting. I promise I won't forget.
I'd really like to see you.
And I have a message for Yato.

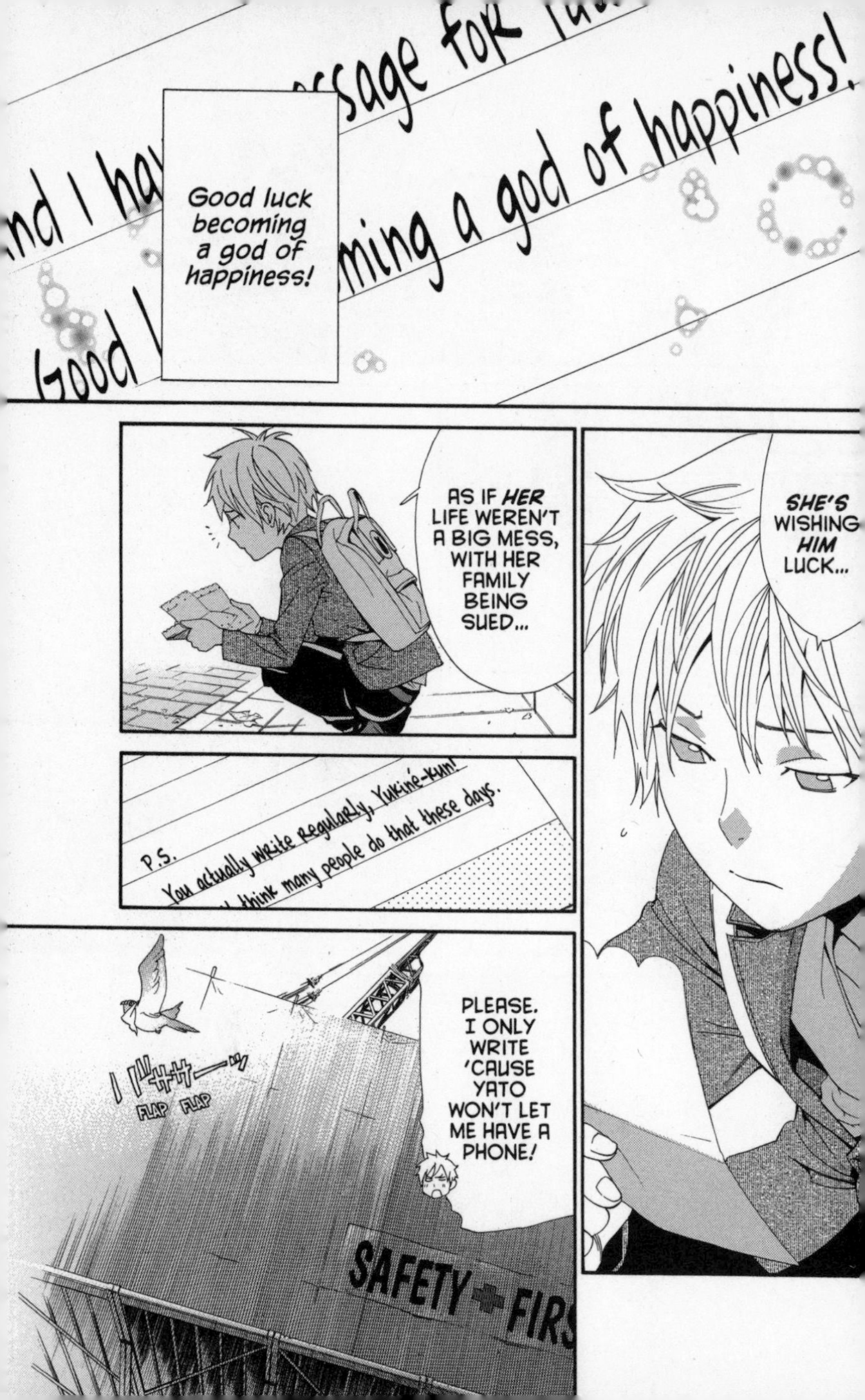

Good luck becoming a god of happiness!
SHE'S WISHING HIM LUCK...
AS IF HER LIFE WEREN'T A BIG MESS, WITH HER FAMILY BEING SUED...
P.S.
You actually write regularly, Yukiné-kun!
think many people do that these days.
PLEASE. I ONLY WRITE 'CAUSE YATO WON'T LET ME HAVE A PHONE!
FLAP FLAP
SAFETY FIRS

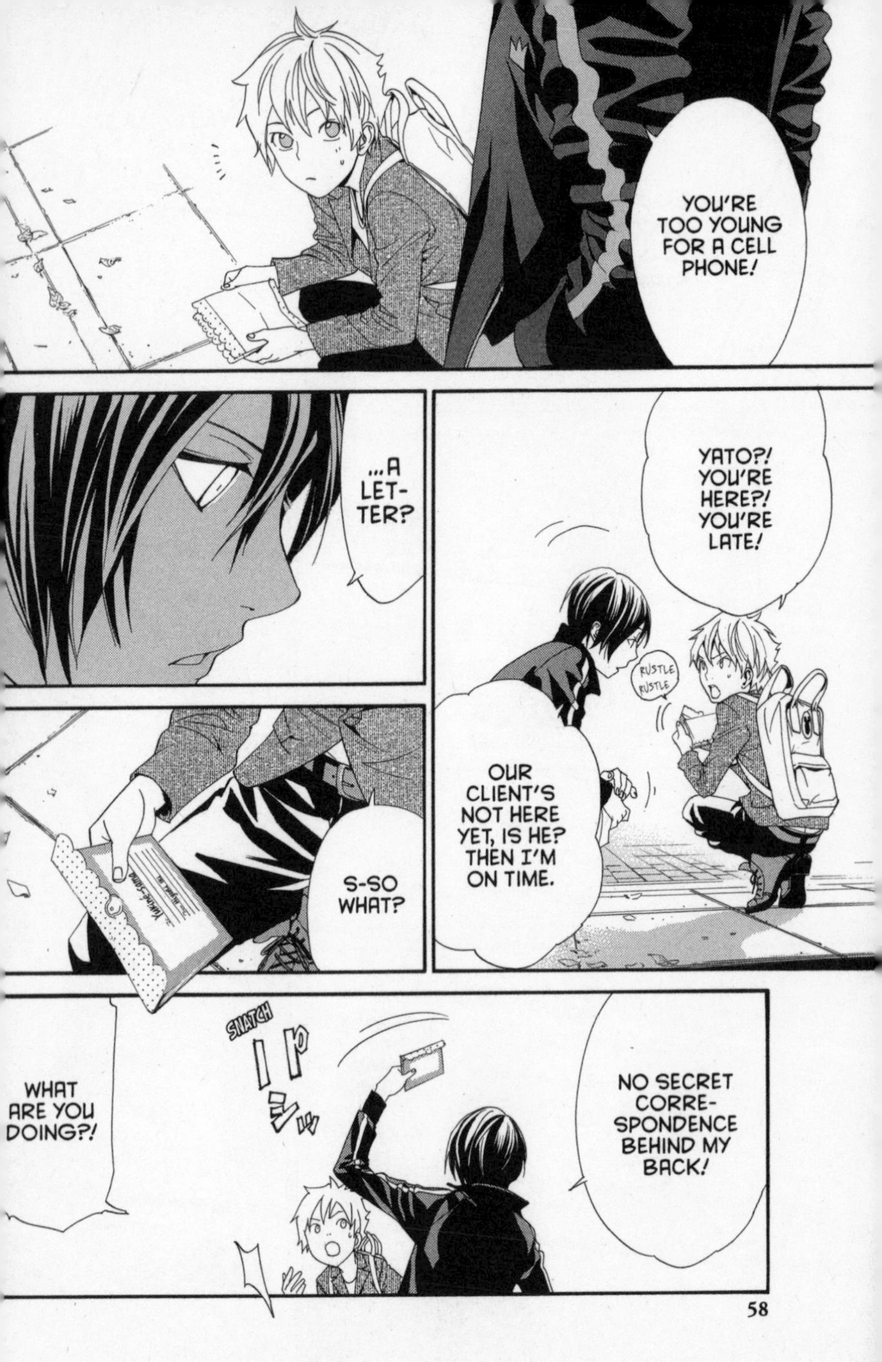
YOU'RE TOO YOUNG FOR A CELL PHONE!
YATO?! YOU'RE HERE?! YOU'RE LATE!
RUSTLE RUSTLE
OUR CLIENT'S NOT HERE YET, IS HE? THEN I'M ON TIME.
...A LET-TER?
S-SO WHAT?
NO SECRET CORRE-SPONDENCE BEHIND MY BACK!
SNATCH
WHAT ARE YOU DOING?!

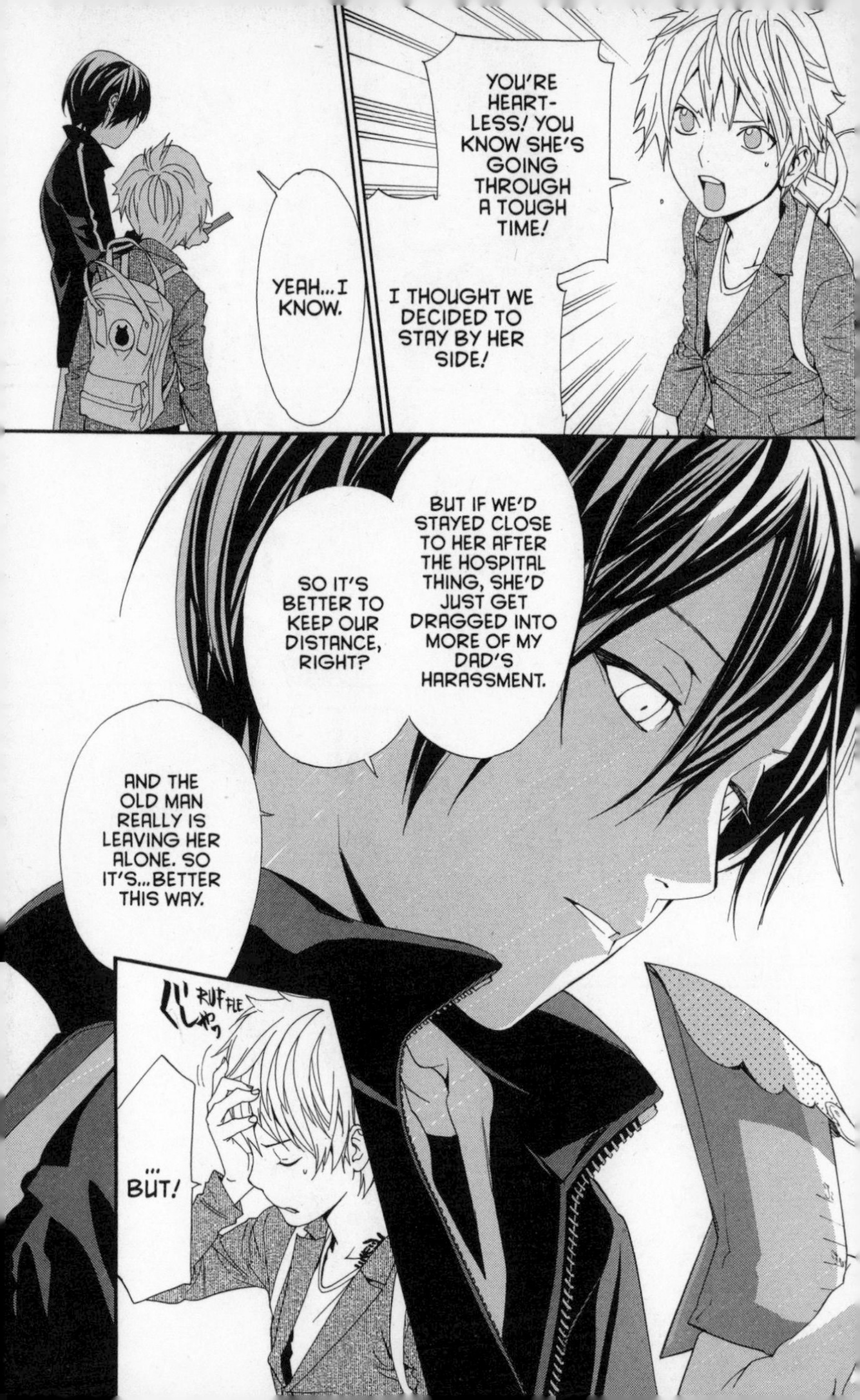
YOU'RE HEART-LESS! YOU KNOW SHE'S GOING THROUGH A TOUGH TIME!
I THOUGHT WE DECIDED TO STAY BY HER SIDE!
YEAH...I KNOW.
BUT IF WE'D STAYED CLOSE TO HER AFTER THE HOSPITAL THING, SHE'D JUST GET DRAGGED INTO MORE OF MY DAD'S HARASSMENT.
SO IT'S BETTER TO KEEP OUR DISTANCE, RIGHT?
AND THE OLD MAN REALLY IS LEAVING HER ALONE. SO IT'S...BETTER THIS WAY.
くしゃっ RUFFLE
...BUT!

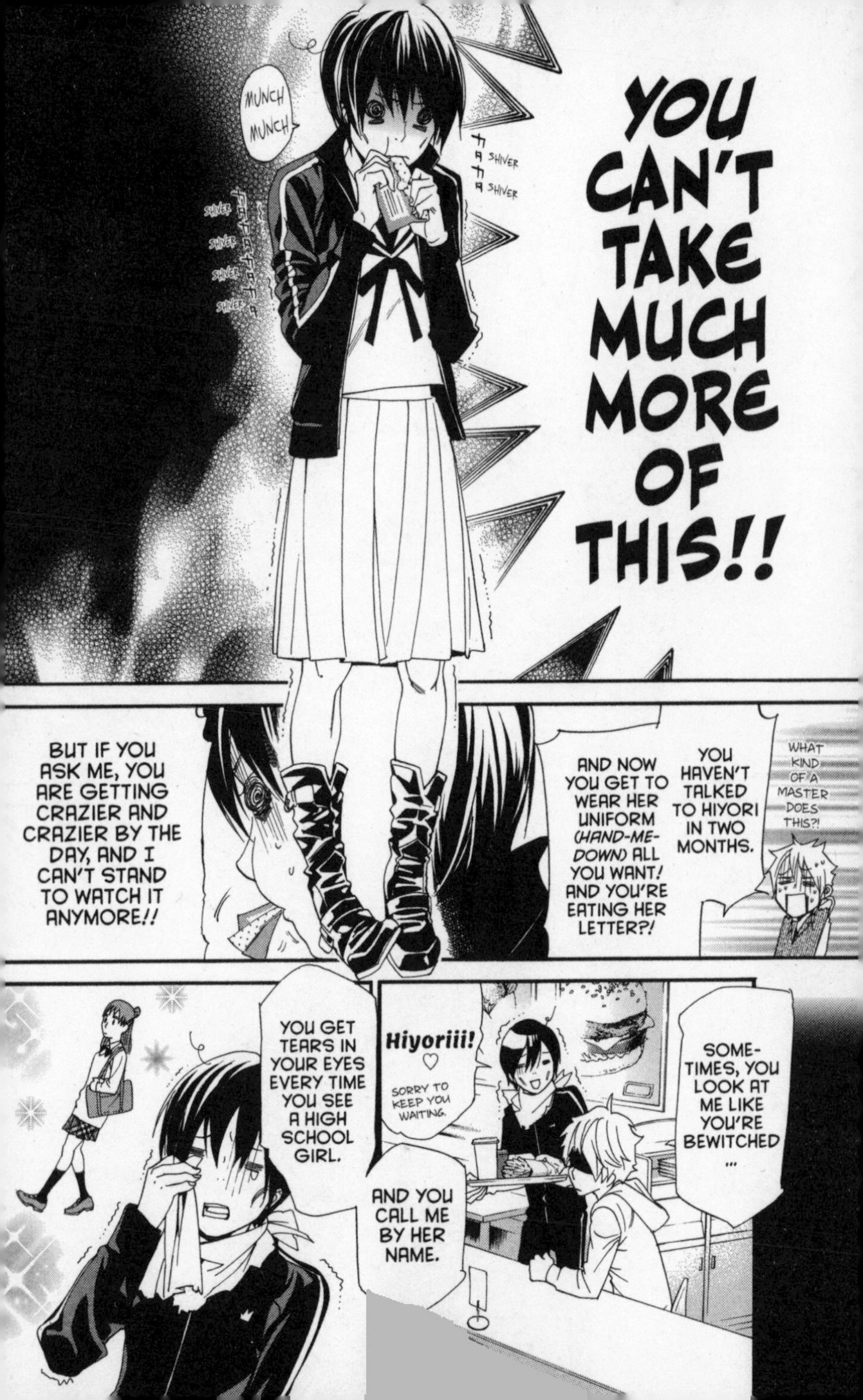
YOU CAN'T TAKE MUCH MORE OF THIS!!
SHIVER
SHIVER
MUNCH MUNCH
SHIVER
SHIVER
SHIVER
SHIVER
WHAT KIND OF A MASTER DOES THIS?!
YOU HAVEN'T TALKED TO HIYORI IN TWO MONTHS.
AND NOW YOU GET TO WEAR HER UNIFORM (HAND-ME-DOWN) ALL YOU WANT! AND YOU'RE EATING HER LETTER?!
BUT IF YOU ASK ME, YOU ARE GETTING CRAZIER AND CRAZIER BY THE DAY, AND I CAN'T STAND TO WATCH IT ANYMORE!!
SOME-TIMES, YOU LOOK AT ME LIKE YOU'RE BEWITCHED ...
Hiyoriii! ♡
SORRY TO KEEP YOU WAITING.
YOU GET TEARS IN YOUR EYES EVERY TIME YOU SEE A HIGH SCHOOL GIRL.
AND YOU CALL ME BY HER NAME.

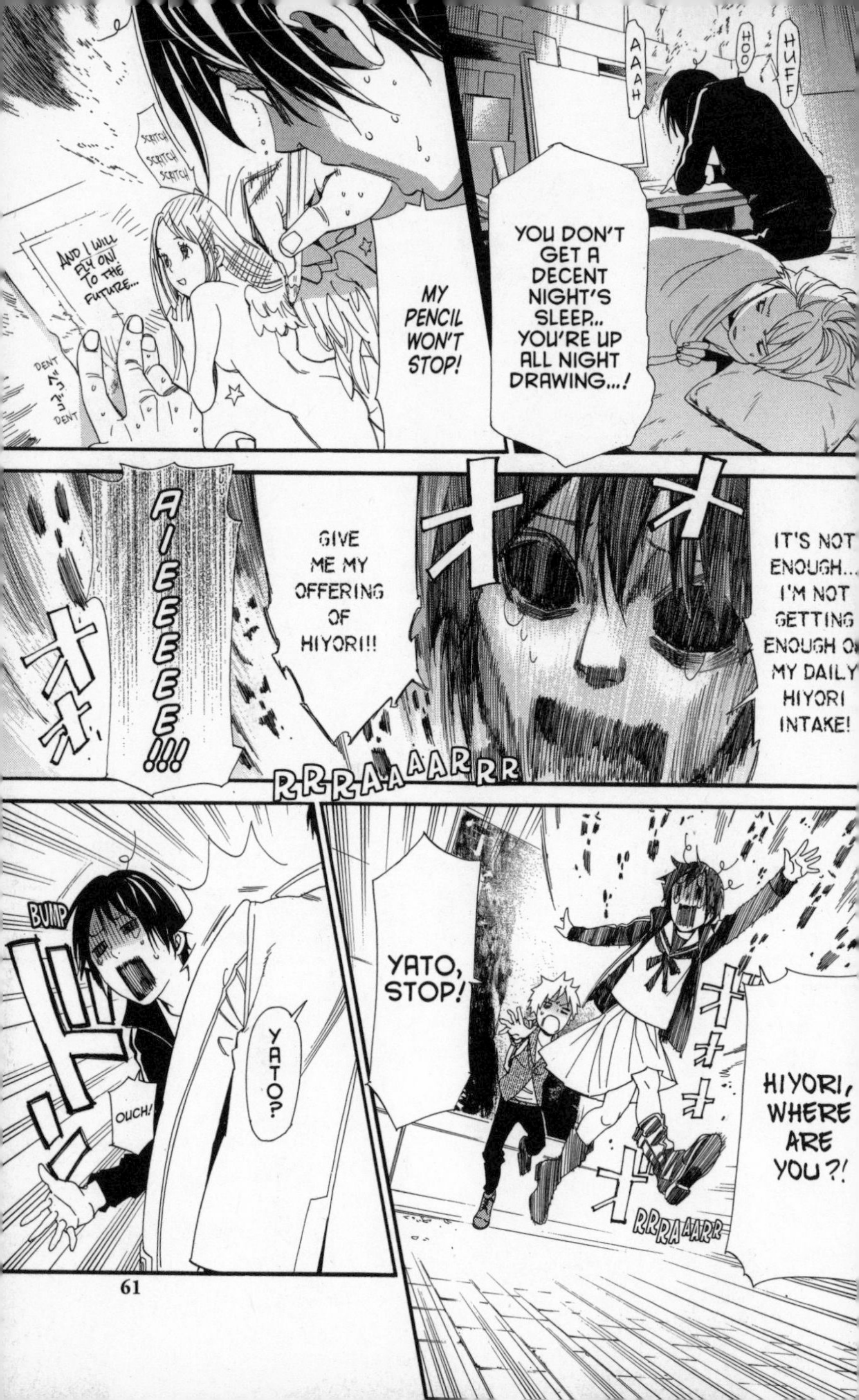
HUFF
HOO
AAAH
YOU DON'T GET A DECENT NIGHT'S SLEEP... YOU'RE UP ALL NIGHT DRAWING...!
MY PENCIL WON'T STOP!
SCRATCH SCRATCH SCRATCH
AND I WILL FLY ON! TO THE FUTURE...
DENT DENT
IT'S NOT ENOUGH... I'M NOT GETTING ENOUGH O MY DAILY HIYORI INTAKE!
GIVE ME MY OFFERING OF HIYORI!!!
RRRRAAAARRRR
AIEEEEEE!!!
HIYORI, WHERE ARE YOU?!
RRRAAARR
YATO, STOP!
YATO?
BUMP
OUCH!

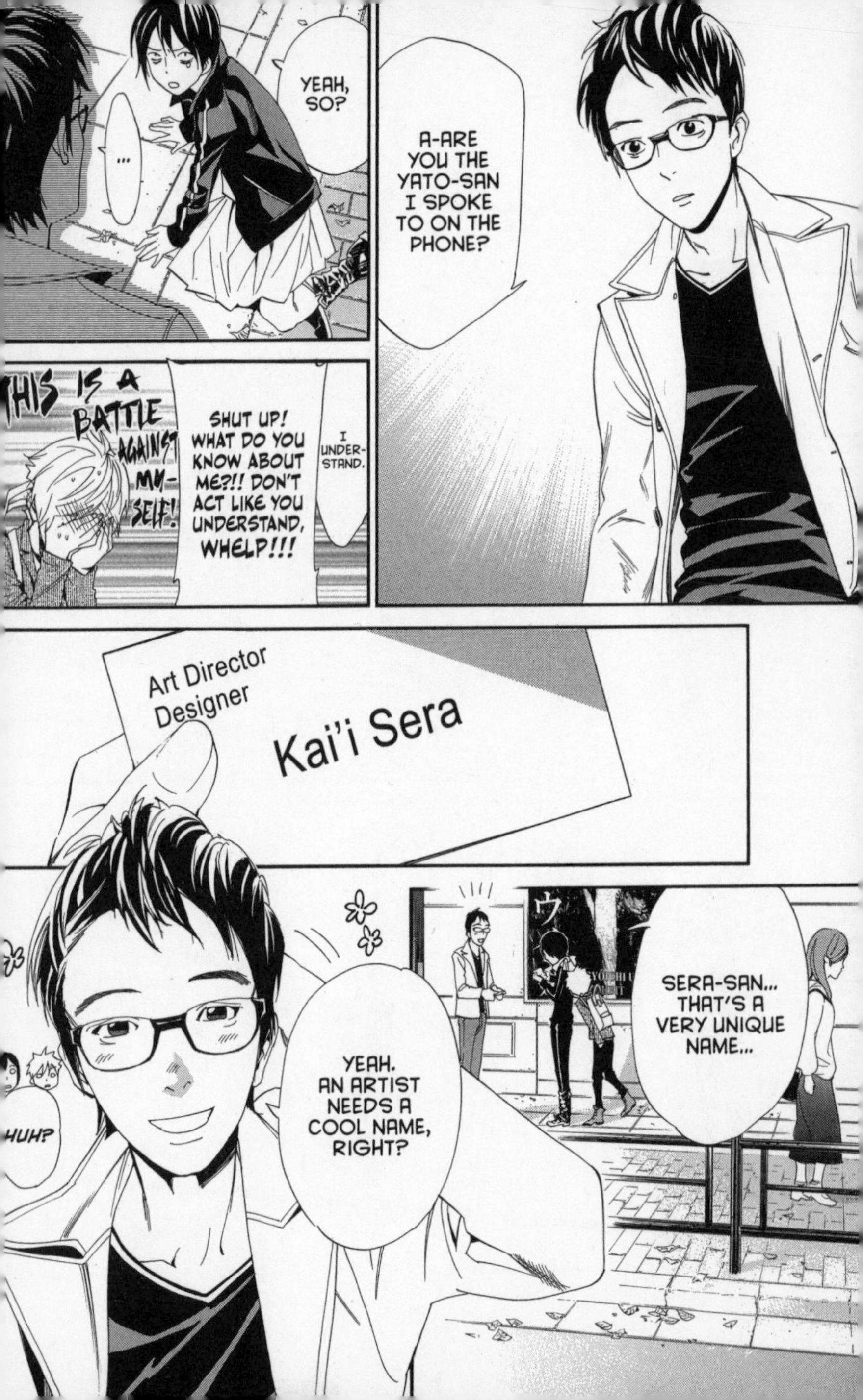
A-ARE YOU THE YATO-SAN I SPOKE TO ON THE PHONE?
YEAH, SO?
...
I UNDER-STAND.
SHUT UP! WHAT DO YOU KNOW ABOUT ME?!! DON'T ACT LIKE YOU UNDERSTAND, WHELP!!!
THIS IS A BATTLE AGAINST MY-SELF!
Art Director
Designer
Kai'i Sera
SERA-SAN... THAT'S A VERY UNIQUE NAME...
YEAH. AN ARTIST NEEDS A COOL NAME, RIGHT?
HUH?

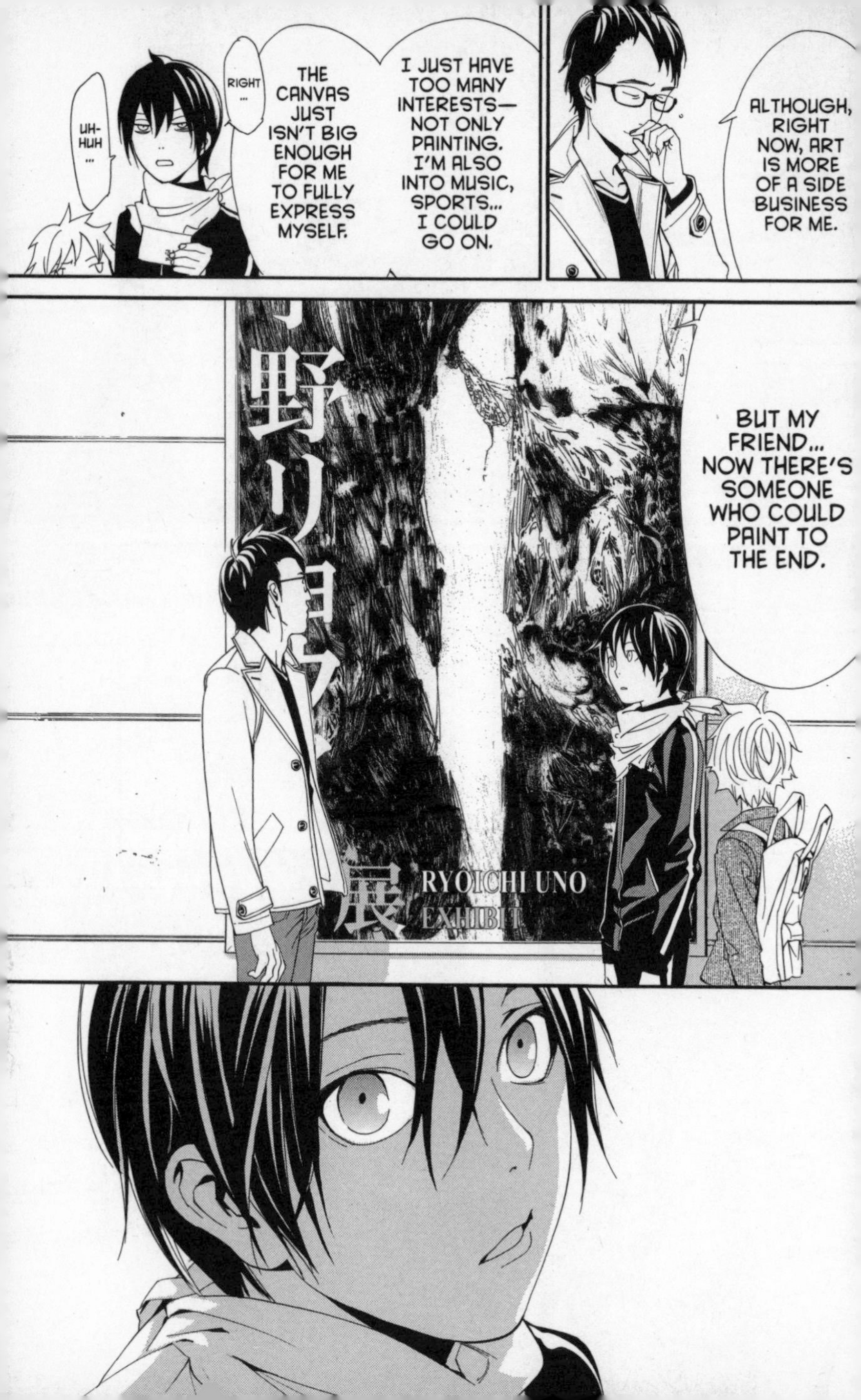
ALTHOUGH, RIGHT NOW, ART IS MORE OF A SIDE BUSINESS FOR ME.
I JUST HAVE TOO MANY INTERESTS— NOT ONLY PAINTING. I'M ALSO INTO MUSIC, SPORTS... I COULD GO ON.
THE CANVAS JUST ISN'T BIG ENOUGH FOR ME TO FULLY EXPRESS MYSELF.
RIGHT ...
UH-HUH ...
BUT MY FRIEND... NOW THERE'S SOMEONE WHO COULD PAINT TO THE END.
RYOICHI UNO
EXHIBIT

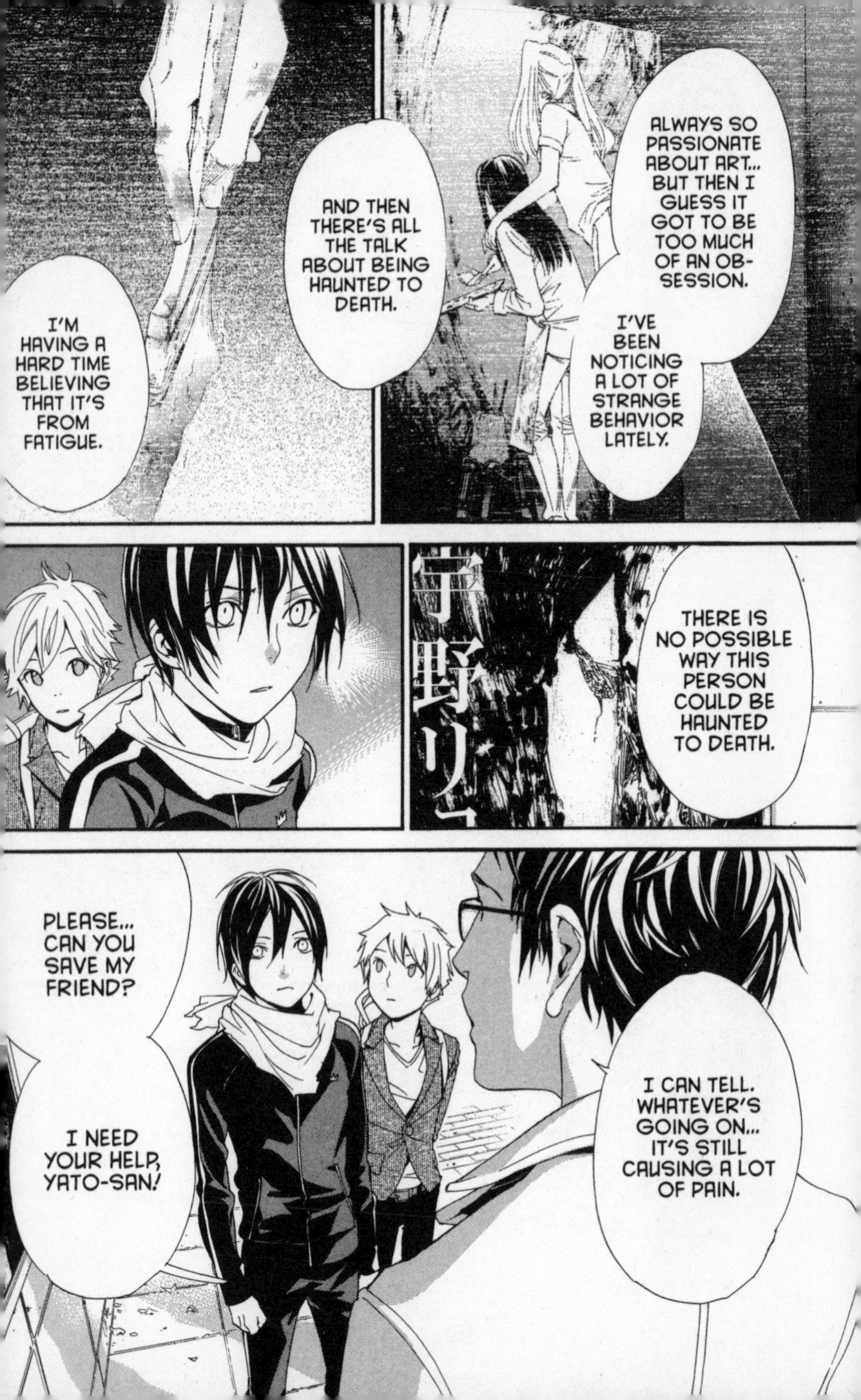
ALWAYS SO PASSIONATE ABOUT ART... BUT THEN I GUESS IT GOT TO BE TOO MUCH OF AN OB-SESSION.
I'VE BEEN NOTICING A LOT OF STRANGE BEHAVIOR LATELY.
AND THEN THERE'S ALL THE TALK ABOUT BEING HAUNTED TO DEATH.
I'M HAVING A HARD TIME BELIEVING THAT IT'S FROM FATIGUE.
THERE IS NO POSSIBLE WAY THIS PERSON COULD BE HAUNTED TO DEATH.
I CAN TELL. WHATEVER'S GOING ON... IT'S STILL CAUSING A LOT OF PAIN.
PLEASE... CAN YOU SAVE MY FRIEND?
I NEED YOUR HELP, YATO-SAN!

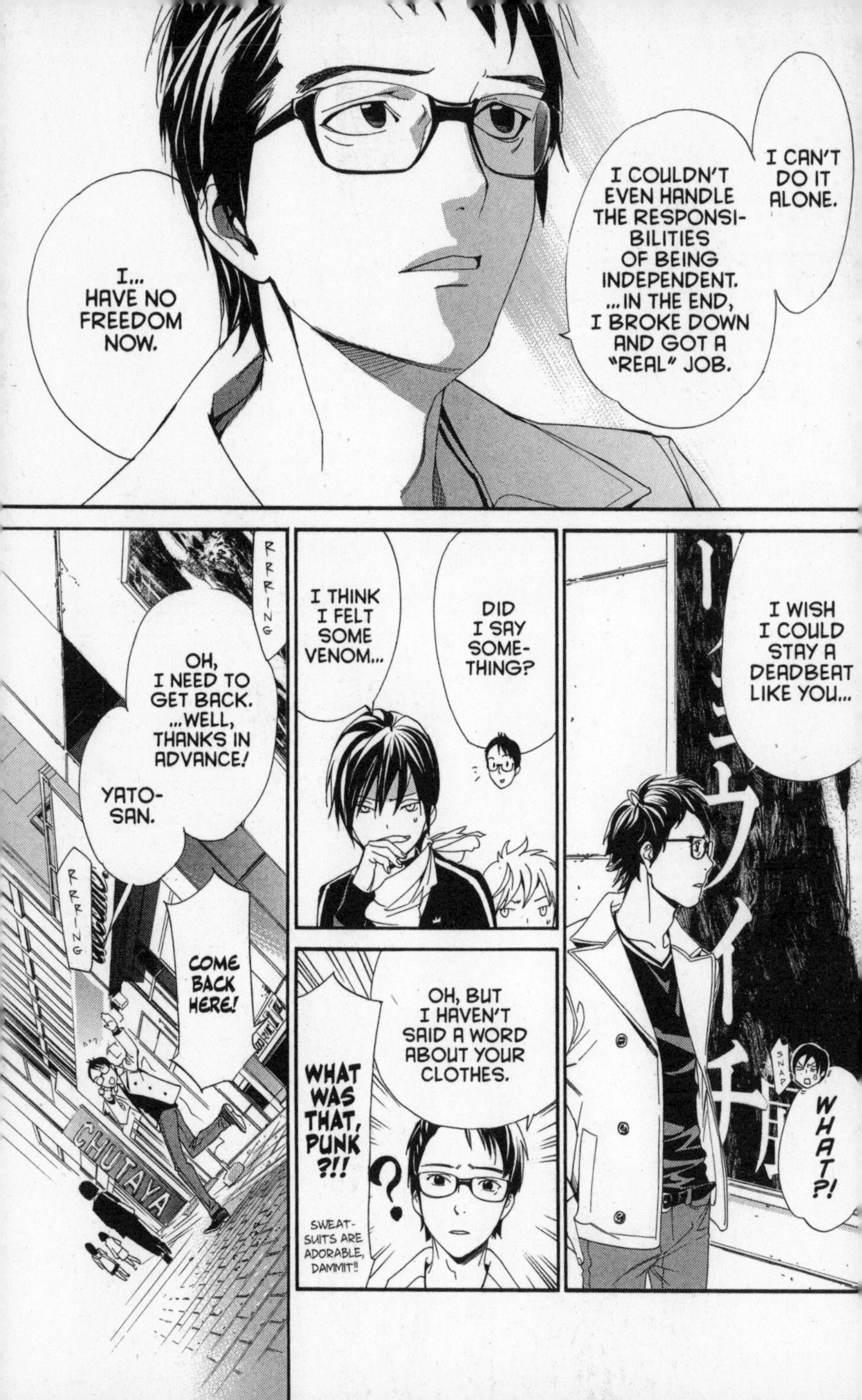
I CAN'T DO IT ALONE.
I COULDN'T EVEN HANDLE THE RESPONSIBILITIES OF BEING INDEPENDENT. ...IN THE END, I BROKE DOWN AND GOT A "REAL" JOB.
I... HAVE NO FREEDOM NOW.
I WISH I COULD STAY A DEADBEAT LIKE YOU...
SNAP
WHAT?!
DID I SAY SOMETHING?
I THINK I FELT SOME VENOM...
OH, BUT I HAVEN'T SAID A WORD ABOUT YOUR CLOTHES.
WHAT WAS THAT, PUNK?!!
SWEATSUITS ARE ADORABLE, DAMMIT!!
RRRING
OH, I NEED TO GET BACK. ...WELL, THANKS IN ADVANCE!
YATO-SAN.
RRRING
COME BACK HERE!
CHUTAYA

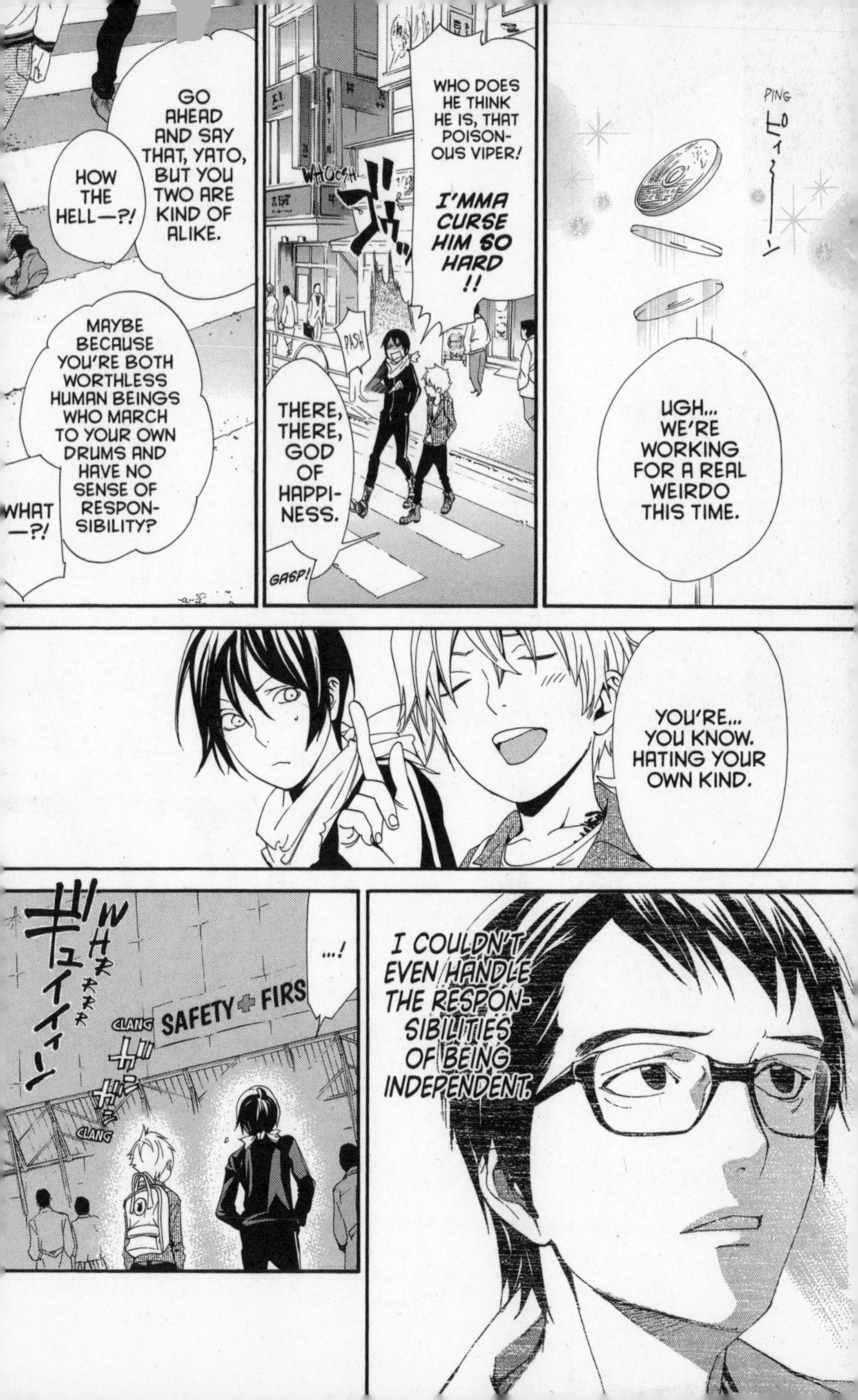
PING
UGH... WE'RE WORKING FOR A REAL WEIRDO THIS TIME.
WHO DOES HE THINK HE IS, THAT POISON-OUS VIPER!
I'MMA CURSE HIM SO HARD !!
WHOOSH
PISH
THERE, THERE, GOD OF HAPPI-NESS.
GASP!
GO AHEAD AND SAY THAT, YATO, BUT YOU TWO ARE KIND OF ALIKE.
HOW THE HELL—?!
MAYBE BECAUSE YOU'RE BOTH WORTHLESS HUMAN BEINGS WHO MARCH TO YOUR OWN DRUMS AND HAVE NO SENSE OF RESPON-SIBILITY?
WHAT —?!
YOU'RE... YOU KNOW. HATING YOUR OWN KIND.
I COULDN'T EVEN HANDLE THE RESPON-SIBILITIES OF BEING INDEPENDENT.
...!
SAFETY FIRS
WHRRRR
CLANG
CLANG

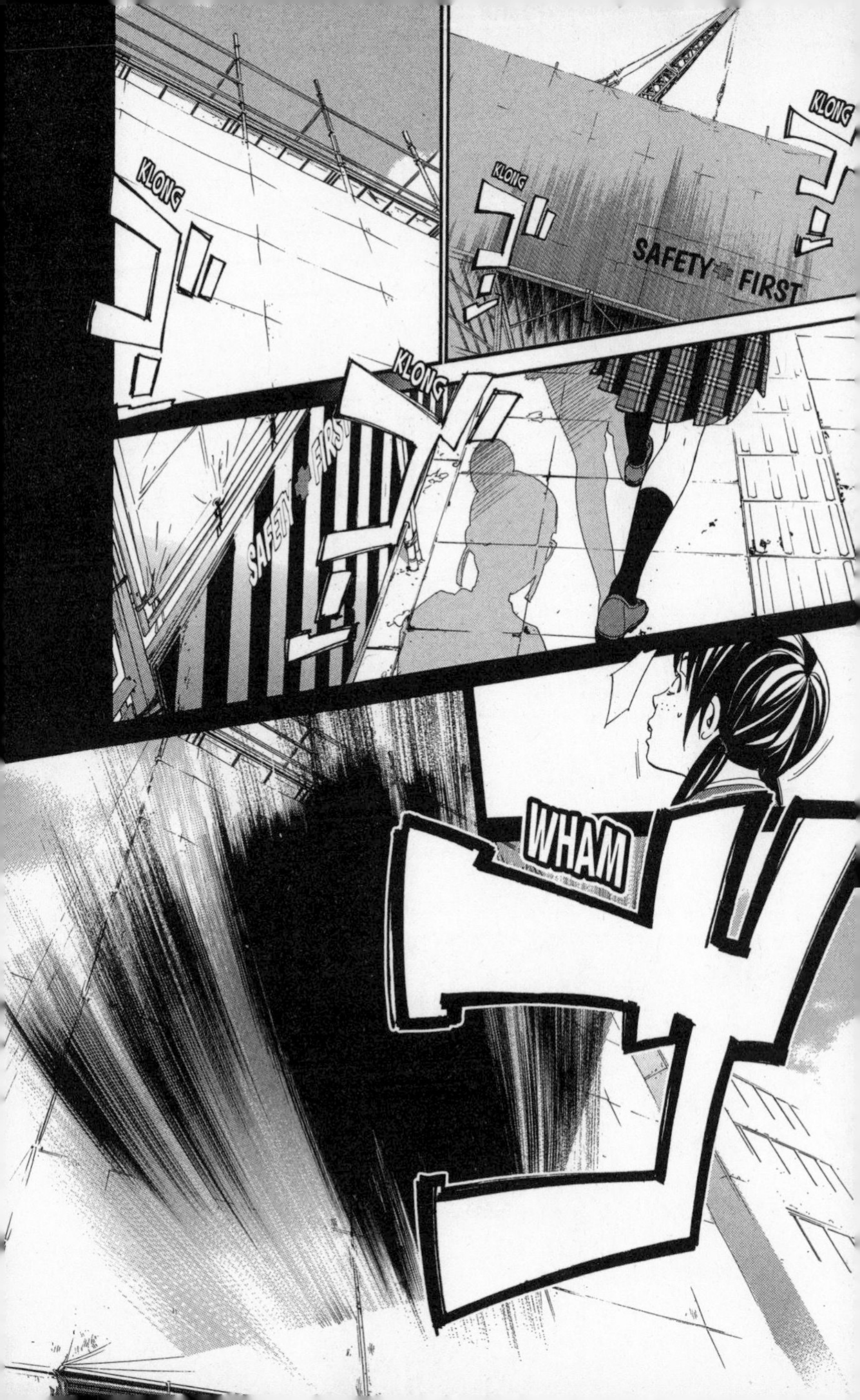
KLONG
KLONG
SAFETY FIRST
KLONG
KLONG
SAFETY FIRST
WHAM

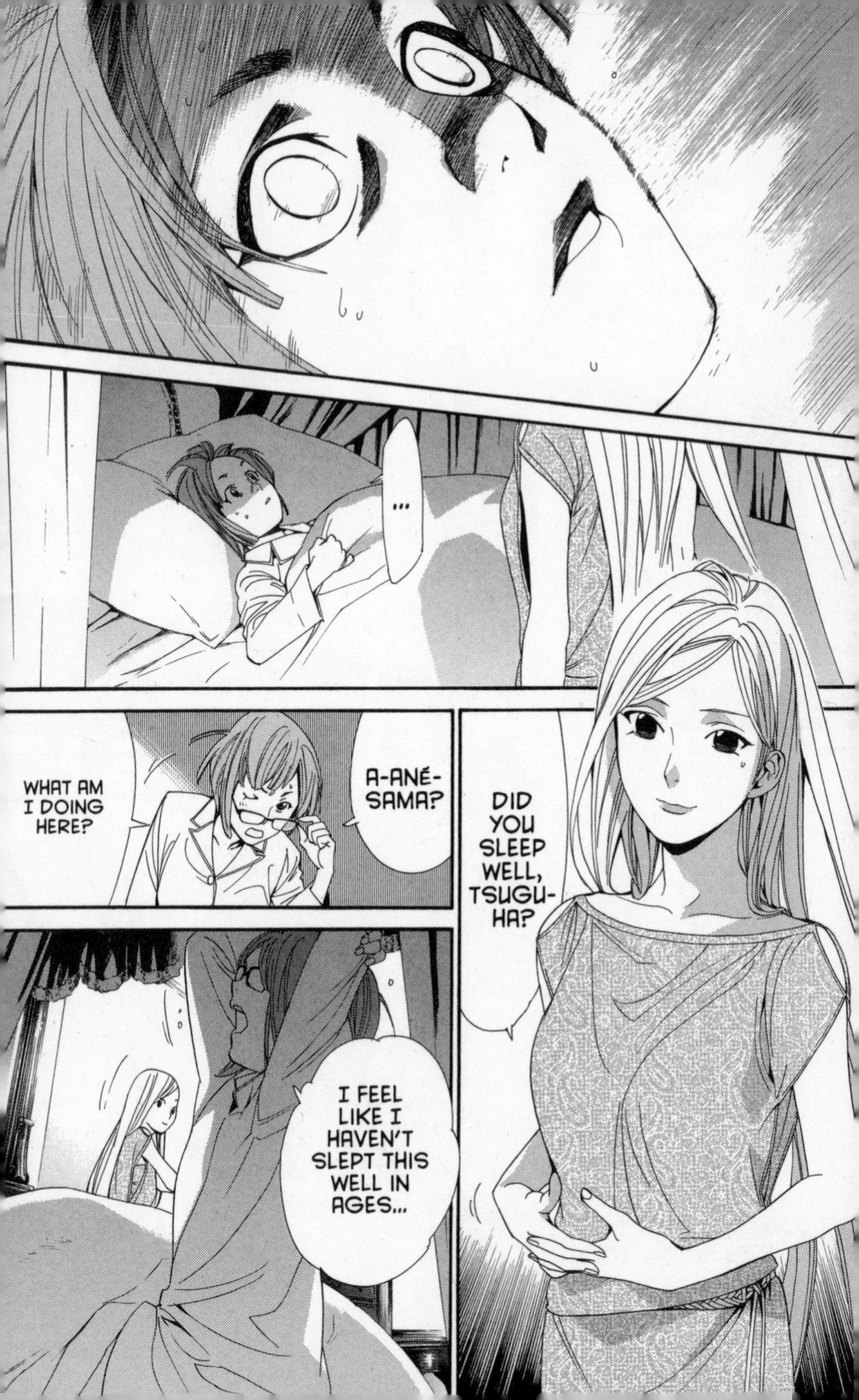
...
DID YOU SLEEP WELL, TSUGUHA?
A-ANÉ-SAMA?
WHAT AM I DOING HERE?
I FEEL LIKE I HAVEN'T SLEPT THIS WELL IN AGES...

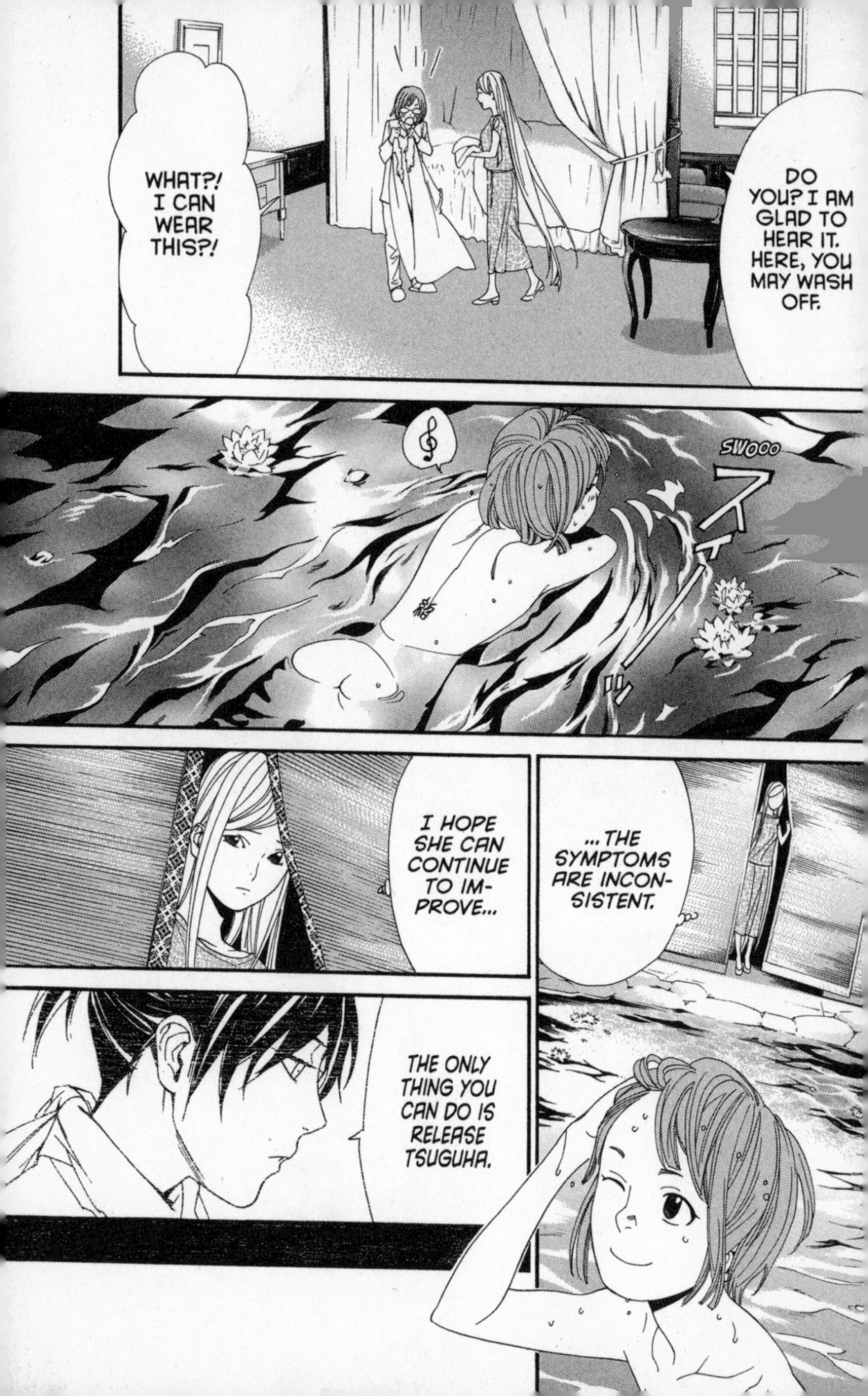
WHAT?! I CAN WEAR THIS?!
DO YOU? I AM GLAD TO HEAR IT. HERE, YOU MAY WASH OFF.
SWOOO
...THE SYMPTOMS ARE INCON-SISTENT.
I HOPE SHE CAN CONTINUE TO IM-PROVE...
THE ONLY THING YOU CAN DO IS RELEASE TSUGUHA.

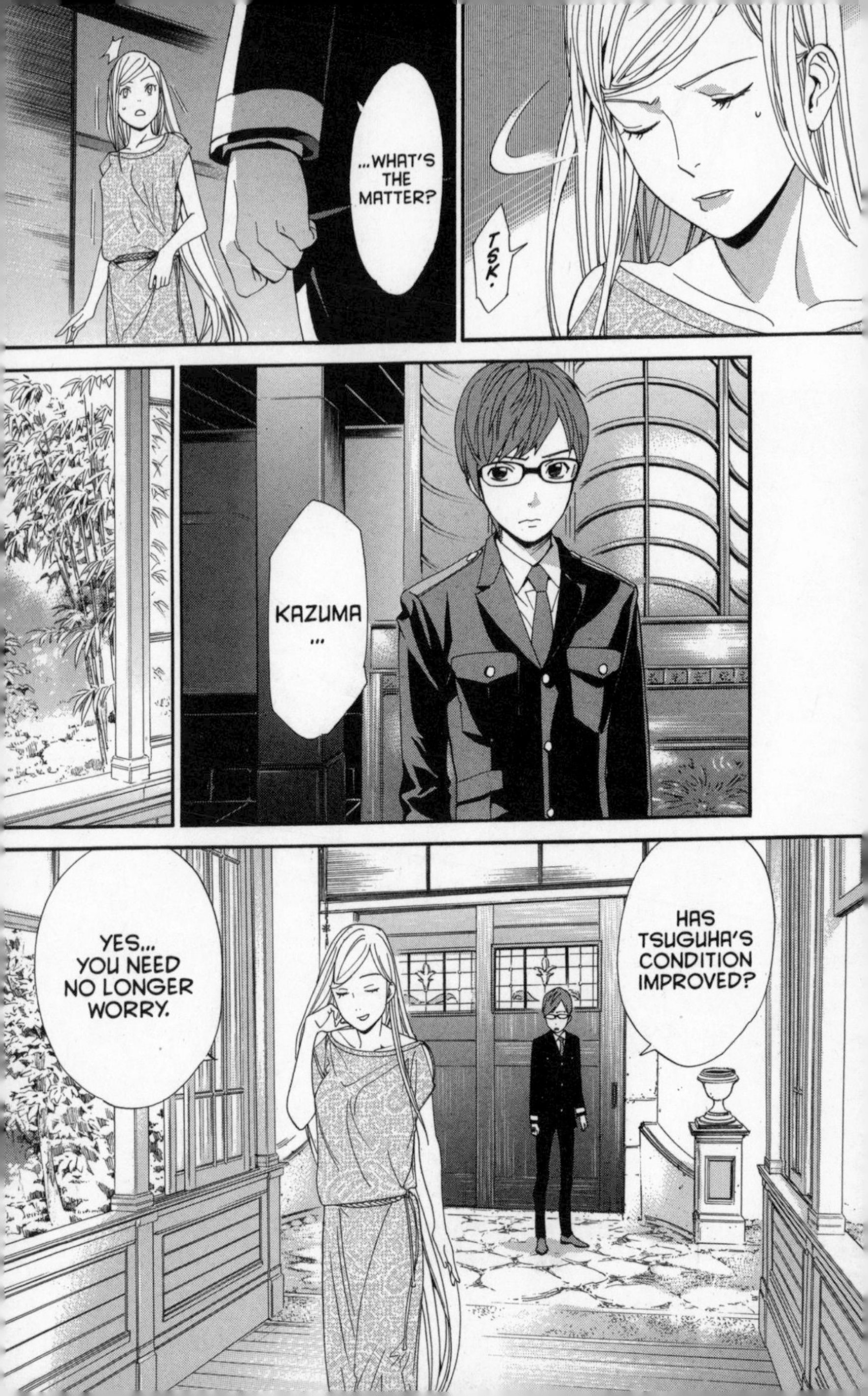
TSK.
...WHAT'S THE MATTER?
KAZUMA ...
HAS TSUGUHA'S CONDITION IMPROVED?
YES... YOU NEED NO LONGER WORRY.

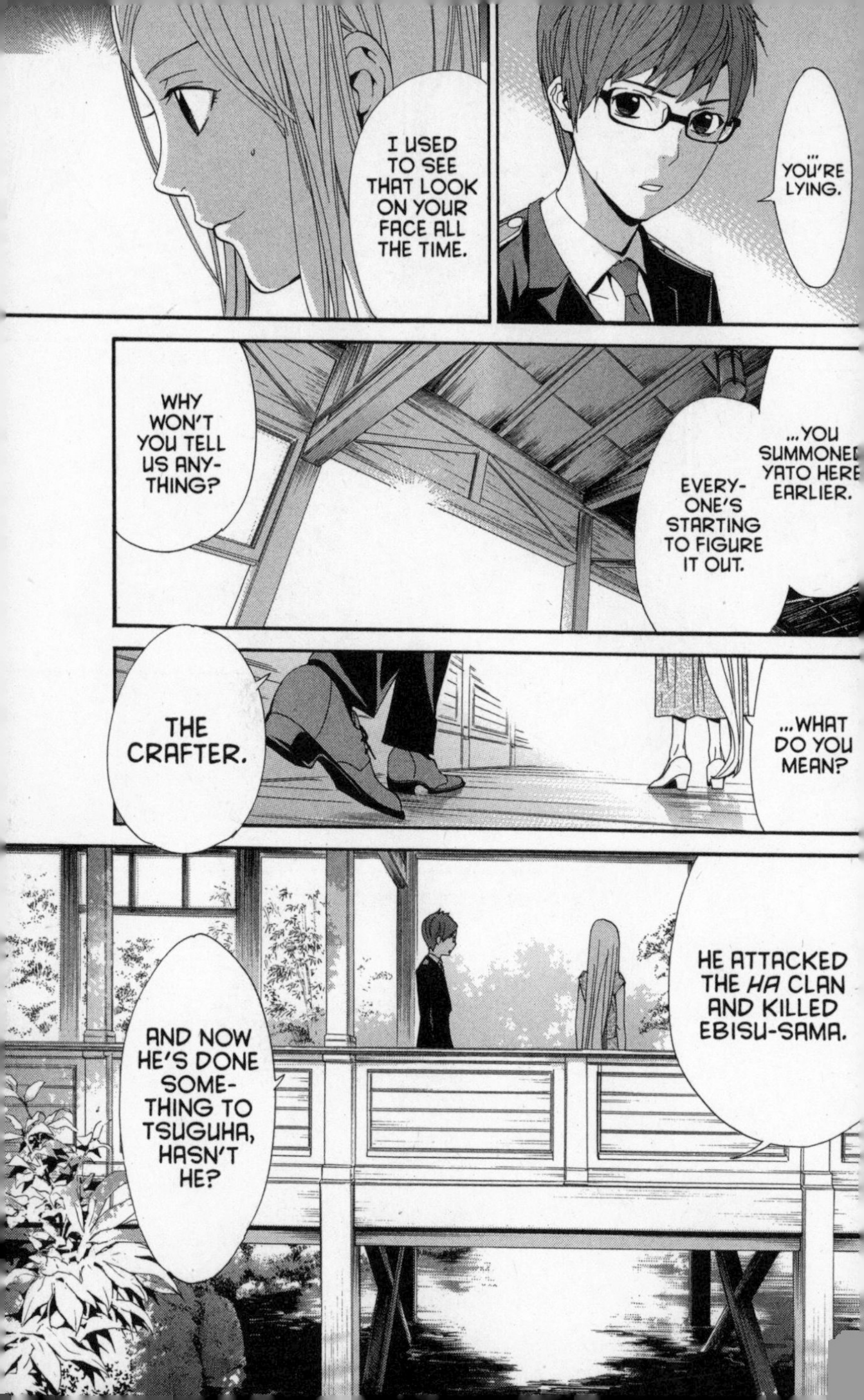
...YOU'RE LYING.
I USED TO SEE THAT LOOK ON YOUR FACE ALL THE TIME.
...YOU SUMMONED YATO HERE EARLIER.
EVERYONE'S STARTING TO FIGURE IT OUT.
WHY WON'T YOU TELL US ANYTHING?
...WHAT DO YOU MEAN?
THE CRAFTER.
HE ATTACKED THE *HA* CLAN AND KILLED EBISU-SAMA.
AND NOW HE'S DONE SOMETHING TO TSUGUHA, HASN'T HE?

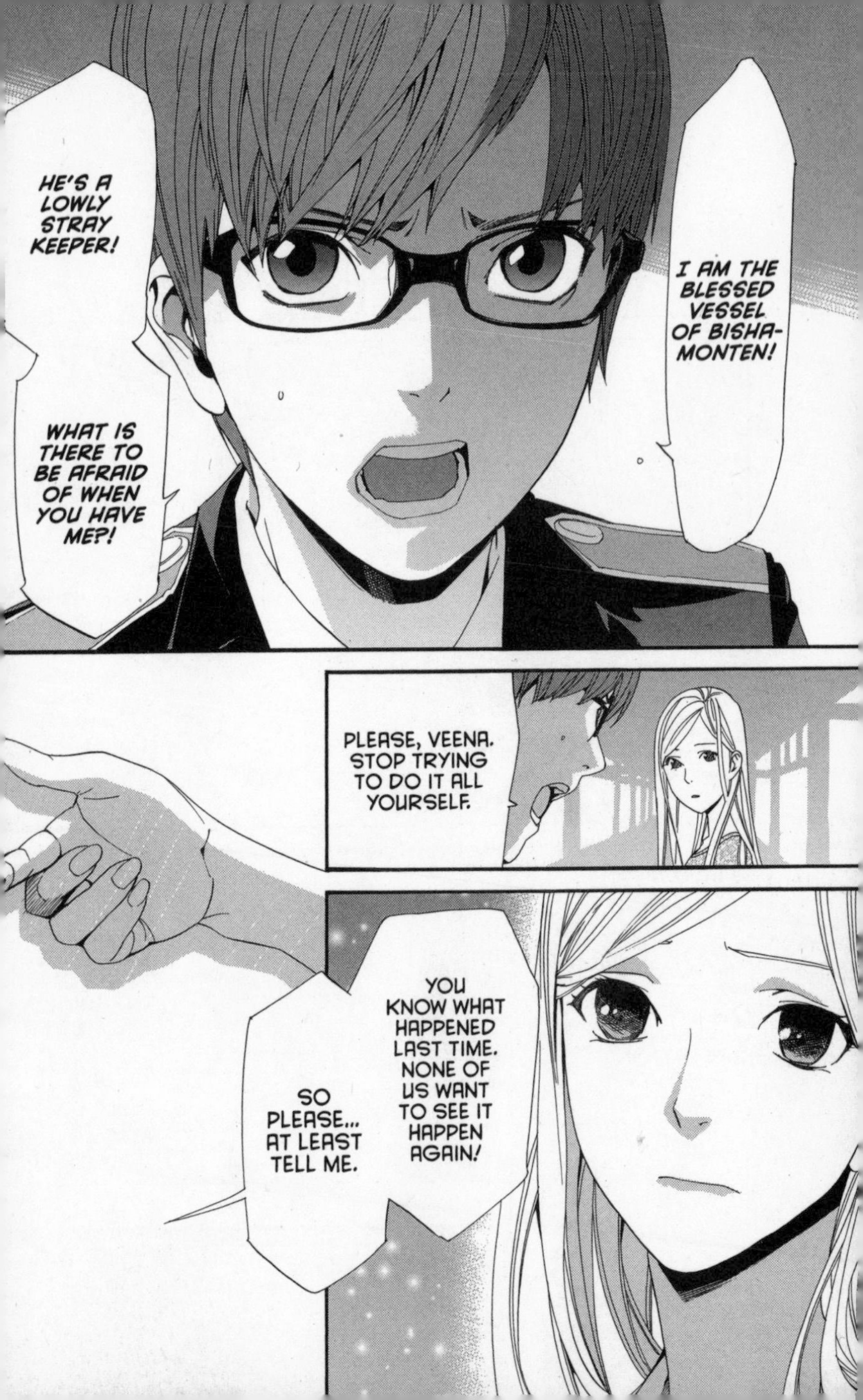
I AM THE BLESSED VESSEL OF BISHA-MONTEN!
HE'S A LOWLY STRAY KEEPER!
WHAT IS THERE TO BE AFRAID OF WHEN YOU HAVE ME?!
PLEASE, VEENA. STOP TRYING TO DO IT ALL YOURSELF.
YOU KNOW WHAT HAPPENED LAST TIME. NONE OF US WANT TO SEE IT HAPPEN AGAIN!
SO PLEASE... AT LEAST TELL ME.

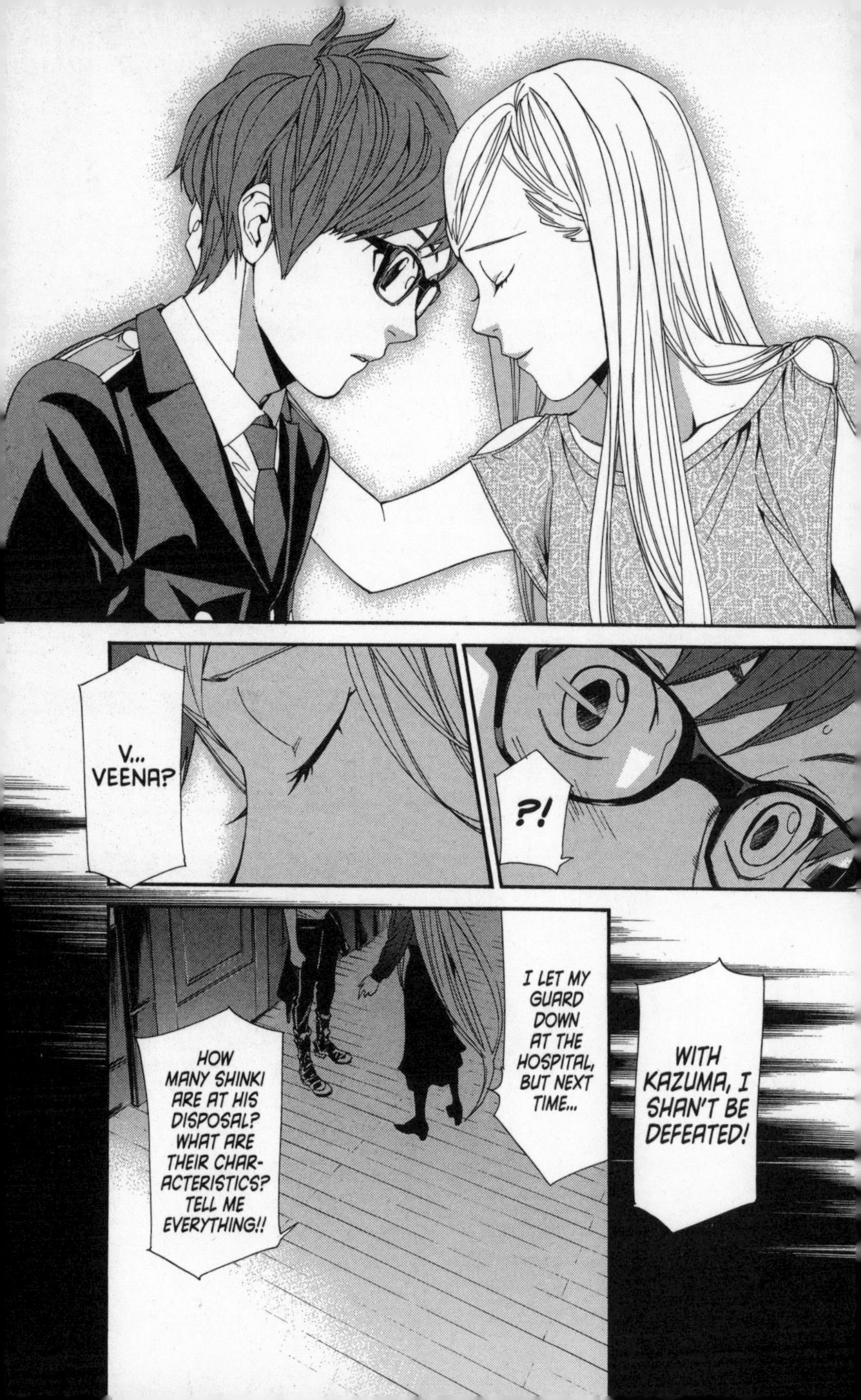
?!
V... VEENA?
I LET MY GUARD DOWN AT THE HOSPITAL, BUT NEXT TIME...
WITH KAZUMA, I SHAN'T BE DEFEATED!
HOW MANY SHINKI ARE AT HIS DISPOSAL? WHAT ARE THEIR CHAR-ACTERISTICS? TELL ME EVERYTHING!!

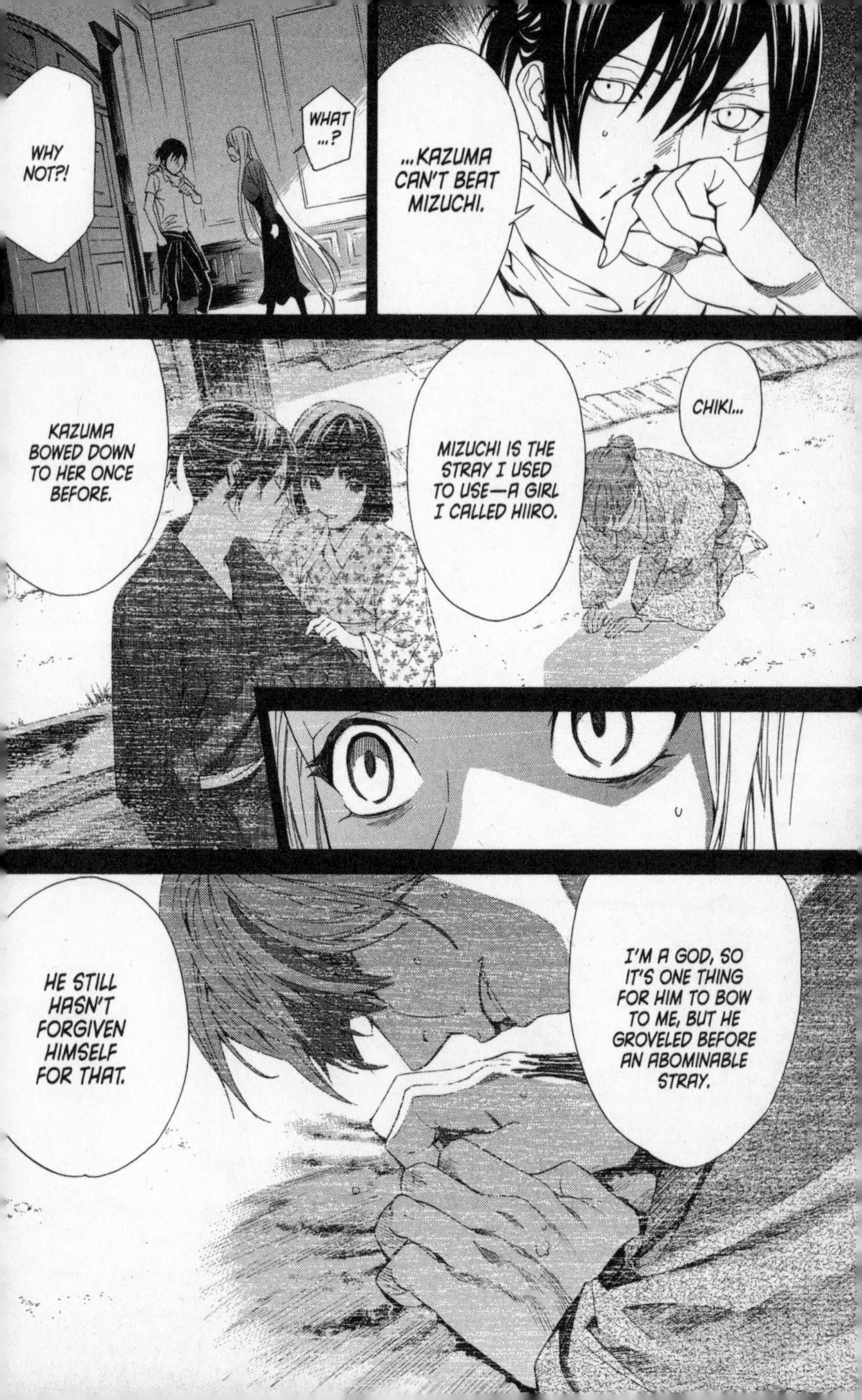
...KAZUMA CAN'T BEAT MIZUCHI.
WHAT ...?
WHY NOT?!
CHIKI...
MIZUCHI IS THE STRAY I USED TO USE—A GIRL I CALLED HIIRO.
KAZUMA BOWED DOWN TO HER ONCE BEFORE.
I'M A GOD, SO IT'S ONE THING FOR HIM TO BOW TO ME, BUT HE GROVELED BEFORE AN ABOMINABLE STRAY.
HE STILL HASN'T FORGIVEN HIMSELF FOR THAT.

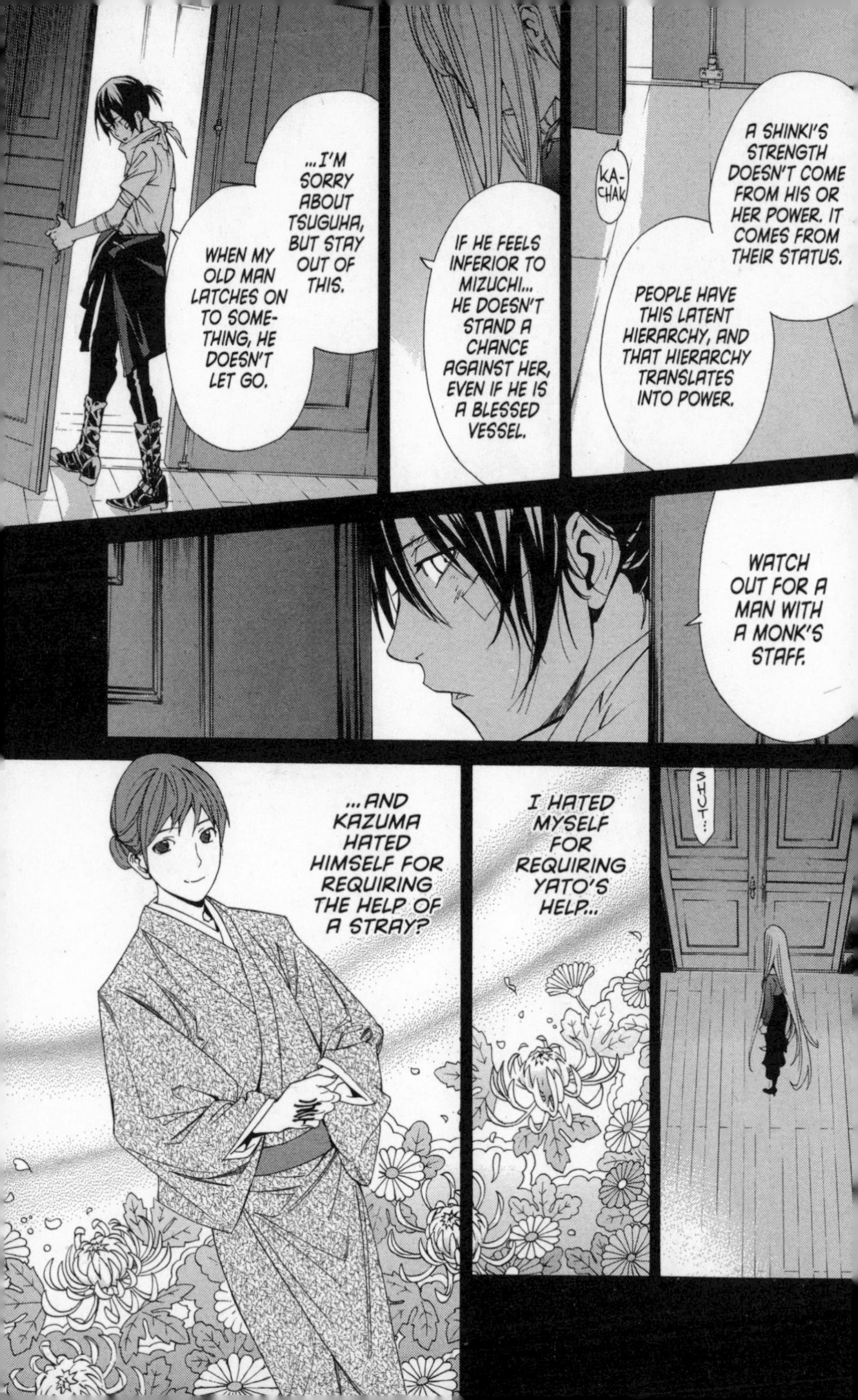
A SHINKI'S STRENGTH DOESN'T COME FROM HIS OR HER POWER. IT COMES FROM THEIR STATUS.
KA-CHAK
PEOPLE HAVE THIS LATENT HIERARCHY, AND THAT HIERARCHY TRANSLATES INTO POWER.
IF HE FEELS INFERIOR TO MIZUCHI... HE DOESN'T STAND A CHANCE AGAINST HER, EVEN IF HE IS A BLESSED VESSEL.
...I'M SORRY ABOUT TSUGUHA, BUT STAY OUT OF THIS.
WHEN MY OLD MAN LATCHES ON TO SOME-THING, HE DOESN'T LET GO.
WATCH OUT FOR A MAN WITH A MONK'S STAFF.
SHUT...
I HATED MYSELF FOR REQUIRING YATO'S HELP...
...AND KAZUMA HATED HIMSELF FOR REQUIRING THE HELP OF A STRAY?

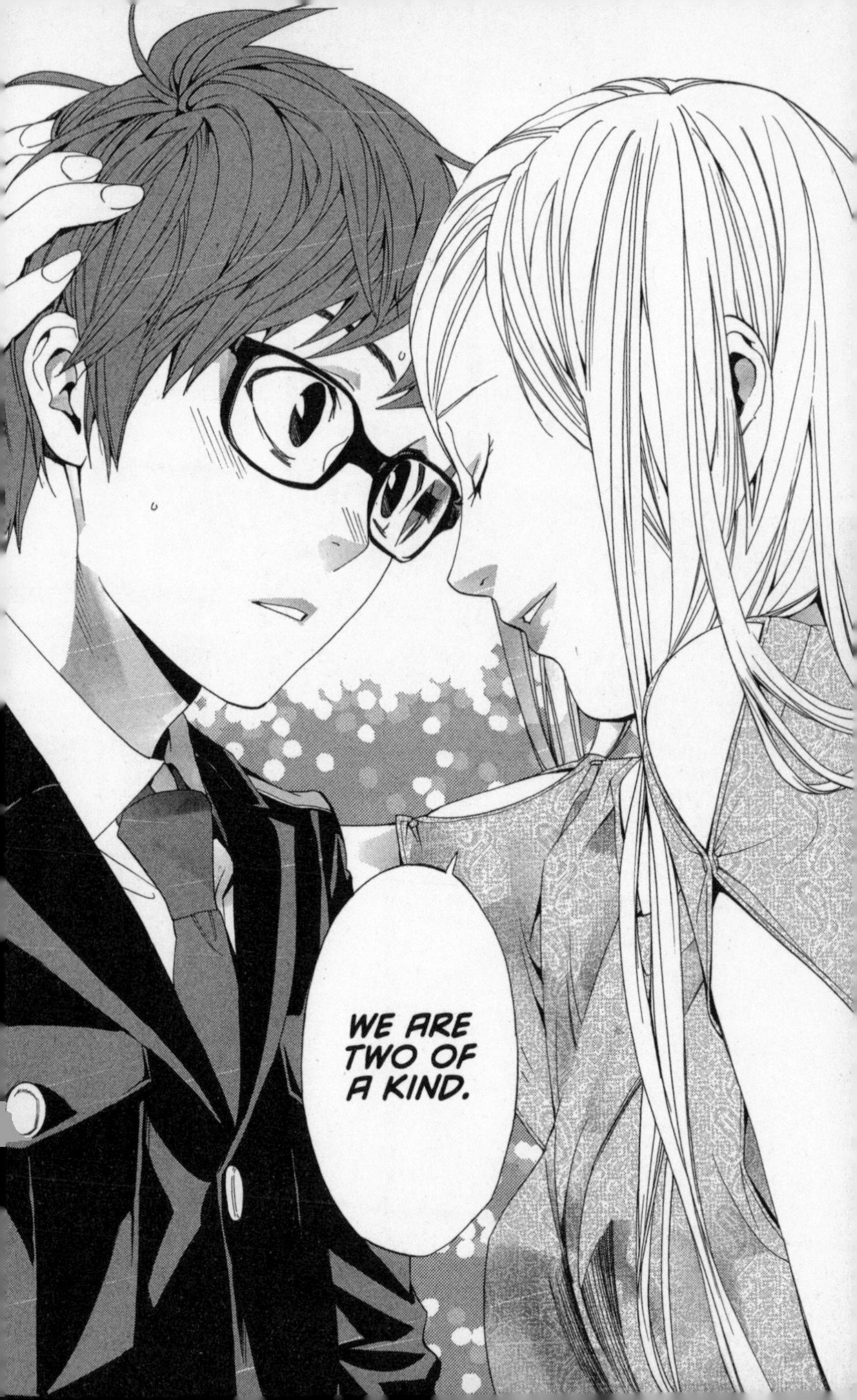
WE ARE TWO OF A KIND.

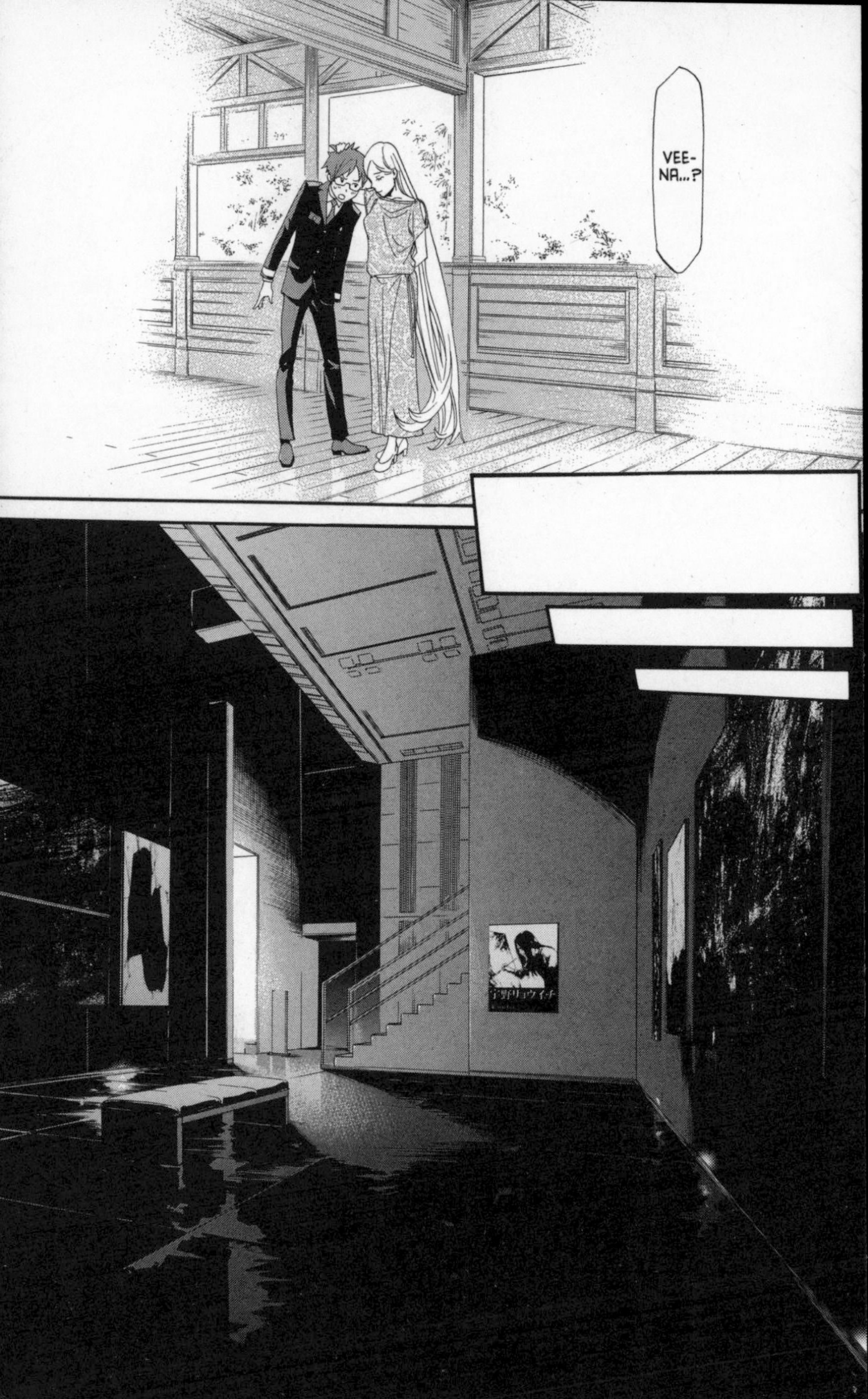
VEE-NA...?

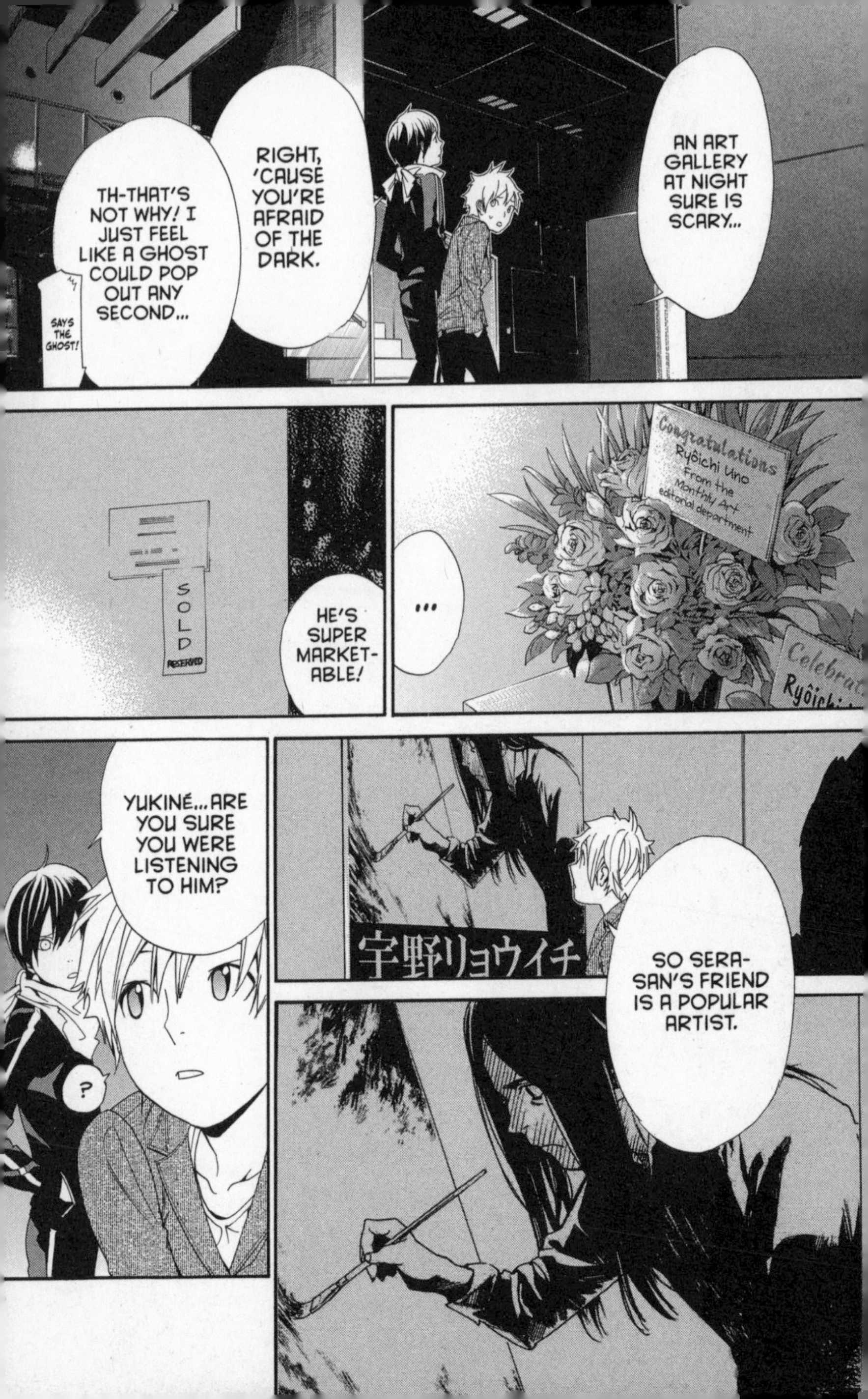
AN ART GALLERY AT NIGHT SURE IS SCARY...
RIGHT, 'CAUSE YOU'RE AFRAID OF THE DARK.
TH-THAT'S NOT WHY! I JUST FEEL LIKE A GHOST COULD POP OUT ANY SECOND...
SAYS THE GHOST!
Congratulations Ryôichi Uno From the Monthly Art editorial department
...
HE'S SUPER MARKETABLE!
SOLD
RESERVED
宇野リョウイチ
SO SERA-SAN'S FRIEND IS A POPULAR ARTIST.
YUKINÉ...ARE YOU SURE YOU WERE LISTENING TO HIM?
?

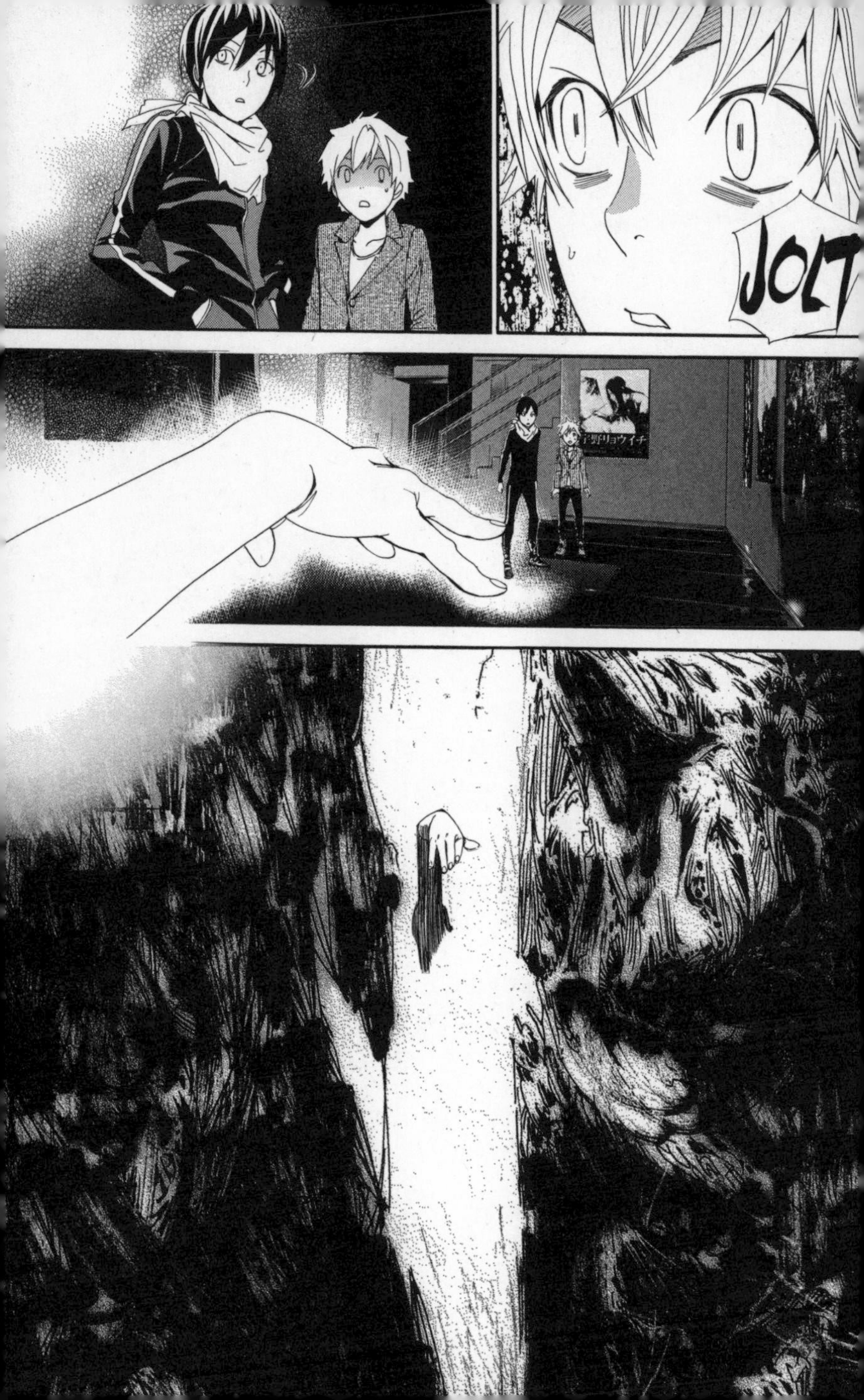
JOLT

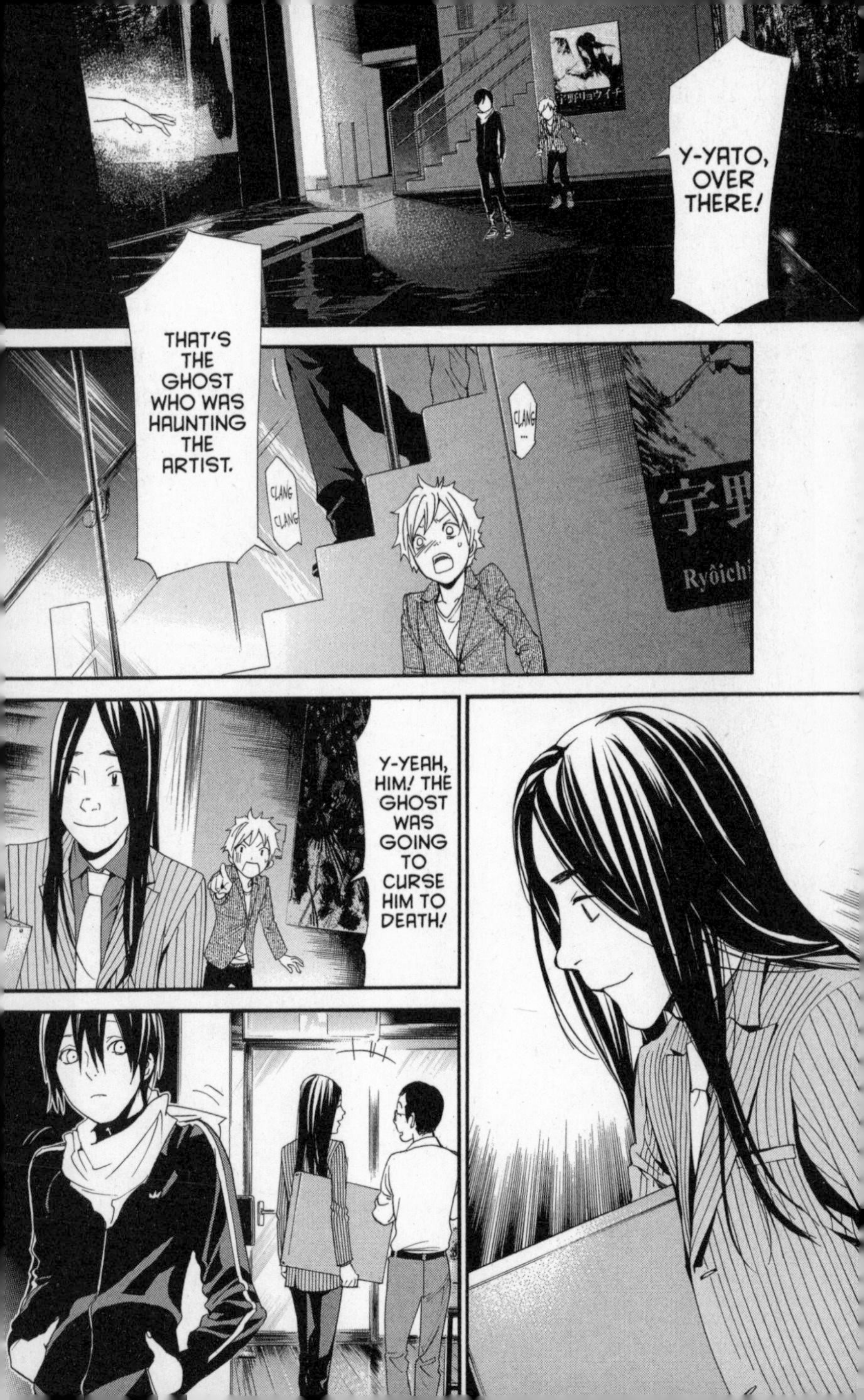
宇野リョウイチ
Y-YATO, OVER THERE!
THAT'S THE GHOST WHO WAS HAUNTING THE ARTIST.
CLANG ...
宇野
Ryôichi
CLANG CLANG
Y-YEAH, HIM! THE GHOST WAS GOING TO CURSE HIM TO DEATH!

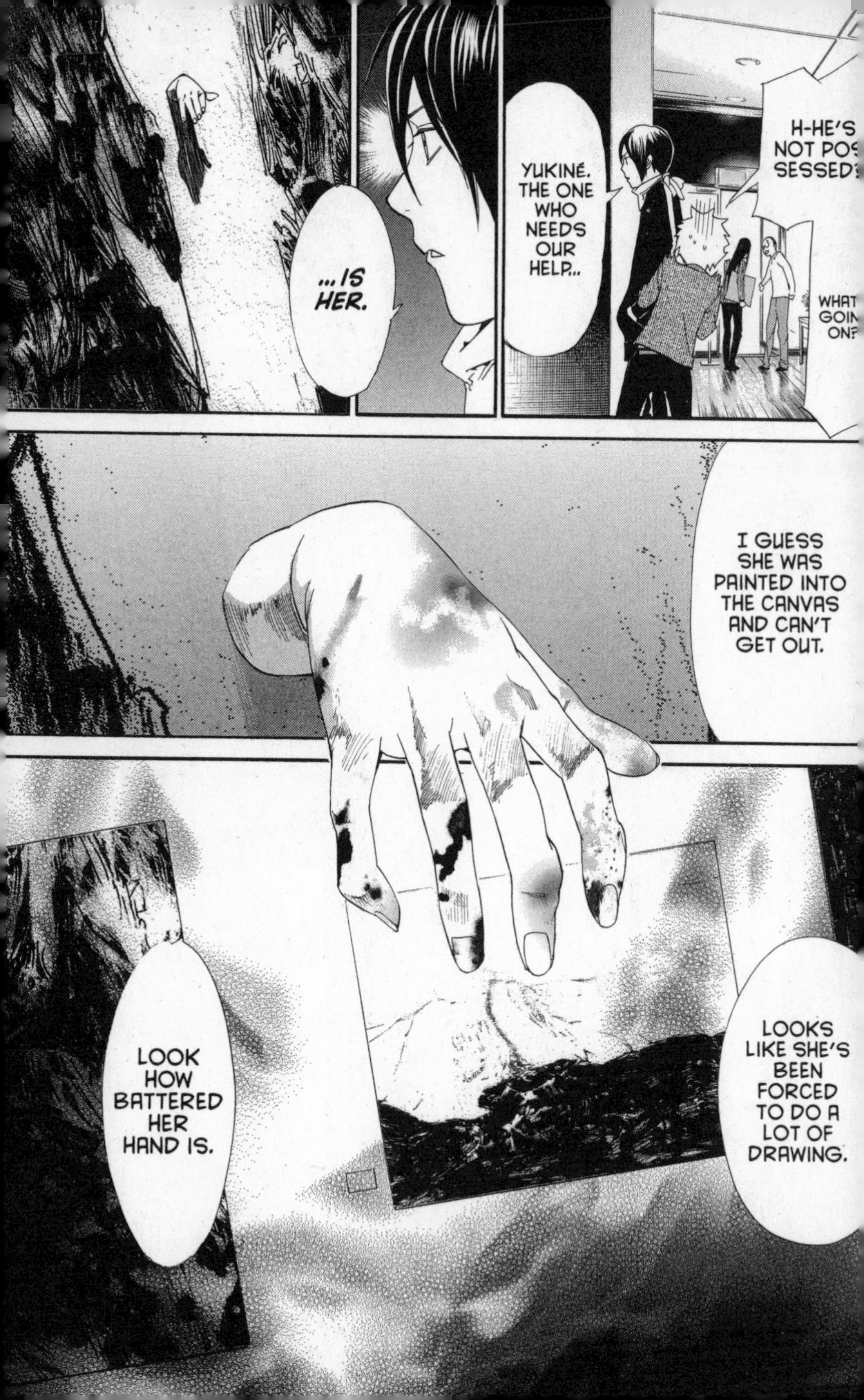
H-HE'S NOT POS SESSED?
WHAT GOIN ON?
YUKINÉ. THE ONE WHO NEEDS OUR HELP...
...IS HER.
I GUESS SHE WAS PAINTED INTO THE CANVAS AND CAN'T GET OUT.
LOOKS LIKE SHE'S BEEN FORCED TO DO A LOT OF DRAWING.
LOOK HOW BATTERED HER HAND IS.

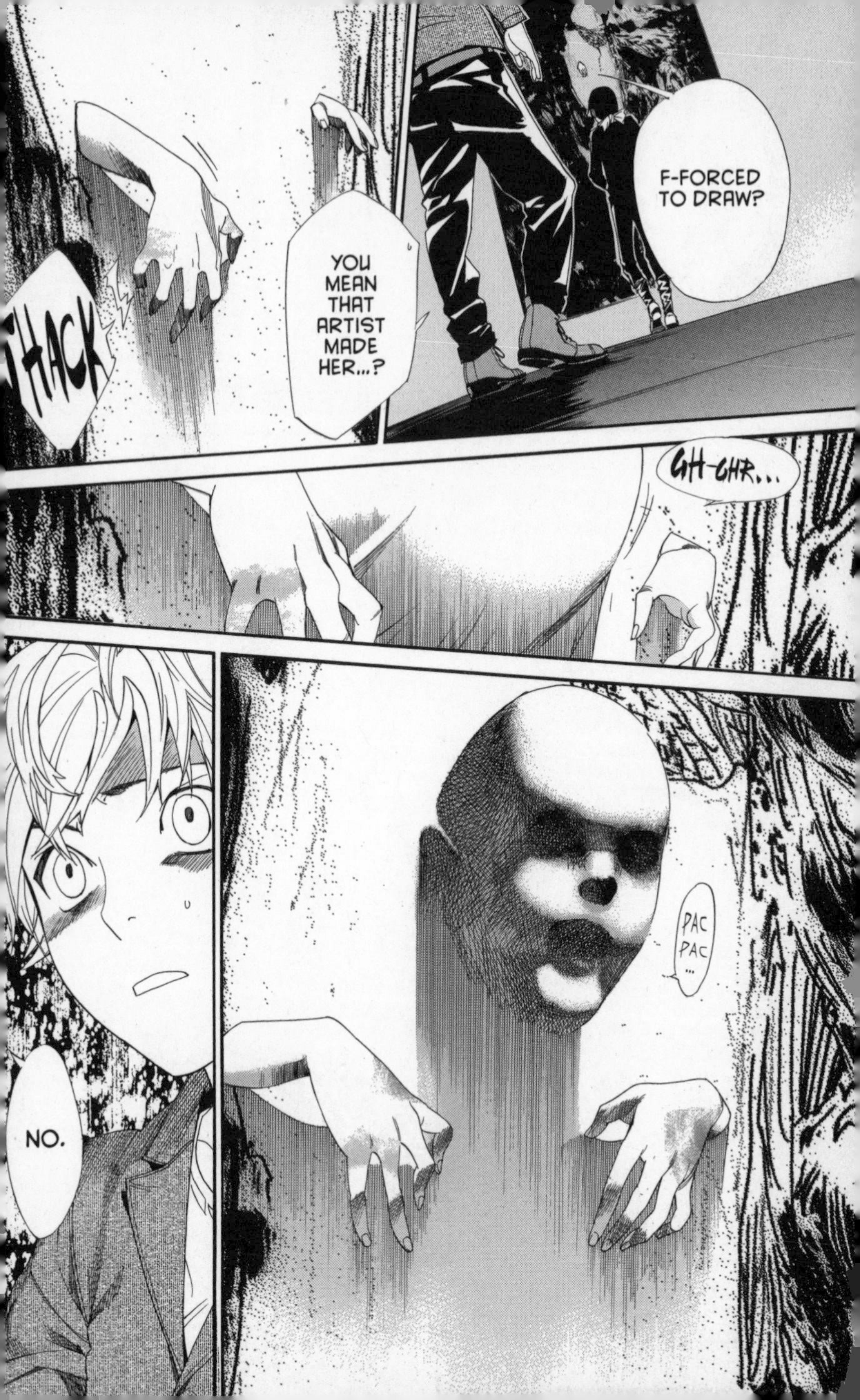
F-FORCED TO DRAW?
YOU MEAN THAT ARTIST MADE HER...?
THACK
GH-GHR...
PAC PAC ...
NO.

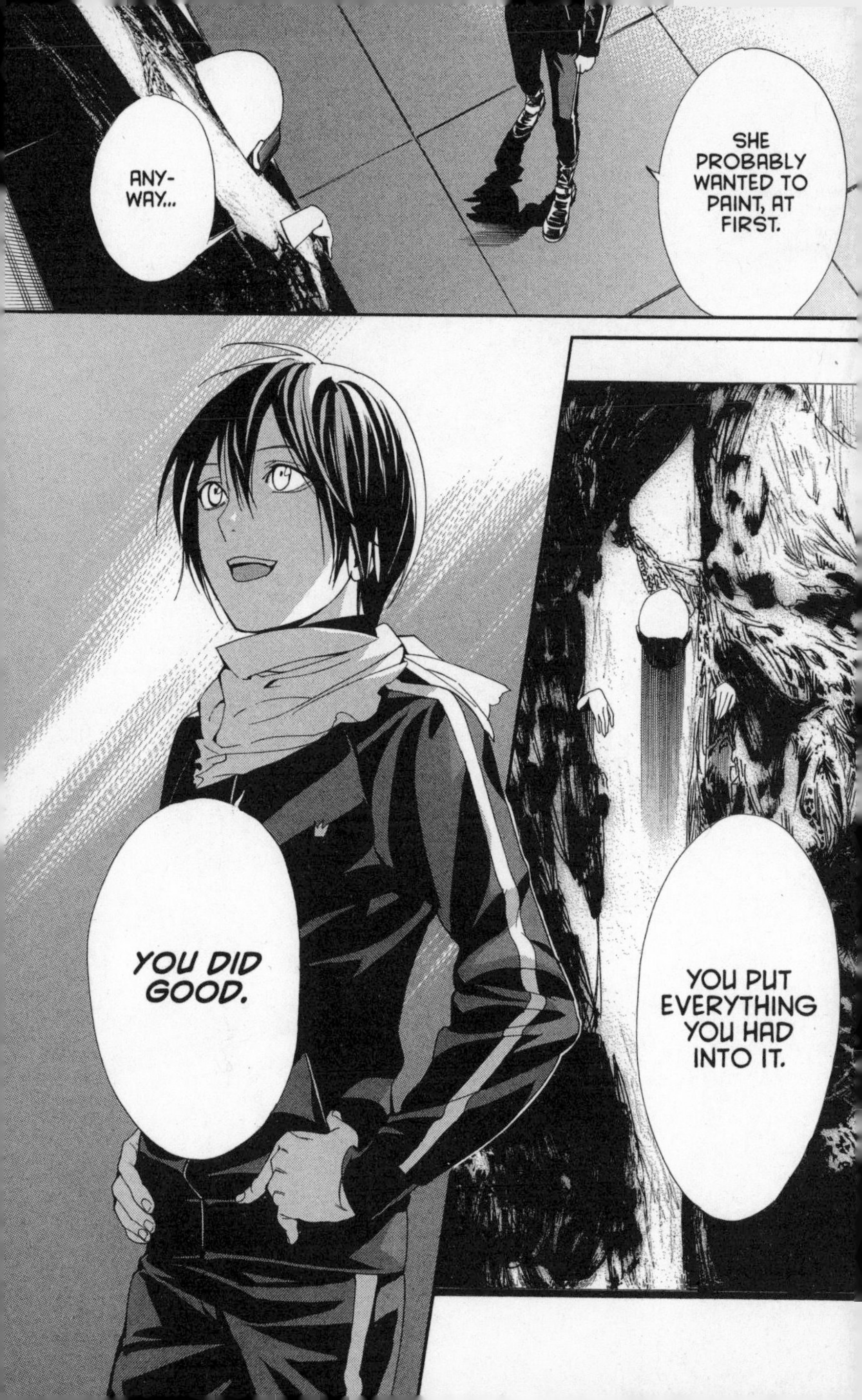
SHE PROBABLY WANTED TO PAINT, AT FIRST.
ANY-WAY...
YOU PUT EVERYTHING YOU HAD INTO IT.
YOU DID GOOD.

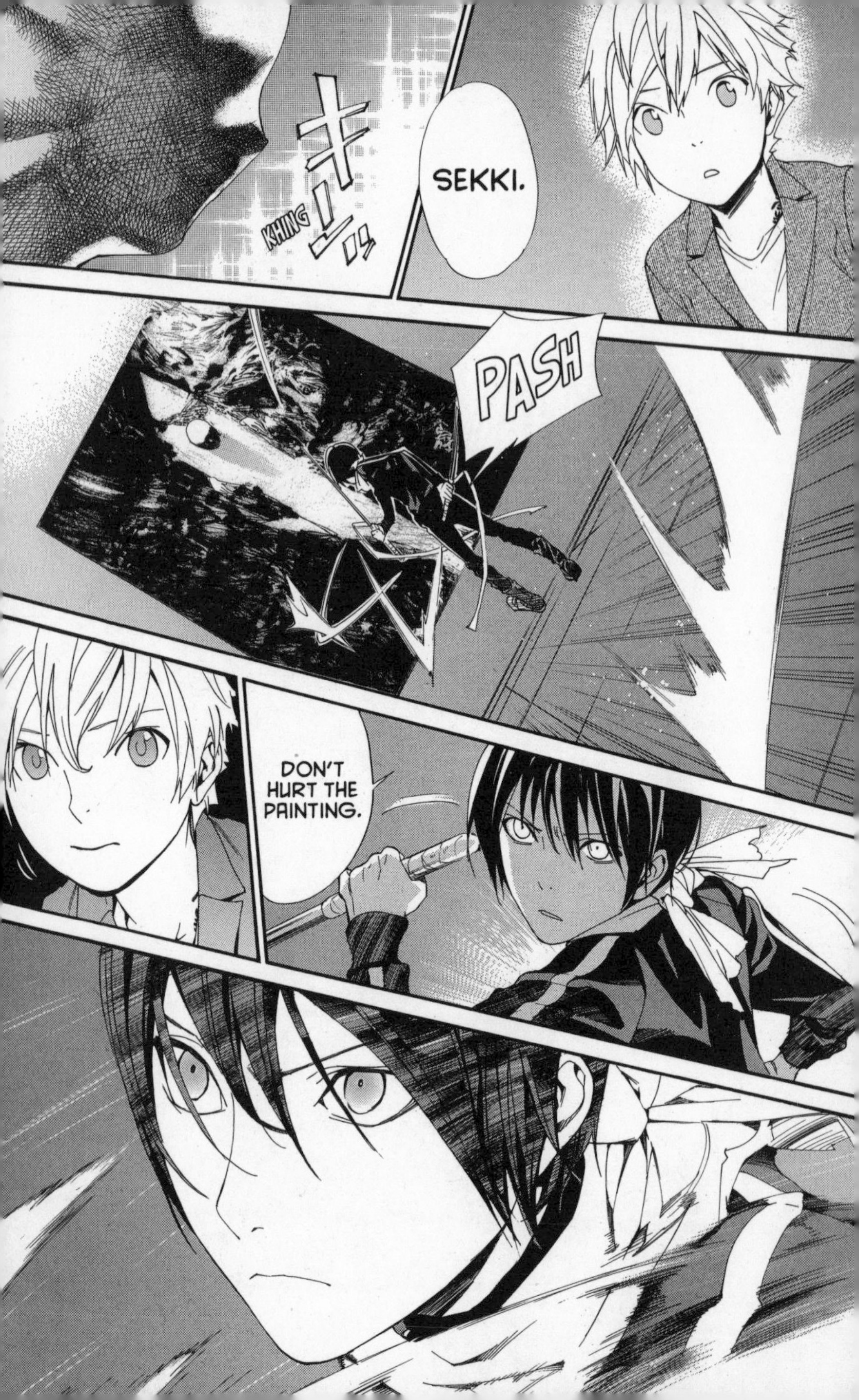
SEKKI.
KHING
PASH
DON'T HURT THE PAINTING.

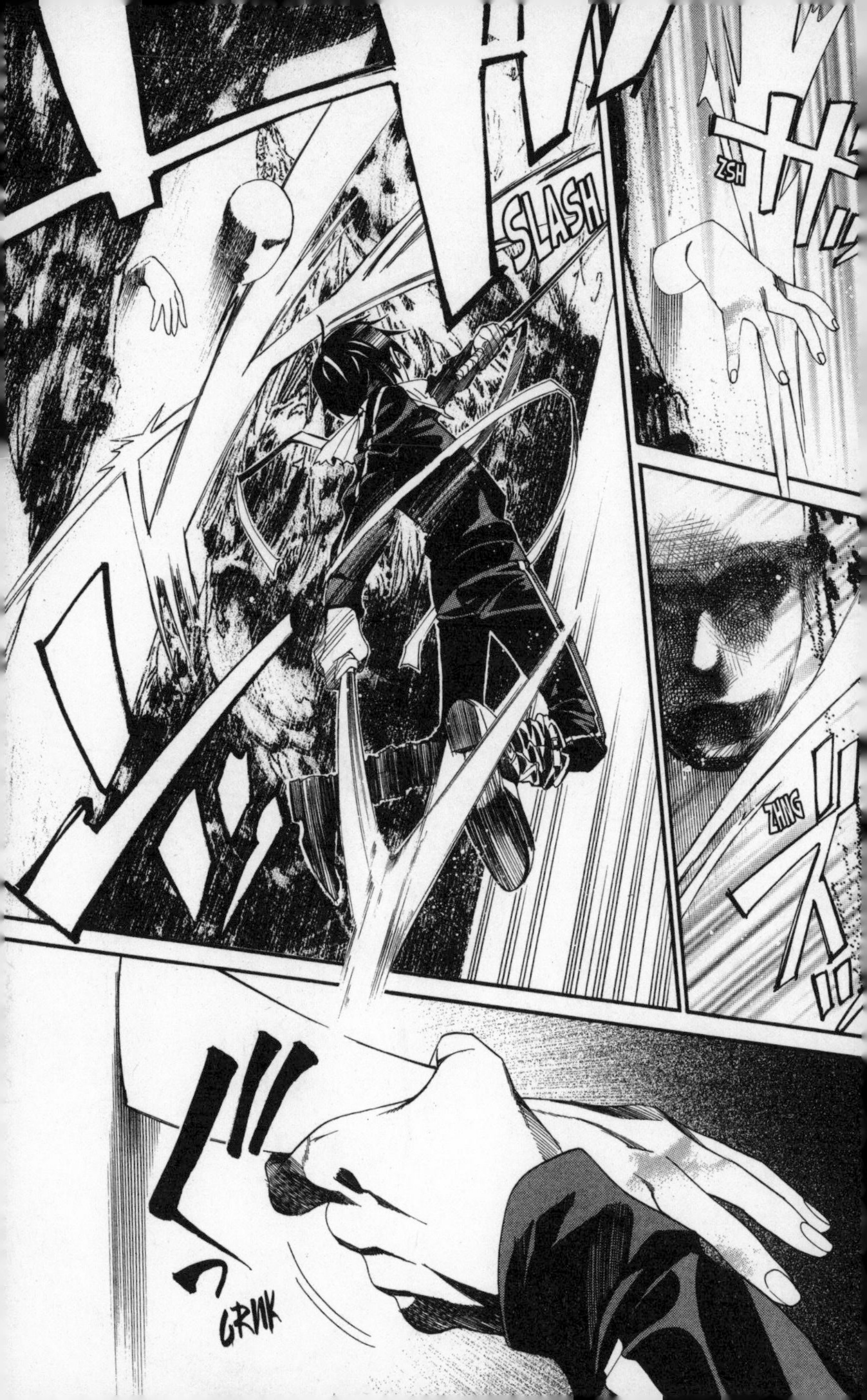
ZSH
SLASH
ZHING
GRNK

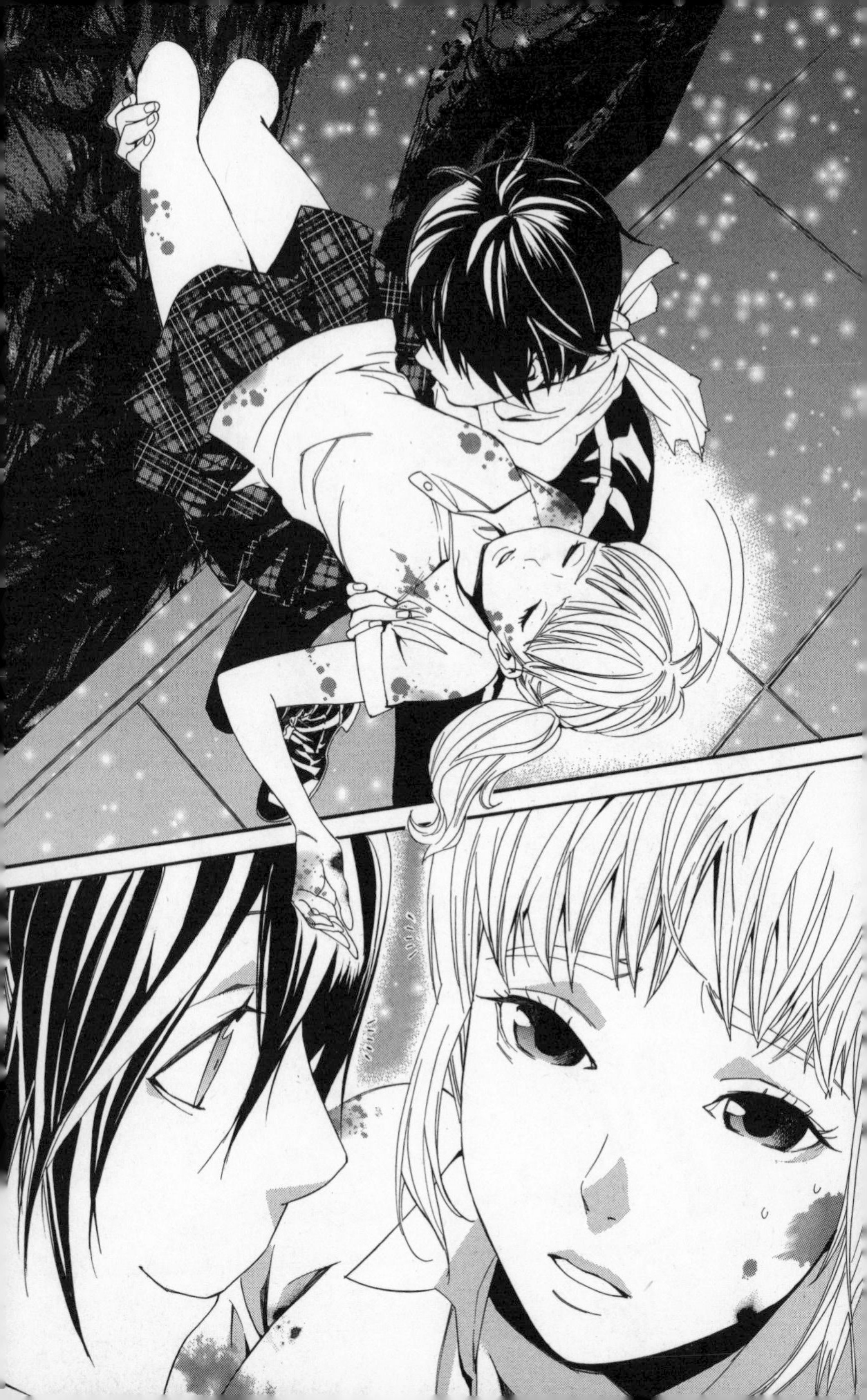

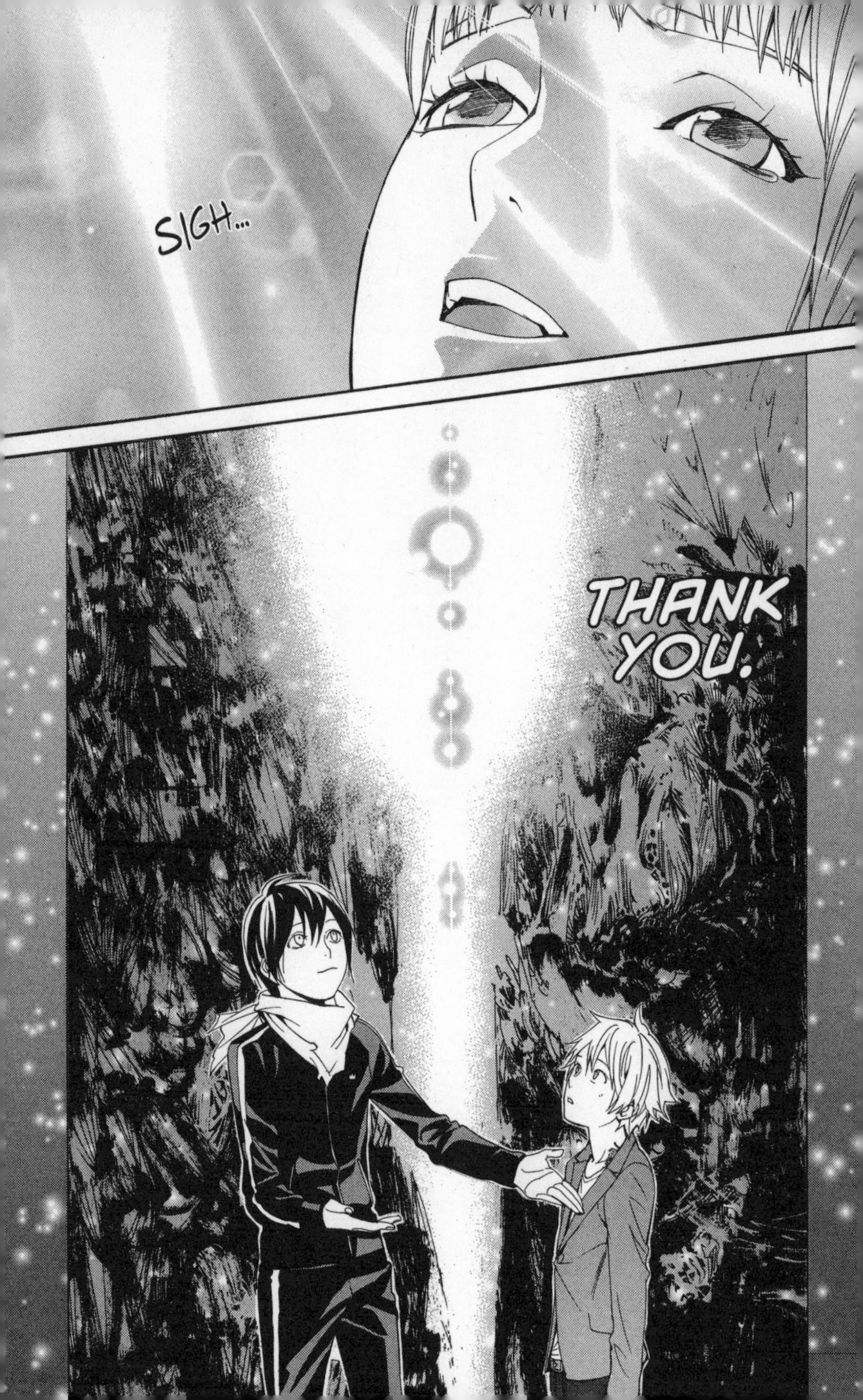
SIGH...
THANK YOU.

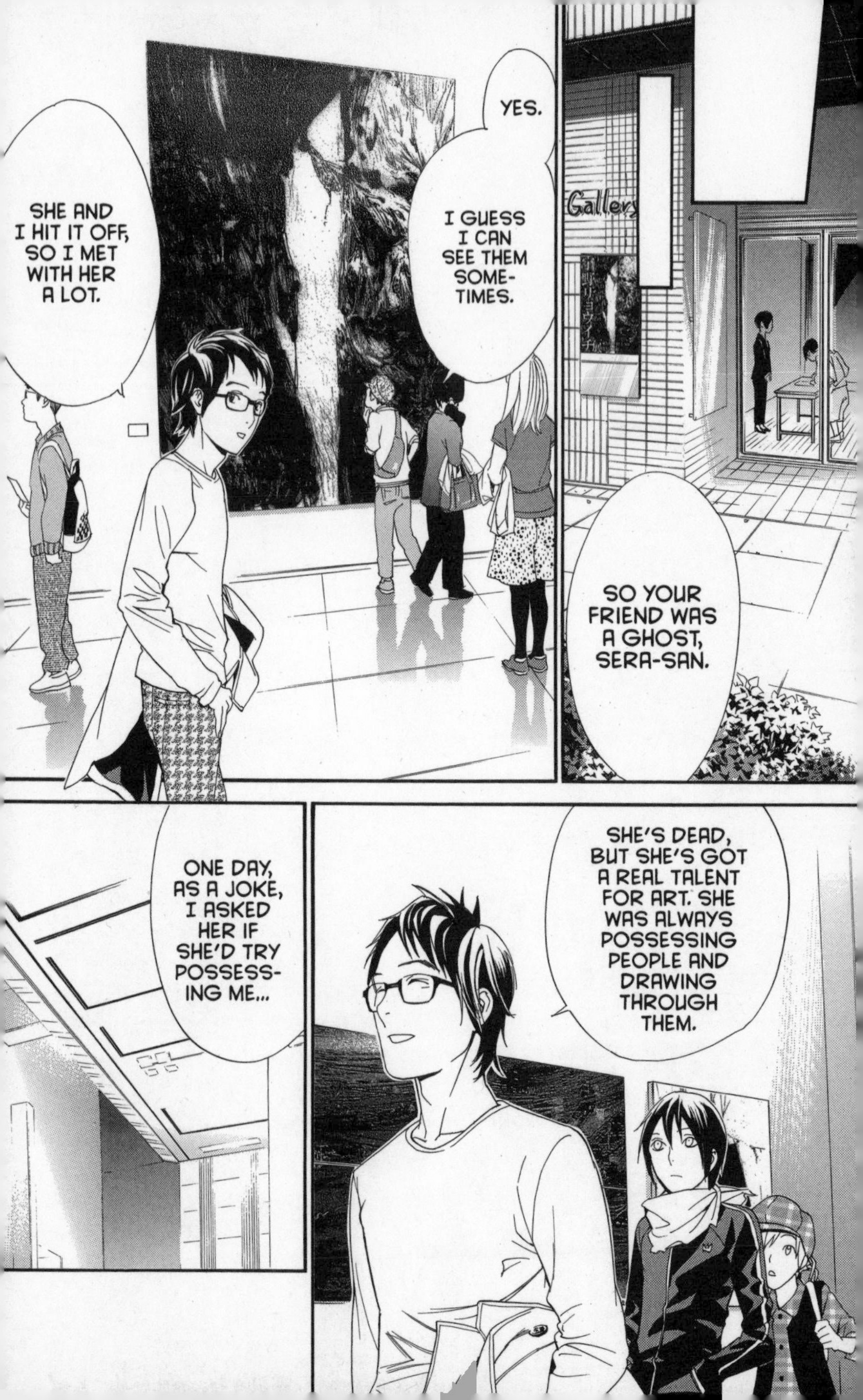
SO YOUR FRIEND WAS A GHOST, SERA-SAN.
YES.
I GUESS I CAN SEE THEM SOME-TIMES.
SHE AND I HIT IT OFF, SO I MET WITH HER A LOT.
SHE'S DEAD, BUT SHE'S GOT A REAL TALENT FOR ART. SHE WAS ALWAYS POSSESSING PEOPLE AND DRAWING THROUGH THEM.
ONE DAY, AS A JOKE, I ASKED HER IF SHE'D TRY POSSESS-ING ME...

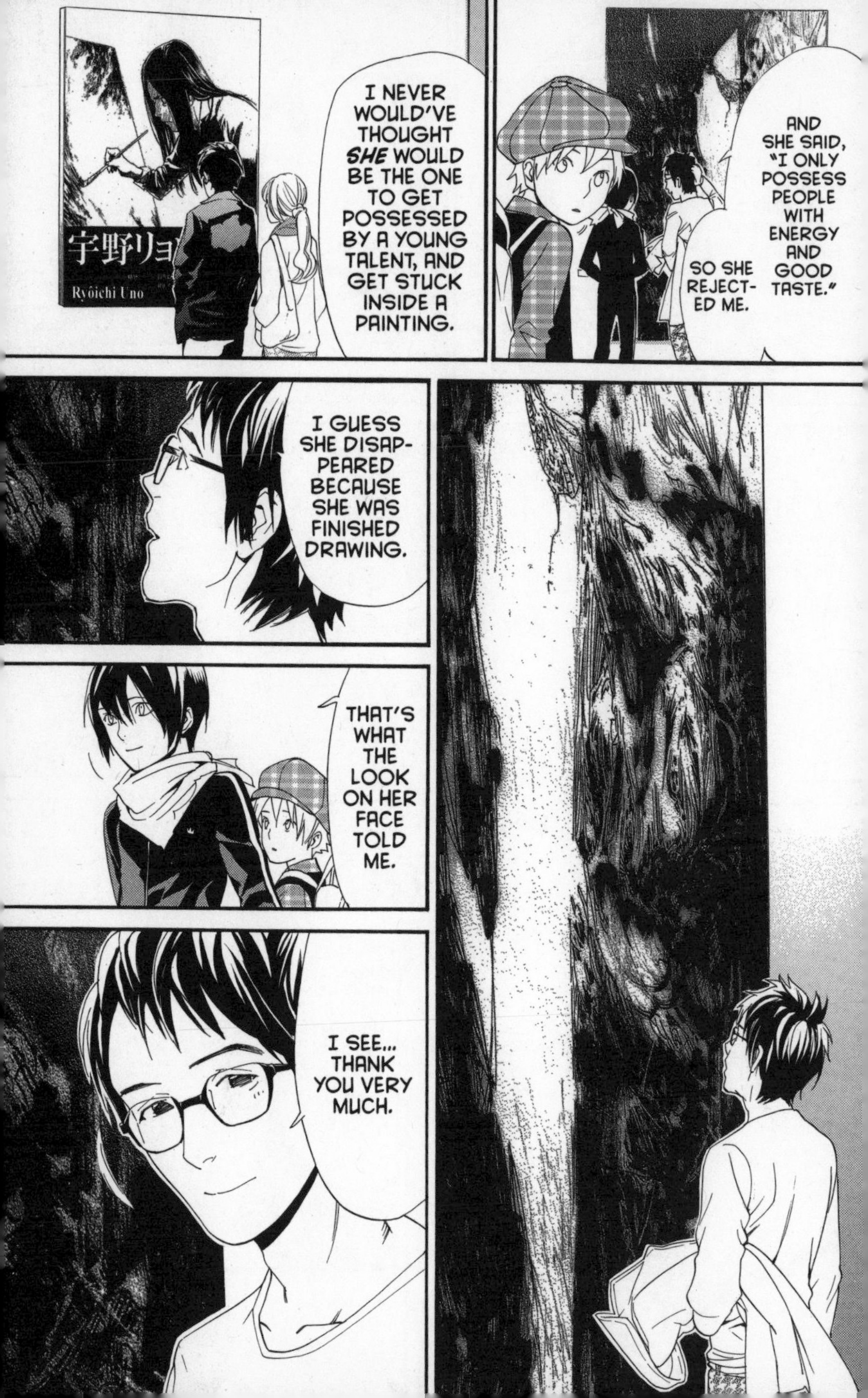
AND SHE SAID, "I ONLY POSSESS PEOPLE WITH ENERGY AND GOOD TASTE."
SO SHE REJECTED ME.
I NEVER WOULD'VE THOUGHT *SHE* WOULD BE THE ONE TO GET POSSESSED BY A YOUNG TALENT, AND GET STUCK INSIDE A PAINTING.
宇野リョ
Ryôichi Uno
I GUESS SHE DISAPPEARED BECAUSE SHE WAS FINISHED DRAWING.
THAT'S WHAT THE LOOK ON HER FACE TOLD ME.
I SEE... THANK YOU VERY MUCH.

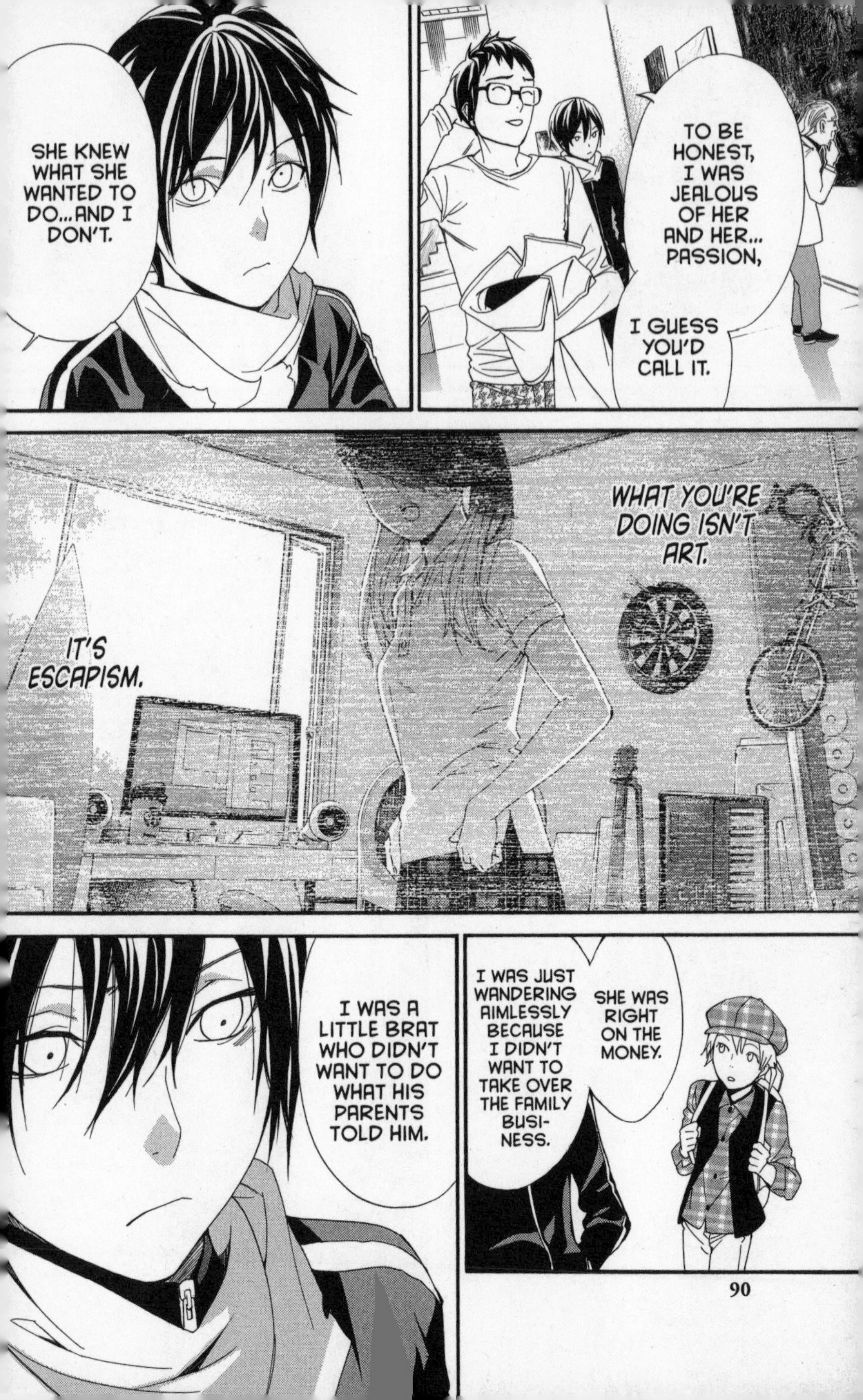
TO BE HONEST, I WAS JEALOUS OF HER AND HER... PASSION,
I GUESS YOU'D CALL IT.
SHE KNEW WHAT SHE WANTED TO DO...AND I DON'T.
WHAT YOU'RE DOING ISN'T ART.
IT'S ESCAPISM.
SHE WAS RIGHT ON THE MONEY.
I WAS JUST WANDERING AIMLESSLY BECAUSE I DIDN'T WANT TO TAKE OVER THE FAMILY BUSI- NESS.
I WAS A LITTLE BRAT WHO DIDN'T WANT TO DO WHAT HIS PARENTS TOLD HIM.

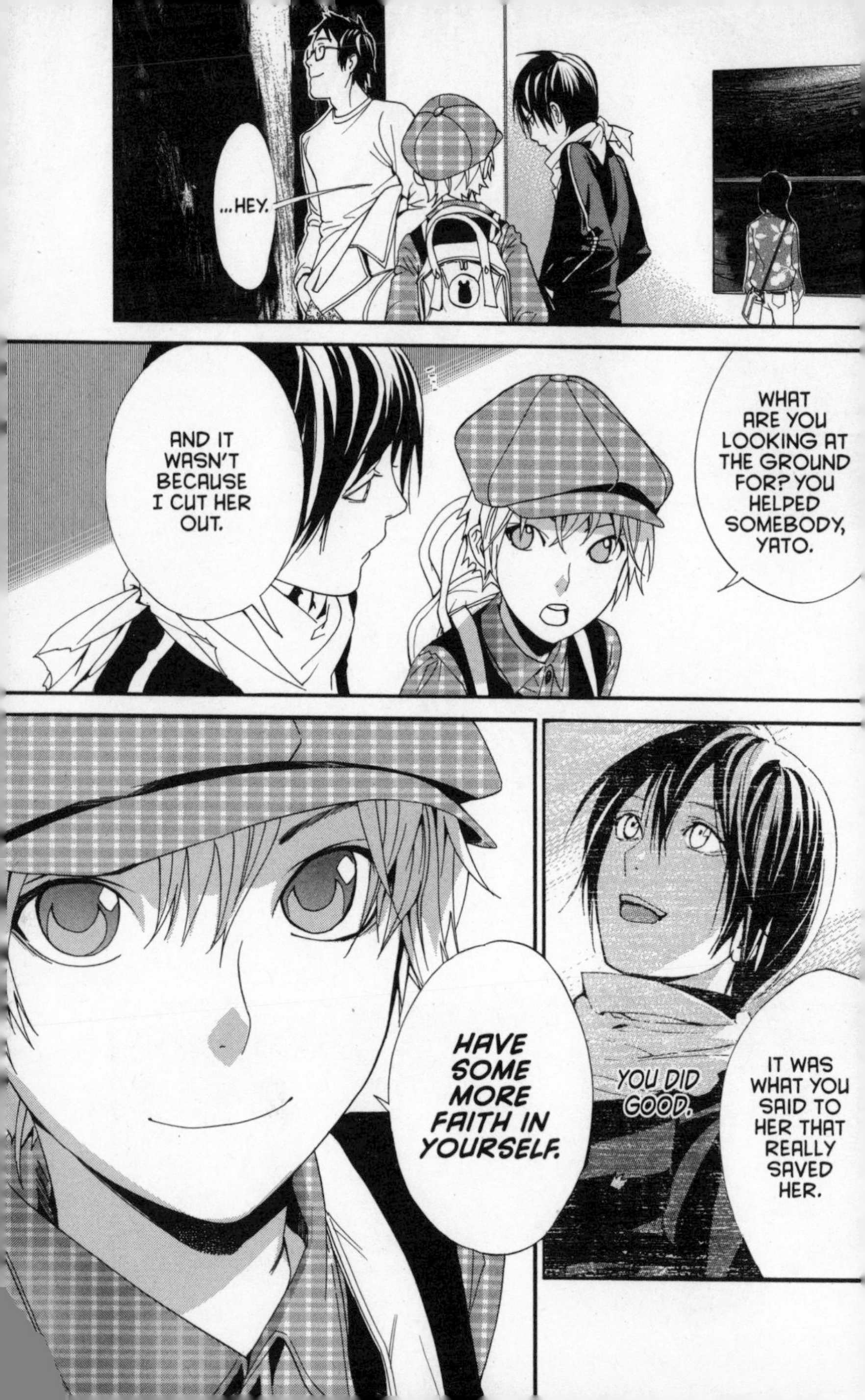
...HEY.
WHAT ARE YOU LOOKING AT THE GROUND FOR? YOU HELPED SOMEBODY, YATO.
AND IT WASN'T BECAUSE I CUT HER OUT.
IT WAS WHAT YOU SAID TO HER THAT REALLY SAVED HER.
YOU DID GOOD.
HAVE SOME MORE FAITH IN YOURSELF.

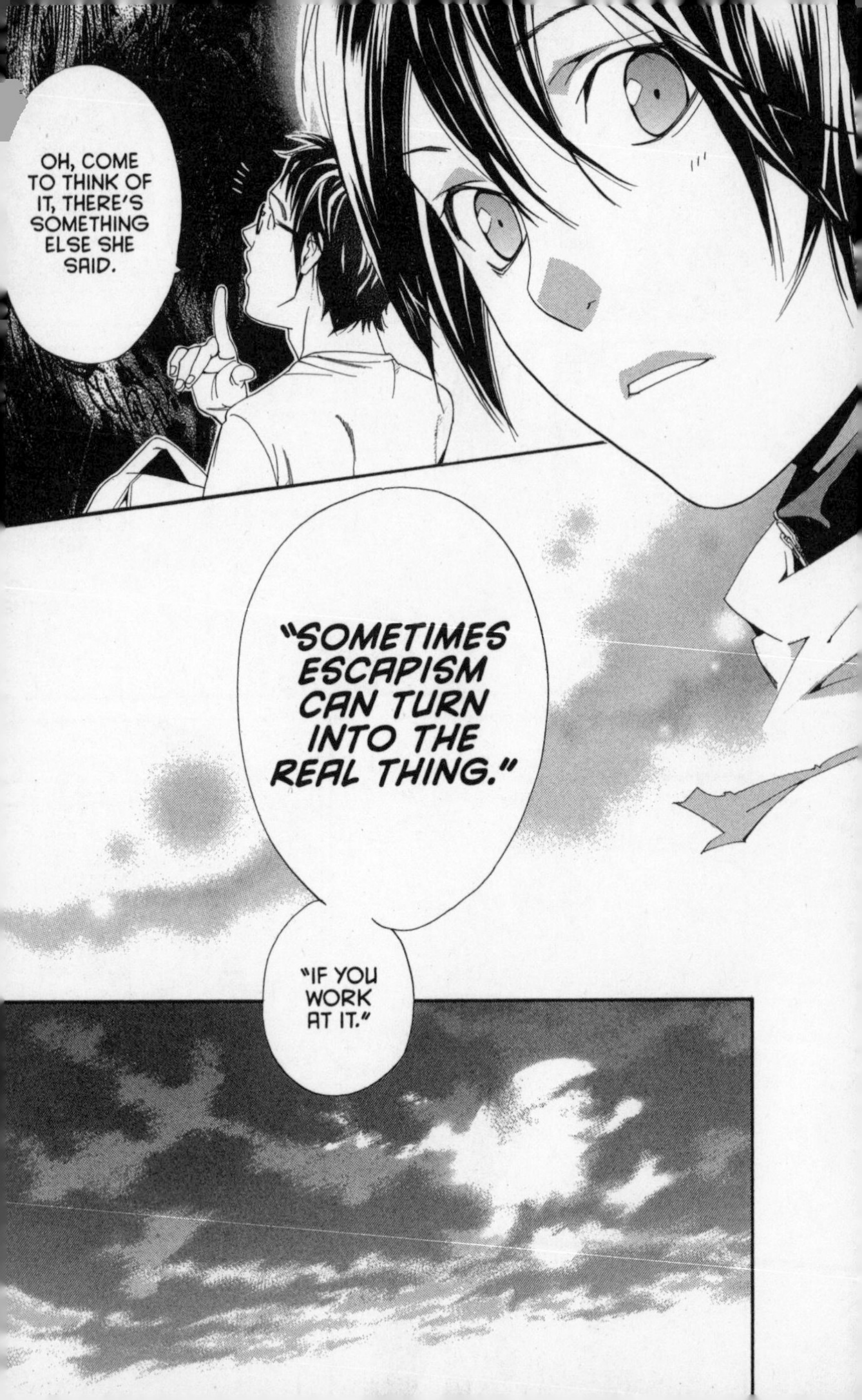
OH, COME TO THINK OF IT, THERE'S SOMETHING ELSE SHE SAID.
"SOMETIMES ESCAPISM CAN TURN INTO THE REAL THING."
"IF YOU WORK AT IT."

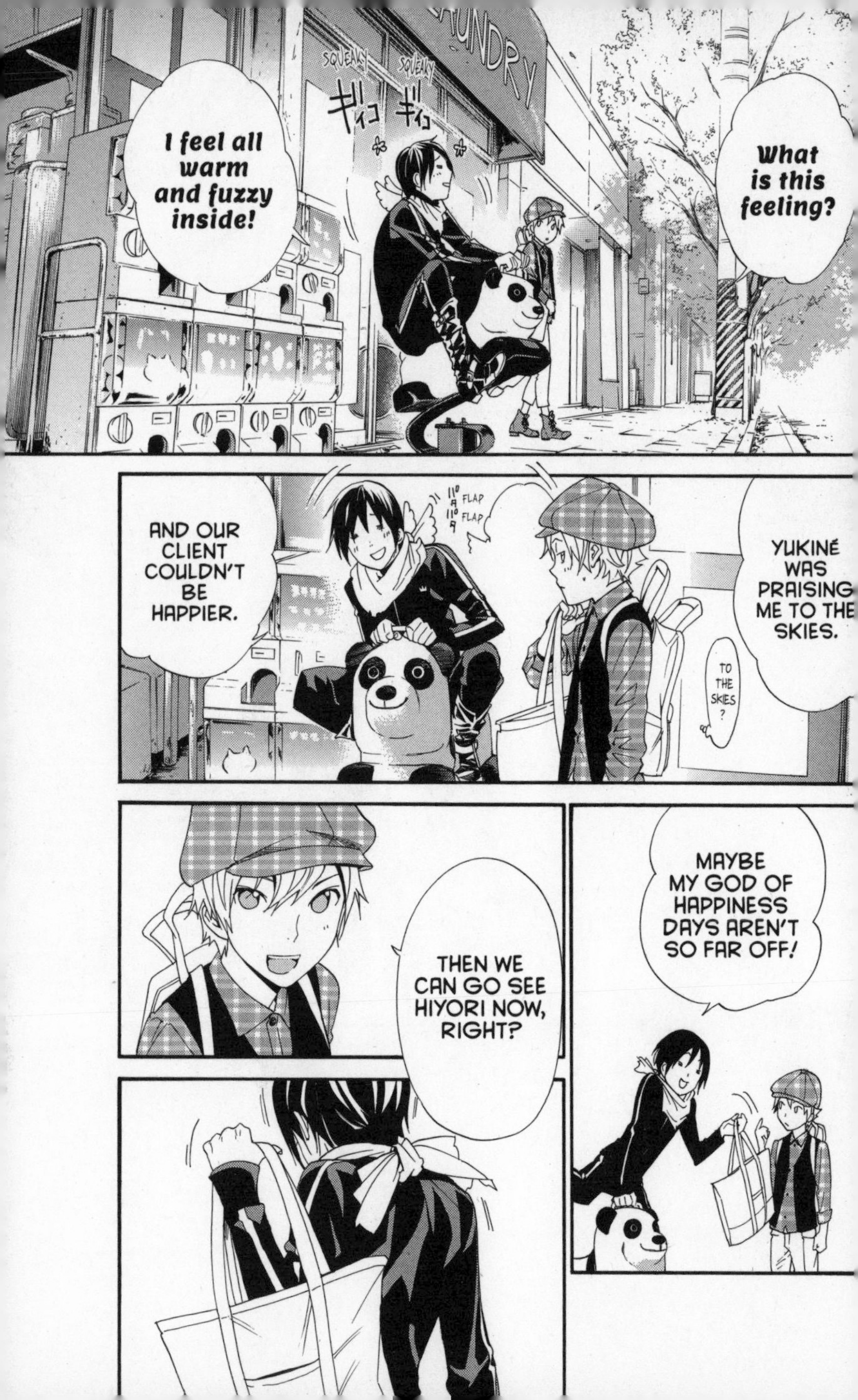
SQUEAKY SQUEAKY
ギイコ ギイコ
What is this feeling?
I feel all warm and fuzzy inside!
YUKINÉ WAS PRAISING ME TO THE SKIES.
TO THE SKIES?
FLAP FLAP
AND OUR CLIENT COULDN'T BE HAPPIER.
MAYBE MY GOD OF HAPPINESS DAYS AREN'T SO FAR OFF!
THEN WE CAN GO SEE HIYORI NOW, RIGHT?

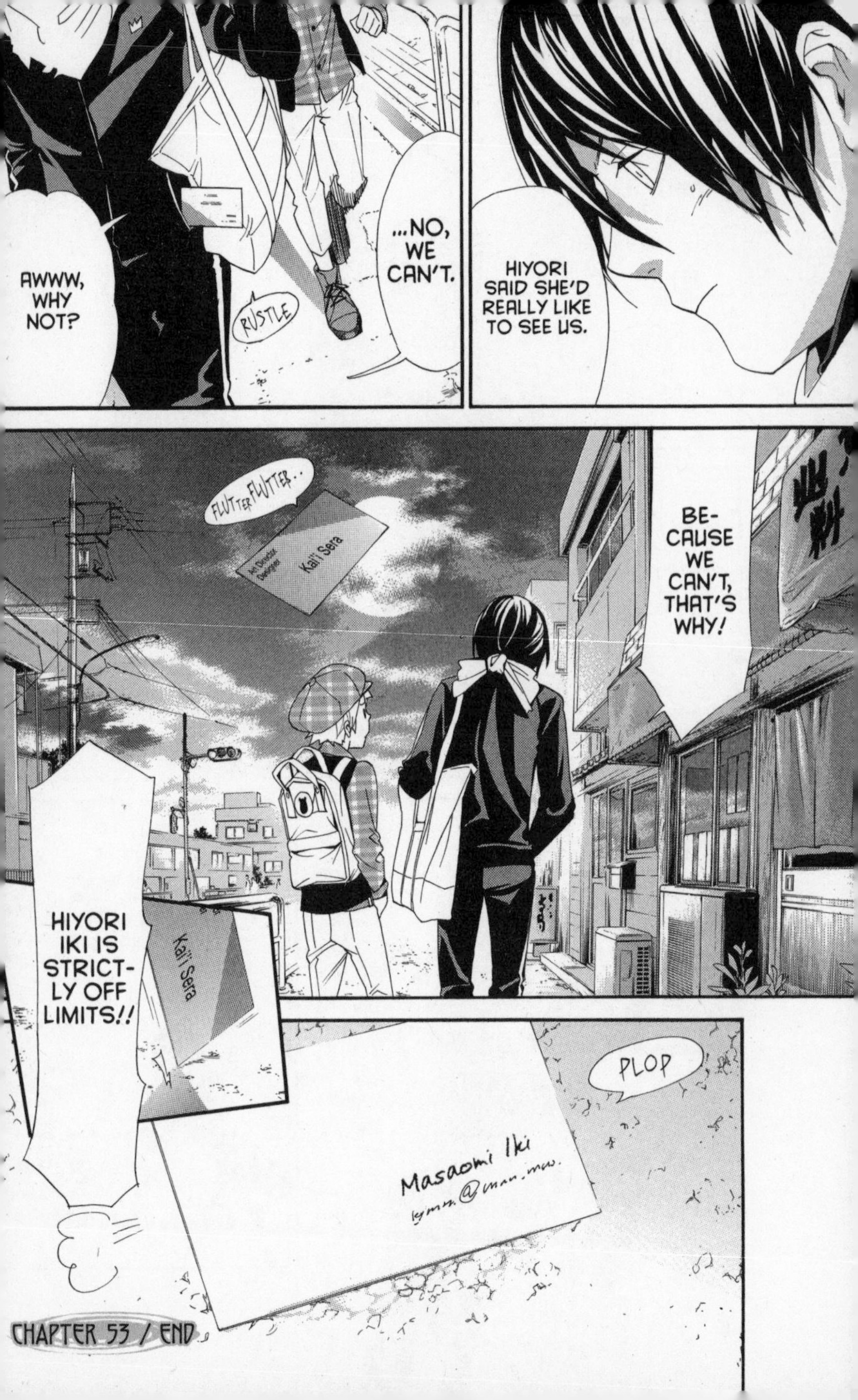
HIYORI SAID SHE'D REALLY LIKE TO SEE US.
...NO, WE CAN'T.
RUSTLE
AWWW, WHY NOT?
BE-CAUSE WE CAN'T, THAT'S WHY!
FLUTTER FLUTTER...
Kai'i Sera
HIYORI IKI IS STRICT-LY OFF LIMITS!!
Kai'i Sera
PLOP
Masaomi Iki
CHAPTER 53 / END

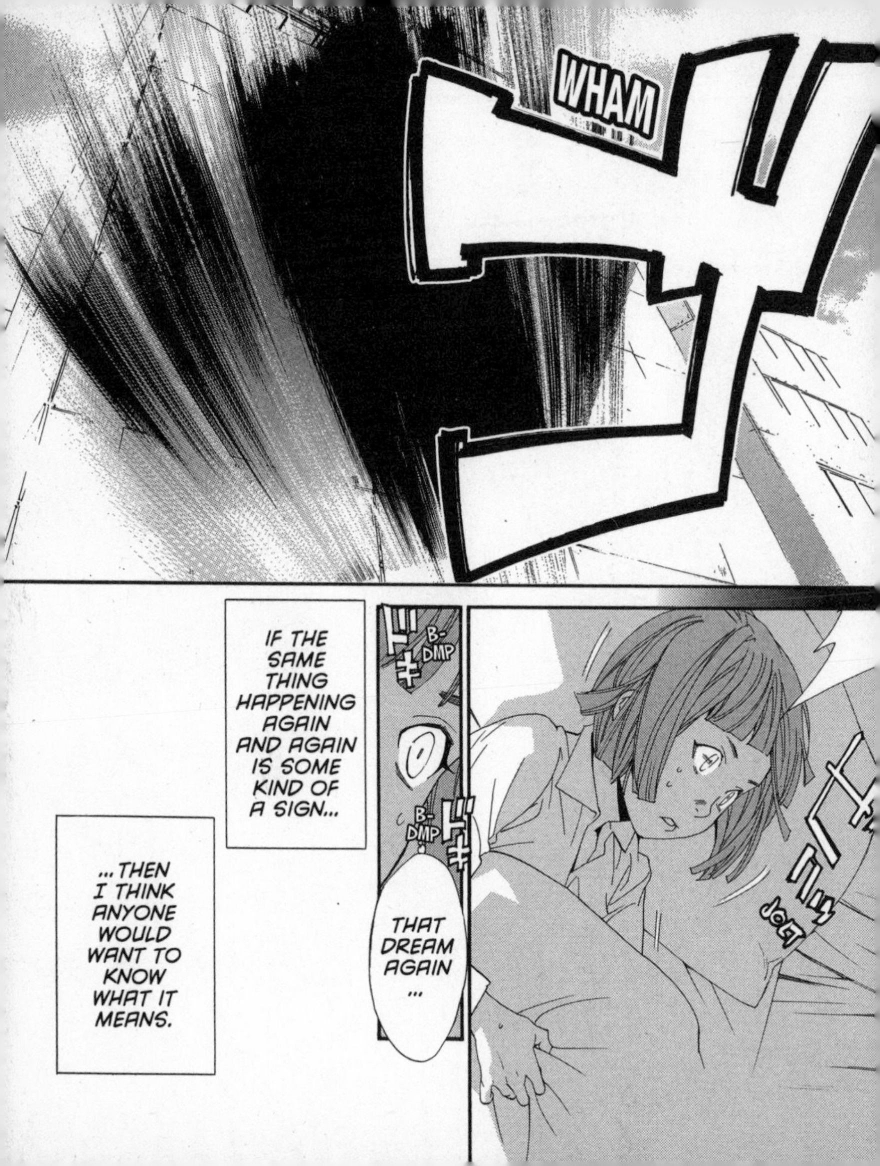
WHAM
B-DMP
B-DMP
THAT DREAM AGAIN ...
IF THE SAME THING HAPPENING AGAIN AND AGAIN IS SOME KIND OF A SIGN...
...THEN I THINK ANYONE WOULD WANT TO KNOW WHAT IT MEANS.

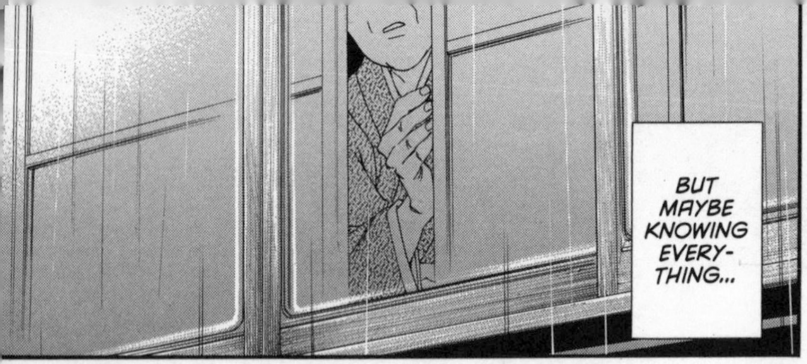
BUT MAYBE KNOWING EVERY-THING...

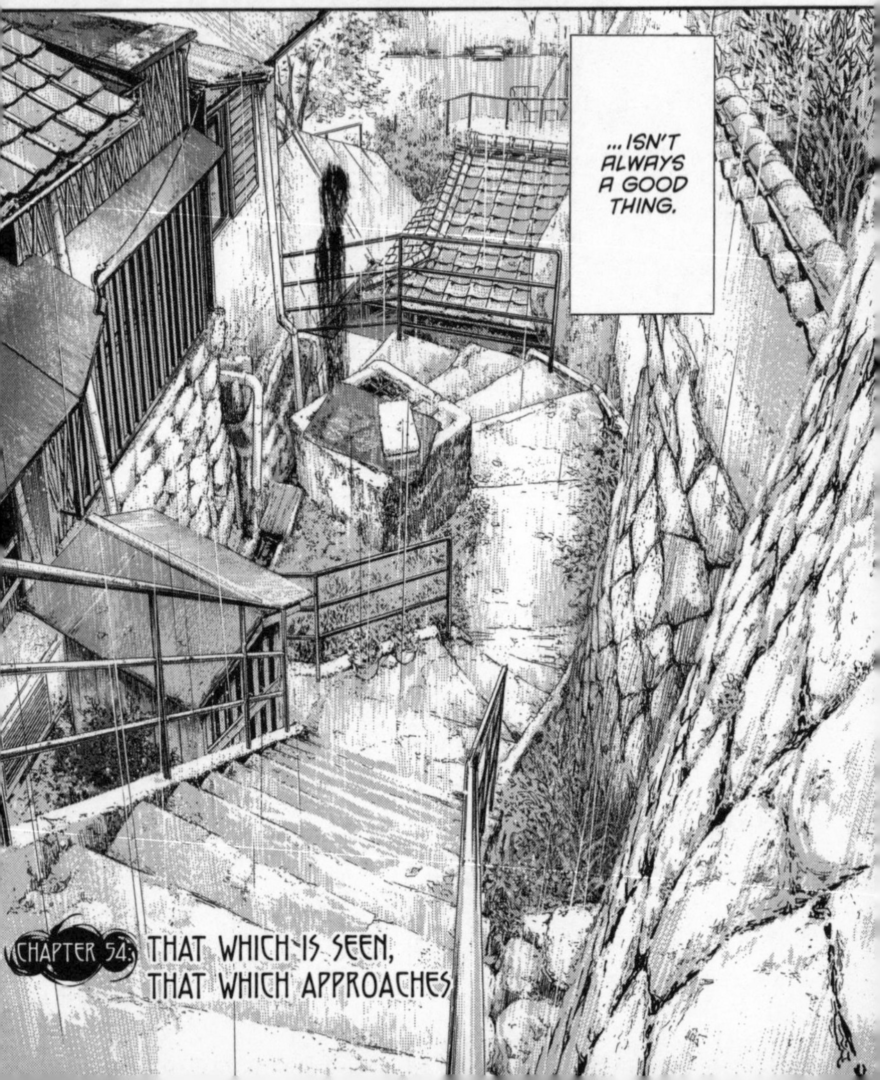
...ISN'T ALWAYS A GOOD THING.
CHAPTER 54: THAT WHICH IS SEEN, THAT WHICH APPROACHES

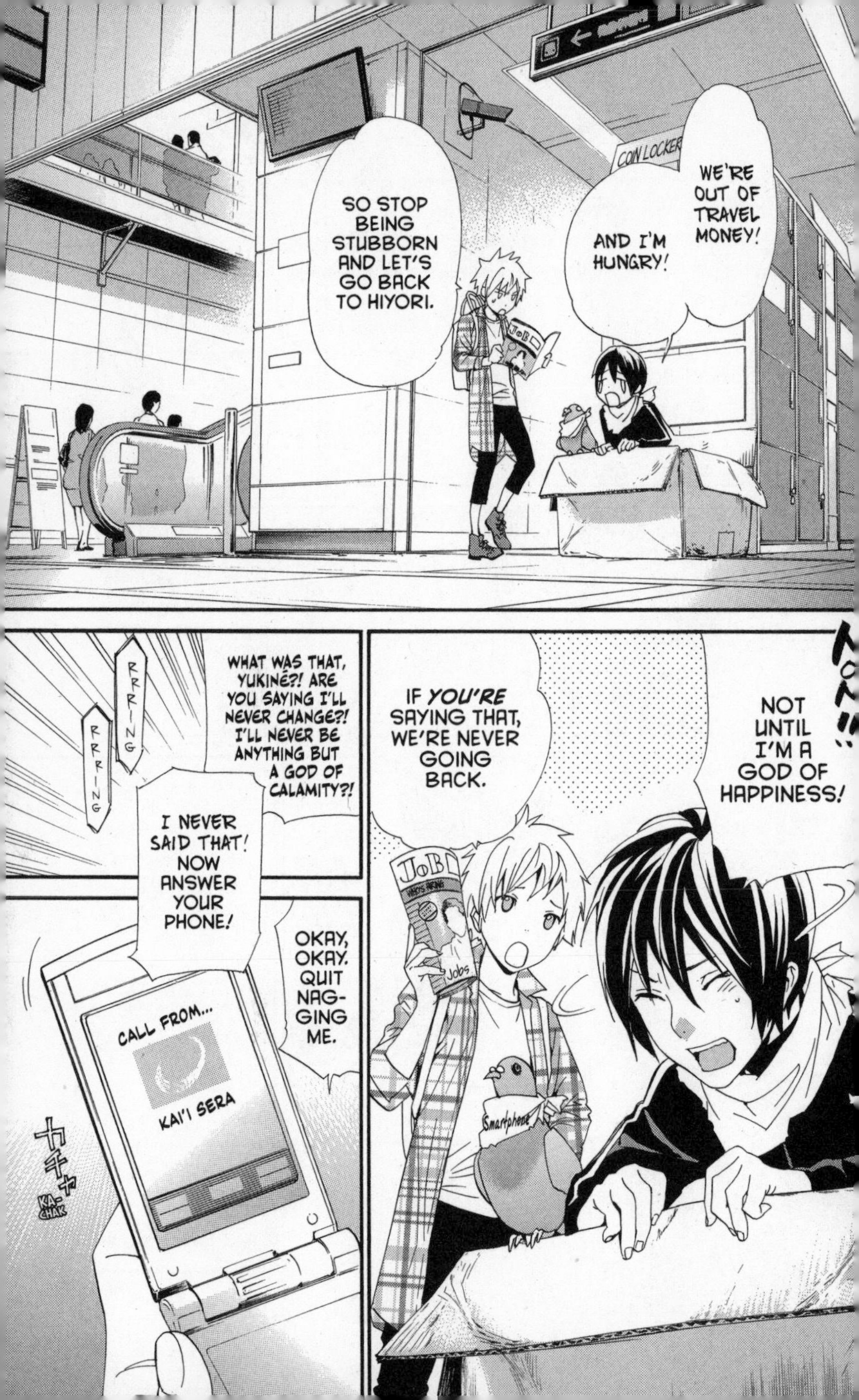
COIN LOCKER
WE'RE OUT OF TRAVEL MONEY!
AND I'M HUNGRY!
SO STOP BEING STUBBORN AND LET'S GO BACK TO HIYORI.
JOB
NOT UNTIL I'M A GOD OF HAPPINESS!
IF *YOU'RE* SAYING THAT, WE'RE NEVER GOING BACK.
JOB
Jobs
Smartphone
WHAT WAS THAT, YUKINÉ?! ARE YOU SAYING I'LL NEVER CHANGE?! I'LL NEVER BE ANYTHING BUT A GOD OF CALAMITY?!
RRRING
RRRING
I NEVER SAID THAT! NOW ANSWER YOUR PHONE!
OKAY, OKAY. QUIT NAG-GING ME.
CALL FROM...
KAI'I SERA
KA-CHAK

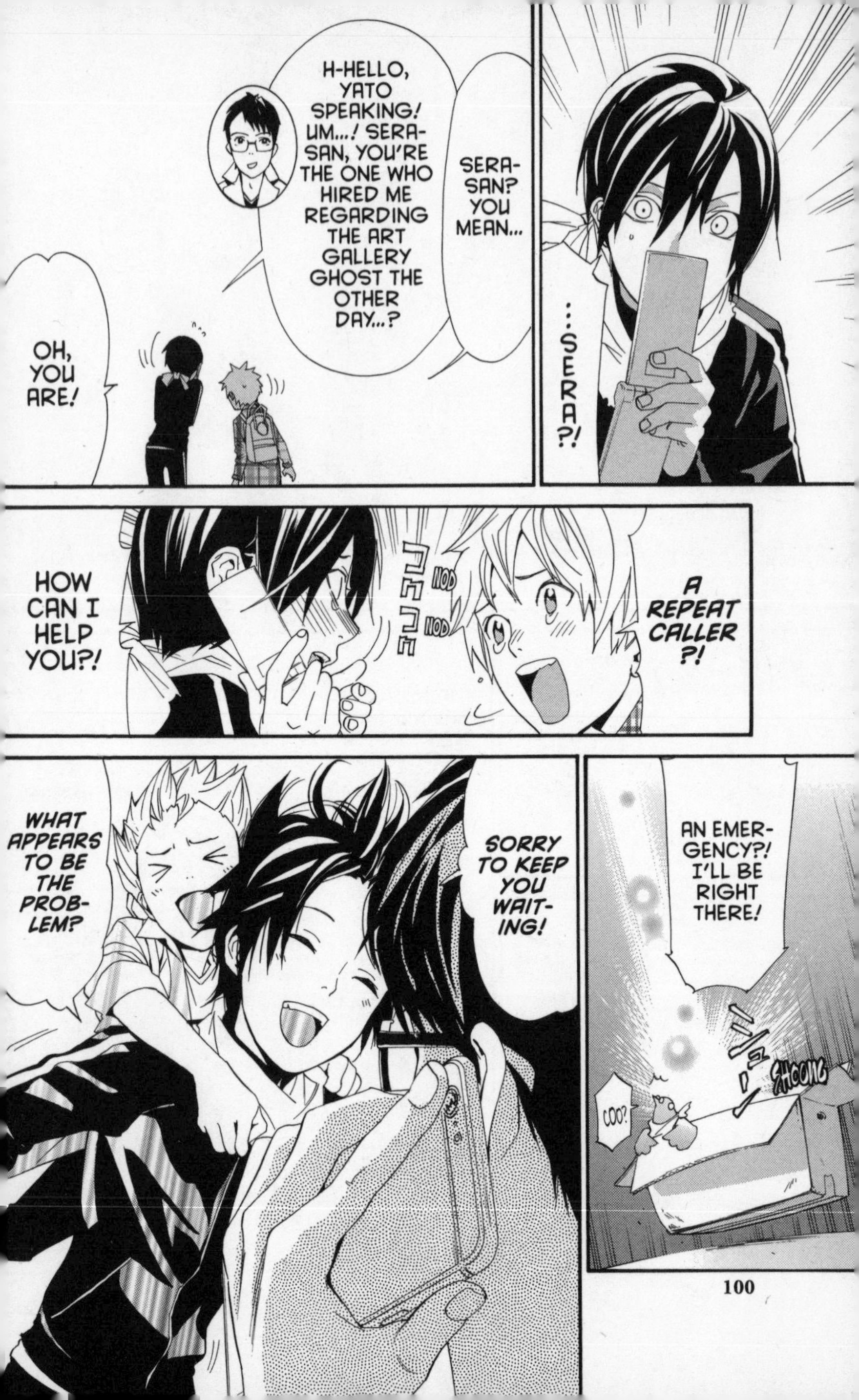
...SERA?!
SERA-SAN? YOU MEAN...
H-HELLO, YATO SPEAKING! UM...! SERA-SAN, YOU'RE THE ONE WHO HIRED ME REGARDING THE ART GALLERY GHOST THE OTHER DAY...?
OH, YOU ARE!
A REPEAT CALLER?!
NOD NOD
HOW CAN I HELP YOU?!
AN EMERGENCY?! I'LL BE RIGHT THERE!
SHOOM
COO?
SORRY TO KEEP YOU WAITING!
WHAT APPEARS TO BE THE PROBLEM?

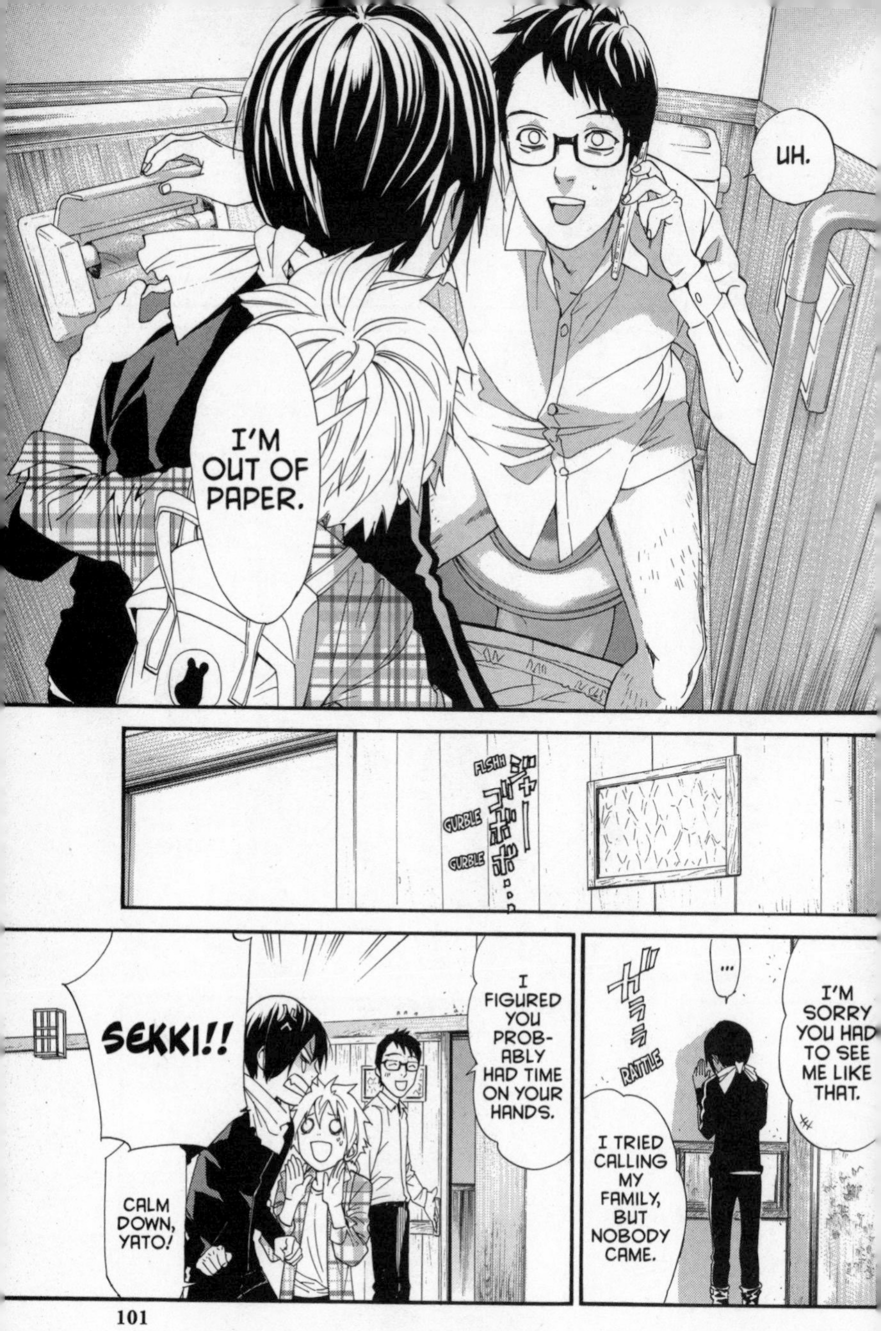
UH.
I'M OUT OF PAPER.
FLSHH
GURBLE
GURBLE
...
I'M SORRY YOU HAD TO SEE ME LIKE THAT.
RATTLE
I TRIED CALLING MY FAMILY, BUT NOBODY CAME.
I FIGURED YOU PROB-ABLY HAD TIME ON YOUR HANDS.
SEKKI!!
CALM DOWN, YATO!

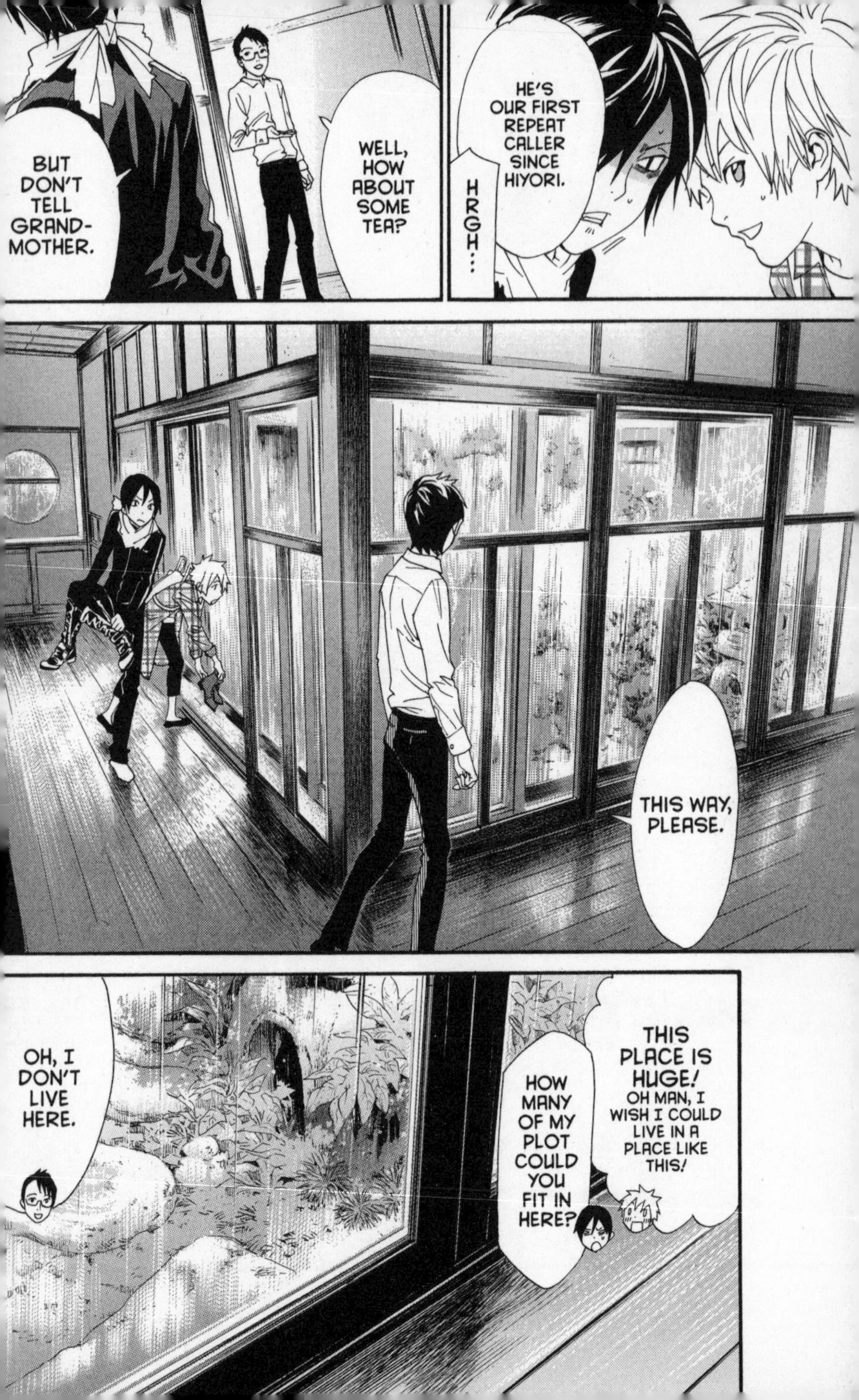
HE'S OUR FIRST REPEAT CALLER SINCE HIYORI.
HRGH...
WELL, HOW ABOUT SOME TEA?
BUT DON'T TELL GRANDMOTHER.
THIS WAY, PLEASE.
THIS PLACE IS HUGE! OH MAN, I WISH I COULD LIVE IN A PLACE LIKE THIS!
HOW MANY OF MY PLOT COULD YOU FIT IN HERE?
OH, I DON'T LIVE HERE.

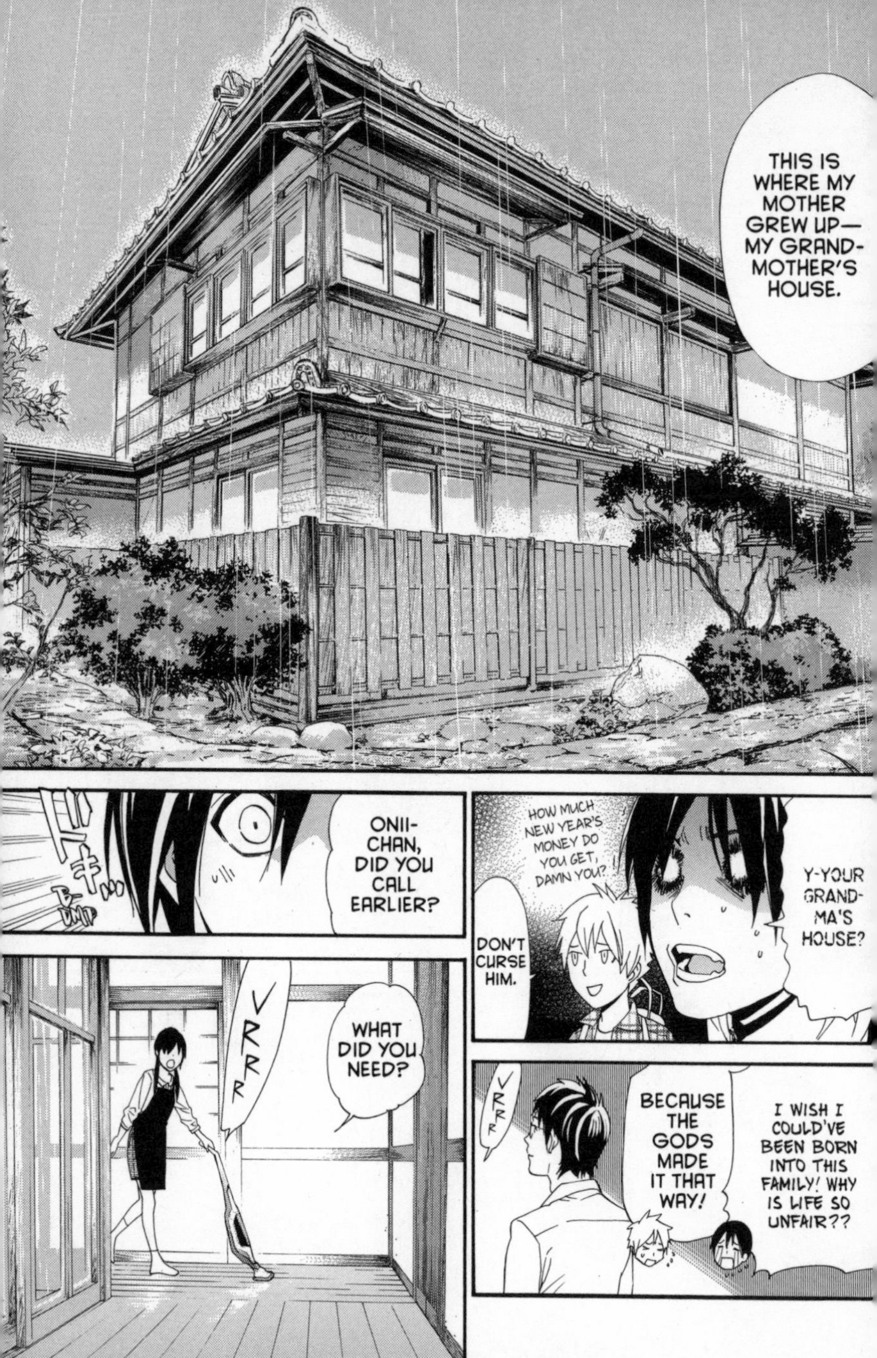
THIS IS WHERE MY MOTHER GREW UP—MY GRAND-MOTHER'S HOUSE.
Y-YOUR GRAND-MA'S HOUSE?
HOW MUCH NEW YEAR'S MONEY DO YOU GET, DAMN YOU?
DON'T CURSE HIM.
ONII-CHAN, DID YOU CALL EARLIER?
B-DUMP
I WISH I COULD'VE BEEN BORN INTO THIS FAMILY! WHY IS LIFE SO UNFAIR??
BECAUSE THE GODS MADE IT THAT WAY!
VRRR
WHAT DID YOU NEED?
VRRR

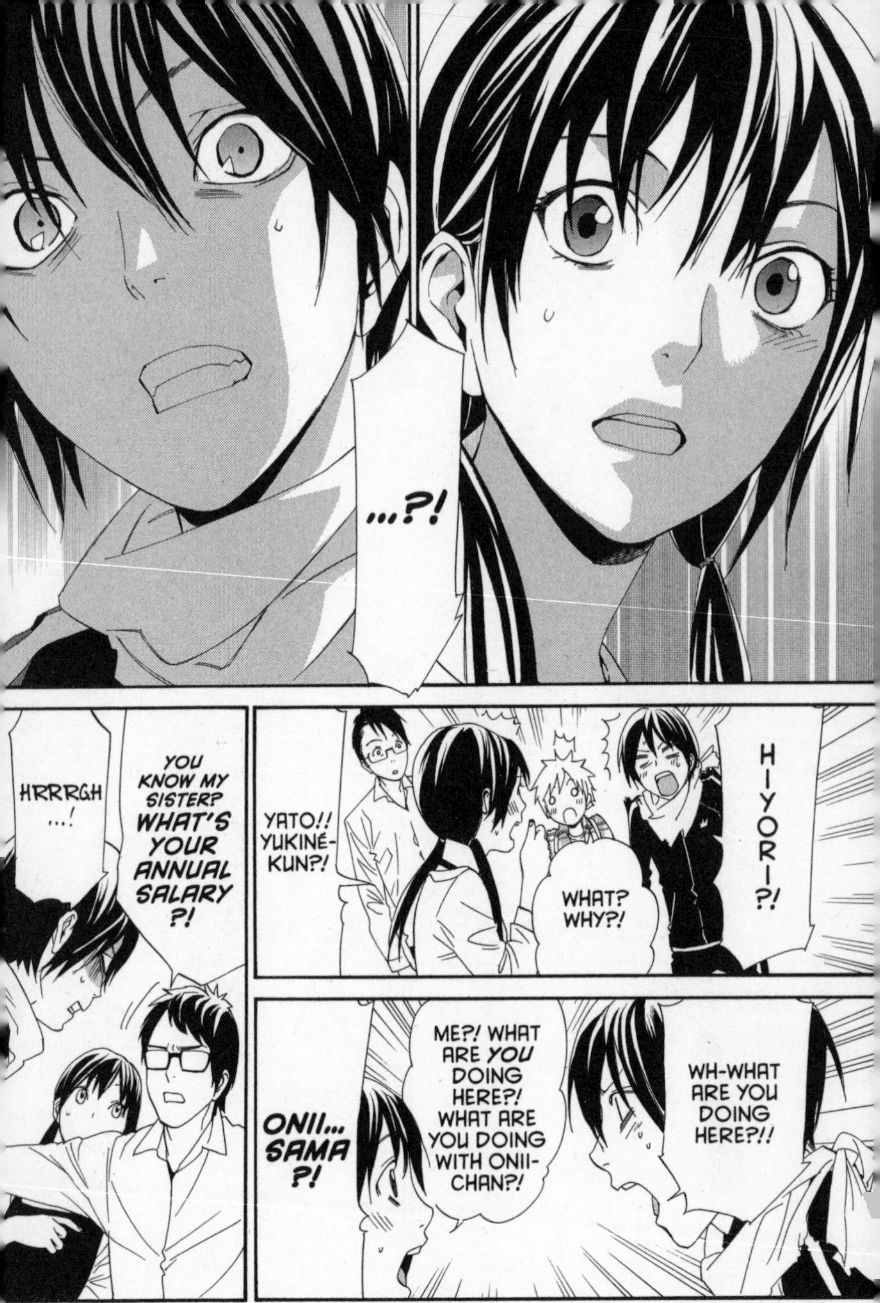
...?!
HIYORI?!
WHAT? WHY?!
YATO!! YUKINÉ-KUN?!
WH-WHAT ARE YOU DOING HERE?!!
ME?! WHAT ARE *YOU* DOING HERE?! WHAT ARE YOU DOING WITH ONII-CHAN?!
ONII... SAMA?!
YOU KNOW MY SISTER? WHAT'S YOUR ANNUAL SALARY?!
HRRRGH ...!

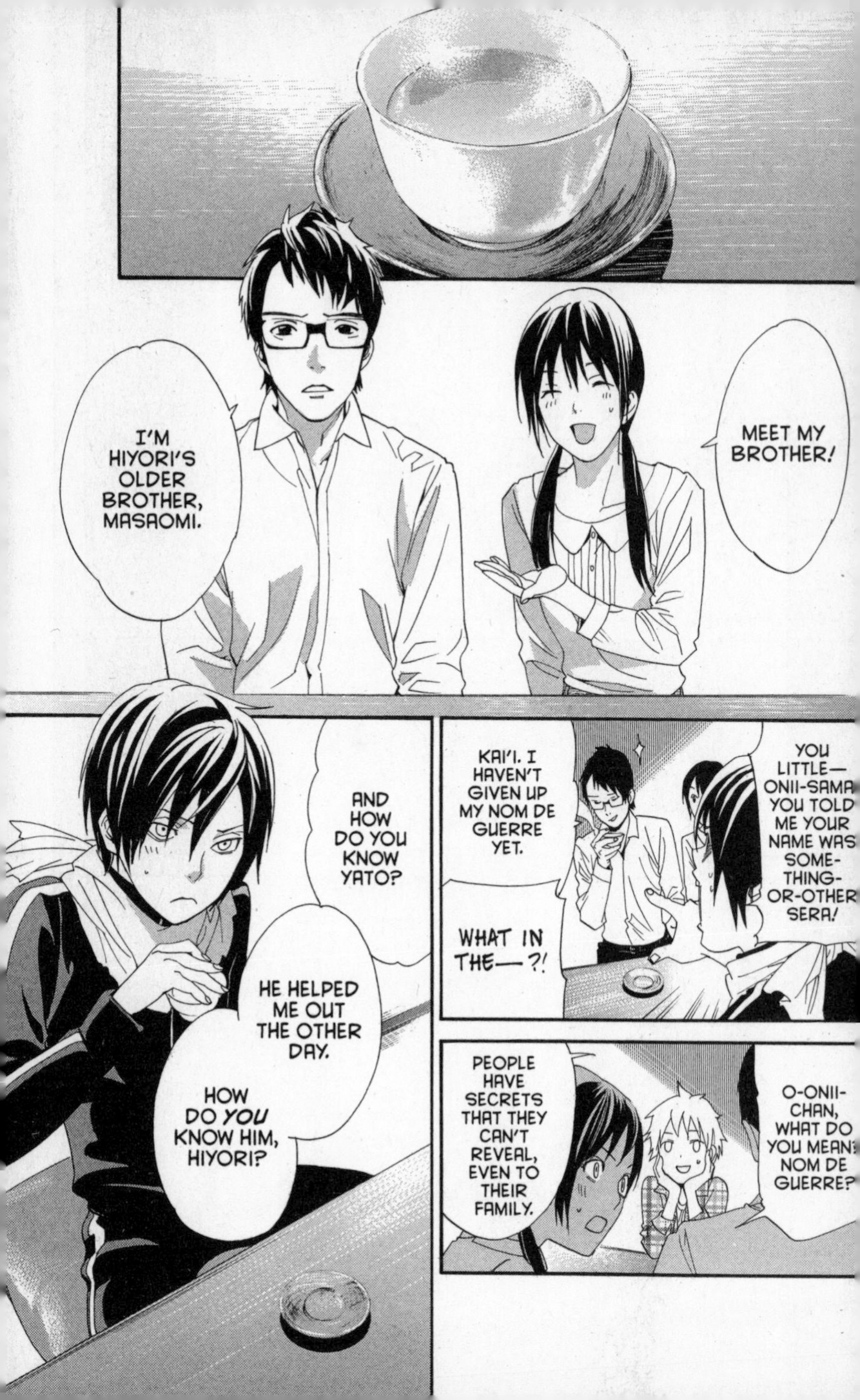
MEET MY BROTHER!
I'M HIYORI'S OLDER BROTHER, MASAOMI.
YOU LITTLE— ONII-SAMA YOU TOLD ME YOUR NAME WAS SOME-THING-OR-OTHER SERA!
KAI'I. I HAVEN'T GIVEN UP MY NOM DE GUERRE YET.
WHAT IN THE—?!
O-ONII-CHAN, WHAT DO YOU MEAN: NOM DE GUERRE?
PEOPLE HAVE SECRETS THAT THEY CAN'T REVEAL, EVEN TO THEIR FAMILY.
AND HOW DO YOU KNOW YATO?
HE HELPED ME OUT THE OTHER DAY.
HOW DO *YOU* KNOW HIM, HIYORI?

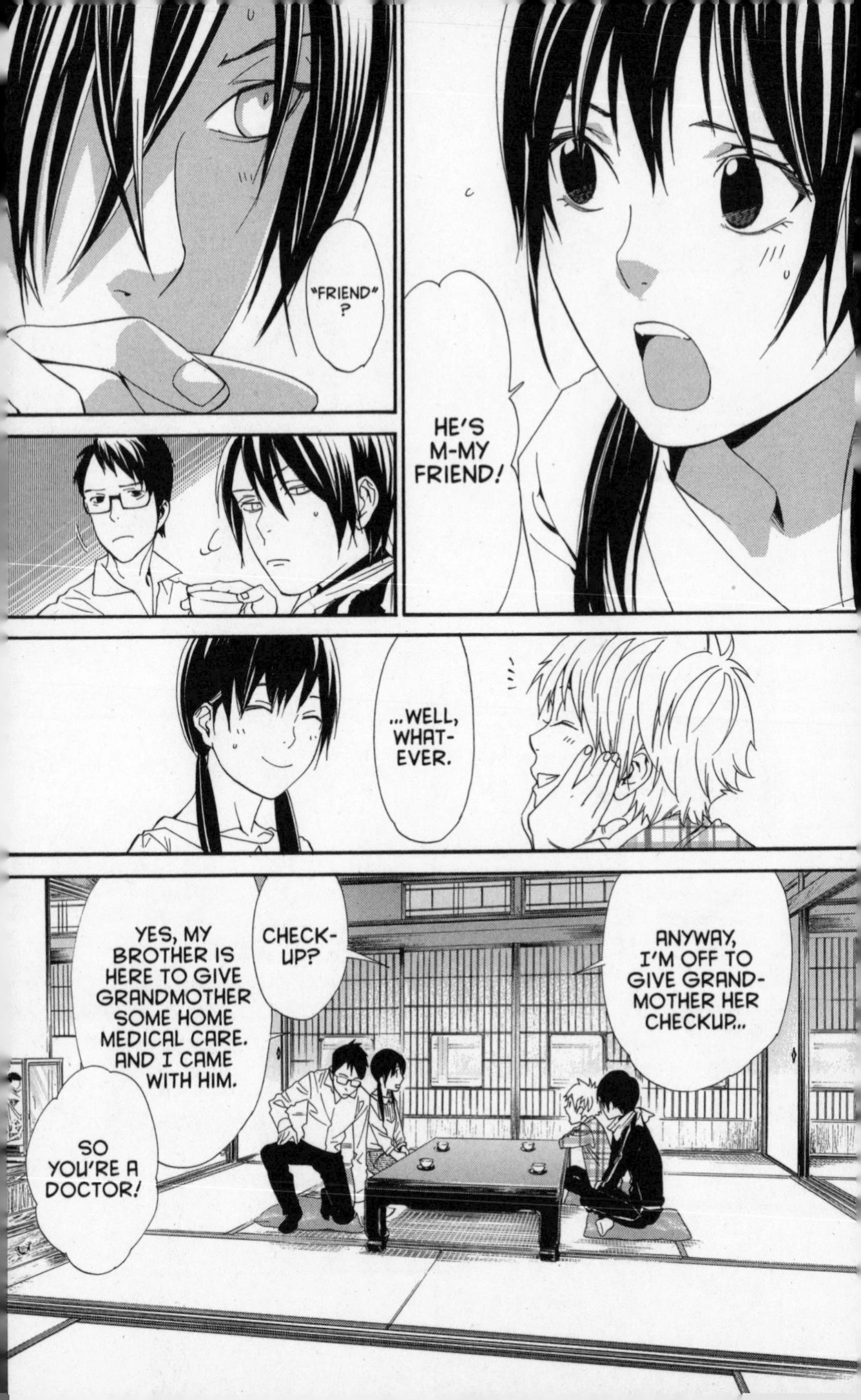
HE'S M-MY FRIEND!
"FRIEND"?
...WELL, WHAT-EVER.
ANYWAY, I'M OFF TO GIVE GRAND-MOTHER HER CHECKUP...
CHECK-UP?
YES, MY BROTHER IS HERE TO GIVE GRANDMOTHER SOME HOME MEDICAL CARE. AND I CAME WITH HIM.
SO YOU'RE A DOCTOR!

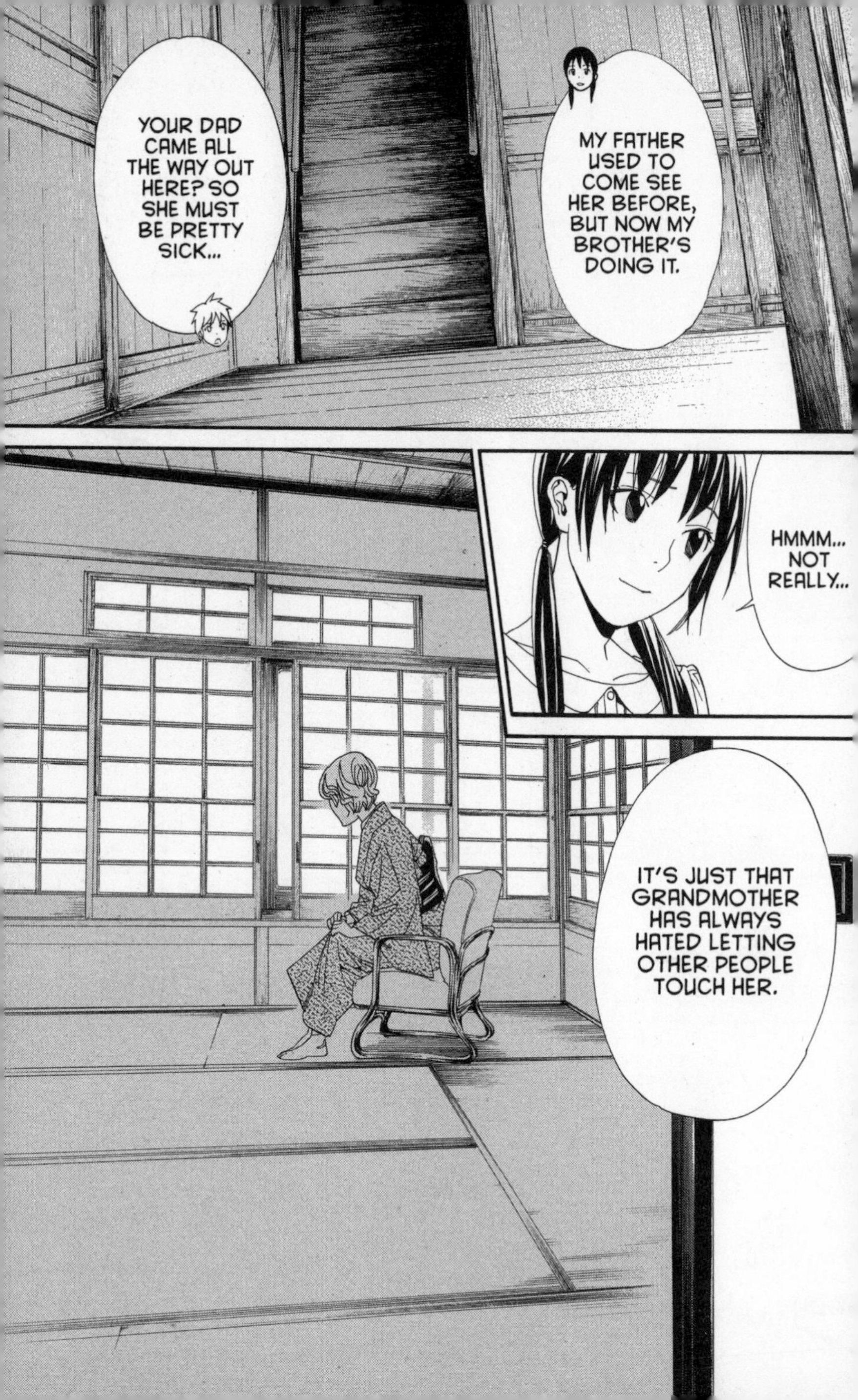
MY FATHER USED TO COME SEE HER BEFORE, BUT NOW MY BROTHER'S DOING IT.
YOUR DAD CAME ALL THE WAY OUT HERE? SO SHE MUST BE PRETTY SICK...
HMMM... NOT REALLY...
IT'S JUST THAT GRANDMOTHER HAS ALWAYS HATED LETTING OTHER PEOPLE TOUCH HER.

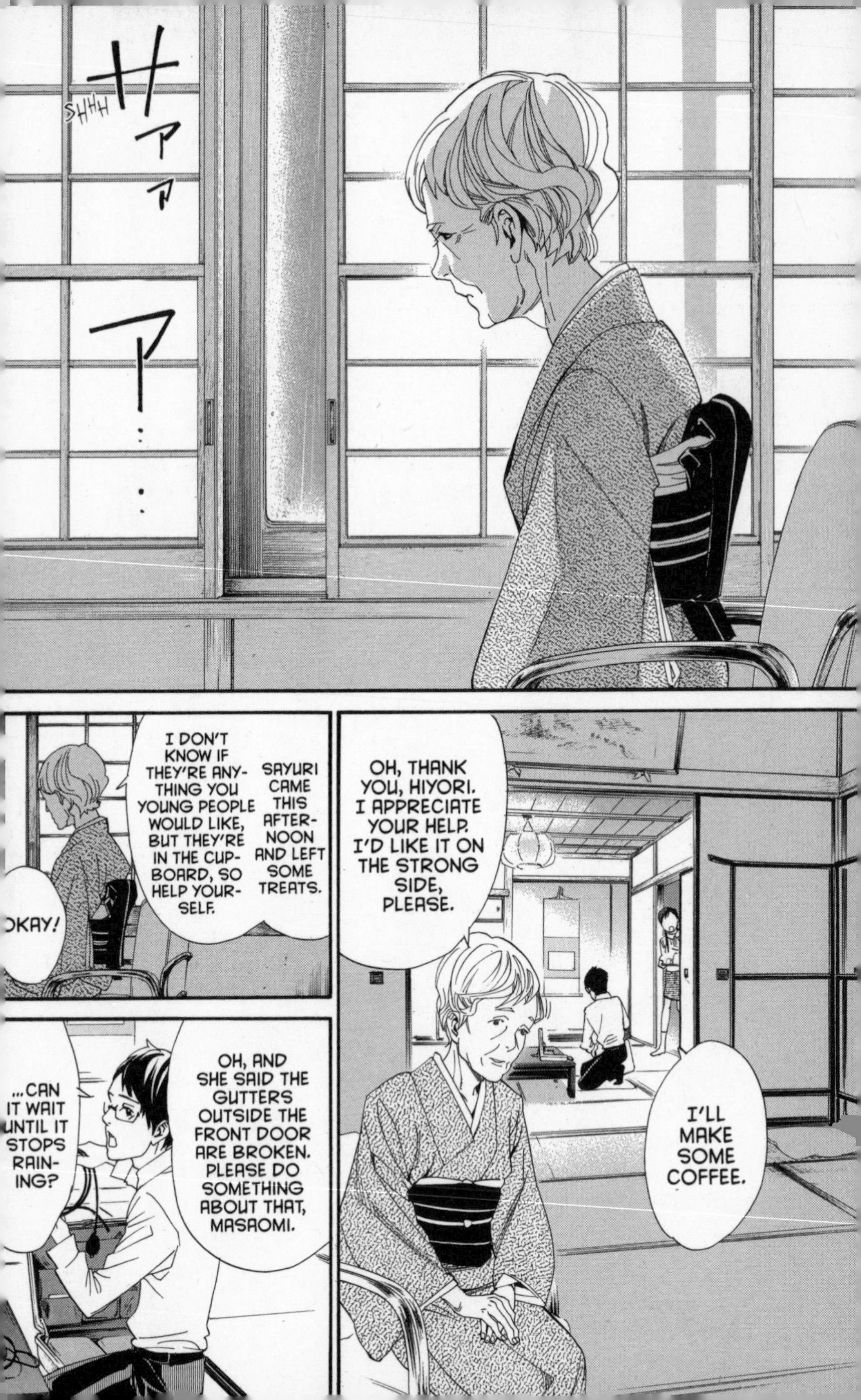
サァァァ…
SHHH
OH, THANK YOU, HIYORI. I APPRECIATE YOUR HELP. I'D LIKE IT ON THE STRONG SIDE, PLEASE.
I'LL MAKE SOME COFFEE.
SAYURI CAME THIS AFTERNOON AND LEFT SOME TREATS.
I DON'T KNOW IF THEY'RE ANYTHING YOU YOUNG PEOPLE WOULD LIKE, BUT THEY'RE IN THE CUPBOARD, SO HELP YOURSELF.
OKAY!
OH, AND SHE SAID THE GUTTERS OUTSIDE THE FRONT DOOR ARE BROKEN. PLEASE DO SOMETHING ABOUT THAT, MASAOMI.
...CAN IT WAIT UNTIL IT STOPS RAINING?

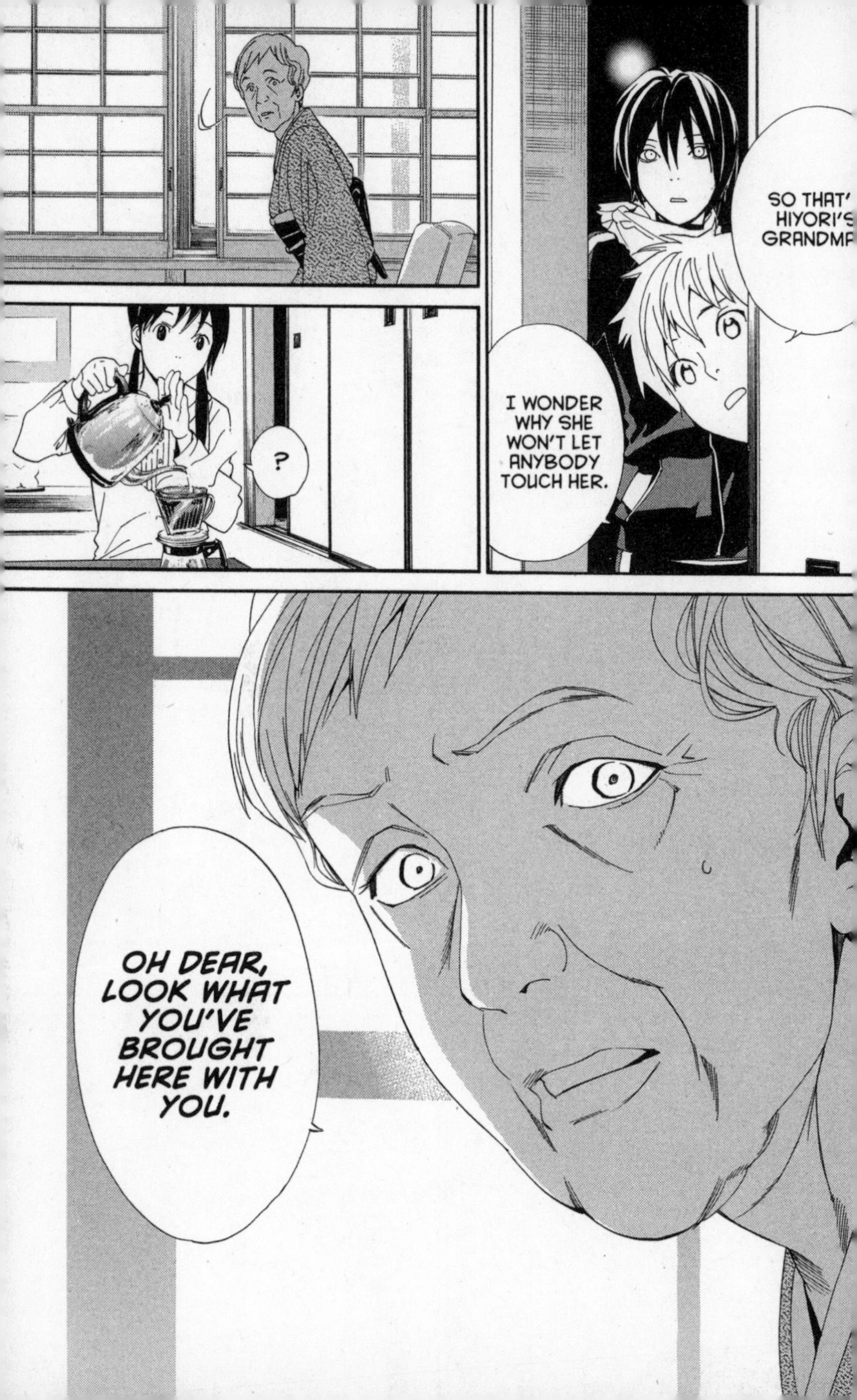
SO THAT' HIYORI'S GRANDMA
I WONDER WHY SHE WON'T LET ANYBODY TOUCH HER.
?
OH DEAR, LOOK WHAT YOU'VE BROUGHT HERE WITH YOU.

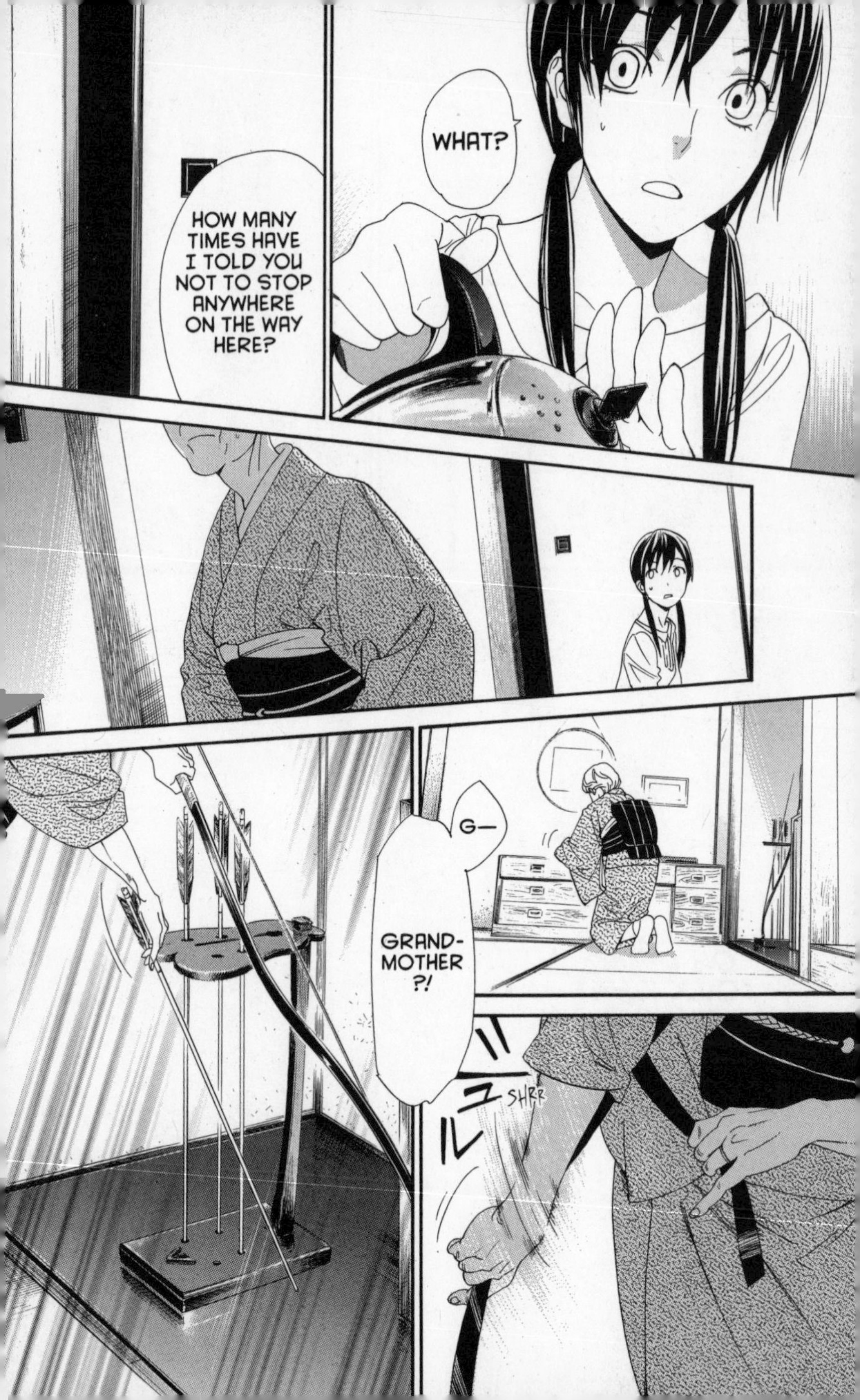
WHAT?
HOW MANY TIMES HAVE I TOLD YOU NOT TO STOP ANYWHERE ON THE WAY HERE?
G—
GRAND-MOTHER?!
SHRR

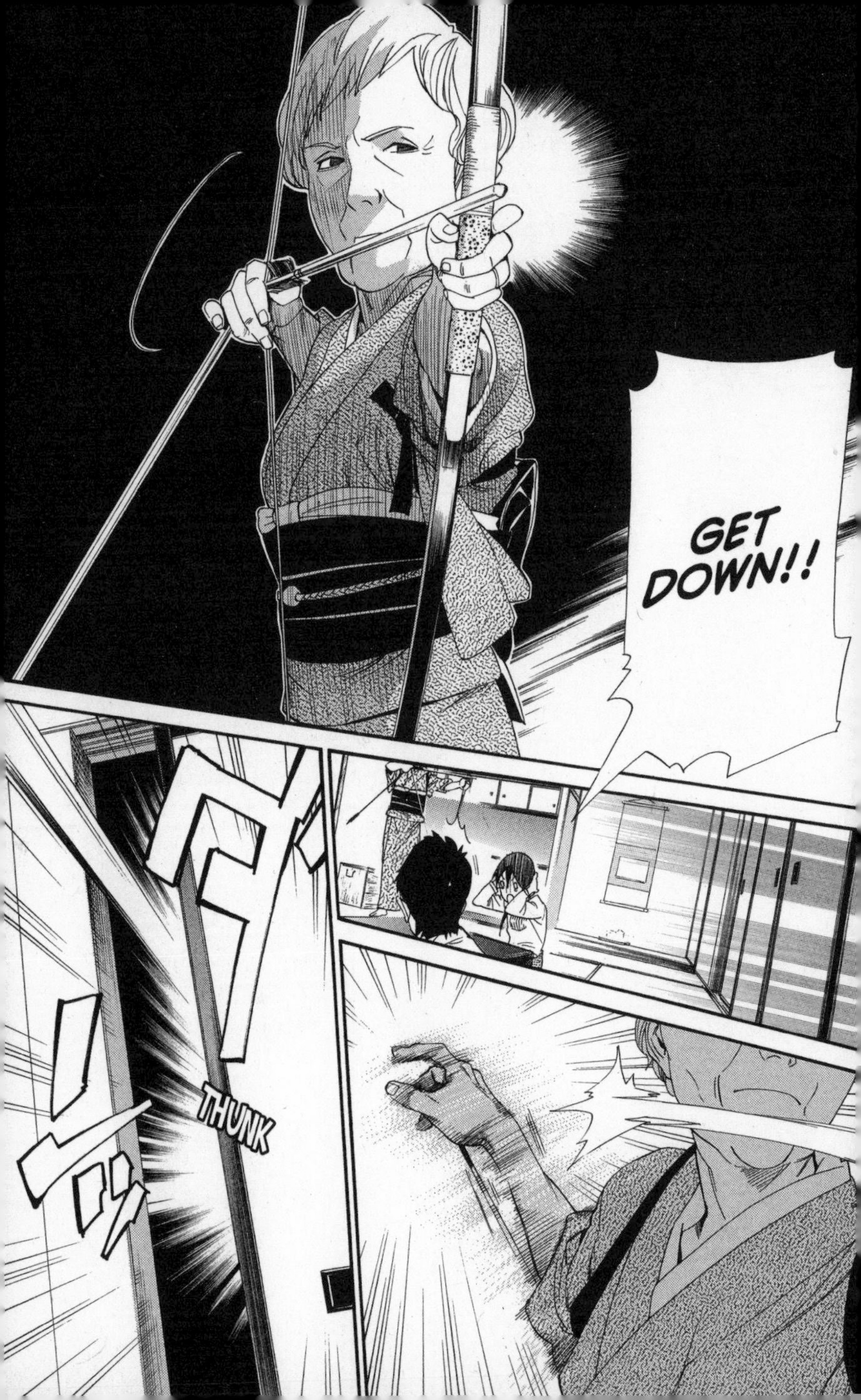
GET DOWN!!
THUNK

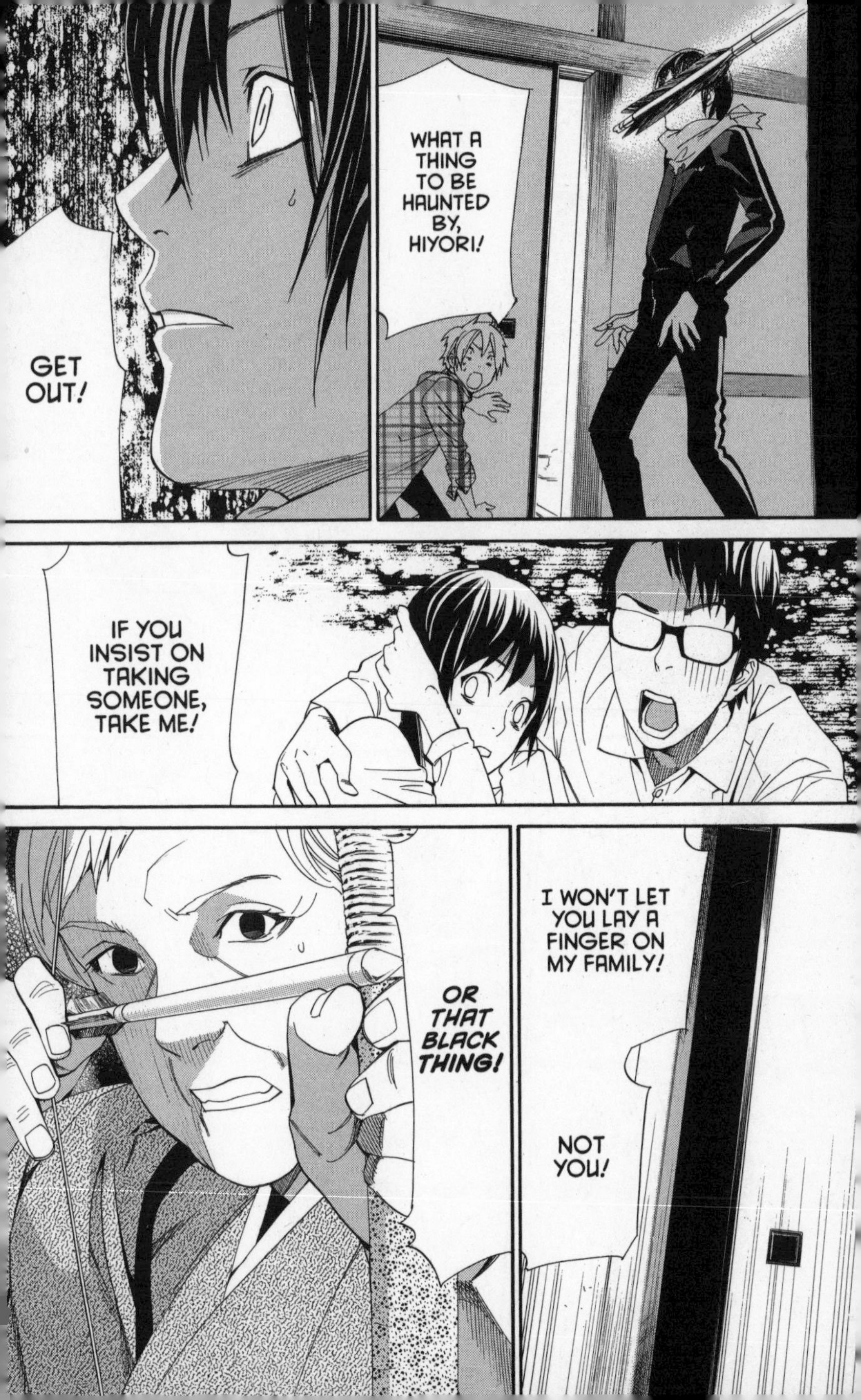
WHAT A THING TO BE HAUNTED BY, HIYORI!
GET OUT!
IF YOU INSIST ON TAKING SOMEONE, TAKE ME!
I WON'T LET YOU LAY A FINGER ON MY FAMILY!
NOT YOU!
OR THAT BLACK THING!

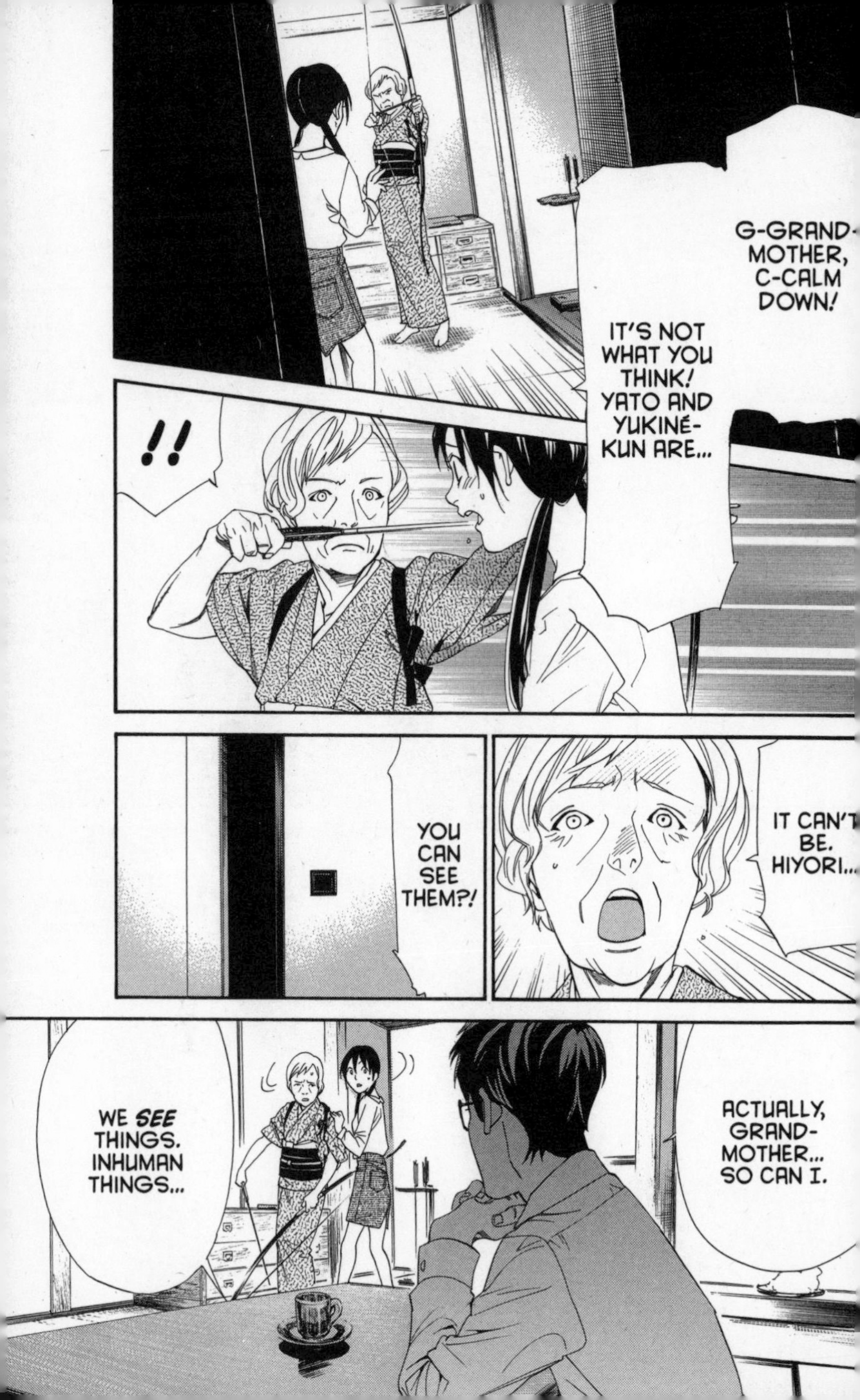

G-GRANDMOTHER, C-CALM DOWN!
IT'S NOT WHAT YOU THINK! YATO AND YUKINÉ-KUN ARE...
!!
IT CAN'T BE. HIYORI...
YOU CAN SEE THEM?!
ACTUALLY, GRANDMOTHER... SO CAN I.
WE *SEE* THINGS. INHUMAN THINGS...

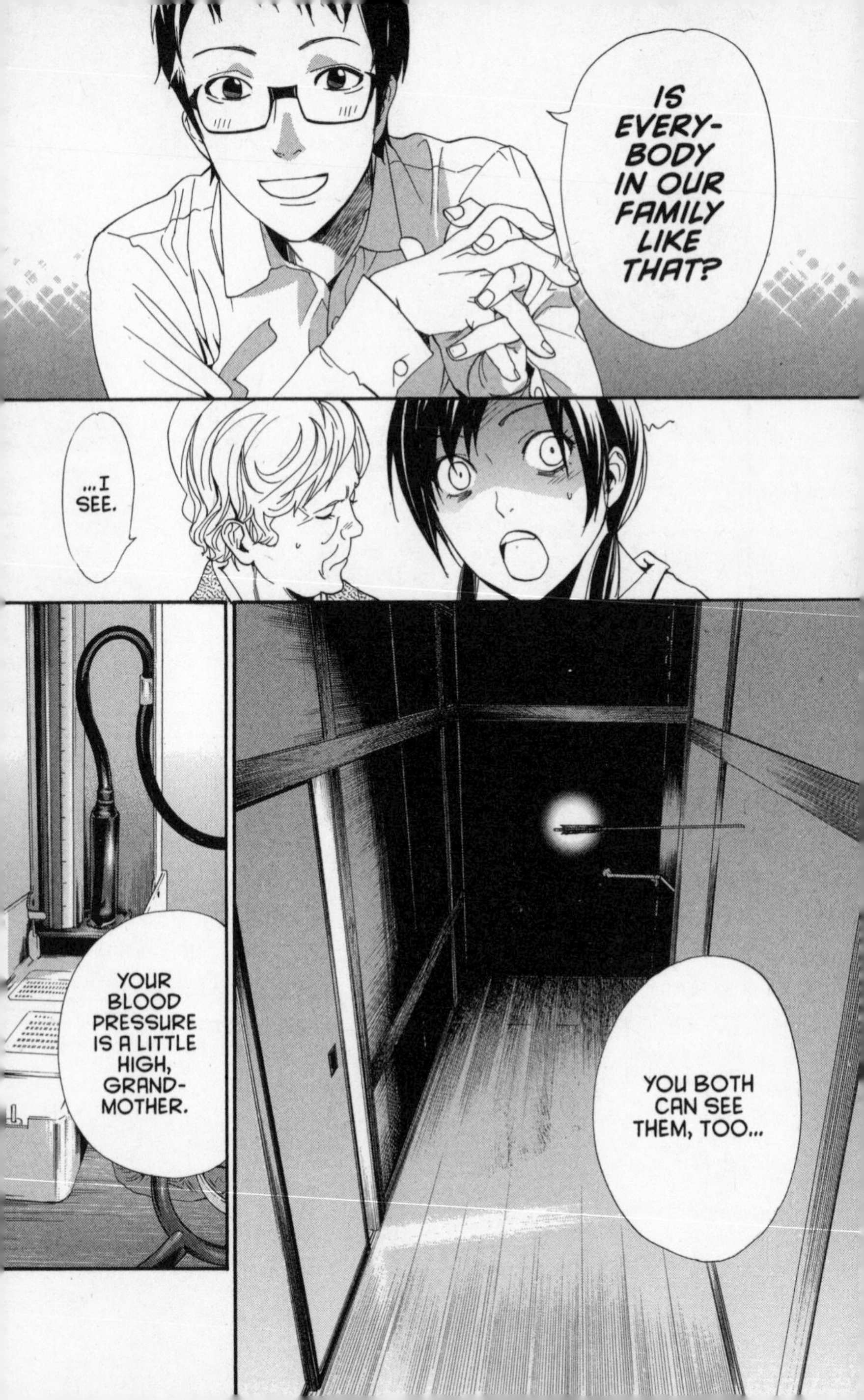
IS EVERY-BODY IN OUR FAMILY LIKE THAT?
...I SEE.
YOU BOTH CAN SEE THEM, TOO...
YOUR BLOOD PRESSURE IS A LITTLE HIGH, GRAND-MOTHER.

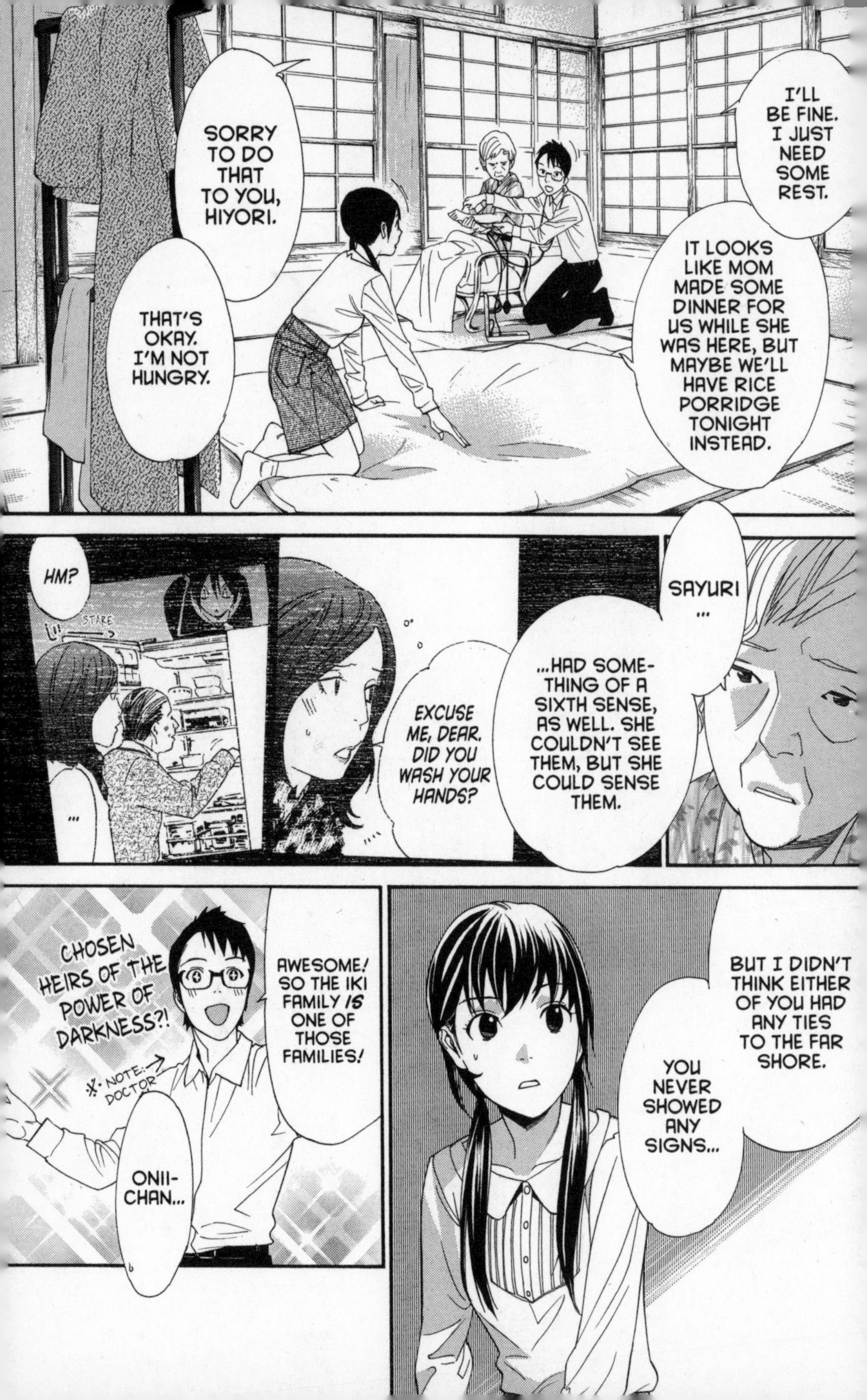
I'LL BE FINE. I JUST NEED SOME REST.
IT LOOKS LIKE MOM MADE SOME DINNER FOR US WHILE SHE WAS HERE, BUT MAYBE WE'LL HAVE RICE PORRIDGE TONIGHT INSTEAD.
SORRY TO DO THAT TO YOU, HIYORI.
THAT'S OKAY. I'M NOT HUNGRY.
SAYURI ...
...HAD SOME-THING OF A SIXTH SENSE, AS WELL. SHE COULDN'T SEE THEM, BUT SHE COULD SENSE THEM.
EXCUSE ME, DEAR. DID YOU WASH YOUR HANDS?
....
HM?
STARE
...
BUT I DIDN'T THINK EITHER OF YOU HAD ANY TIES TO THE FAR SHORE.
YOU NEVER SHOWED ANY SIGNS...
AWESOME! SO THE IKI FAMILY *IS* ONE OF THOSE FAMILIES!
CHOSEN HEIRS OF THE POWER OF DARKNESS?!
※ NOTE: DOCTOR
ONII-CHAN...

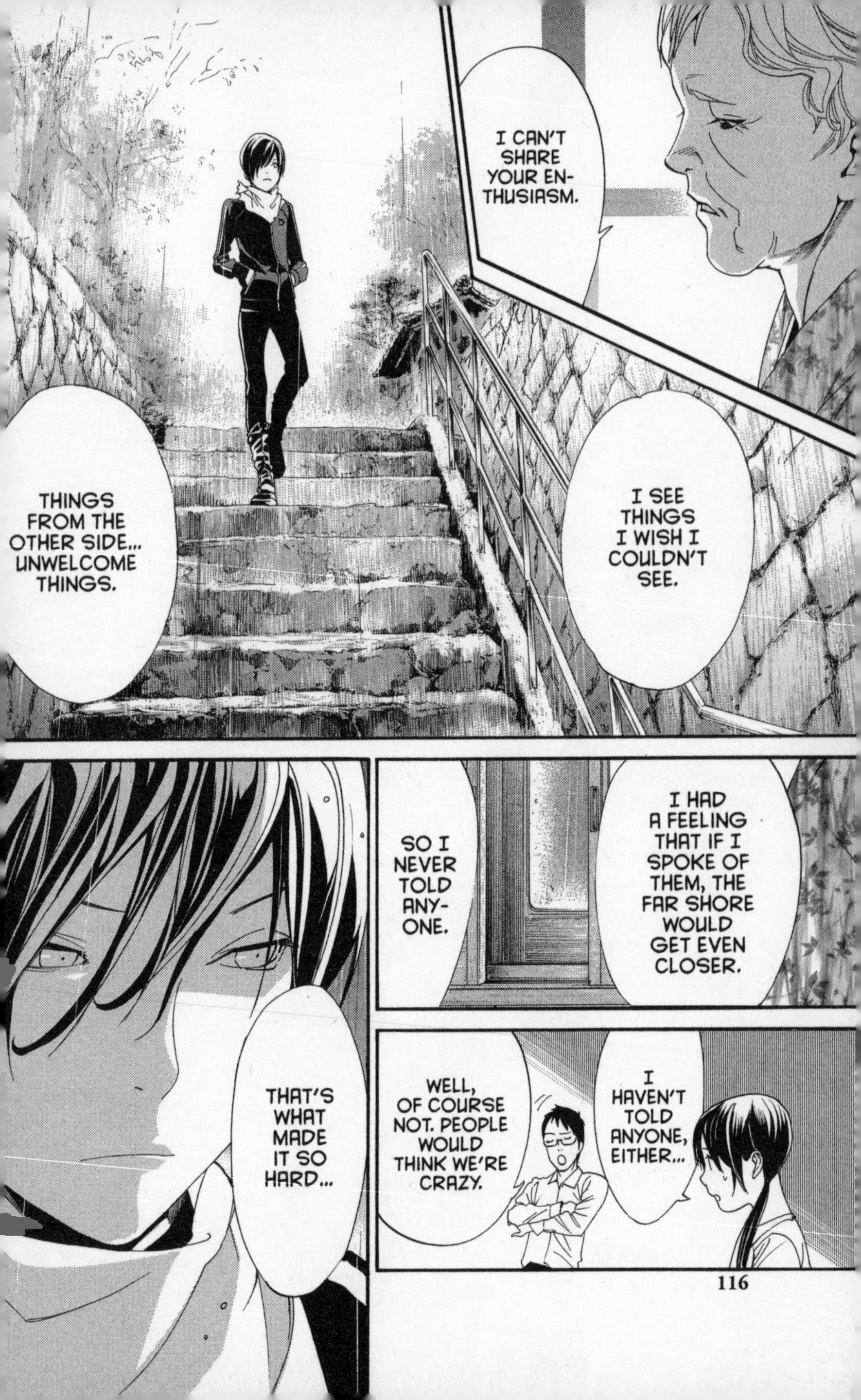
I CAN'T SHARE YOUR EN-THUSIASM.
I SEE THINGS I WISH I COULDN'T SEE.
THINGS FROM THE OTHER SIDE... UNWELCOME THINGS.
I HAD A FEELING THAT IF I SPOKE OF THEM, THE FAR SHORE WOULD GET EVEN CLOSER.
SO I NEVER TOLD ANY-ONE.
I HAVEN'T TOLD ANYONE, EITHER...
WELL, OF COURSE NOT. PEOPLE WOULD THINK WE'RE CRAZY.
THAT'S WHAT MADE IT SO HARD...

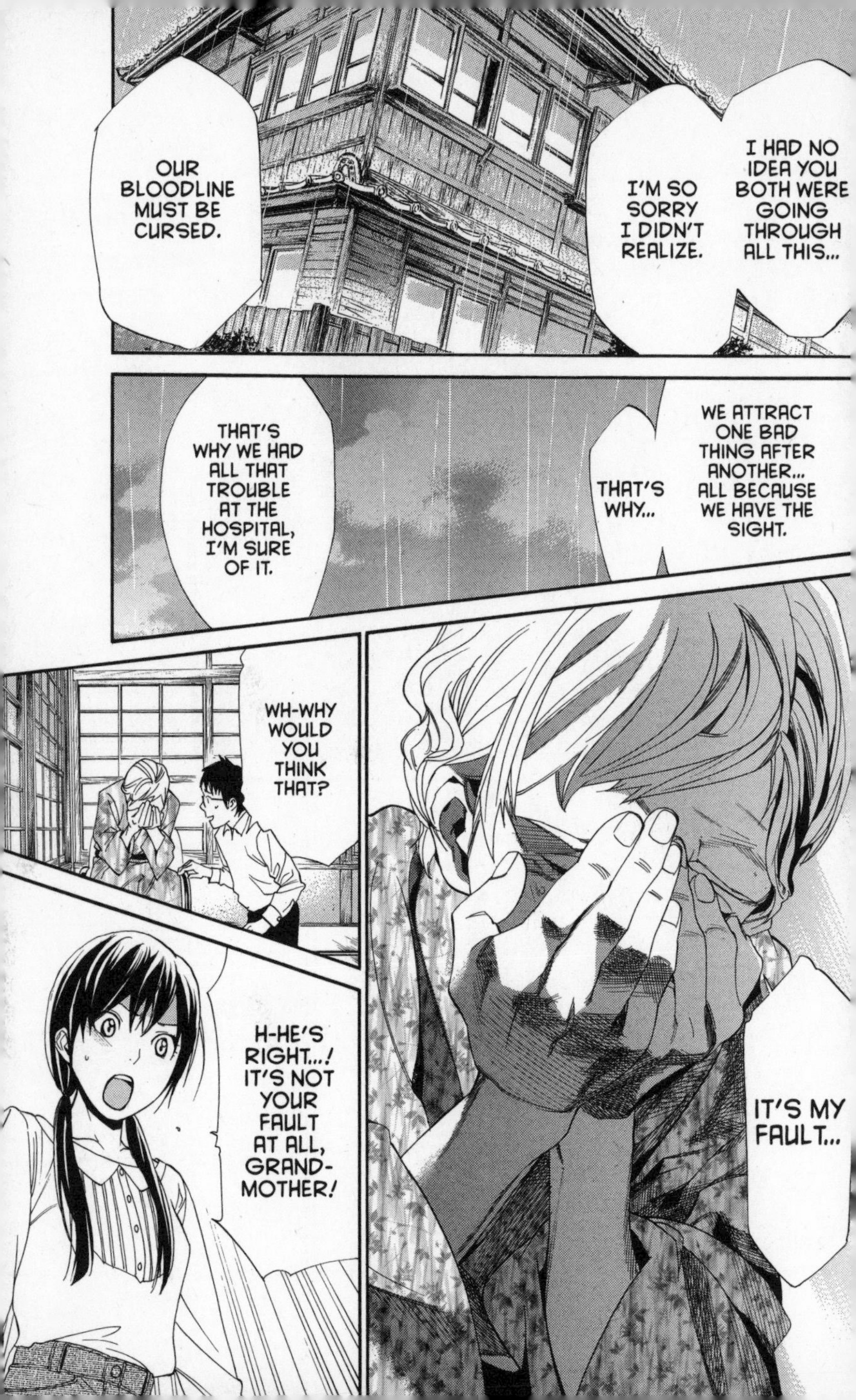
I HAD NO IDEA YOU BOTH WERE GOING THROUGH ALL THIS...
I'M SO SORRY I DIDN'T REALIZE.
OUR BLOODLINE MUST BE CURSED.
WE ATTRACT ONE BAD THING AFTER ANOTHER... ALL BECAUSE WE HAVE THE SIGHT.
THAT'S WHY...
THAT'S WHY WE HAD ALL THAT TROUBLE AT THE HOSPITAL, I'M SURE OF IT.
IT'S MY FAULT...
WH-WHY WOULD YOU THINK THAT?
H-HE'S RIGHT...! IT'S NOT YOUR FAULT AT ALL, GRAND-MOTHER!

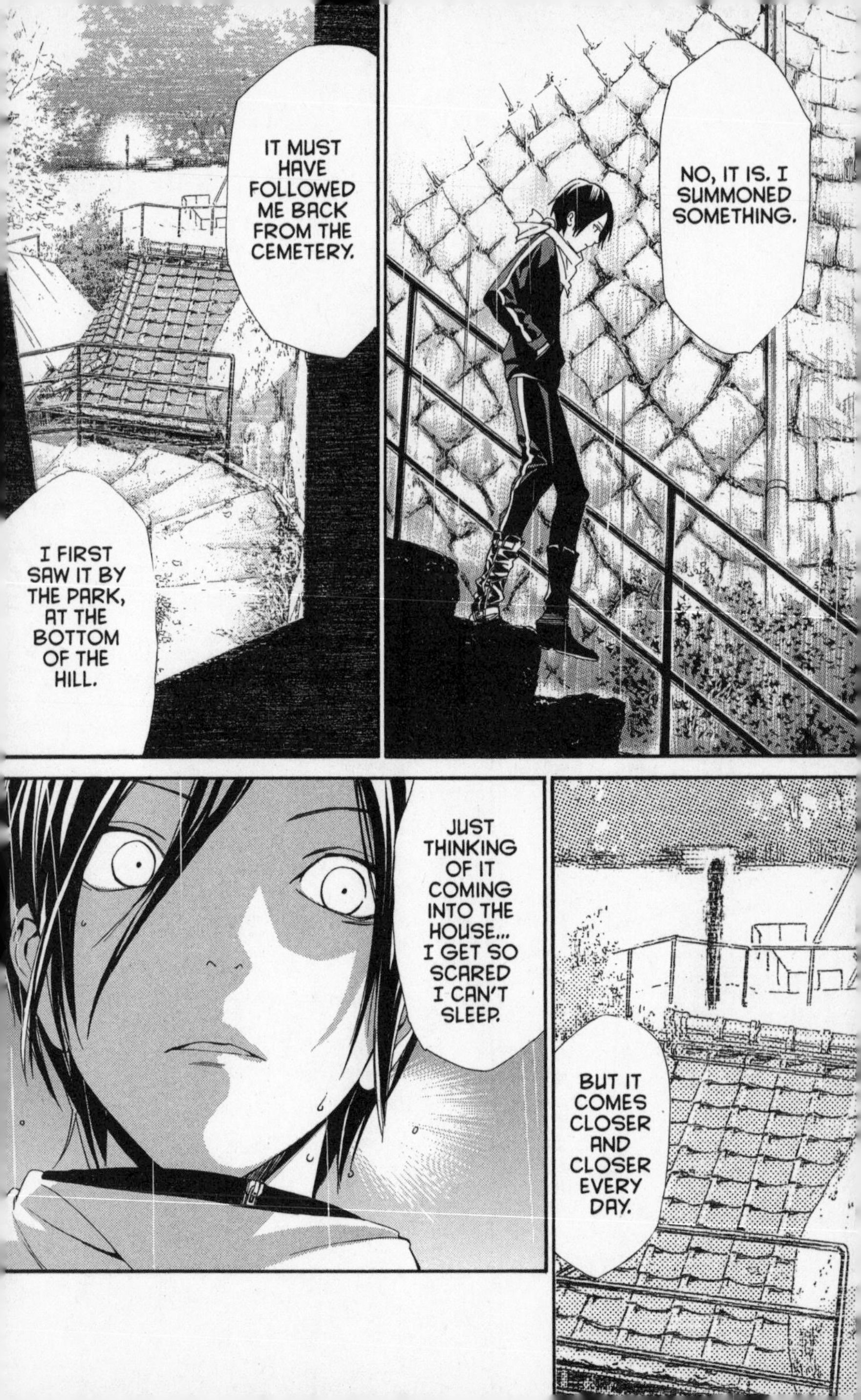
NO, IT IS. I SUMMONED SOMETHING.
IT MUST HAVE FOLLOWED ME BACK FROM THE CEMETERY.
I FIRST SAW IT BY THE PARK, AT THE BOTTOM OF THE HILL.
BUT IT COMES CLOSER AND CLOSER EVERY DAY.
JUST THINKING OF IT COMING INTO THE HOUSE... I GET SO SCARED I CAN'T SLEEP.

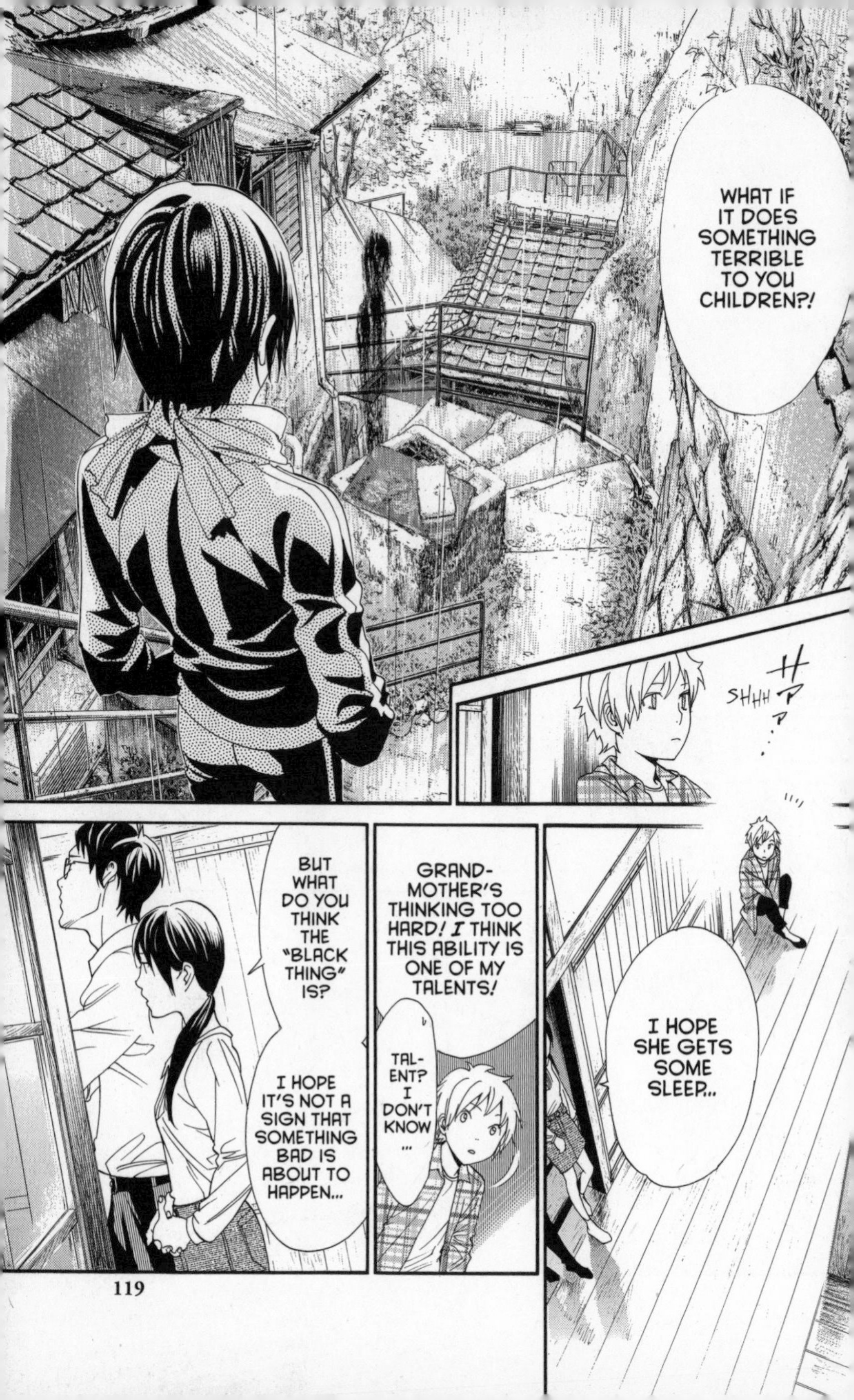
WHAT IF IT DOES SOMETHING TERRIBLE TO YOU CHILDREN?!
SHHH
I HOPE SHE GETS SOME SLEEP...
GRAND-MOTHER'S THINKING TOO HARD! *I* THINK THIS ABILITY IS ONE OF MY TALENTS!
TAL-ENT? I DON'T KNOW ...
BUT WHAT DO YOU THINK THE "BLACK THING" IS?
I HOPE IT'S NOT A SIGN THAT SOMETHING BAD IS ABOUT TO HAPPEN...

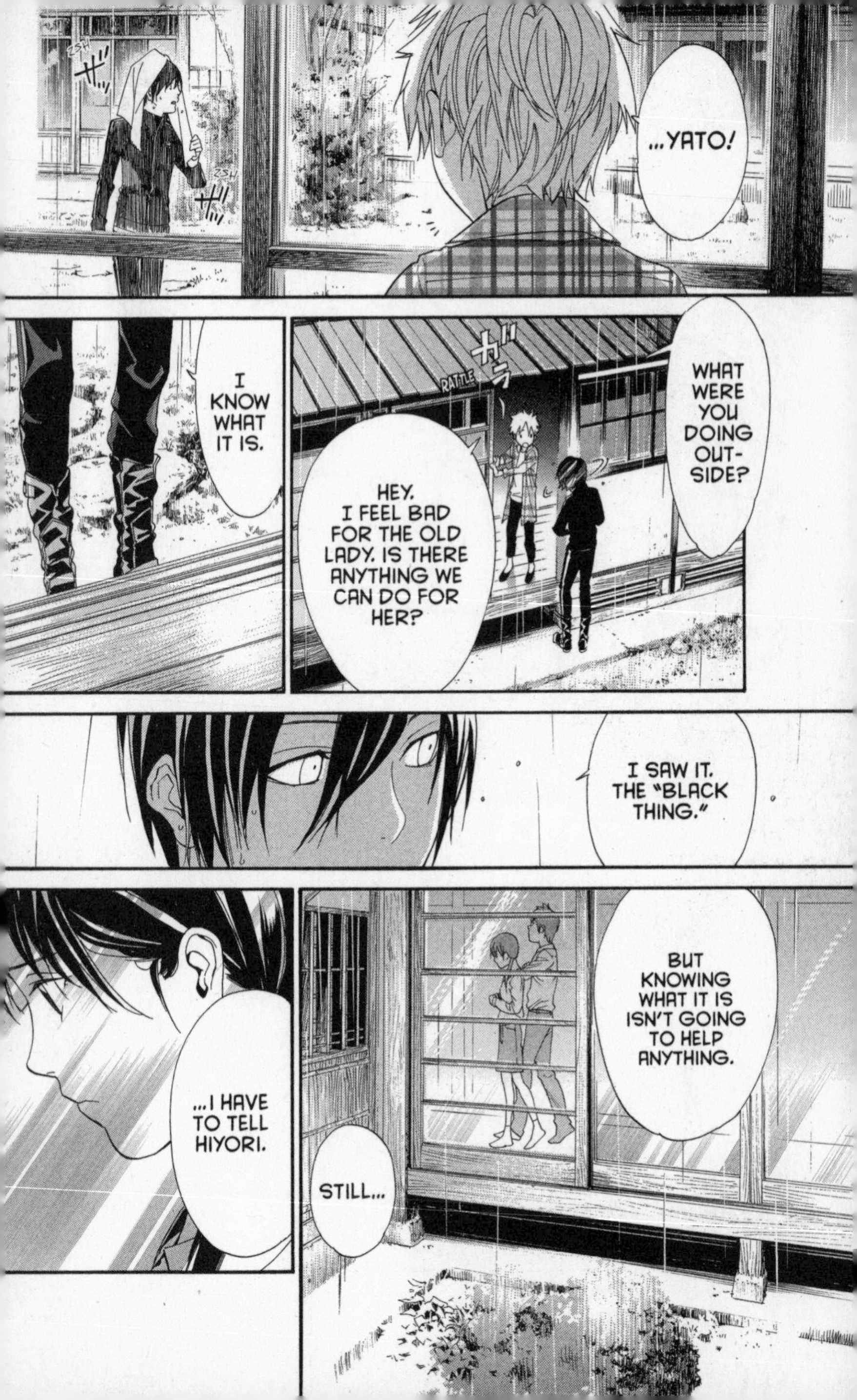
...YATO!
ZSH
ZSH
WHAT WERE YOU DOING OUTSIDE?
RATTLE
HEY. I FEEL BAD FOR THE OLD LADY. IS THERE ANYTHING WE CAN DO FOR HER?
I KNOW WHAT IT IS.
I SAW IT. THE "BLACK THING."
BUT KNOWING WHAT IT IS ISN'T GOING TO HELP ANYTHING.
STILL...
...I HAVE TO TELL HIYORI.

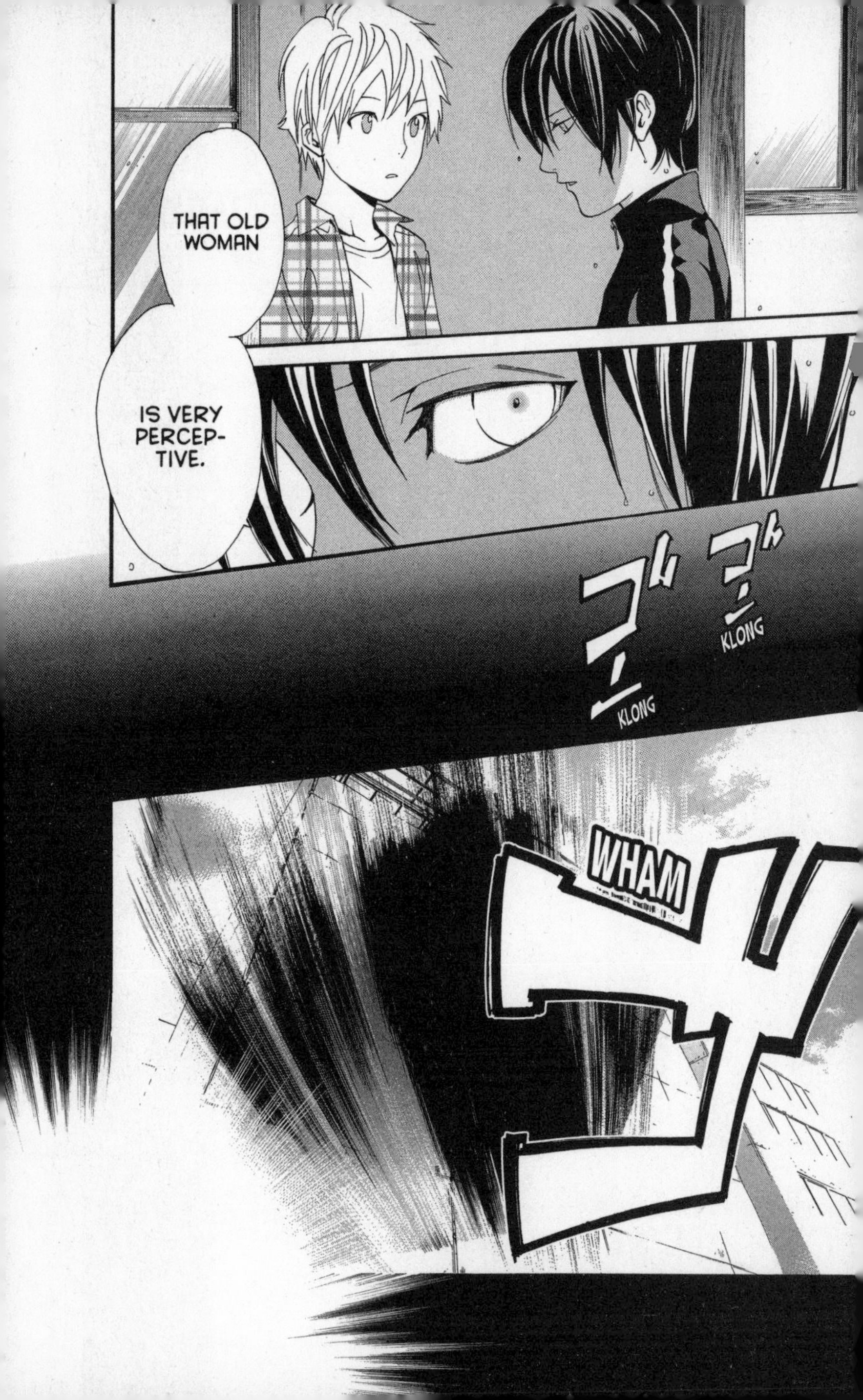
THAT OLD WOMAN
IS VERY PERCEP-TIVE.
KLONG
KLONG
WHAM

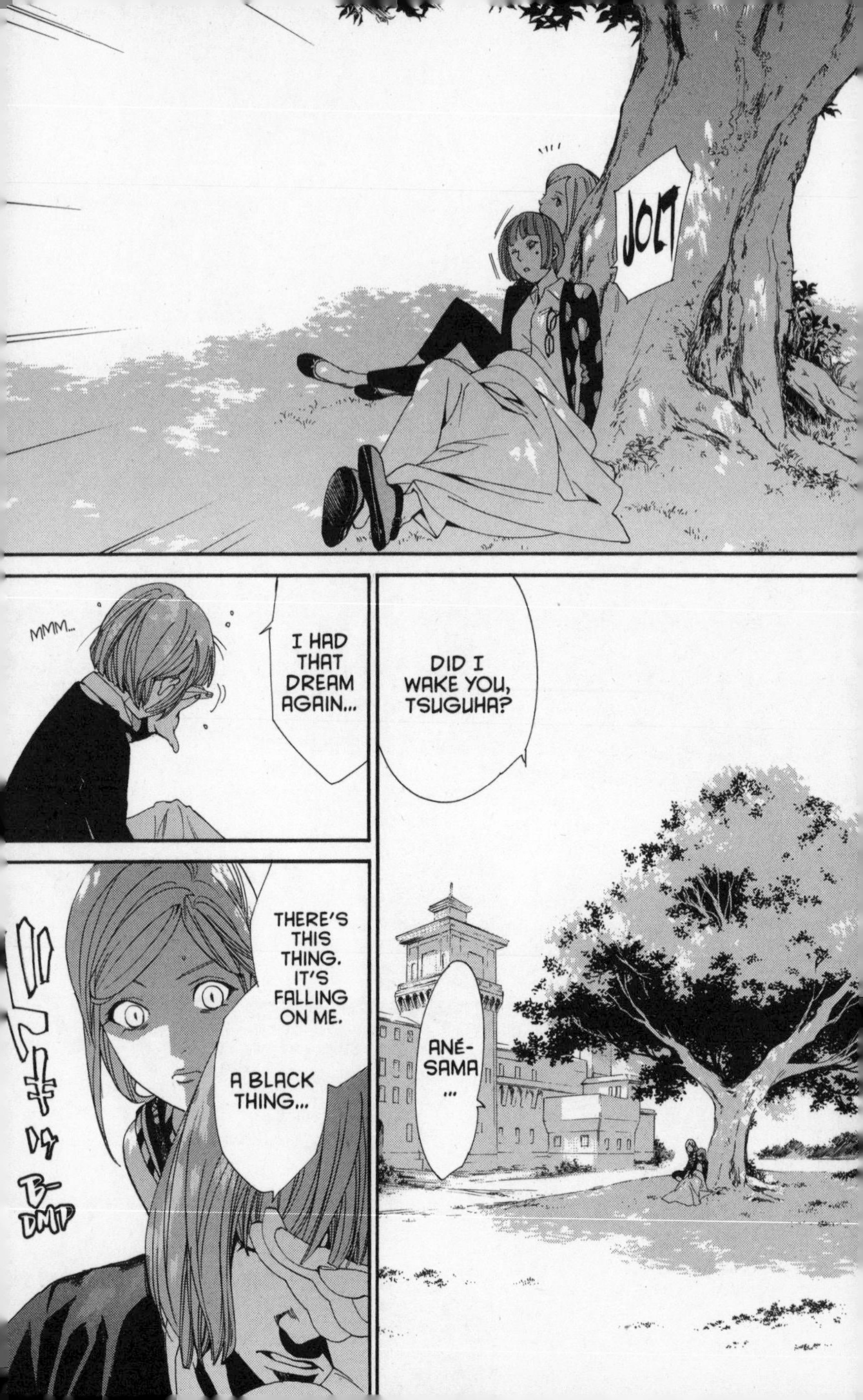
JOLT
DID I WAKE YOU, TSUGUHA?
ANÉ-SAMA ...
MMM...
I HAD THAT DREAM AGAIN...
B-DMP
THERE'S THIS THING. IT'S FALLING ON ME.
A BLACK THING...

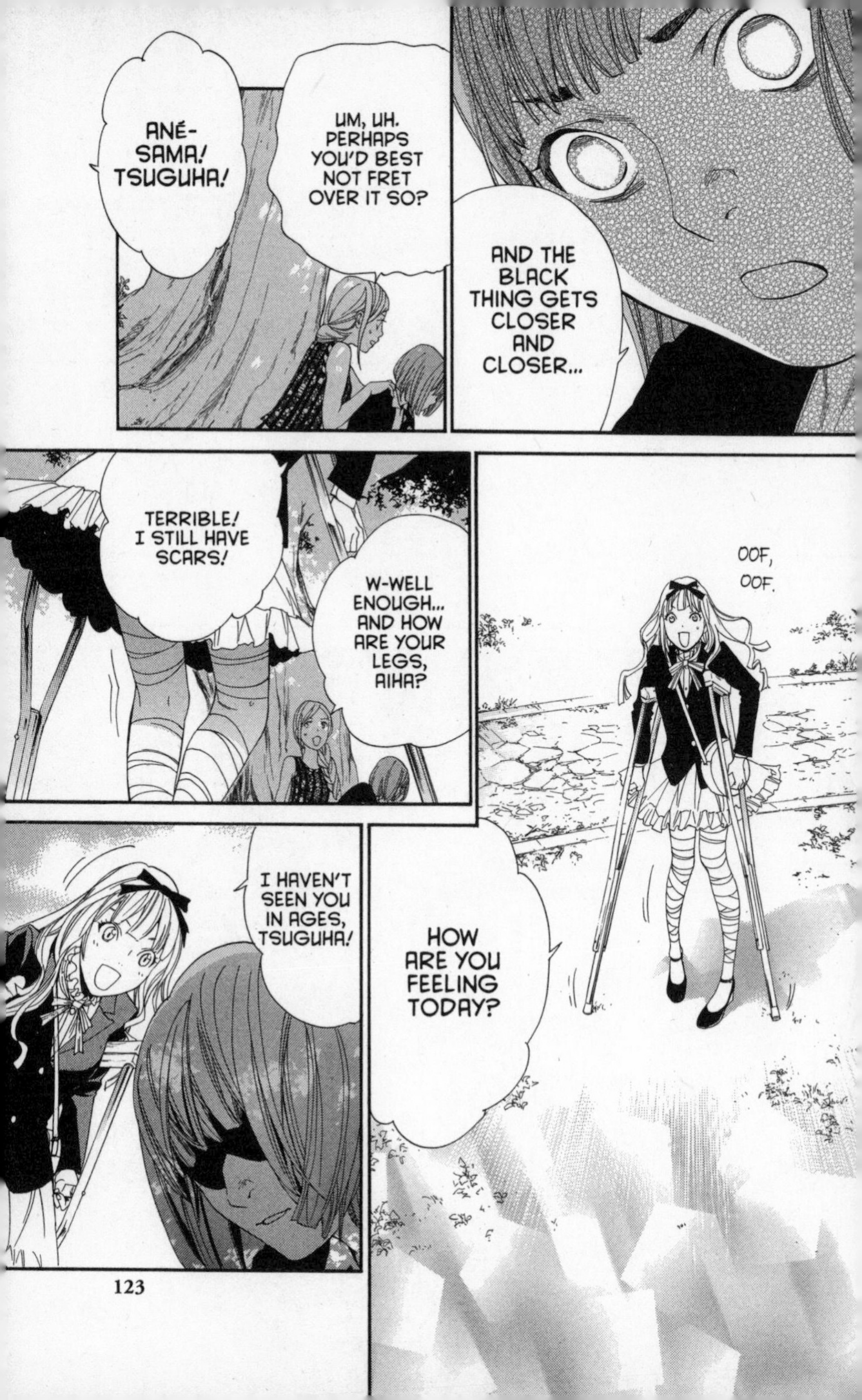
AND THE BLACK THING GETS CLOSER AND CLOSER...
UM, UH. PERHAPS YOU'D BEST NOT FRET OVER IT SO?
ANÉ-SAMA! TSUGUHA!
OOF, OOF.
I HAVEN'T SEEN YOU IN AGES, TSUGUHA!
HOW ARE YOU FEELING TODAY?
W-WELL ENOUGH... AND HOW ARE YOUR LEGS, AIHA?
TERRIBLE! I STILL HAVE SCARS!

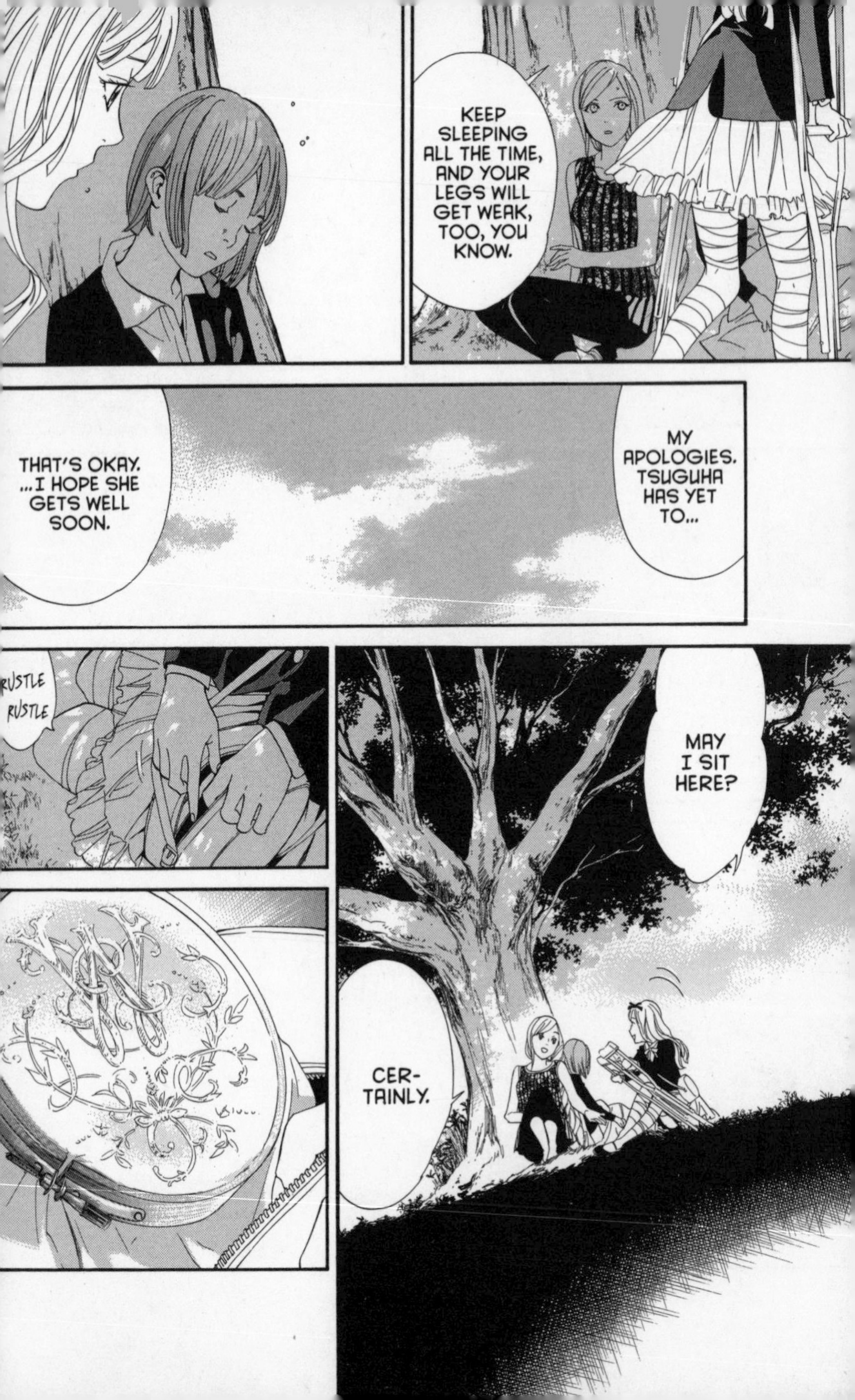
KEEP SLEEPING ALL THE TIME, AND YOUR LEGS WILL GET WEAK, TOO, YOU KNOW.
MY APOLOGIES. TSUGUHA HAS YET TO...
THAT'S OKAY. ...I HOPE SHE GETS WELL SOON.
MAY I SIT HERE?
CER-TAINLY.
RUSTLE
RUSTLE

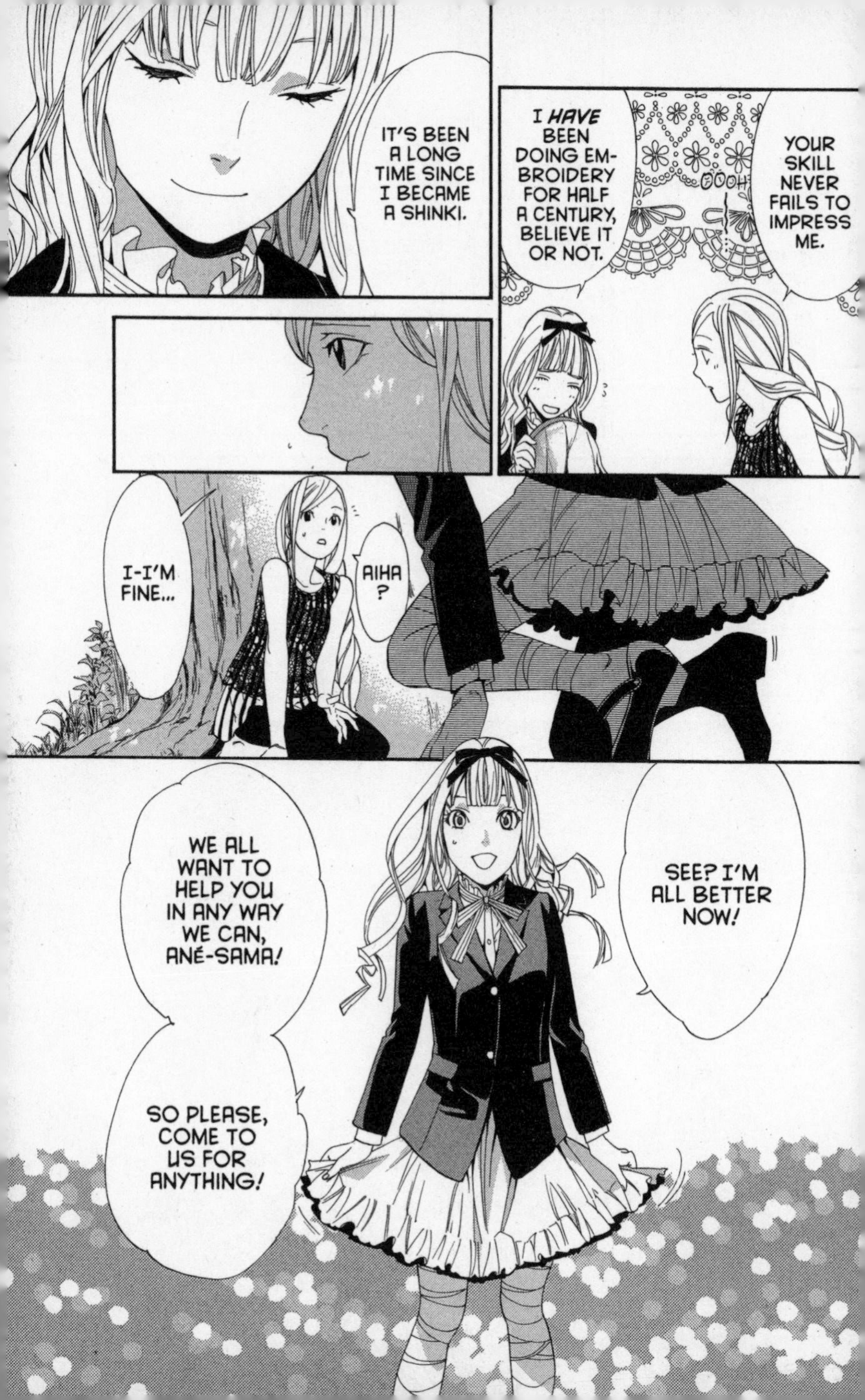
YOUR SKILL NEVER FAILS TO IMPRESS ME.
FOOH
I *HAVE* BEEN DOING EM-BROIDERY FOR HALF A CENTURY, BELIEVE IT OR NOT.
IT'S BEEN A LONG TIME SINCE I BECAME A SHINKI.
AIHA?
I-I'M FINE...
SEE? I'M ALL BETTER NOW!
WE ALL WANT TO HELP YOU IN ANY WAY WE CAN, ANÉ-SAMA!
SO PLEASE, COME TO US FOR ANYTHING!

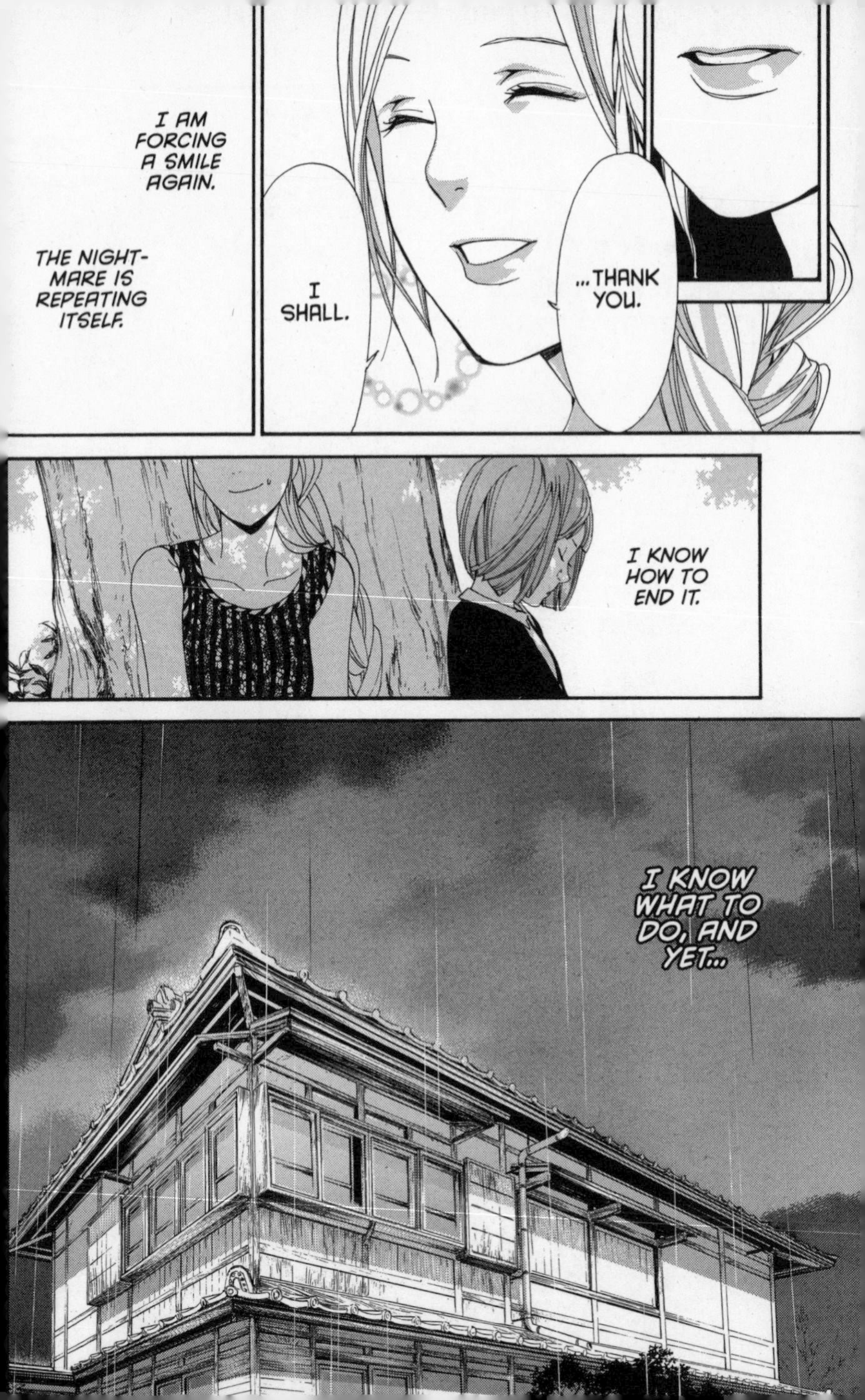
...THANK YOU.
I SHALL.
I AM FORCING A SMILE AGAIN.
THE NIGHT-MARE IS REPEATING ITSELF.
I KNOW HOW TO END IT.
I KNOW WHAT TO DO, AND YET...

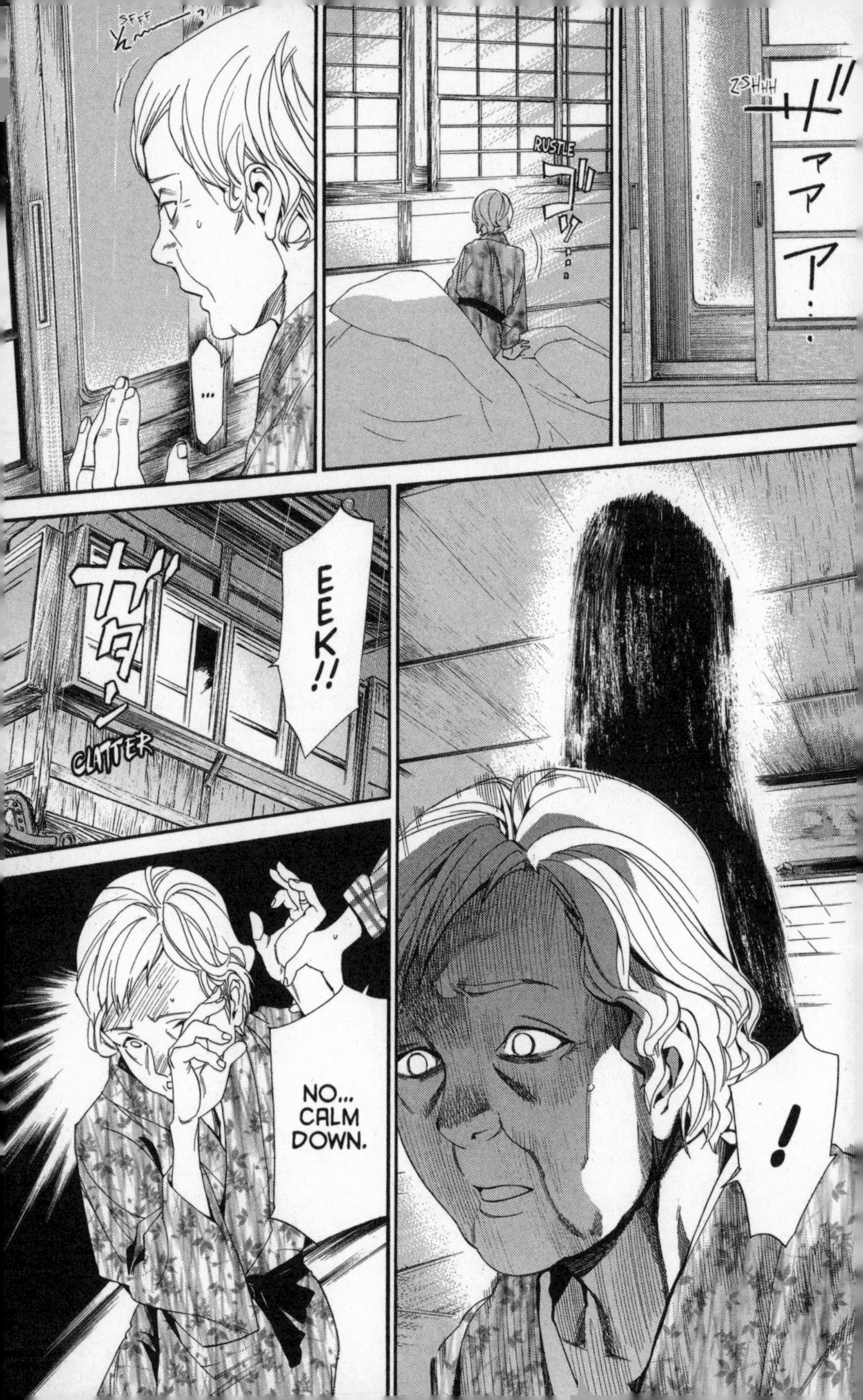
ZSHHH
RUSTLE
SFFF
...
!
EEK!!
CLATTER
NO... CALM DOWN.

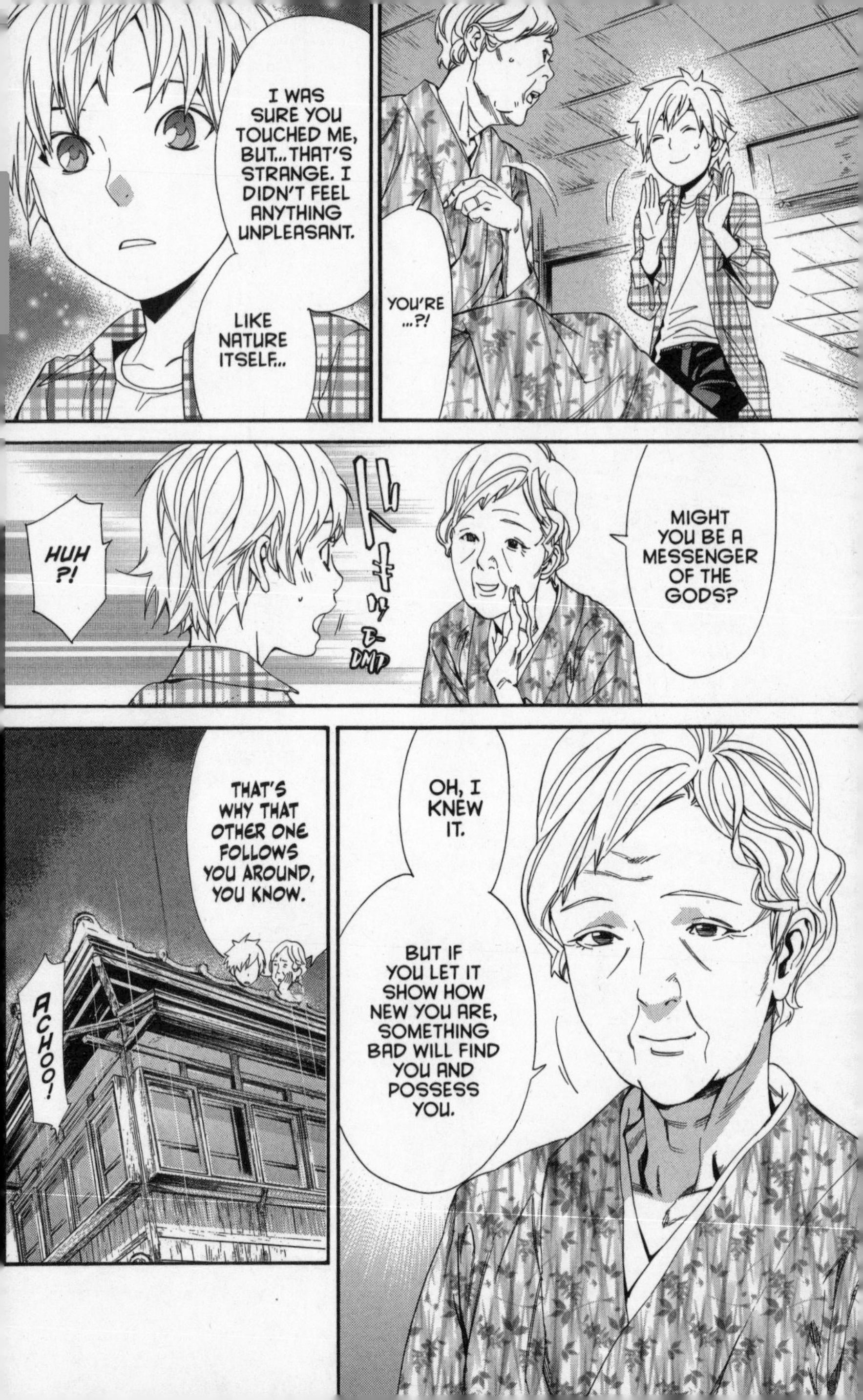
YOU'RE ...?!
I WAS SURE YOU TOUCHED ME, BUT... THAT'S STRANGE. I DIDN'T FEEL ANYTHING UNPLEASANT.
LIKE NATURE ITSELF...
MIGHT YOU BE A MESSENGER OF THE GODS?
T-DMP
HUH ?!
OH, I KNEW IT.
BUT IF YOU LET IT SHOW HOW NEW YOU ARE, SOMETHING BAD WILL FIND YOU AND POSSESS YOU.
THAT'S WHY THAT OTHER ONE FOLLOWS YOU AROUND, YOU KNOW.
ACHOO!

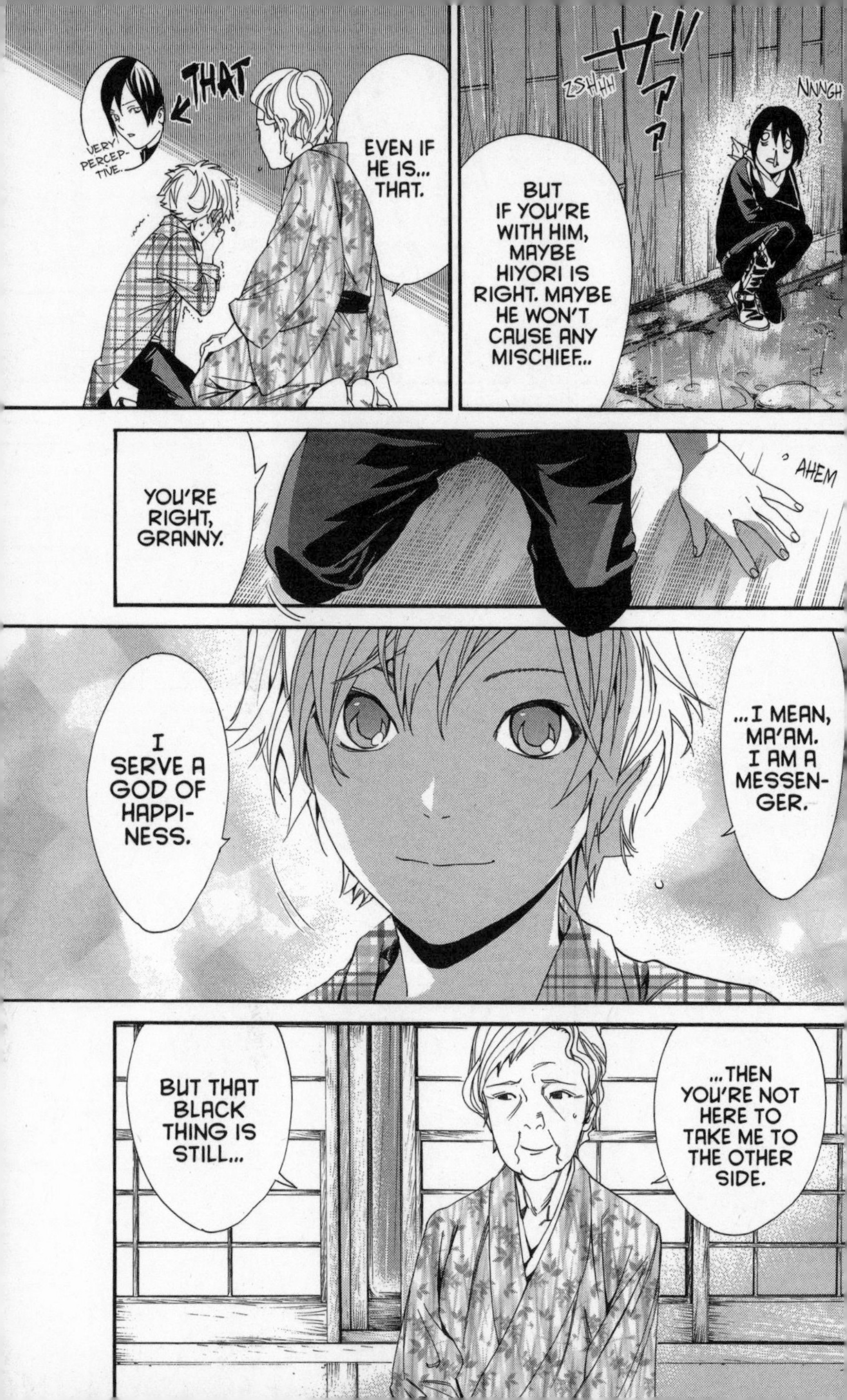
ZSHHH
NNNGH
BUT IF YOU'RE WITH HIM, MAYBE HIYORI IS RIGHT. MAYBE HE WON'T CAUSE ANY MISCHIEF...
EVEN IF HE IS... THAT.
THAT
VERY PERCEPTIVE...
AHEM
YOU'RE RIGHT, GRANNY.
...I MEAN, MA'AM. I AM A MESSENGER.
I SERVE A GOD OF HAPPINESS.
...THEN YOU'RE NOT HERE TO TAKE ME TO THE OTHER SIDE.
BUT THAT BLACK THING IS STILL...

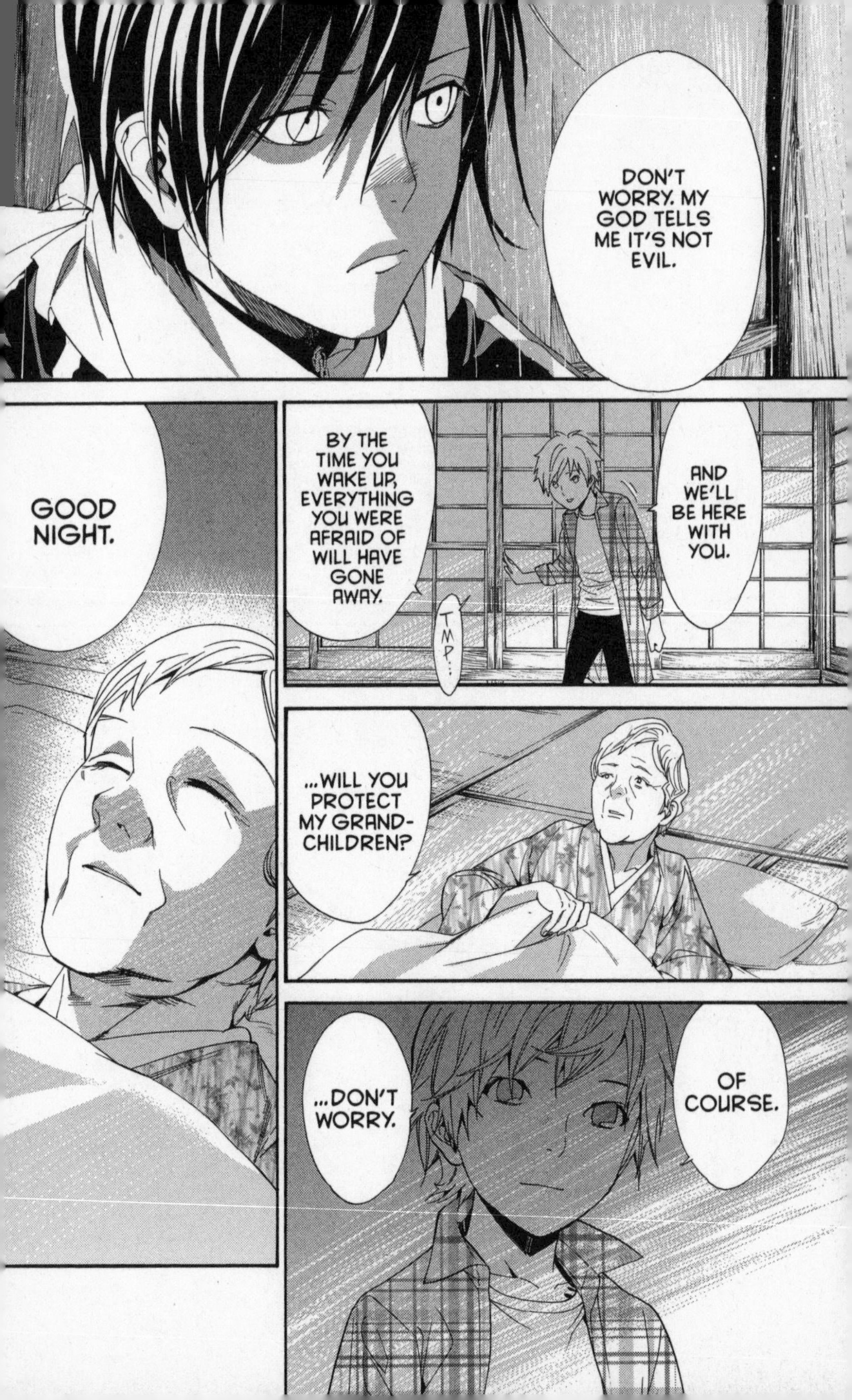
DON'T WORRY. MY GOD TELLS ME IT'S NOT EVIL.
AND WE'LL BE HERE WITH YOU.
BY THE TIME YOU WAKE UP, EVERYTHING YOU WERE AFRAID OF WILL HAVE GONE AWAY.
TMP...
...WILL YOU PROTECT MY GRAND-CHILDREN?
OF COURSE.
...DON'T WORRY.
GOOD NIGHT.

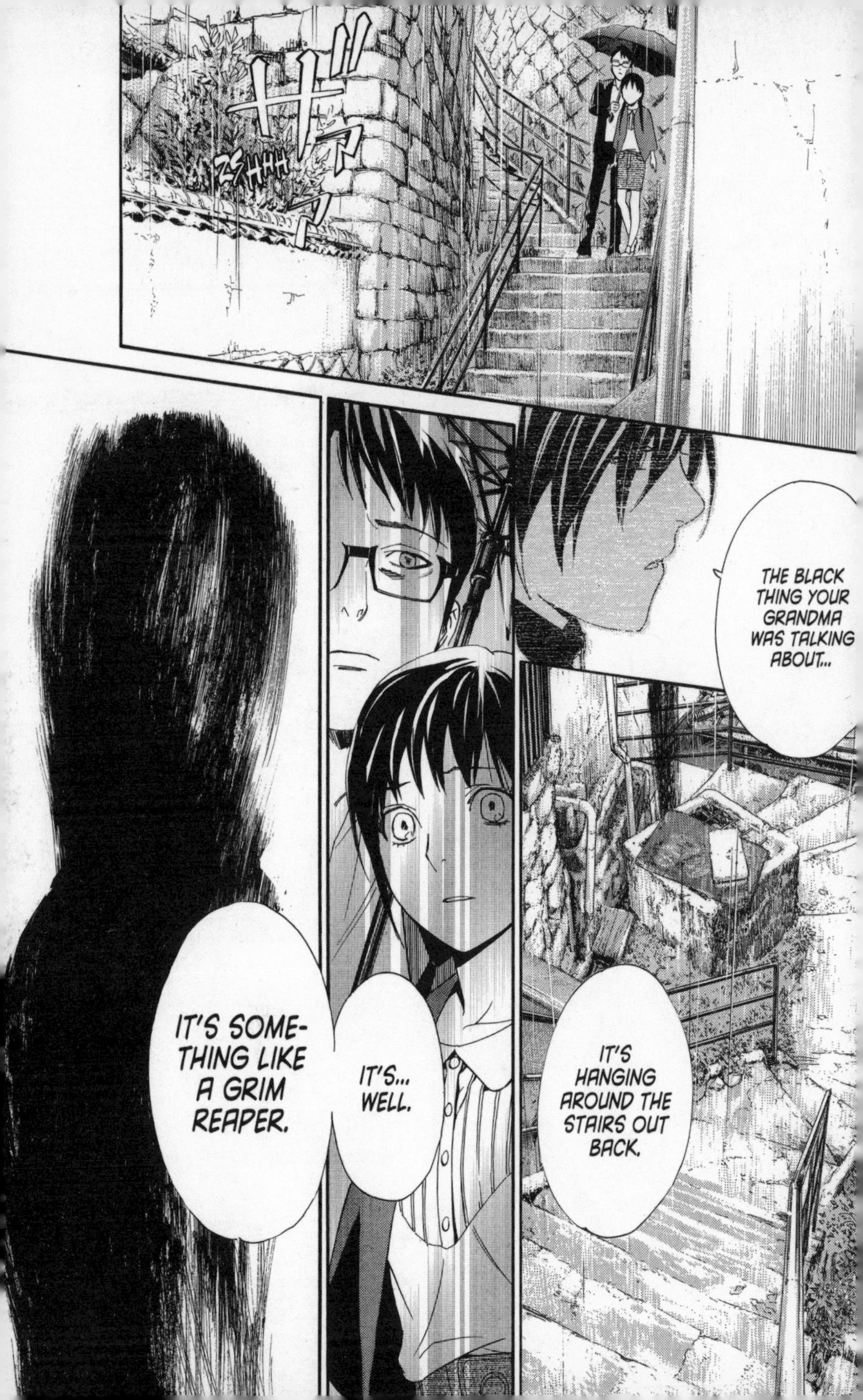
ZSHHH
THE BLACK THING YOUR GRANDMA WAS TALKING ABOUT...
IT'S HANGING AROUND THE STAIRS OUT BACK.
IT'S... WELL.
IT'S SOME-THING LIKE A GRIM REAPER.

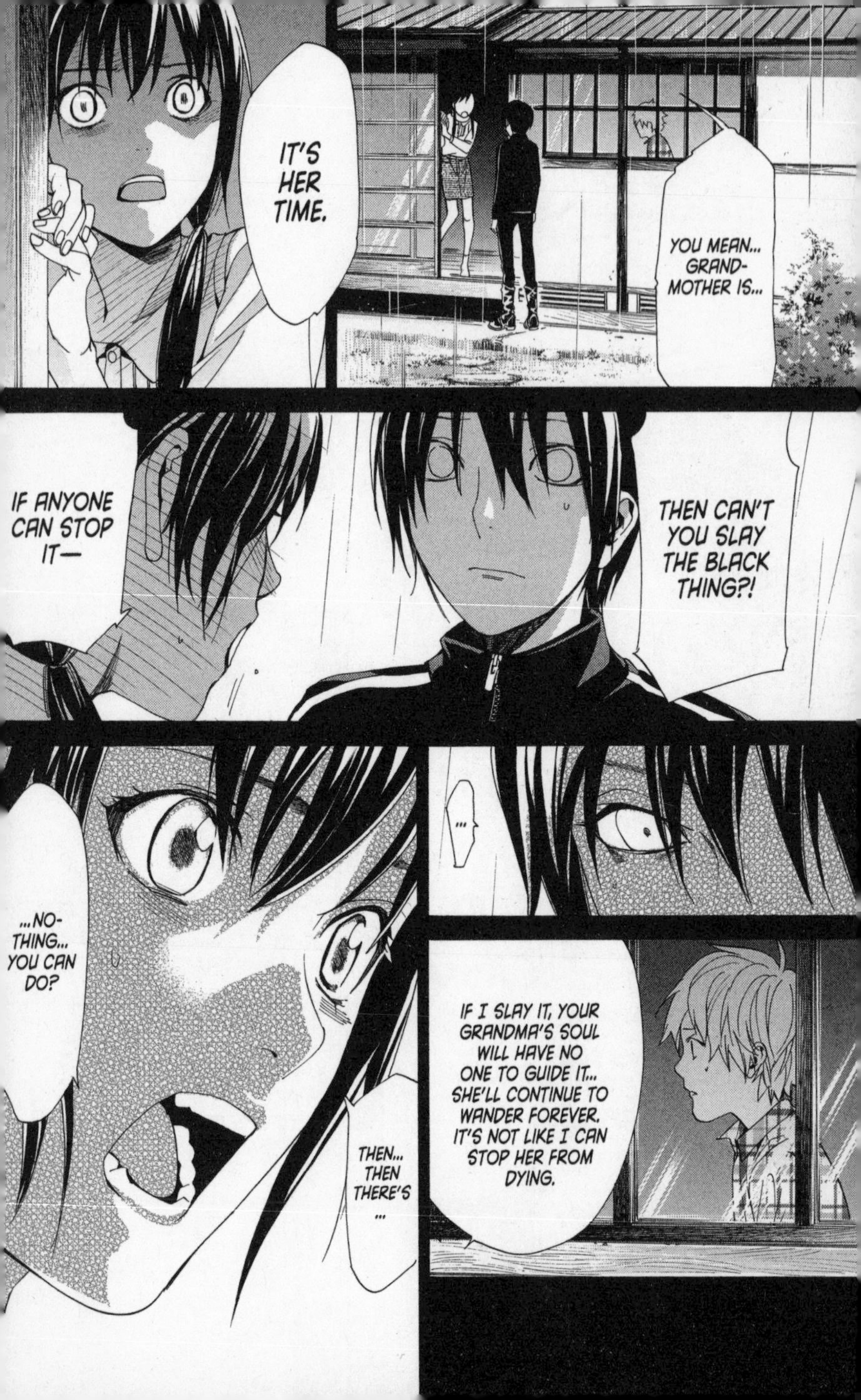
IT'S HER TIME.
YOU MEAN... GRAND-MOTHER IS...
THEN CAN'T YOU SLAY THE BLACK THING?!
IF ANYONE CAN STOP IT—
...
IF I SLAY IT, YOUR GRANDMA'S SOUL WILL HAVE NO ONE TO GUIDE IT... SHE'LL CONTINUE TO WANDER FOREVER. IT'S NOT LIKE I CAN STOP HER FROM DYING.
THEN... THEN THERE'S ...
...NO-THING... YOU CAN DO?

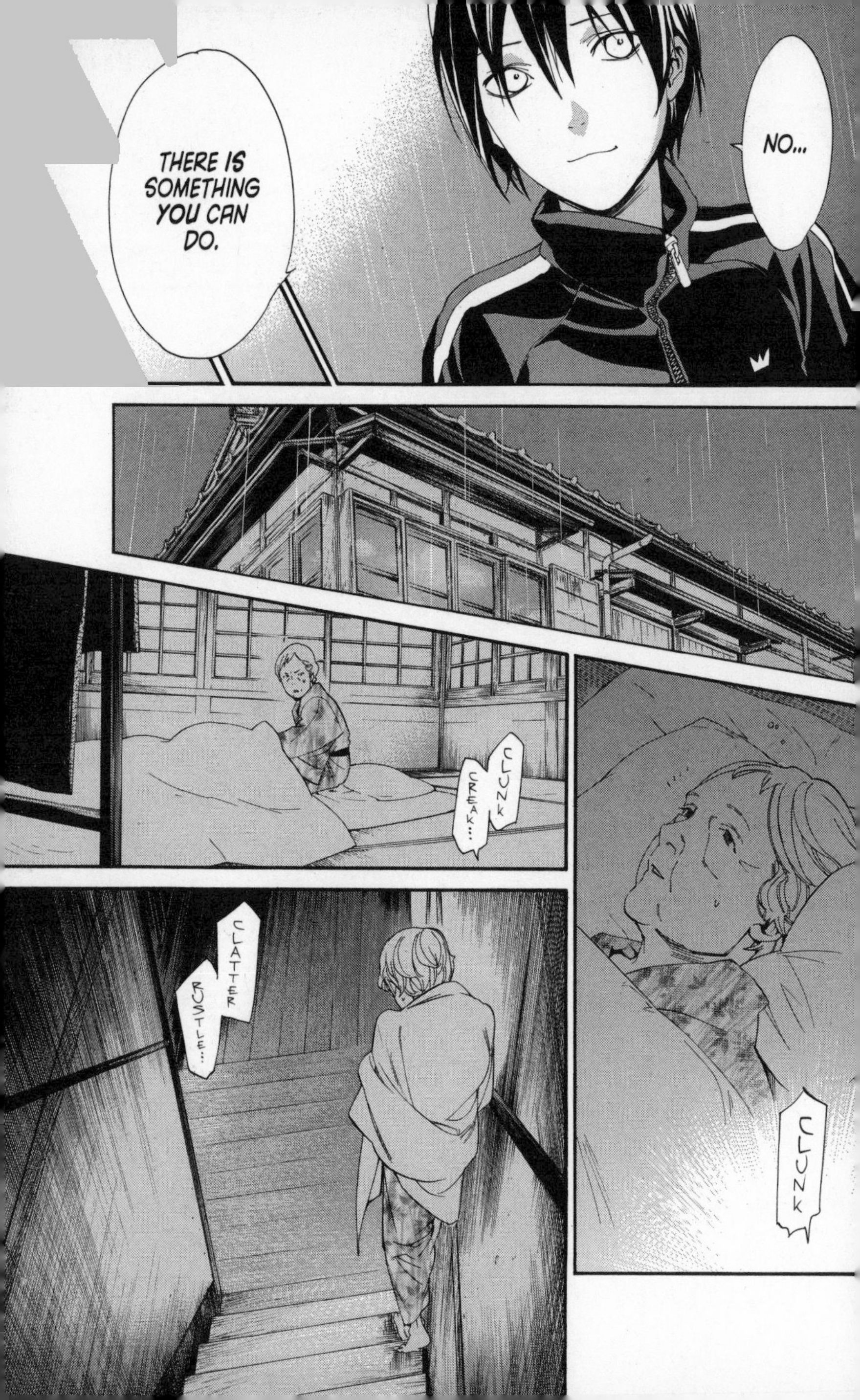
NO...
THERE IS SOMETHING YOU CAN DO.
CLUNK
CREAK...
CLUNK
CLATTER
RUSTLE...

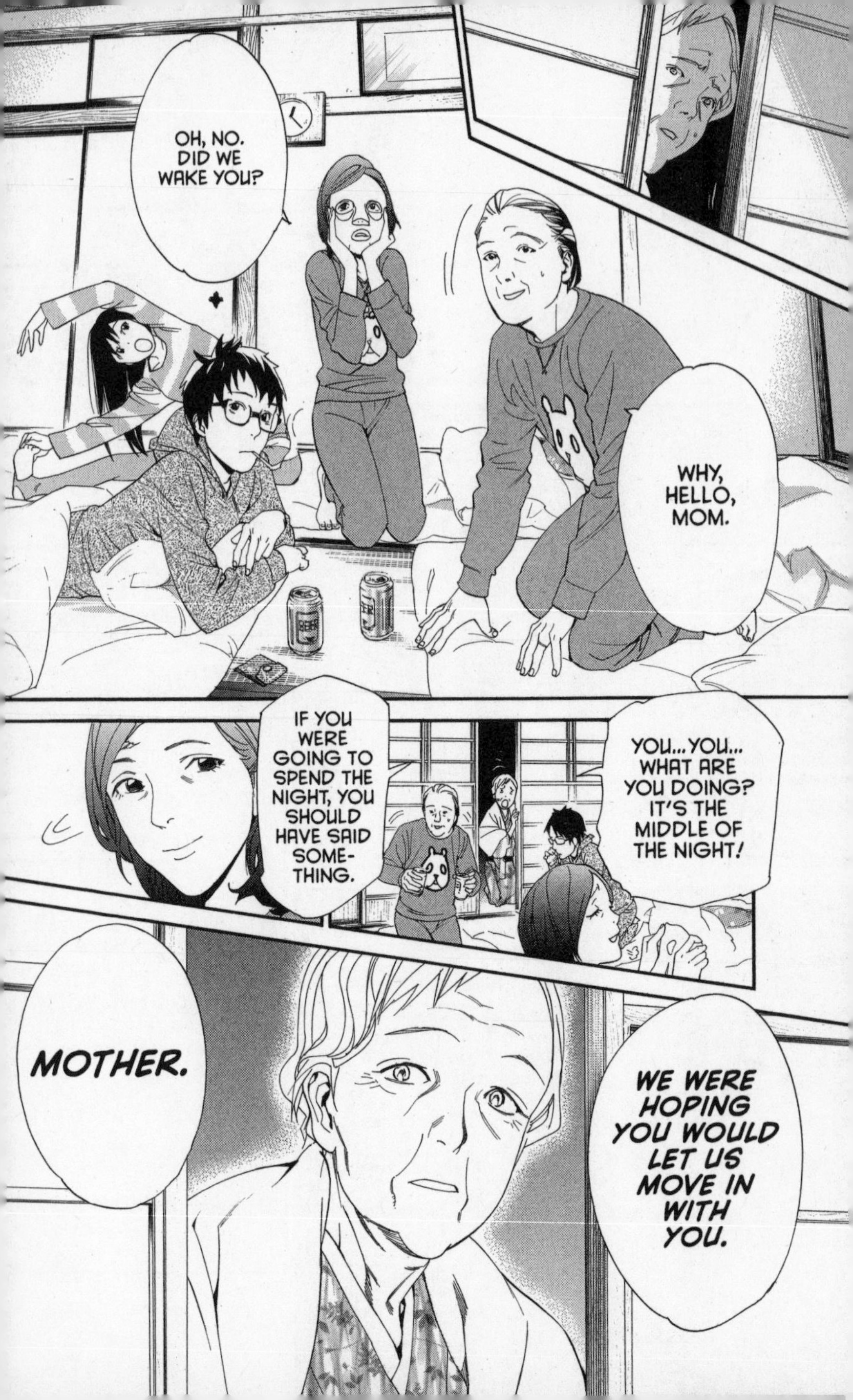
WHY, HELLO, MOM.
OH, NO. DID WE WAKE YOU?
YOU...YOU... WHAT ARE YOU DOING? IT'S THE MIDDLE OF THE NIGHT!
IF YOU WERE GOING TO SPEND THE NIGHT, YOU SHOULD HAVE SAID SOME-THING.
WE WERE HOPING YOU WOULD LET US MOVE IN WITH YOU.
MOTHER.

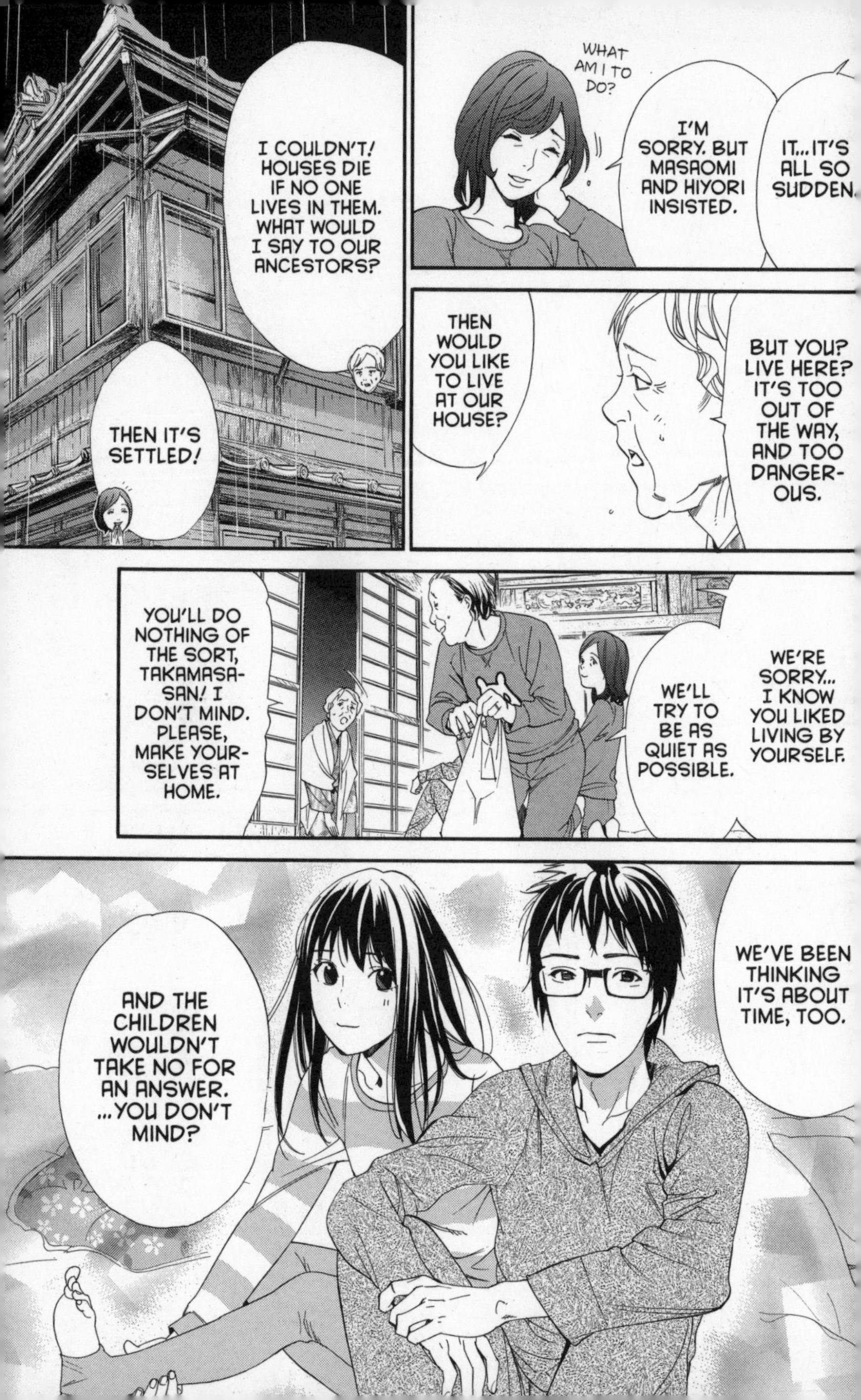
IT... IT'S ALL SO SUDDEN.
I'M SORRY. BUT MASAOMI AND HIYORI INSISTED.
WHAT AM I TO DO?
BUT YOU? LIVE HERE? IT'S TOO OUT OF THE WAY, AND TOO DANGER-OUS.
THEN WOULD YOU LIKE TO LIVE AT OUR HOUSE?
I COULDN'T! HOUSES DIE IF NO ONE LIVES IN THEM. WHAT WOULD I SAY TO OUR ANCESTORS?
THEN IT'S SETTLED!
WE'RE SORRY... I KNOW YOU LIKED LIVING BY YOURSELF.
WE'LL TRY TO BE AS QUIET AS POSSIBLE.
YOU'LL DO NOTHING OF THE SORT, TAKAMASA-SAN! I DON'T MIND. PLEASE, MAKE YOUR-SELVES AT HOME.
WE'VE BEEN THINKING IT'S ABOUT TIME, TOO.
AND THE CHILDREN WOULDN'T TAKE NO FOR AN ANSWER. ...YOU DON'T MIND?

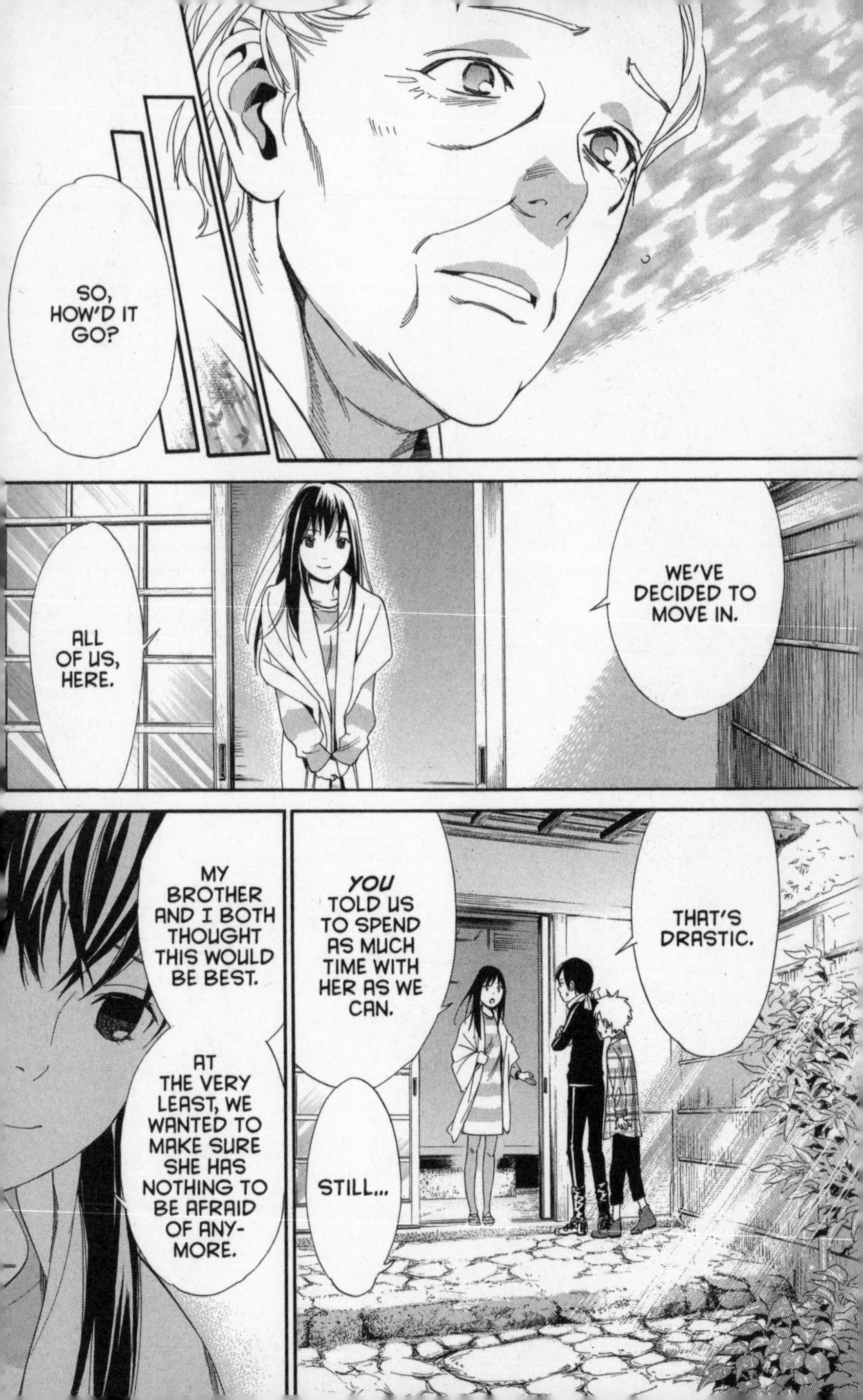
SO, HOW'D IT GO?
WE'VE DECIDED TO MOVE IN.
ALL OF US, HERE.
THAT'S DRASTIC.
YOU TOLD US TO SPEND AS MUCH TIME WITH HER AS WE CAN.
STILL...
MY BROTHER AND I BOTH THOUGHT THIS WOULD BE BEST.
AT THE VERY LEAST, WE WANTED TO MAKE SURE SHE HAS NOTHING TO BE AFRAID OF ANY-MORE.

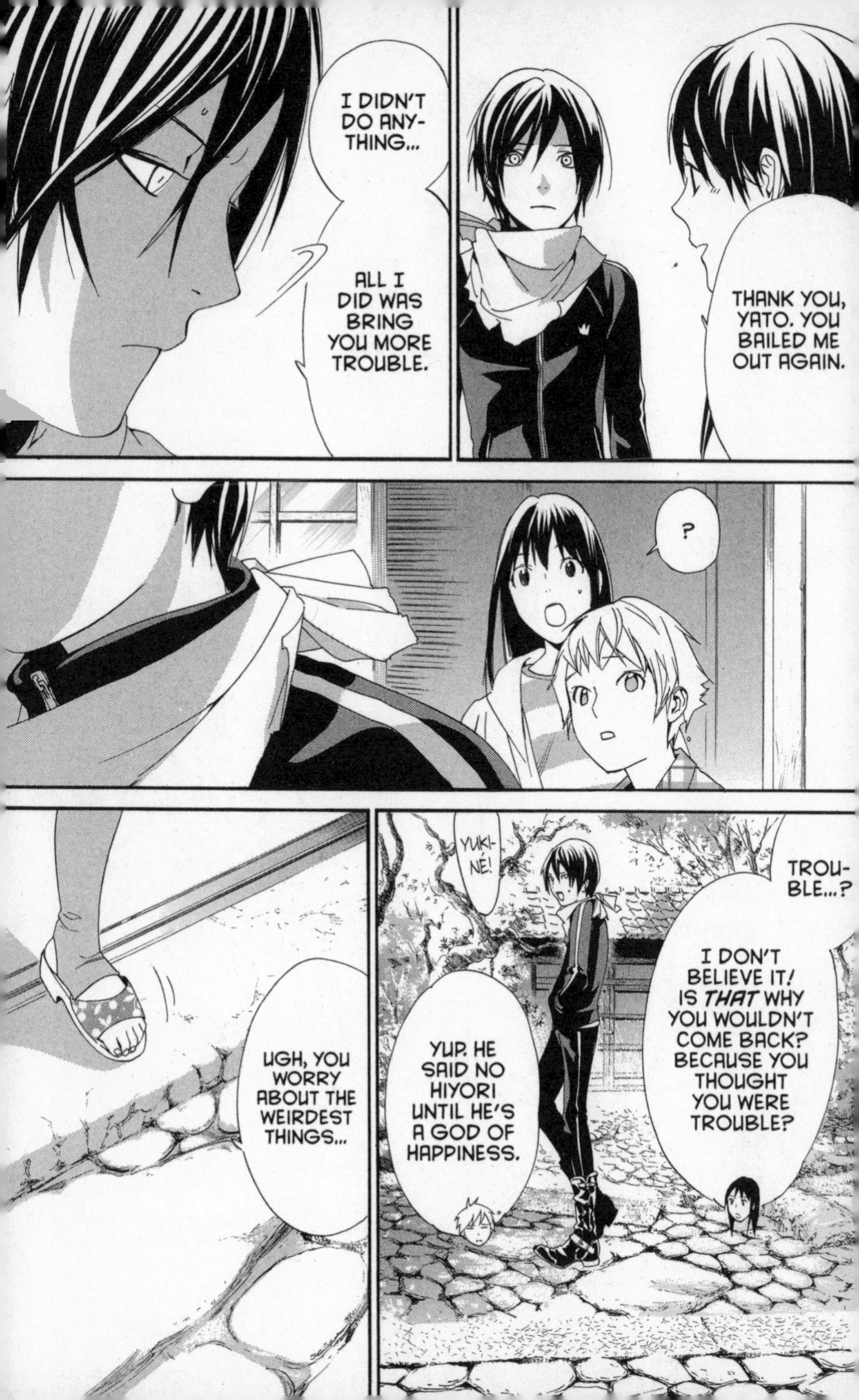
THANK YOU, YATO. YOU BAILED ME OUT AGAIN.
I DIDN'T DO ANYTHING...
ALL I DID WAS BRING YOU MORE TROUBLE.
?
TROUBLE...?
I DON'T BELIEVE IT! IS *THAT* WHY YOU WOULDN'T COME BACK? BECAUSE YOU THOUGHT YOU WERE TROUBLE?
YUKINÉ!
YUP. HE SAID NO HIYORI UNTIL HE'S A GOD OF HAPPINESS.
UGH, YOU WORRY ABOUT THE WEIRDEST THINGS...

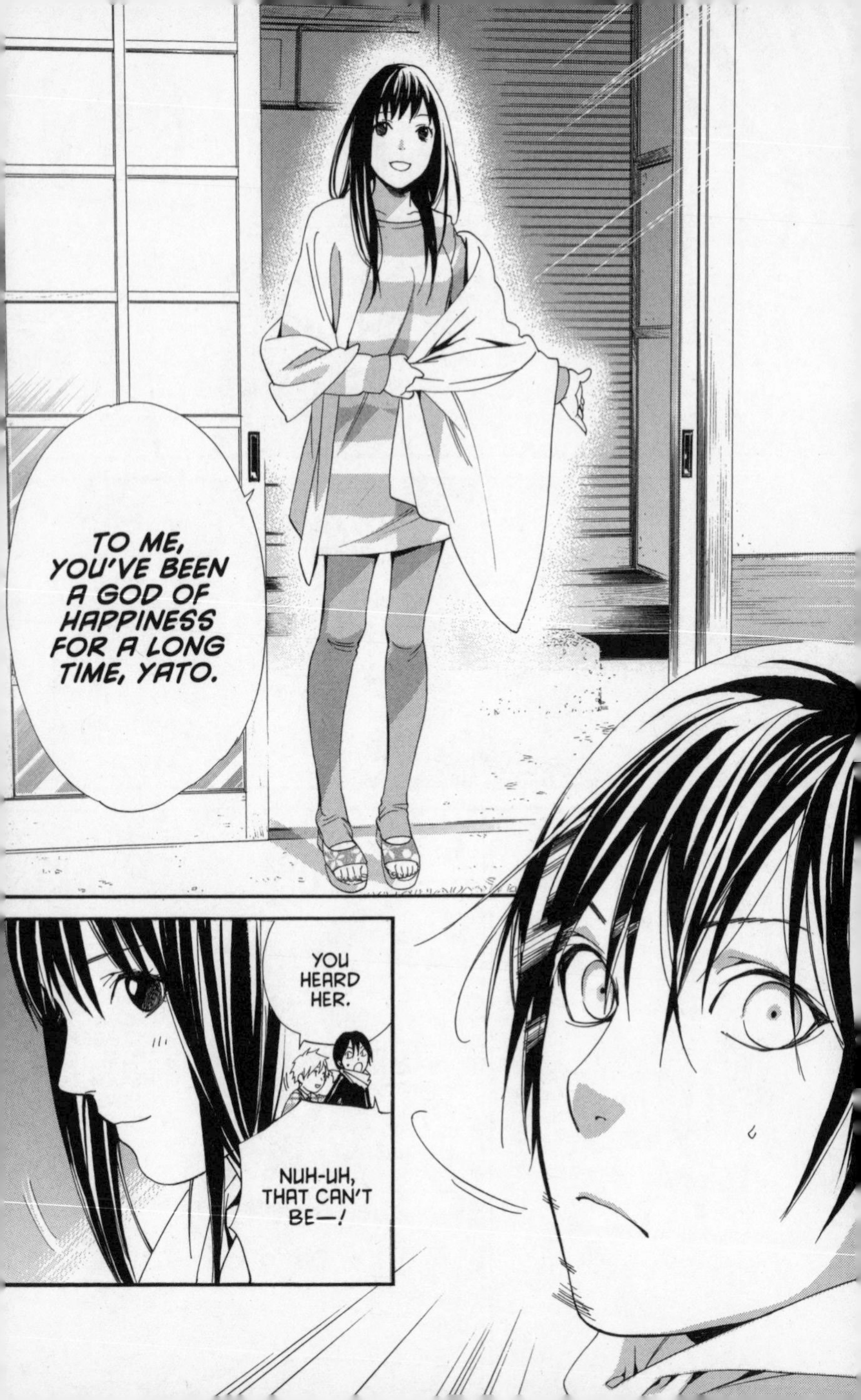
TO ME, YOU'VE BEEN A GOD OF HAPPINESS FOR A LONG TIME, YATO.
YOU HEARD HER.
NUH-UH, THAT CAN'T BE—!

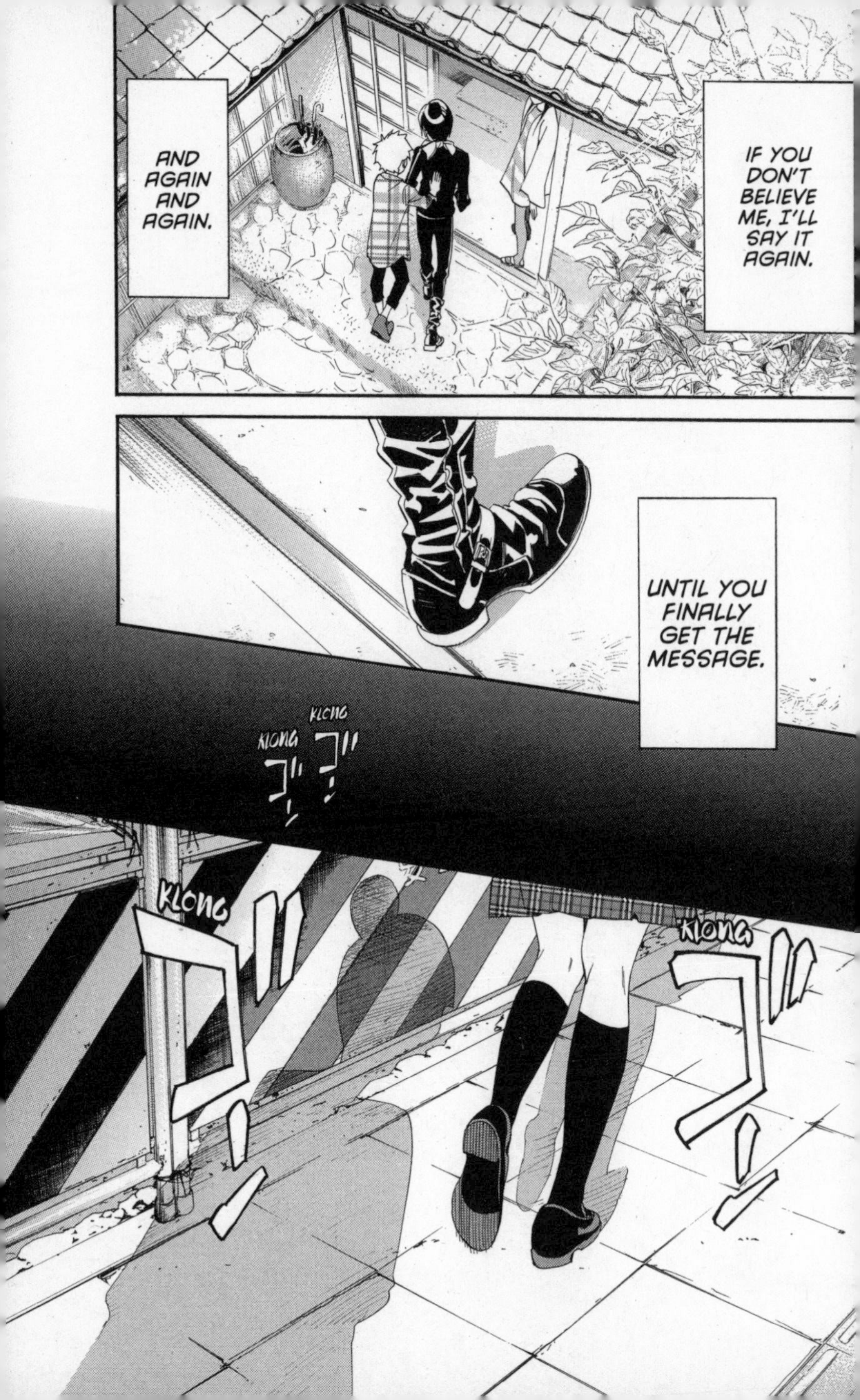

IF YOU DON'T BELIEVE ME, I'LL SAY IT AGAIN.
AND AGAIN AND AGAIN.
UNTIL YOU FINALLY GET THE MESSAGE.
KLONG
KLONG
KLONG
KLONG

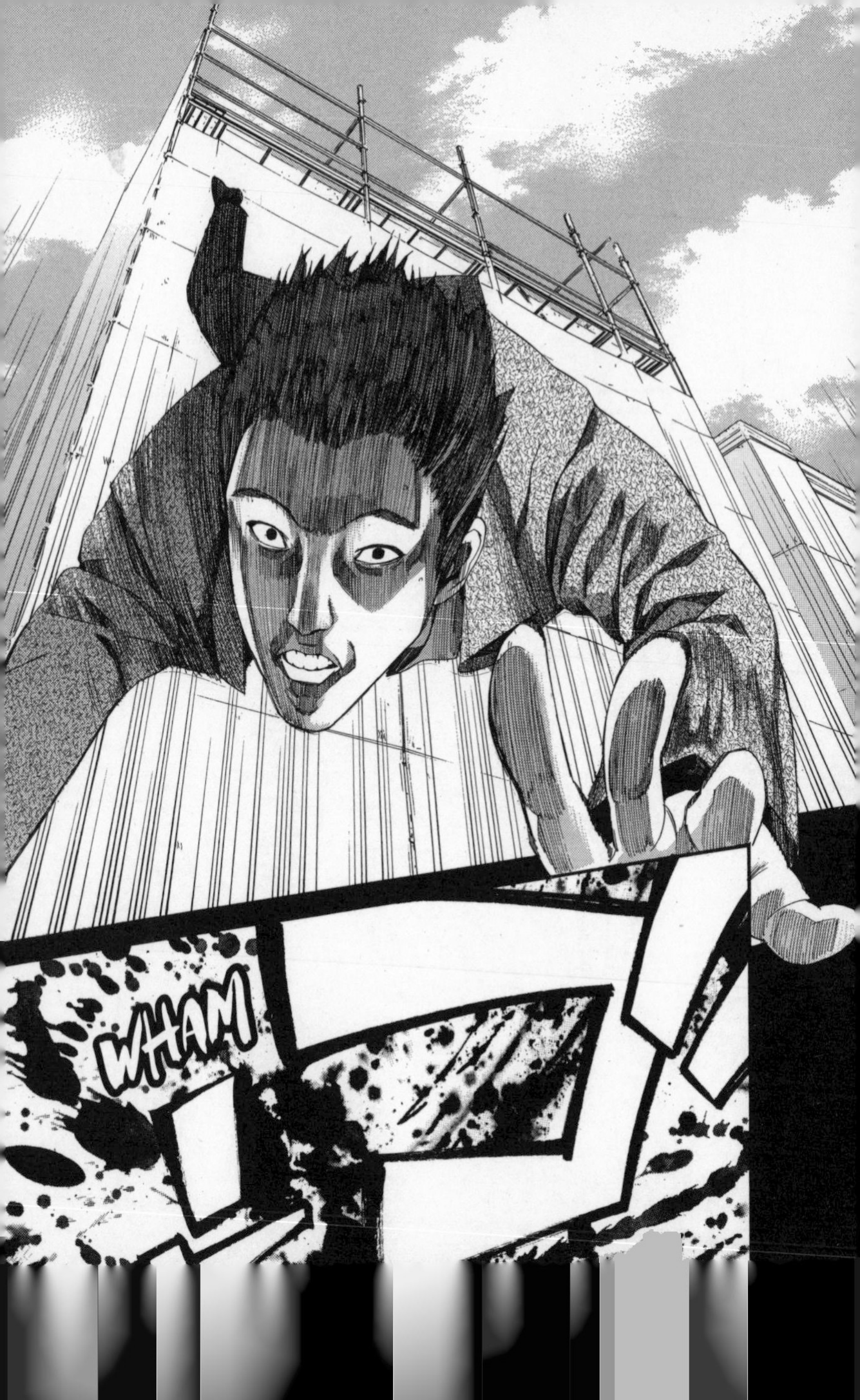
WHAM

野

鬼

神

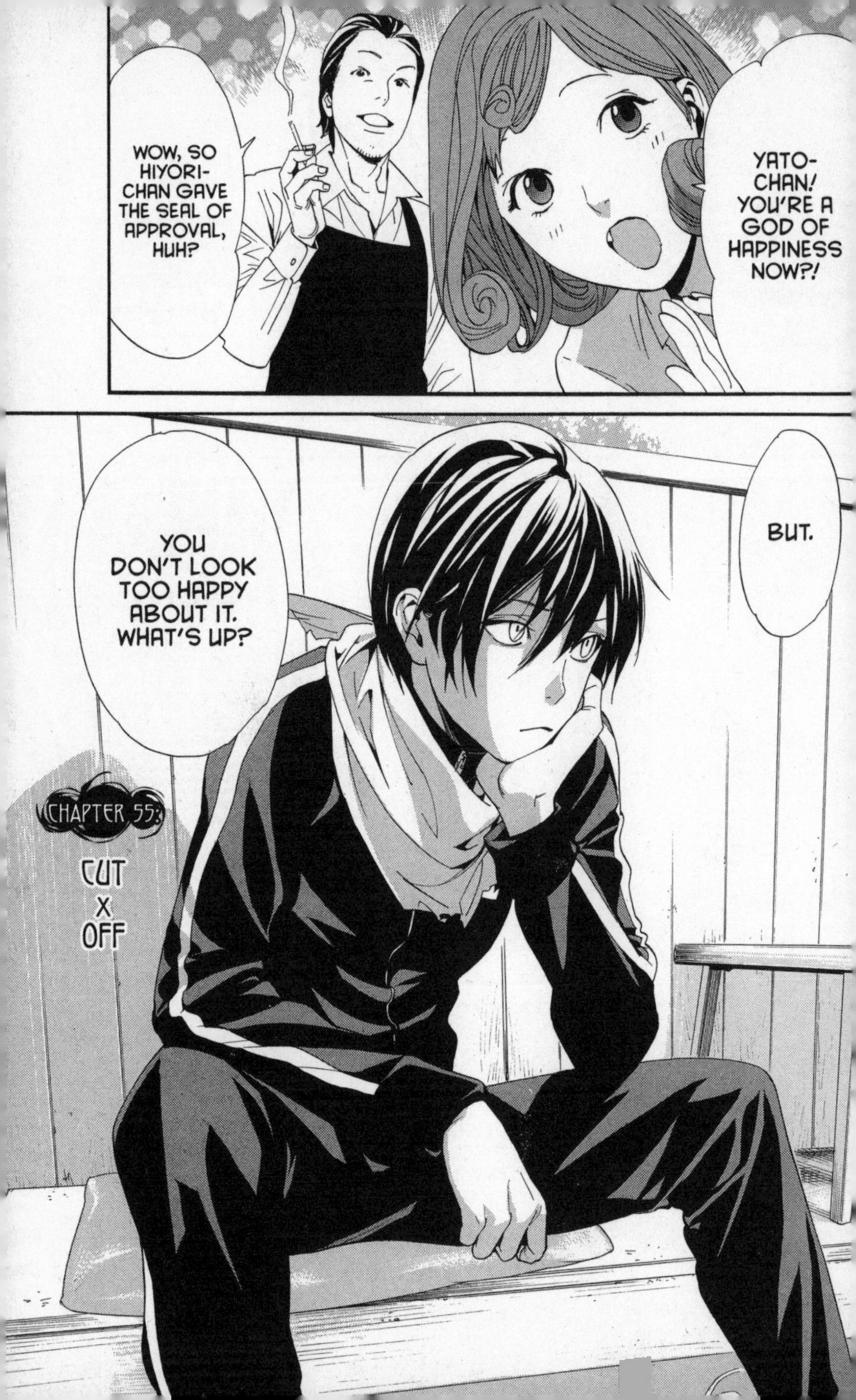
YATO-CHAN! YOU'RE A GOD OF HAPPINESS NOW?!
WOW, SO HIYORI-CHAN GAVE THE SEAL OF APPROVAL, HUH?
BUT.
YOU DON'T LOOK TOO HAPPY ABOUT IT. WHAT'S UP?
CHAPTER 55:
CUT x OFF

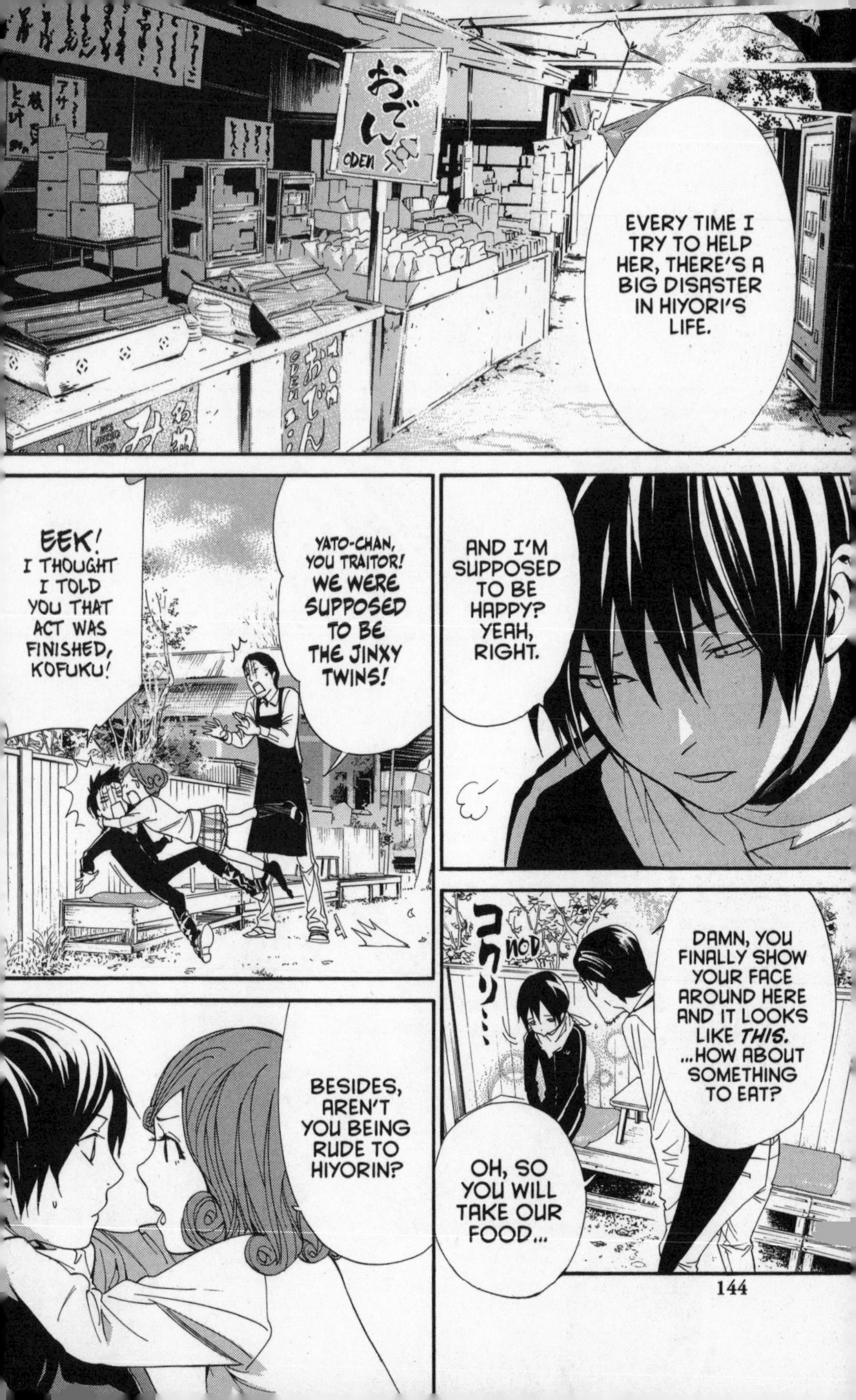
EVERY TIME I TRY TO HELP HER, THERE'S A BIG DISASTER IN HIYORI'S LIFE.
ODEN
AND I'M SUPPOSED TO BE HAPPY? YEAH, RIGHT.
YATO-CHAN, YOU TRAITOR! WE WERE SUPPOSED TO BE THE JINXY TWINS!
EEK! I THOUGHT I TOLD YOU THAT ACT WAS FINISHED, KOFUKU!
DAMN, YOU FINALLY SHOW YOUR FACE AROUND HERE AND IT LOOKS LIKE *THIS.* ...HOW ABOUT SOMETHING TO EAT?
NOD
OH, SO YOU WILL TAKE OUR FOOD...
BESIDES, AREN'T YOU BEING RUDE TO HIYORIN?

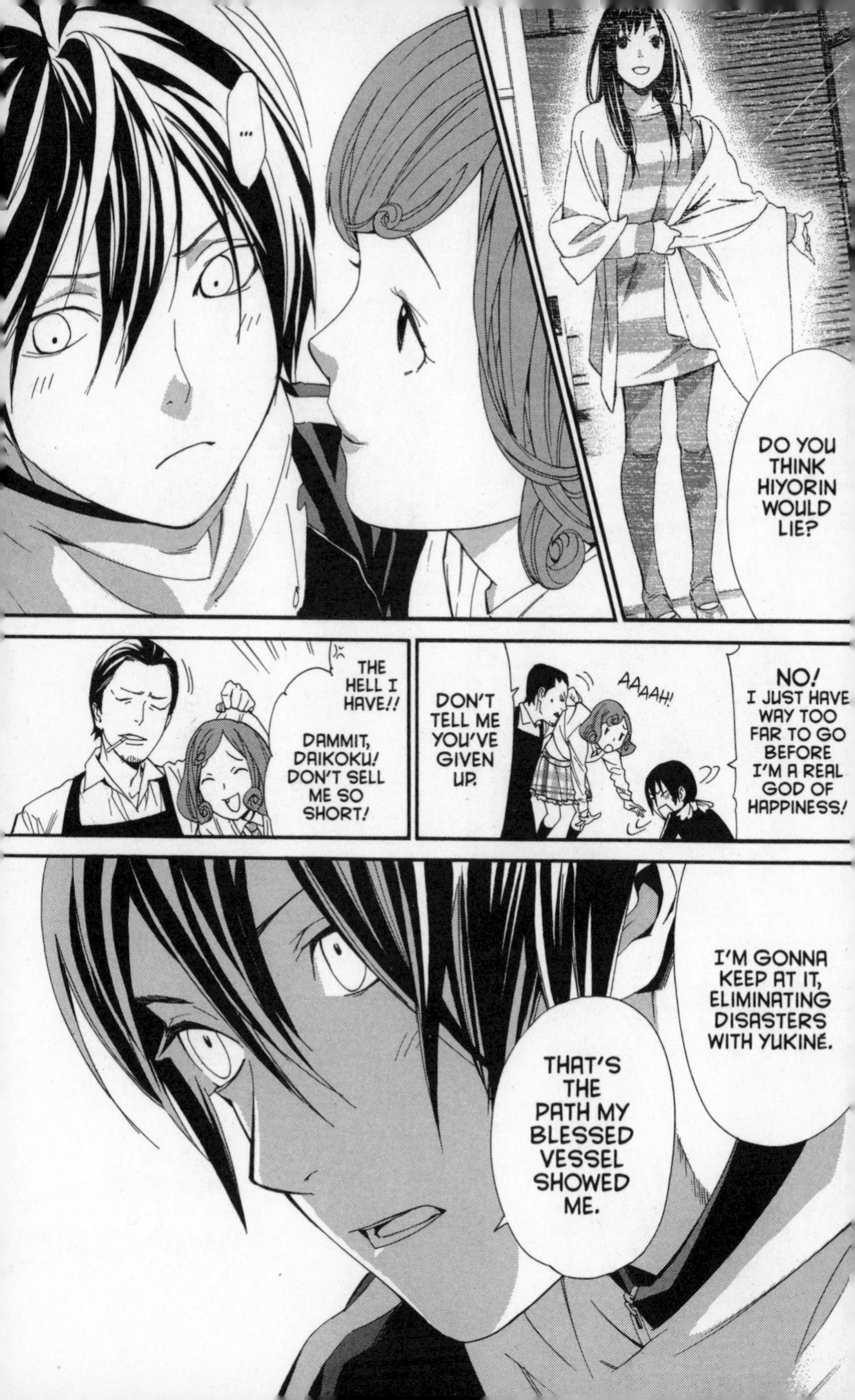
DO YOU THINK HIYORIN WOULD LIE?
...
NO! I JUST HAVE WAY TOO FAR TO GO BEFORE I'M A REAL GOD OF HAPPINESS!
AAAAH!
DON'T TELL ME YOU'VE GIVEN UP.
THE HELL I HAVE!!
DAMMIT, DAIKOKU! DON'T SELL ME SO SHORT!
I'M GONNA KEEP AT IT, ELIMINATING DISASTERS WITH YUKINÉ.
THAT'S THE PATH MY BLESSED VESSEL SHOWED ME.

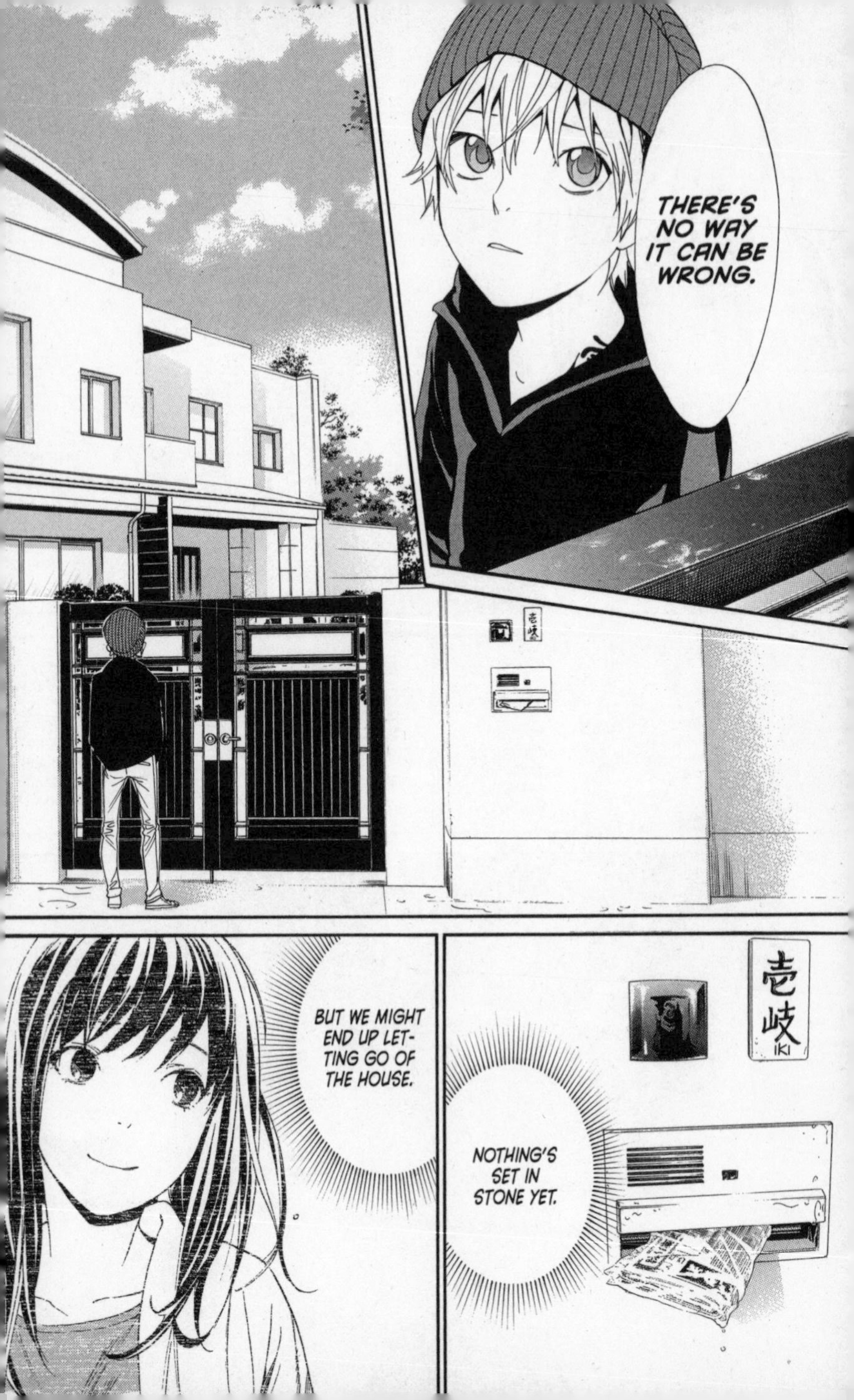
THERE'S NO WAY IT CAN BE WRONG.
壱岐
IKI
NOTHING'S SET IN STONE YET.
BUT WE MIGHT END UP LET-TING GO OF THE HOUSE.

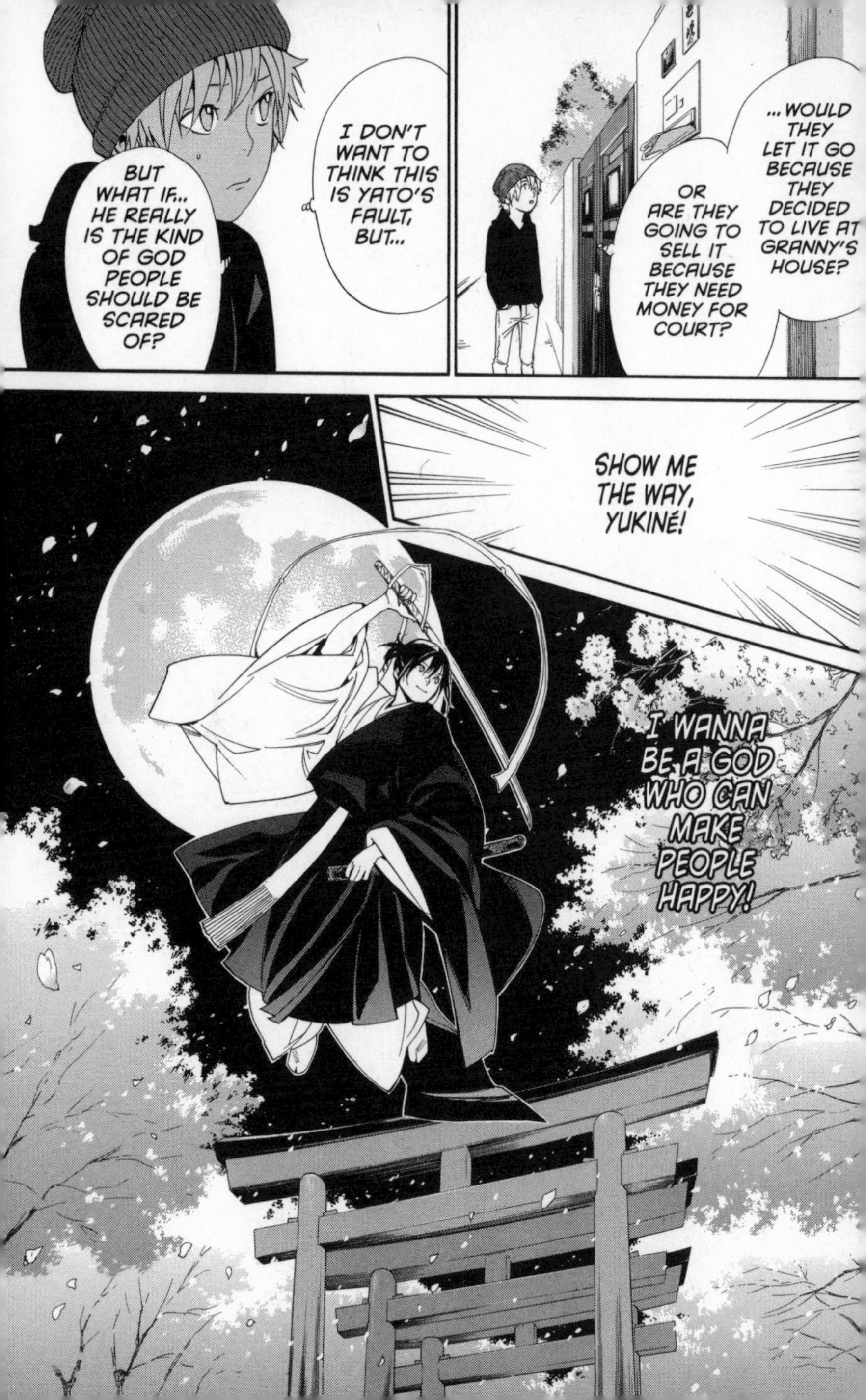
...WOULD THEY LET IT GO BECAUSE THEY DECIDED TO LIVE AT GRANNY'S HOUSE?
OR ARE THEY GOING TO SELL IT BECAUSE THEY NEED MONEY FOR COURT?
I DON'T WANT TO THINK THIS IS YATO'S FAULT, BUT...
BUT WHAT IF... HE REALLY IS THE KIND OF GOD PEOPLE SHOULD BE SCARED OF?
SHOW ME THE WAY, YUKINÉ!
I WANNA BE A GOD WHO CAN MAKE PEOPLE HAPPY!

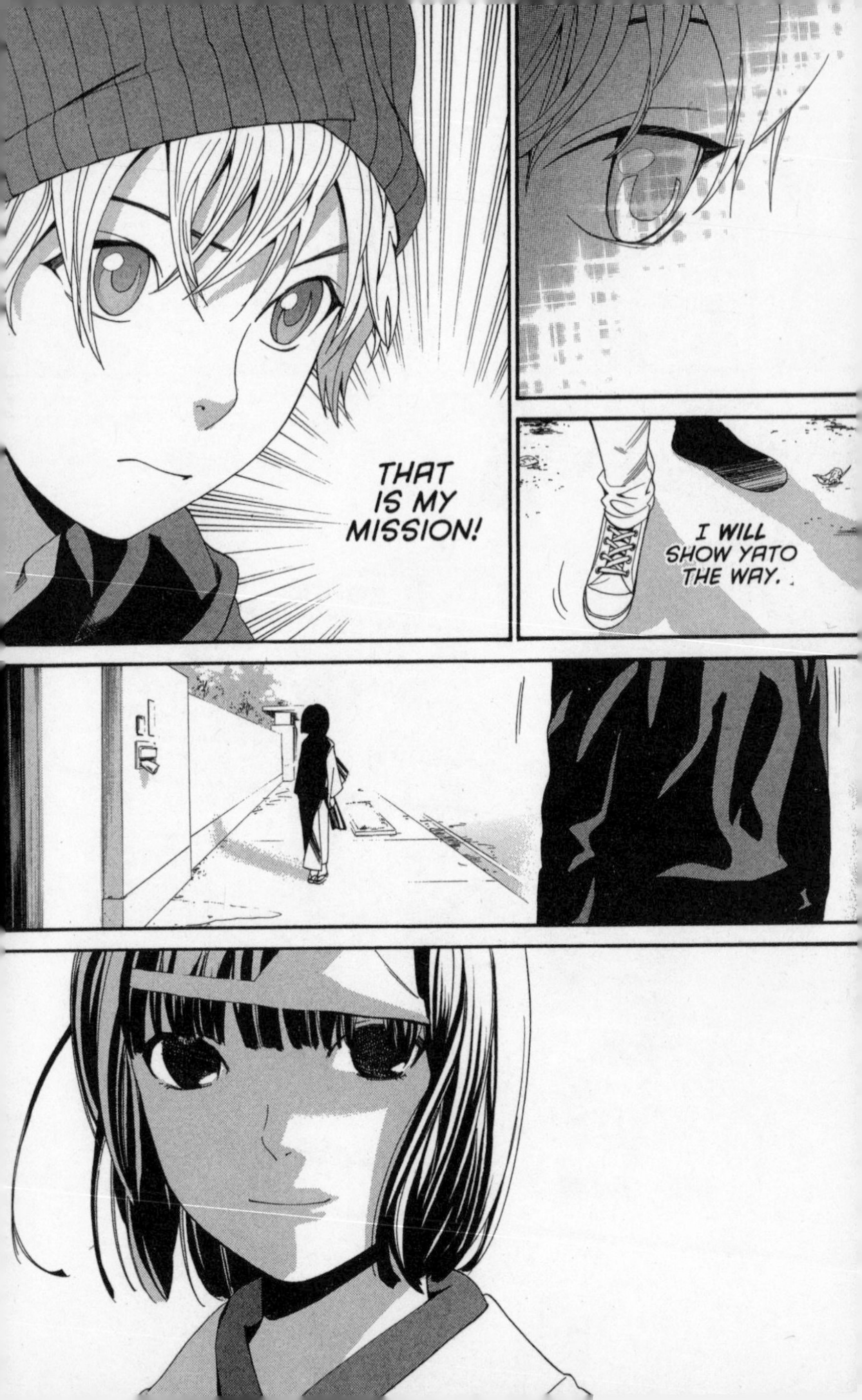
I WILL SHOW YATO THE WAY.
THAT IS MY MISSION!

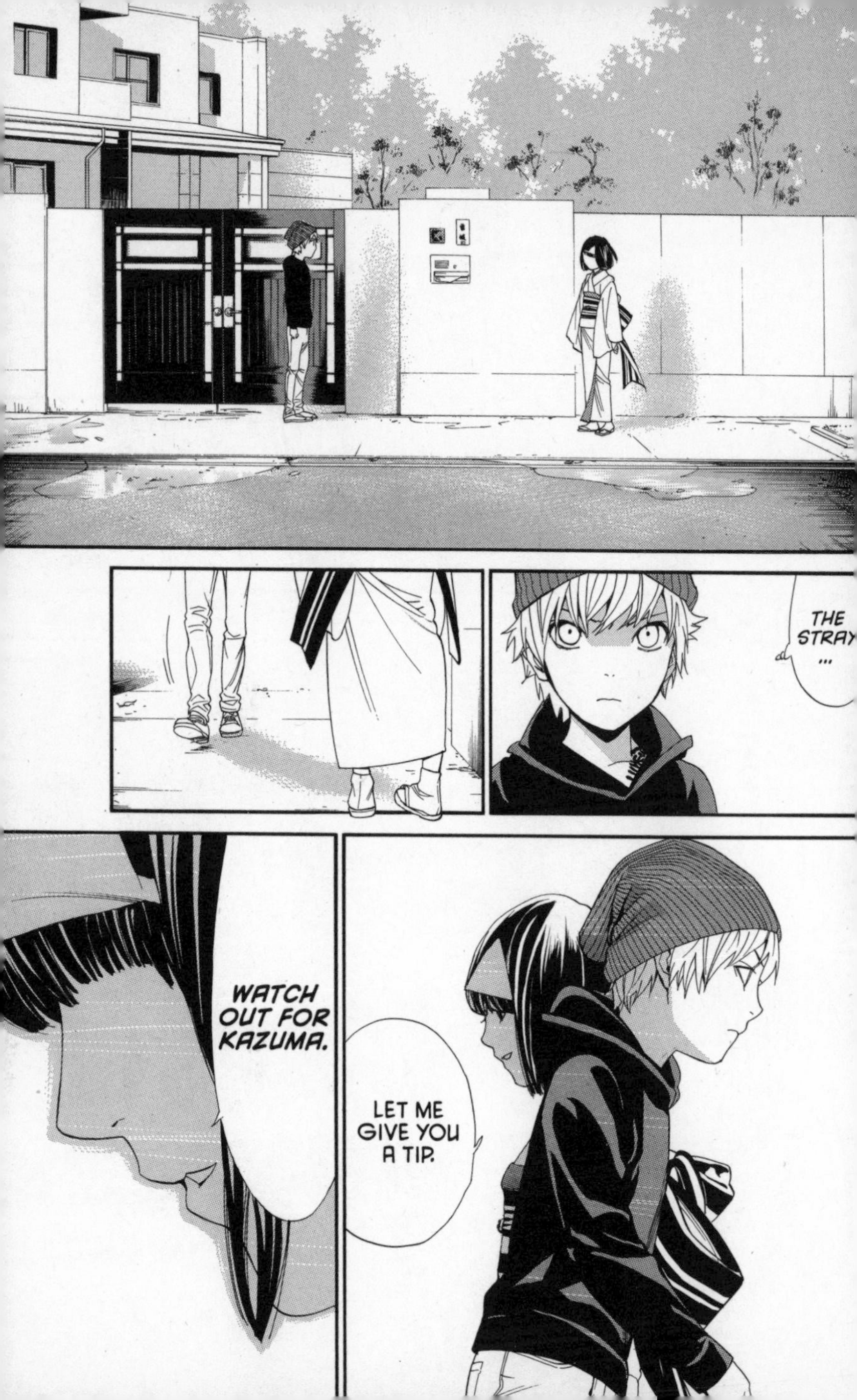
THE STRAY ...
LET ME GIVE YOU A TIP.
WATCH OUT FOR KAZUMA.

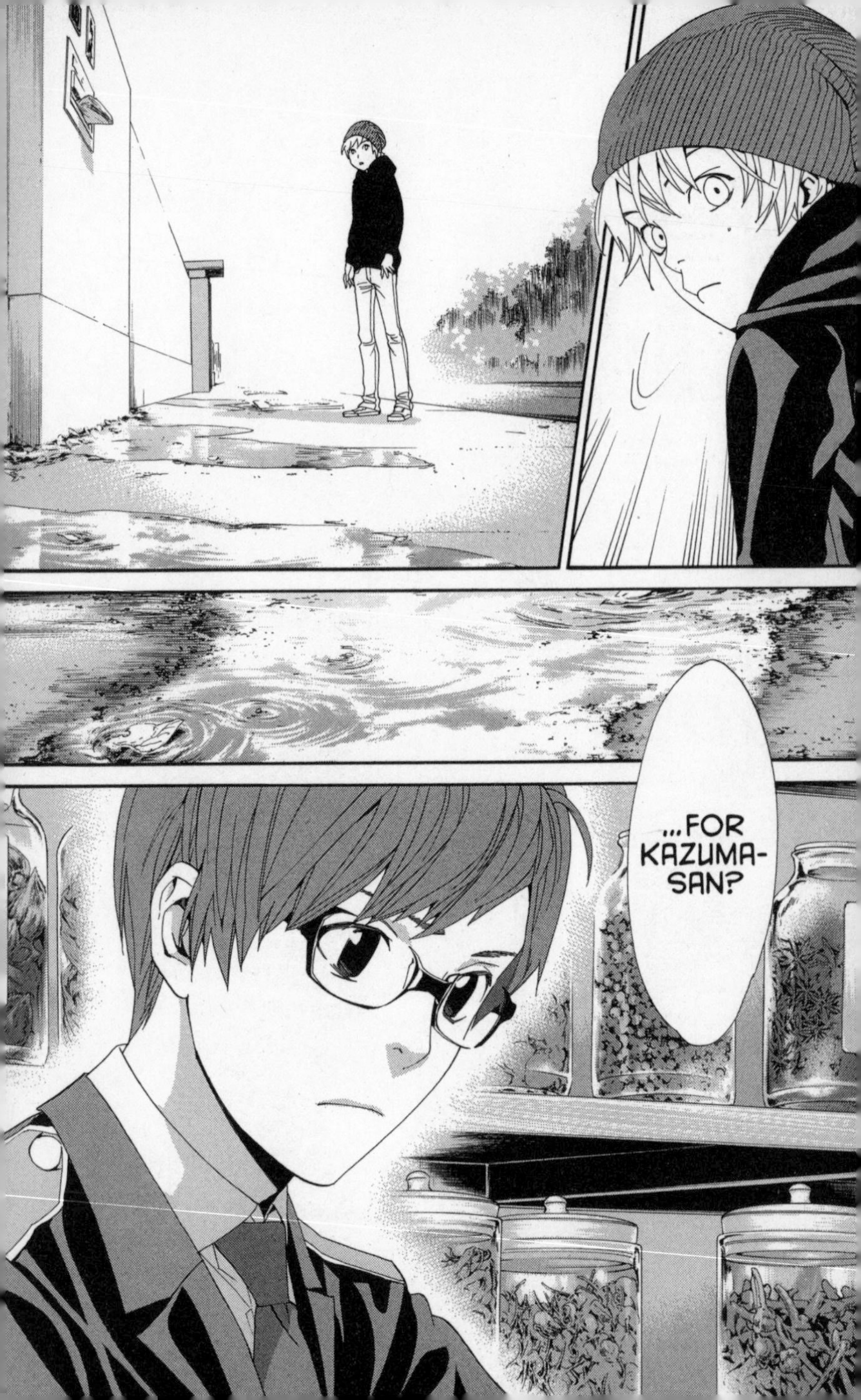
...FOR KAZUMA-SAN?

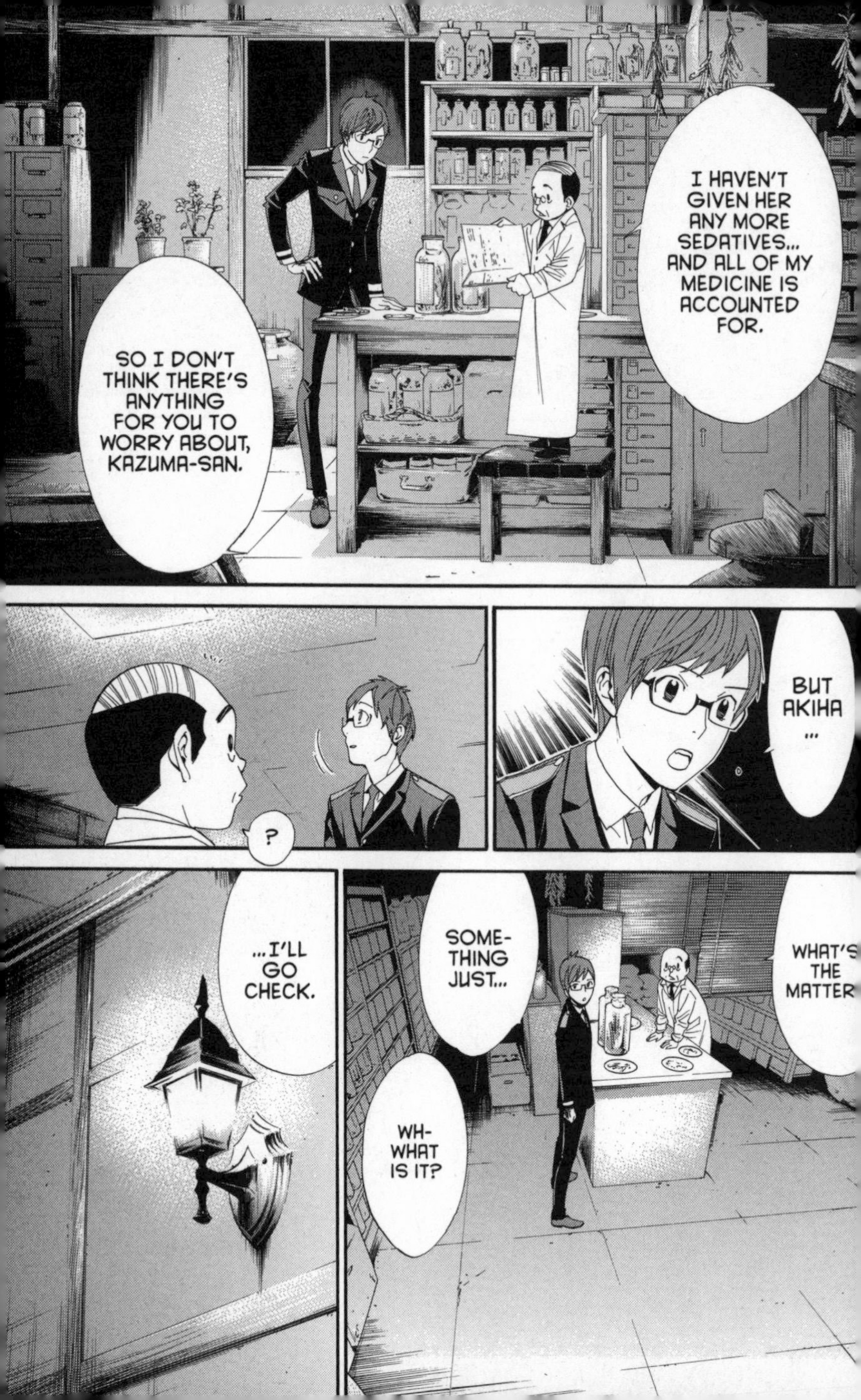
I HAVEN'T GIVEN HER ANY MORE SEDATIVES... AND ALL OF MY MEDICINE IS ACCOUNTED FOR.
SO I DON'T THINK THERE'S ANYTHING FOR YOU TO WORRY ABOUT, KAZUMA-SAN.
BUT AKIHA ...
?
WHAT'S THE MATTER
SOME-THING JUST...
WH-WHAT IS IT?
...I'LL GO CHECK.

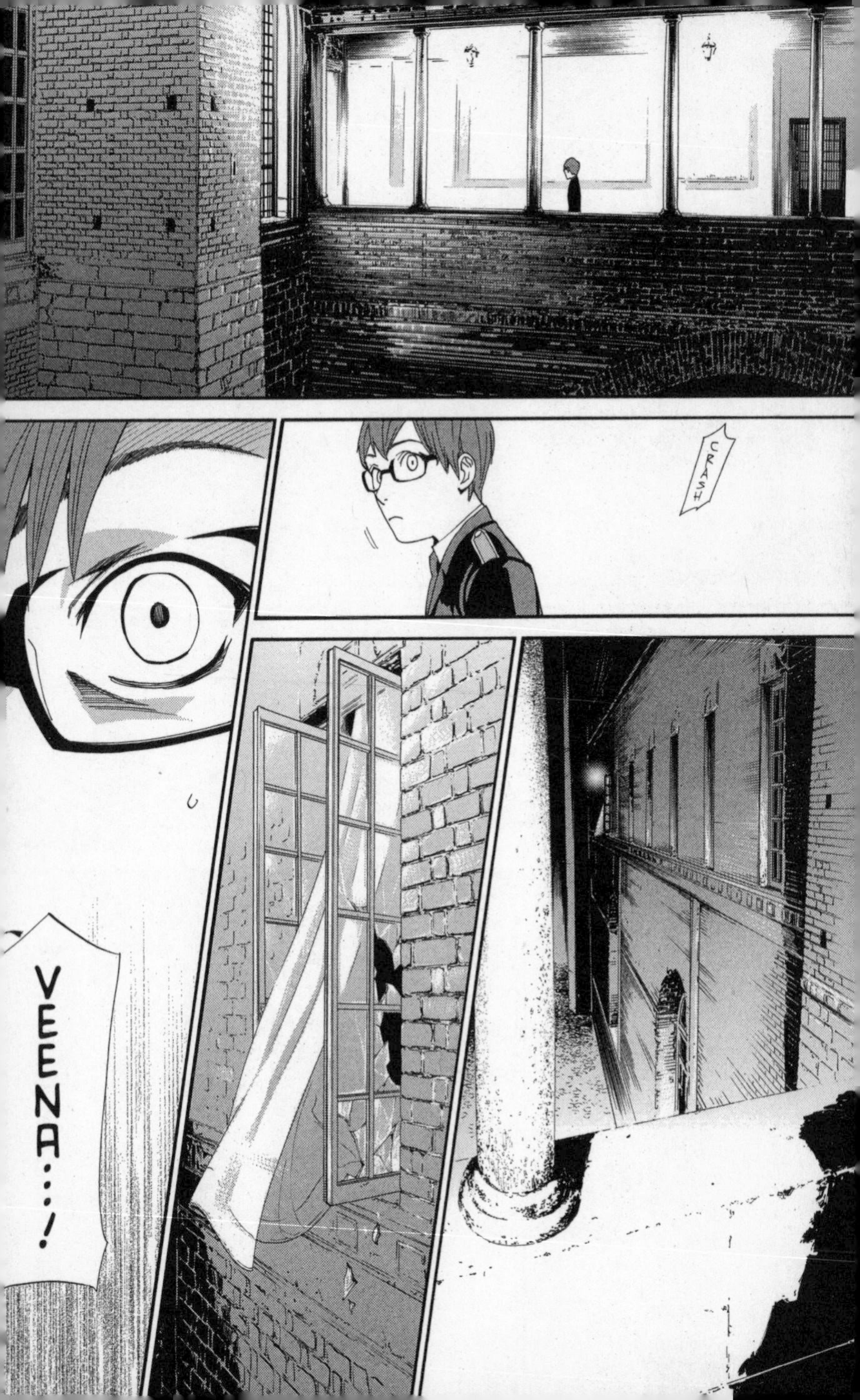
CRASH
VEENA...!

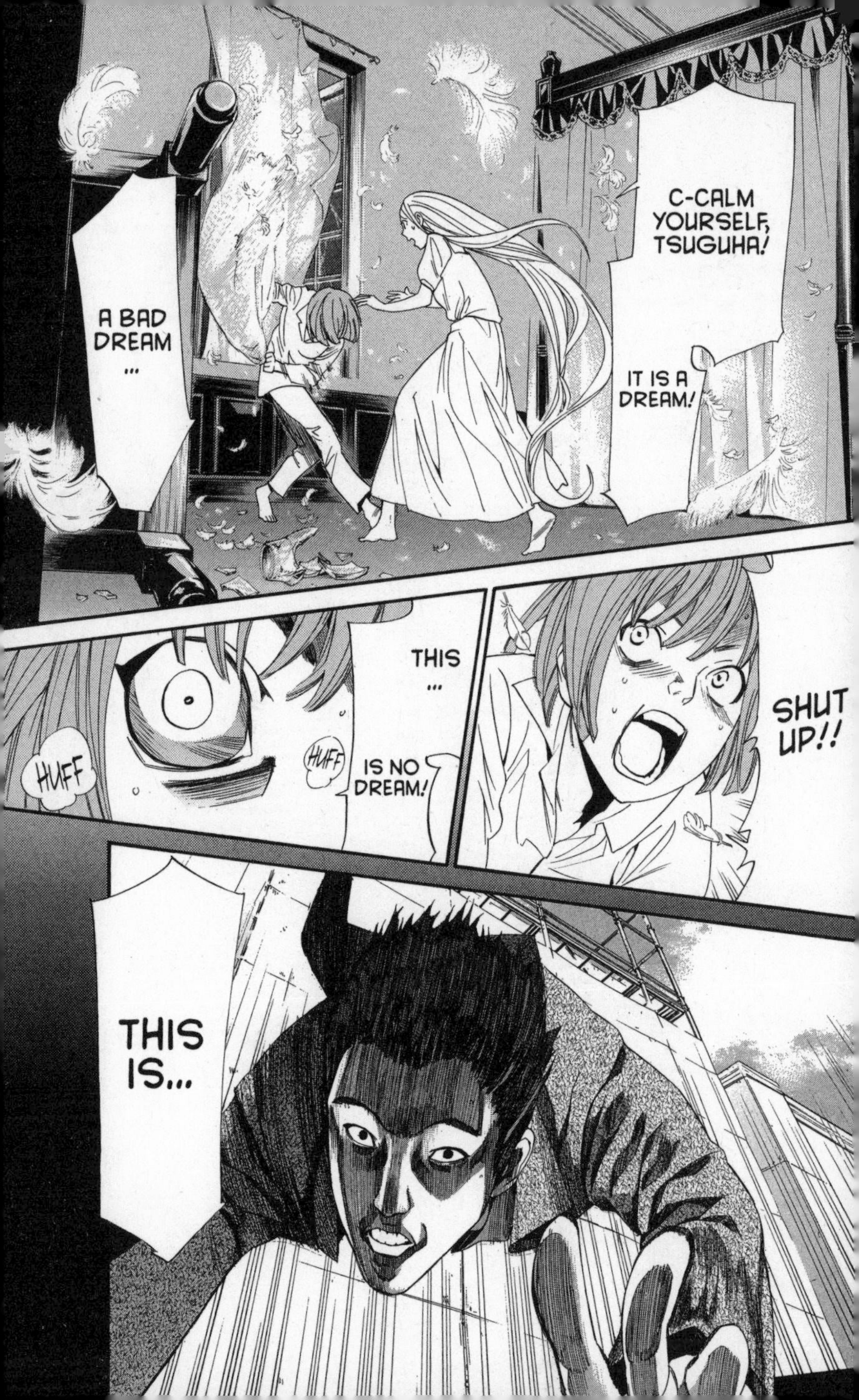
C-CALM YOURSELF, TSUGUHA!
IT IS A DREAM!
A BAD DREAM ...
SHUT UP!!
THIS ...
HUFF
IS NO DREAM!
HUFF
THIS IS...

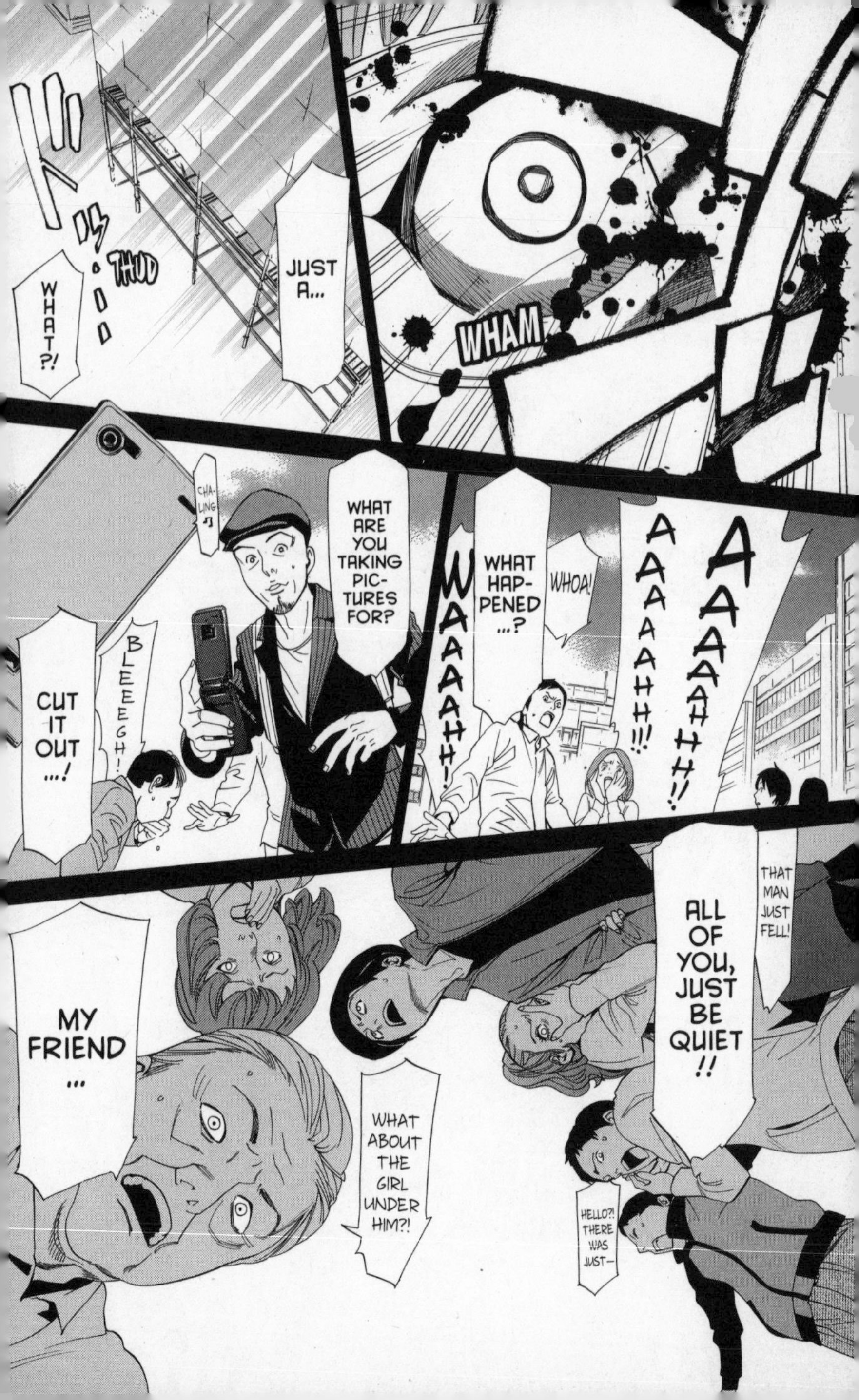
WHAM
JUST A...
THUD
WHAT?!
AAAAAHHH!!
AAAAAHH!!!
WHOA!
WHAT HAPPENED ...?
WAAAAAHH!
WHAT ARE YOU TAKING PICTURES FOR?
CHA-LING ♫
BLEEEGH!
CUT IT OUT ...!
THAT MAN JUST FELL!
ALL OF YOU, JUST BE QUIET!!
HELLO?! THERE WAS JUST—
WHAT ABOUT THE GIRL UNDER HIM?!
MY FRIEND ...

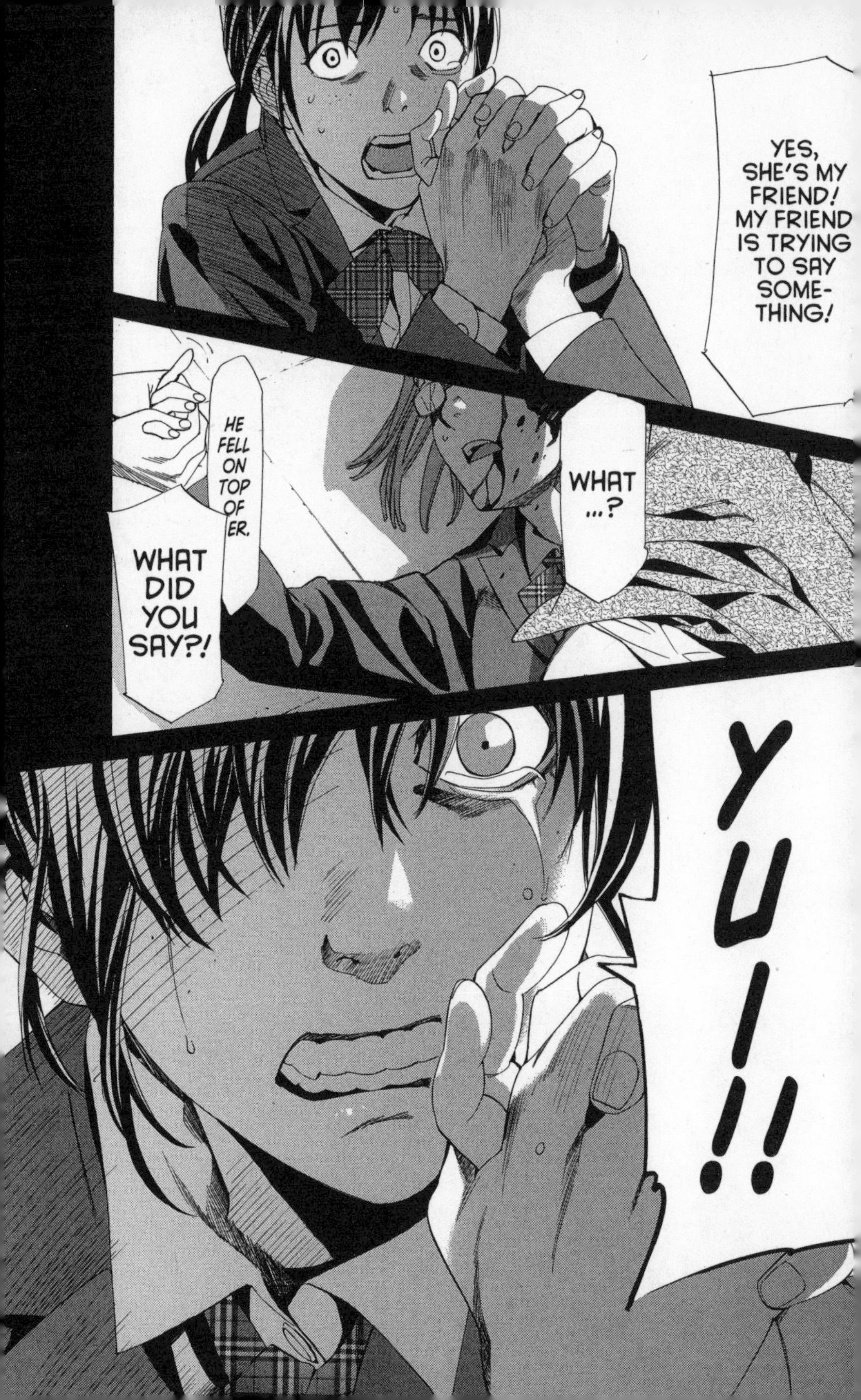
YES, SHE'S MY FRIEND! MY FRIEND IS TRYING TO SAY SOME-THING!
WHAT ...?
HE FELL ON TOP OF ER.
WHAT DID YOU SAY?!
YU—!!

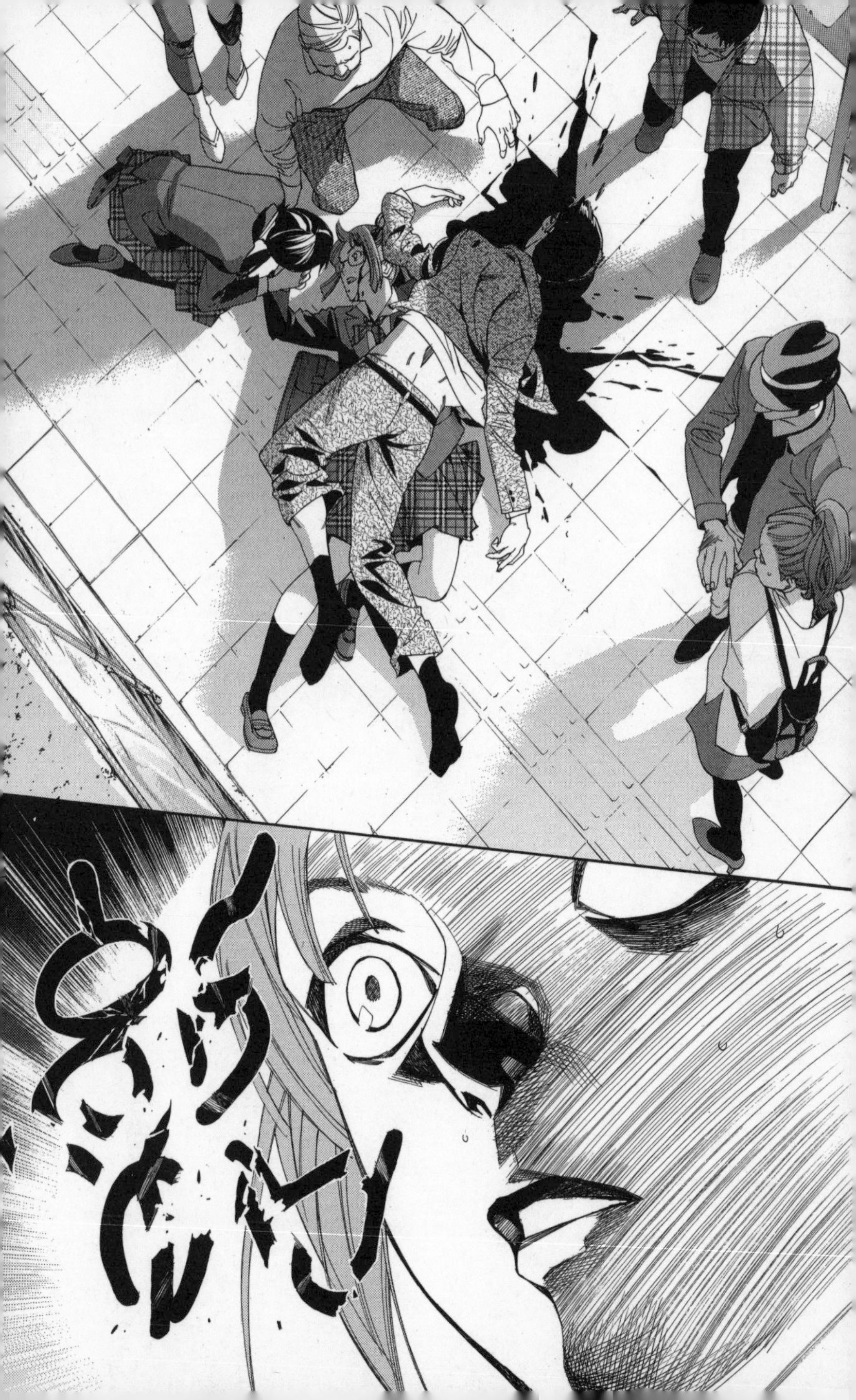

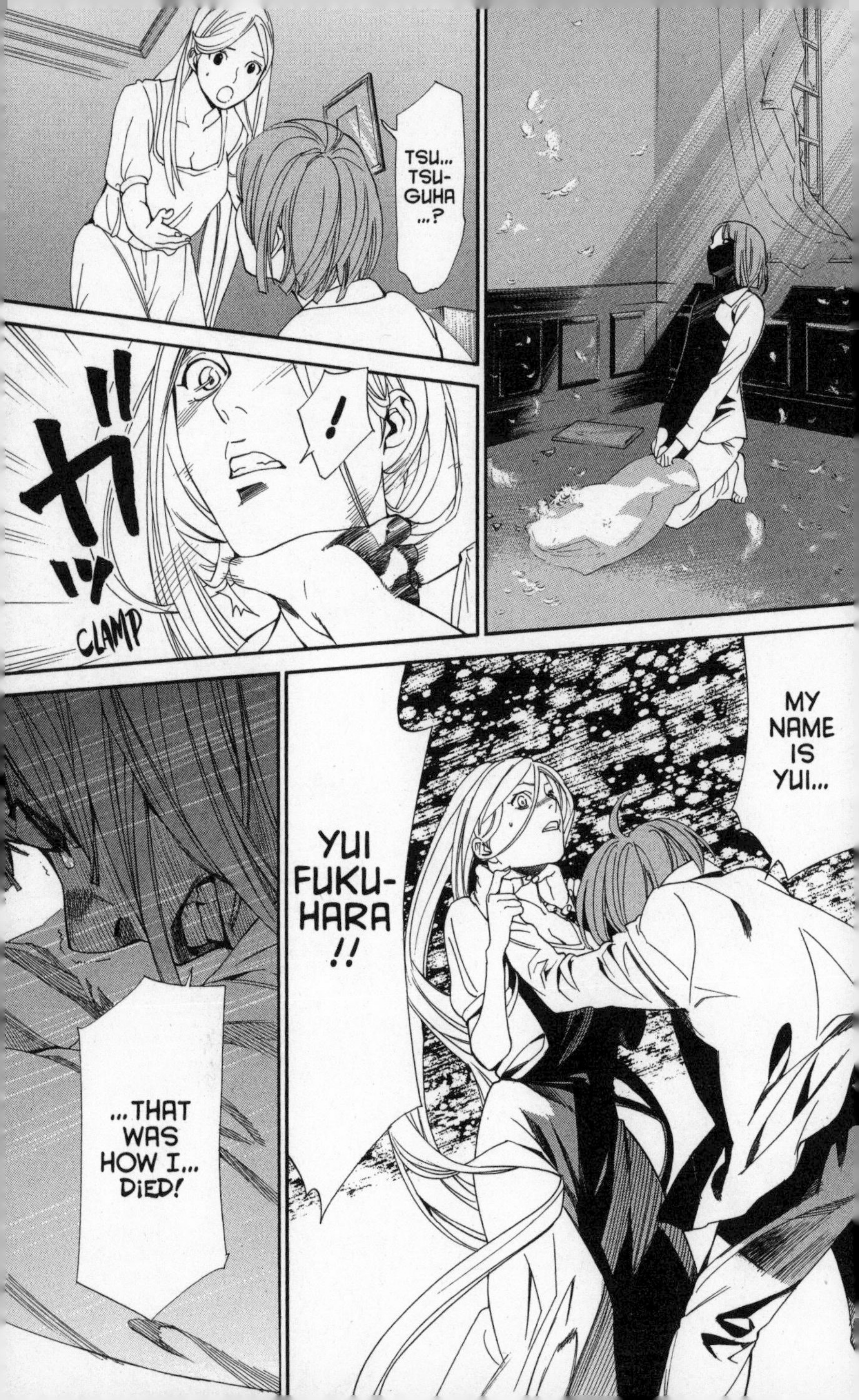
TSU... TSU-GUHA ...?
!
ガッ
CLAMP
MY NAME IS YUI...
YUI FUKU-HARA !!
...THAT WAS HOW I... DIED!

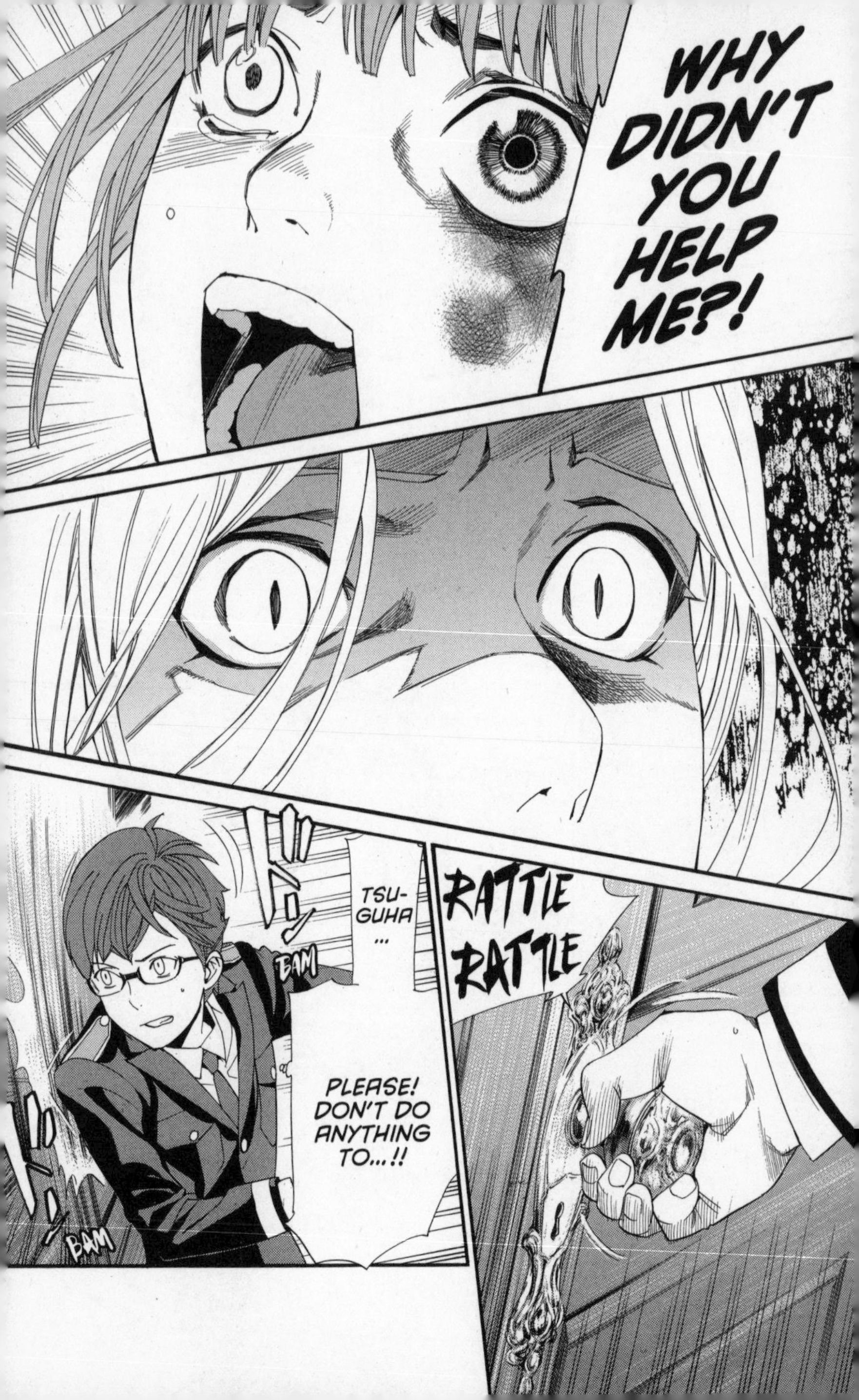
WHY DIDN'T YOU HELP ME?!
RATTLE RATTLE
TSU-GUHA...
BAM
PLEASE! DON'T DO ANYTHING TO...!!
BAM

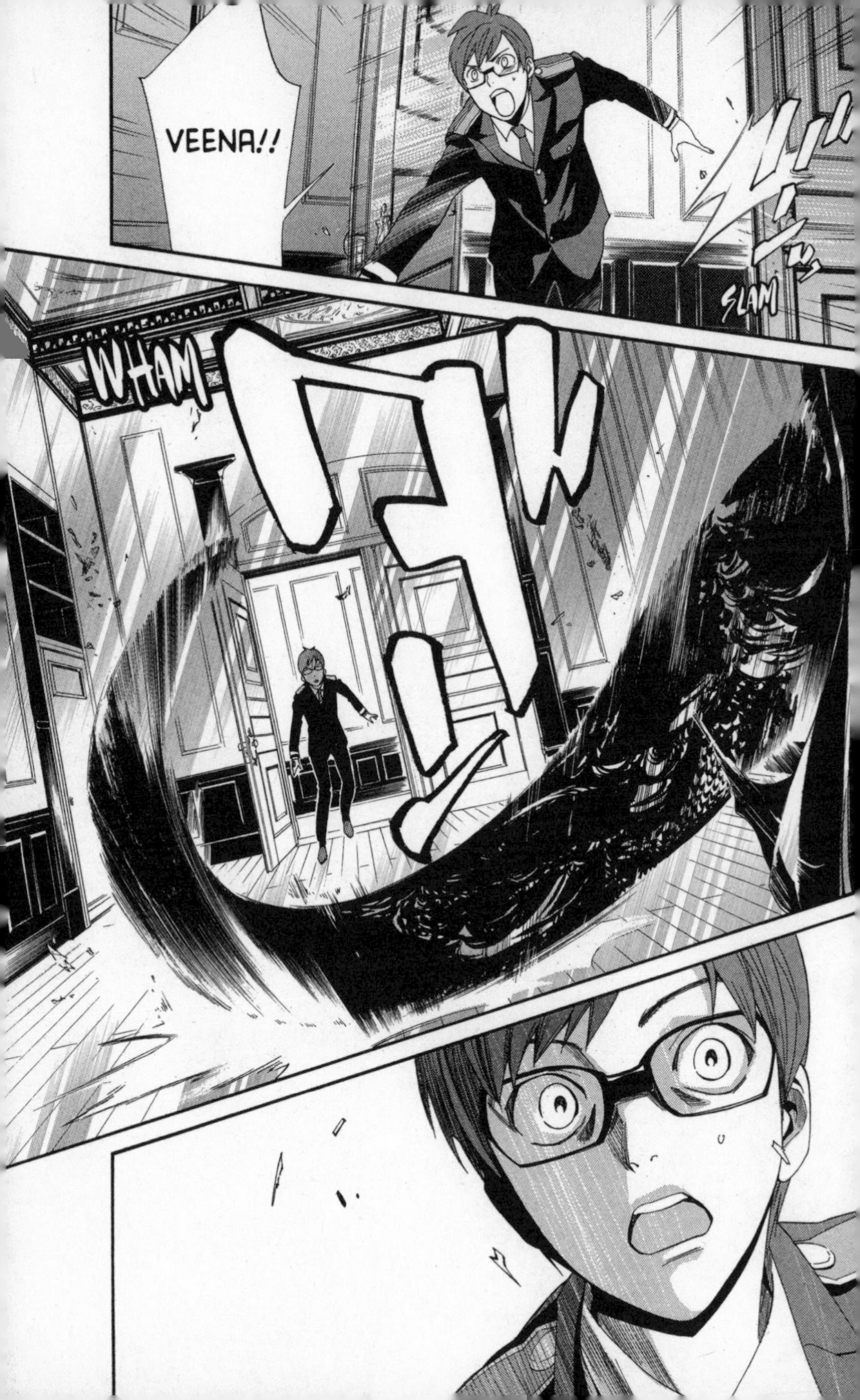
VEENA!!
SLAM
WHAM

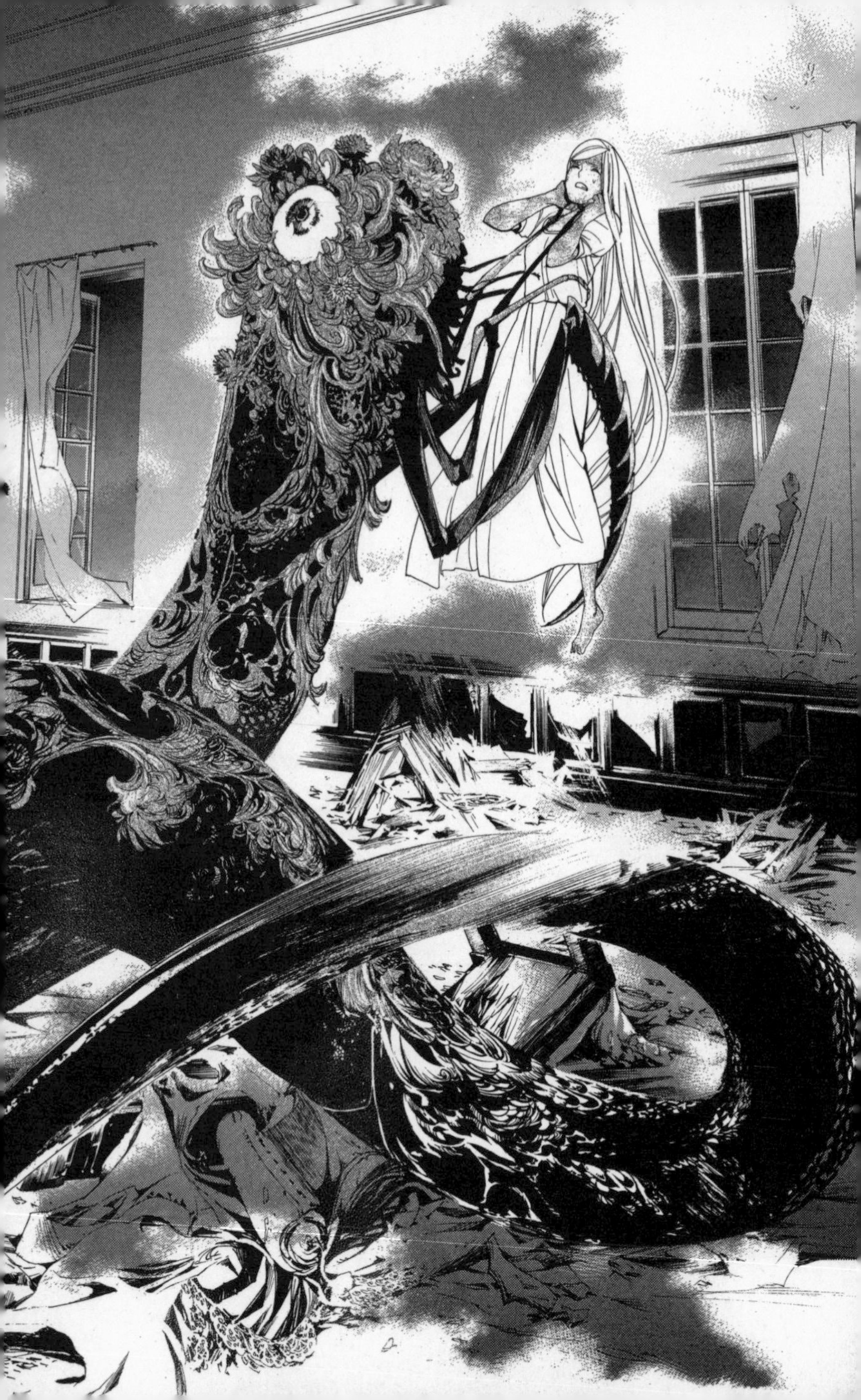

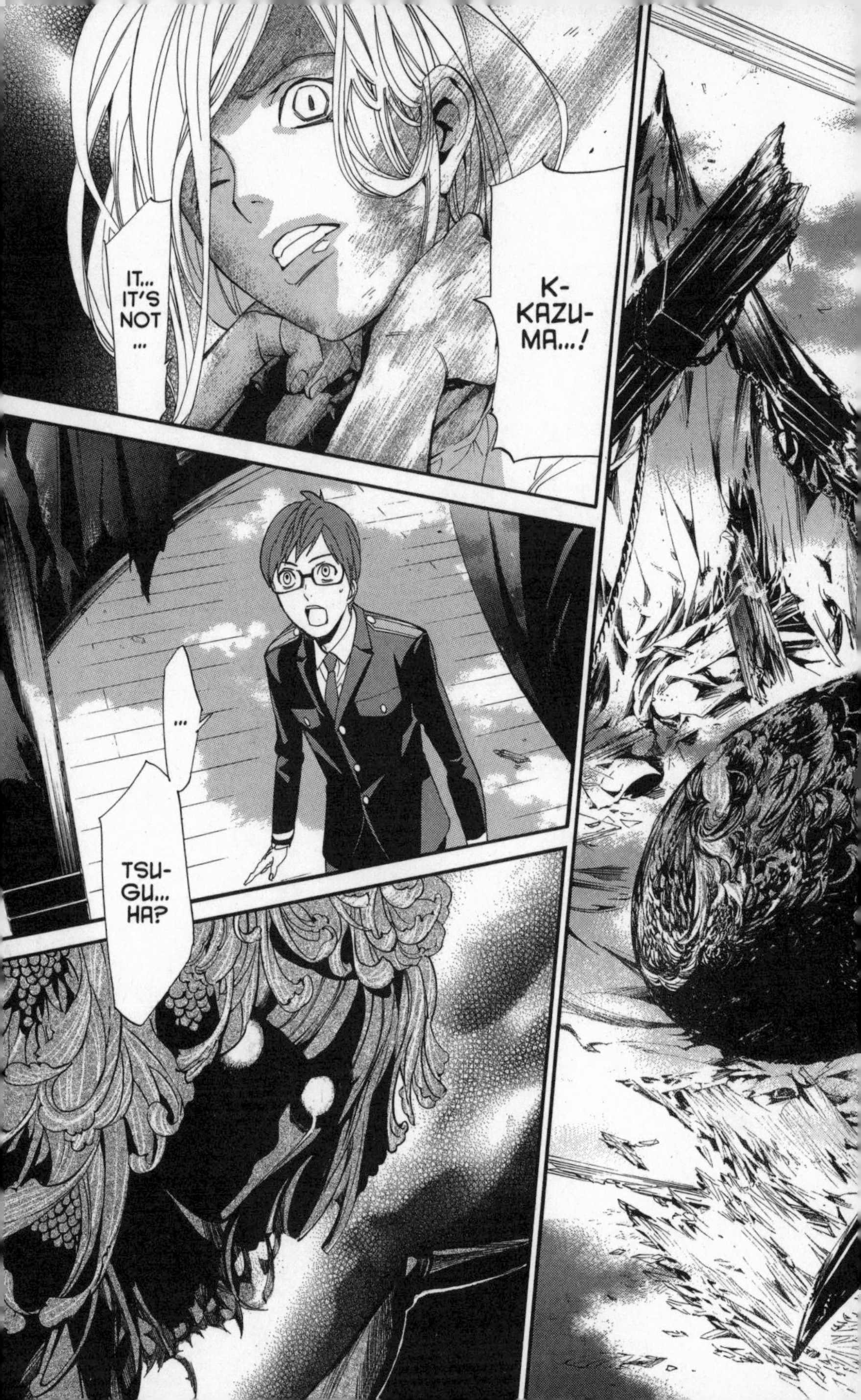
K-KAZUMA...!
IT... IT'S NOT ...
...
TSUGU... HA?

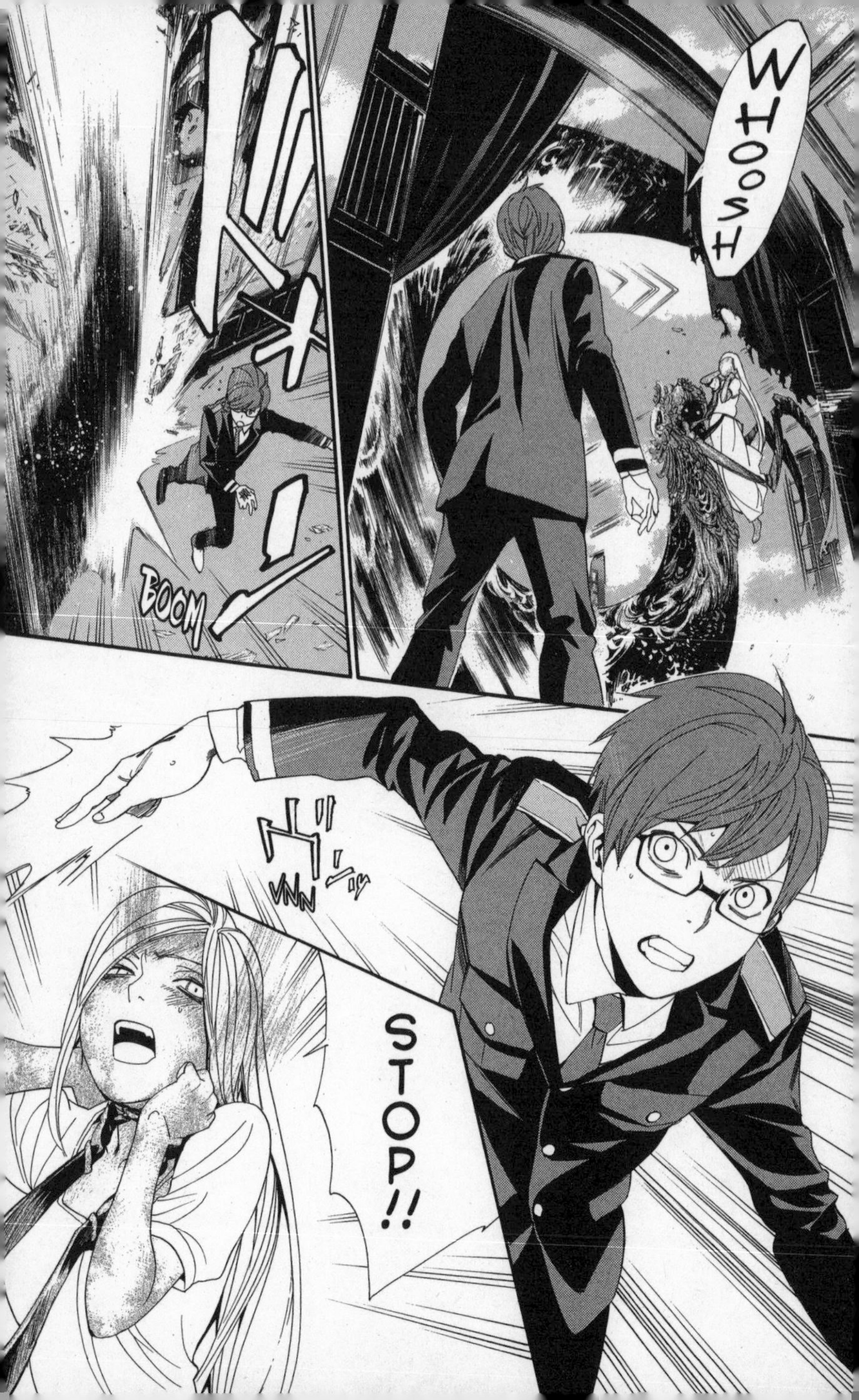
WHOOSH
BOOM
VNN
STOP!!

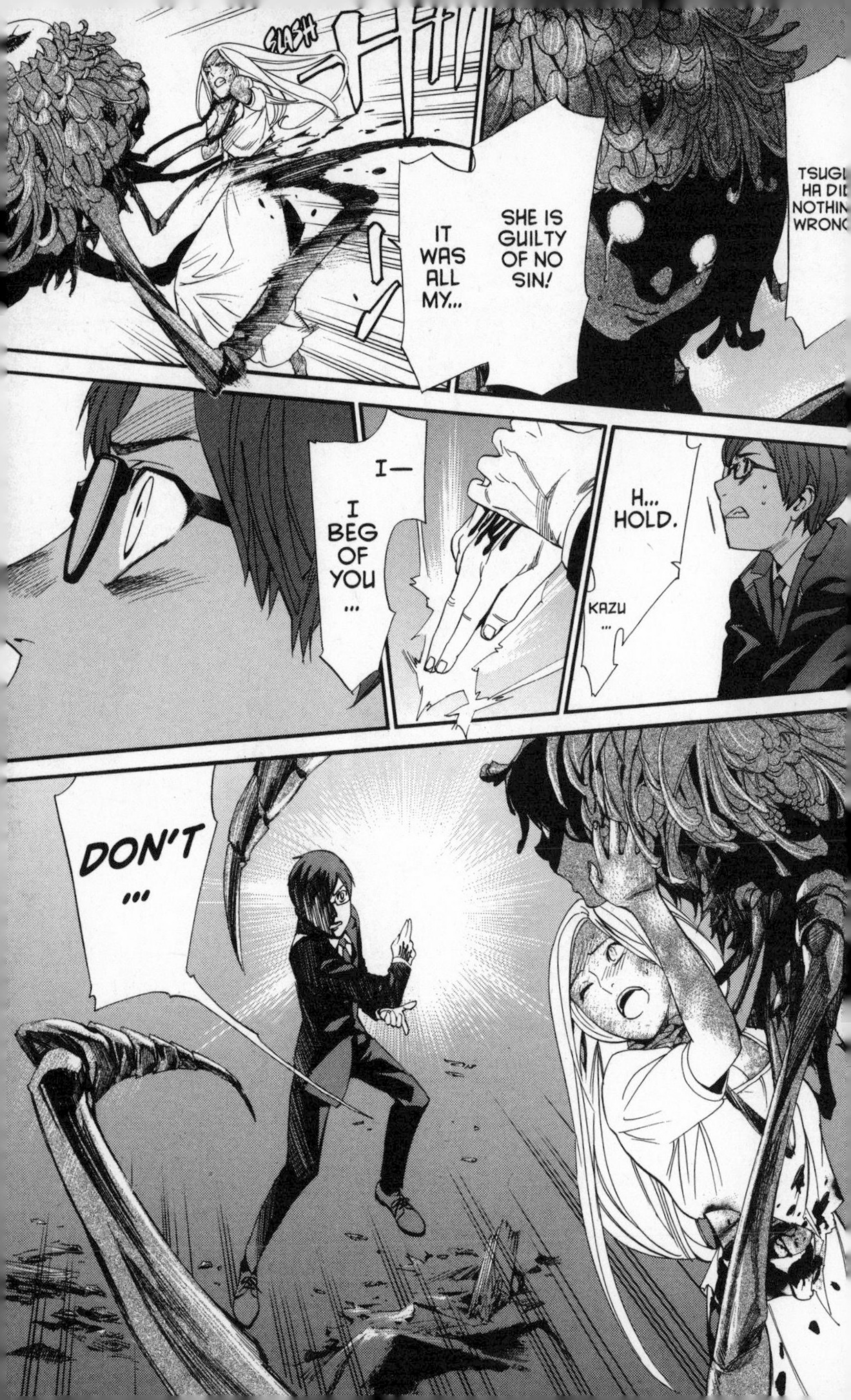

TSUGI HA DI NOTHIN WRONG
SHE IS GUILTY OF NO SIN!
IT WAS ALL MY...
SLASH
H... HOLD.
KAZU ...
I—
I BEG OF YOU ...
DON'T ...

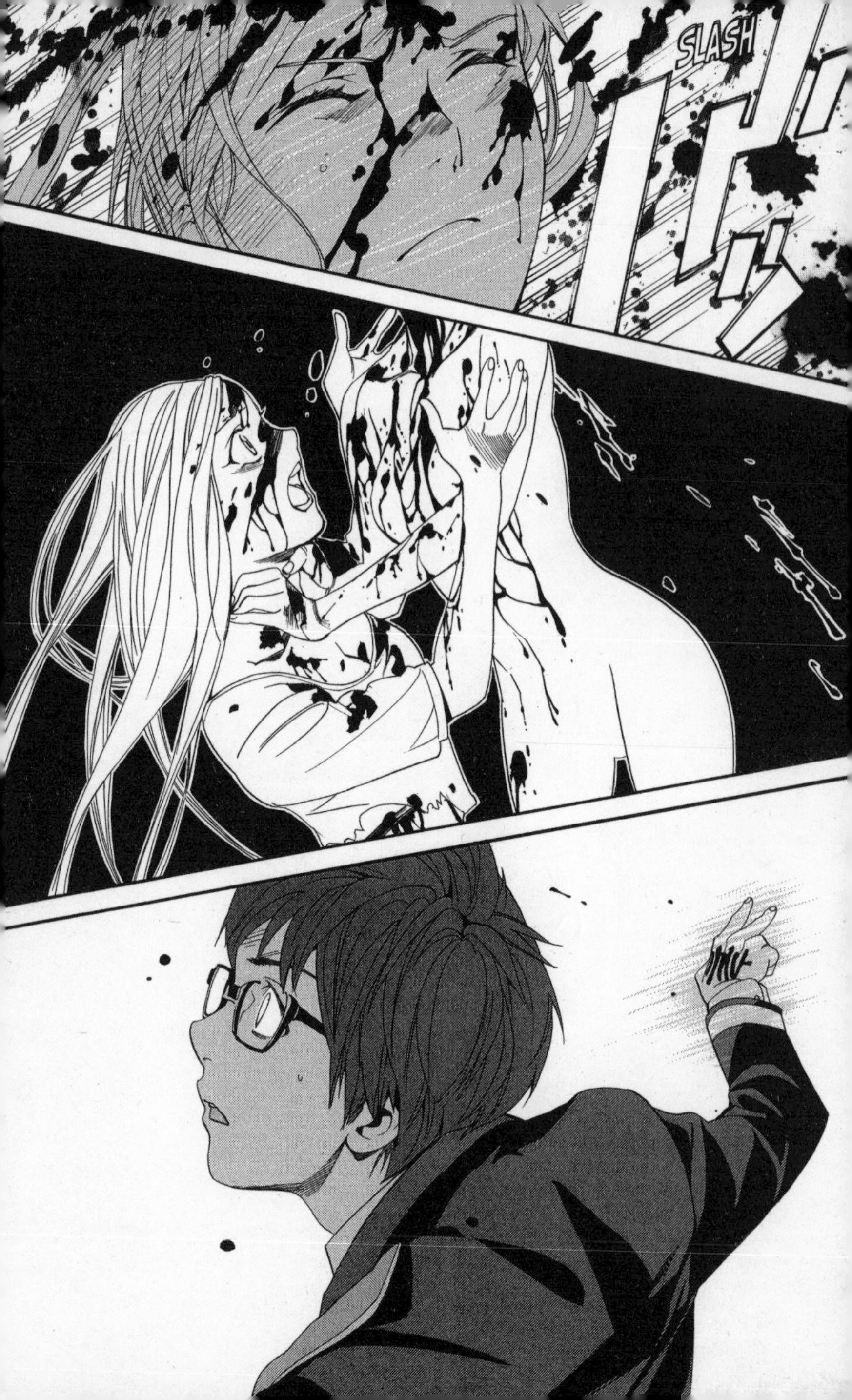
SLASH

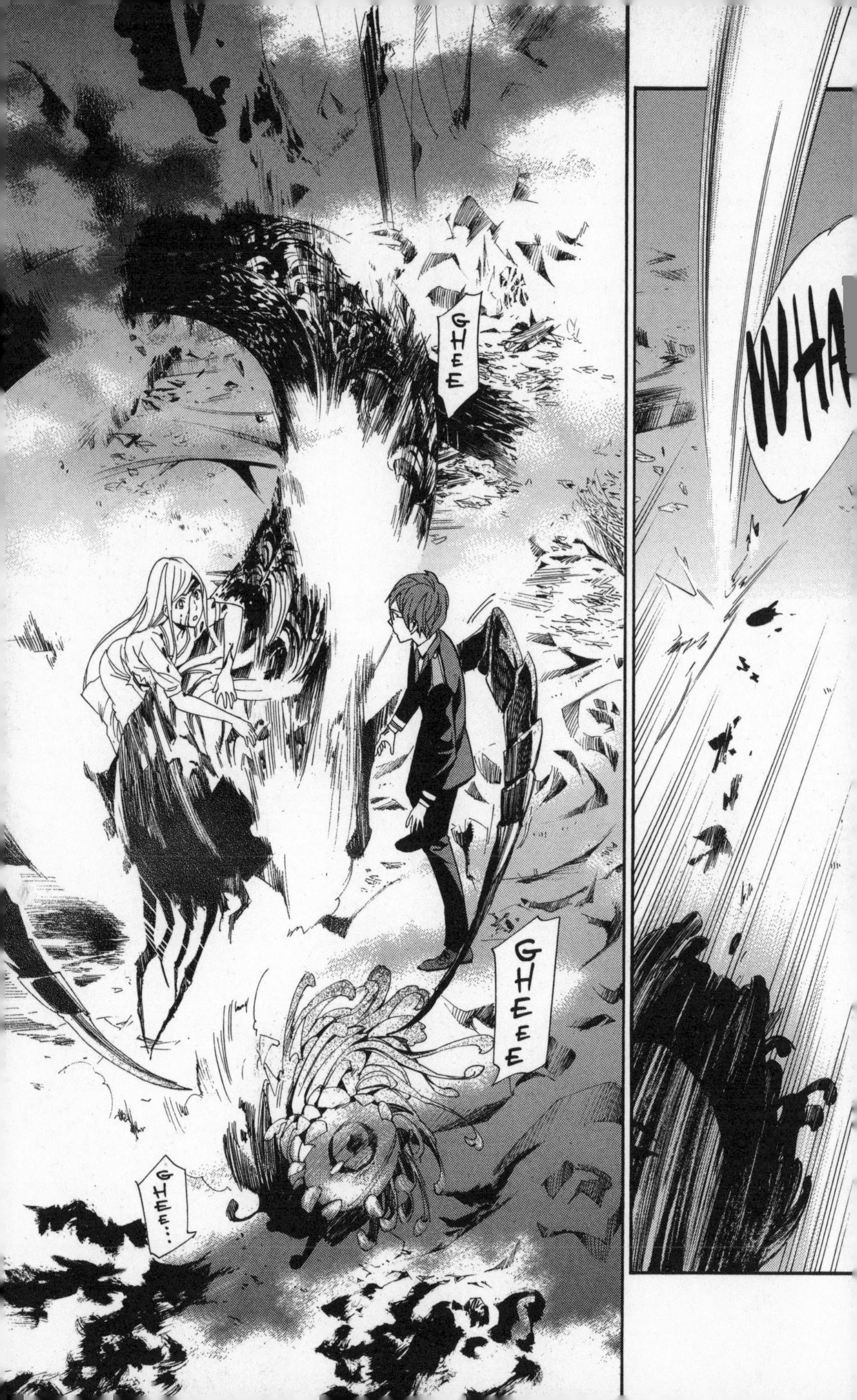
WHA
GHEE
GHEEE
GHEE...

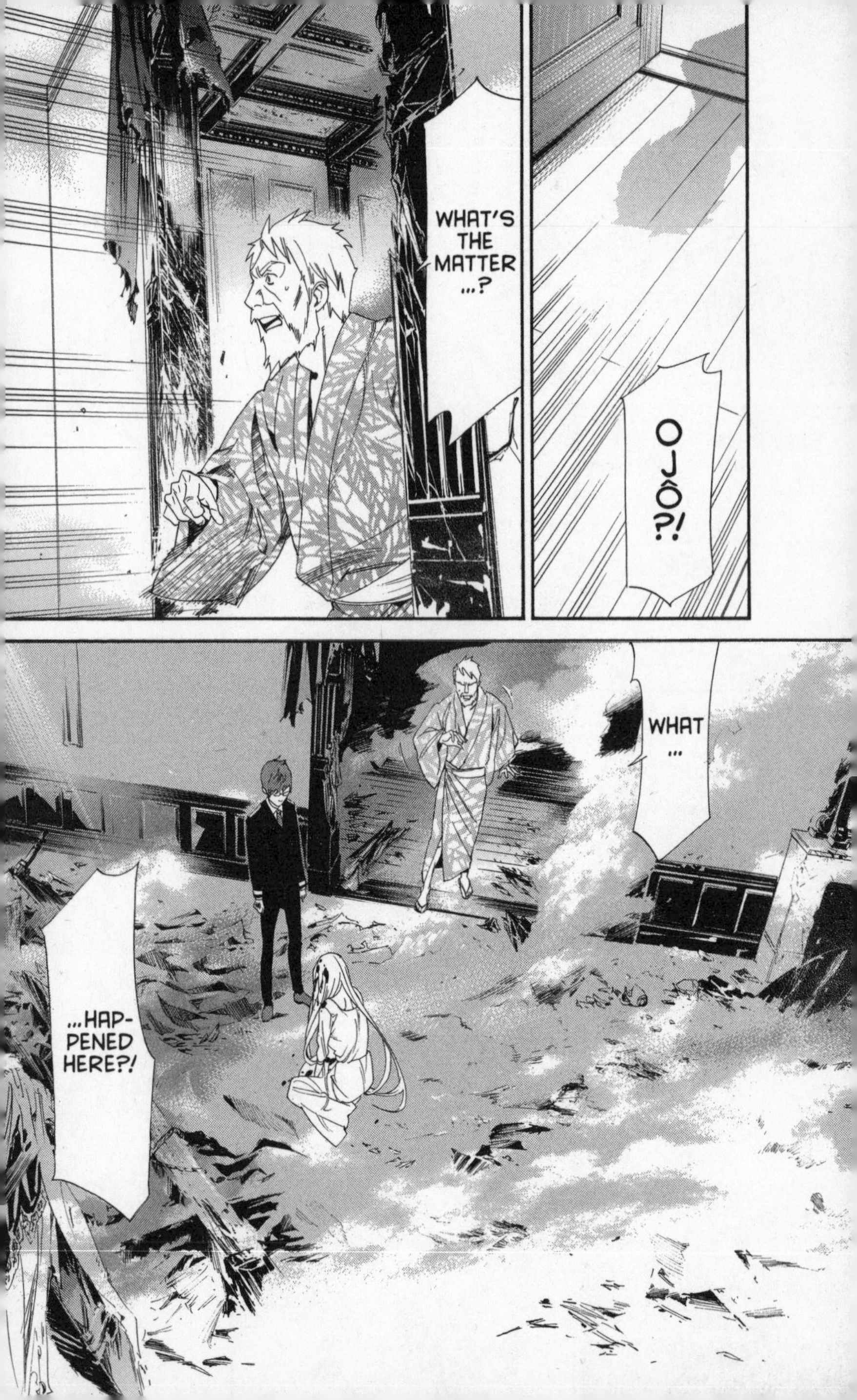
OJÔ?!
WHAT'S THE MATTER ...?
WHAT ...
...HAP-PENED HERE?!

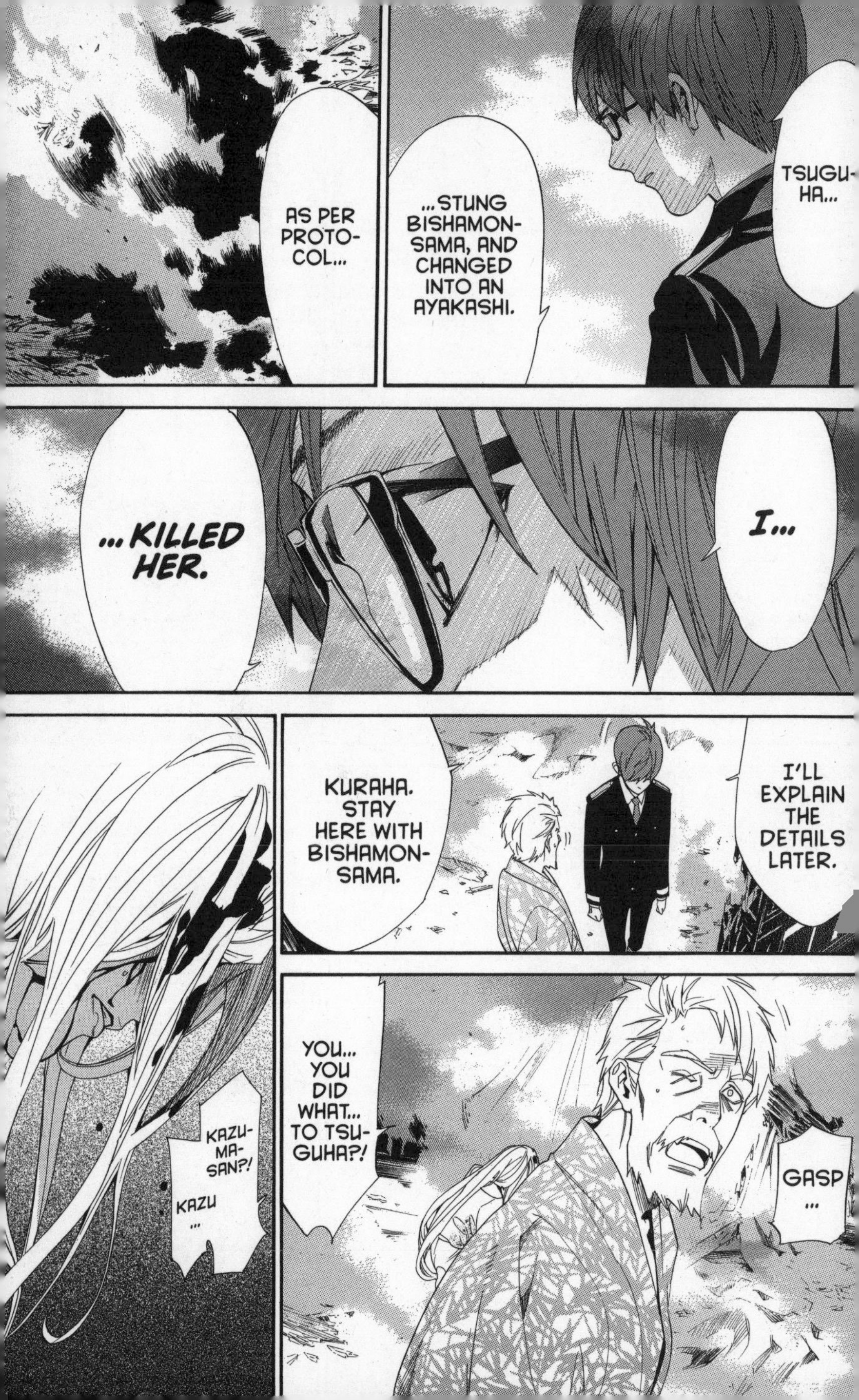
TSUGU-HA...
...STUNG BISHAMON-SAMA, AND CHANGED INTO AN AYAKASHI.
AS PER PROTO-COL...
I...
...KILLED HER.
I'LL EXPLAIN THE DETAILS LATER.
KURAHA. STAY HERE WITH BISHAMON-SAMA.
GASP...
YOU... YOU DID WHAT... TO TSUGUHA?!
KAZU-MA-SAN?!
KAZU...

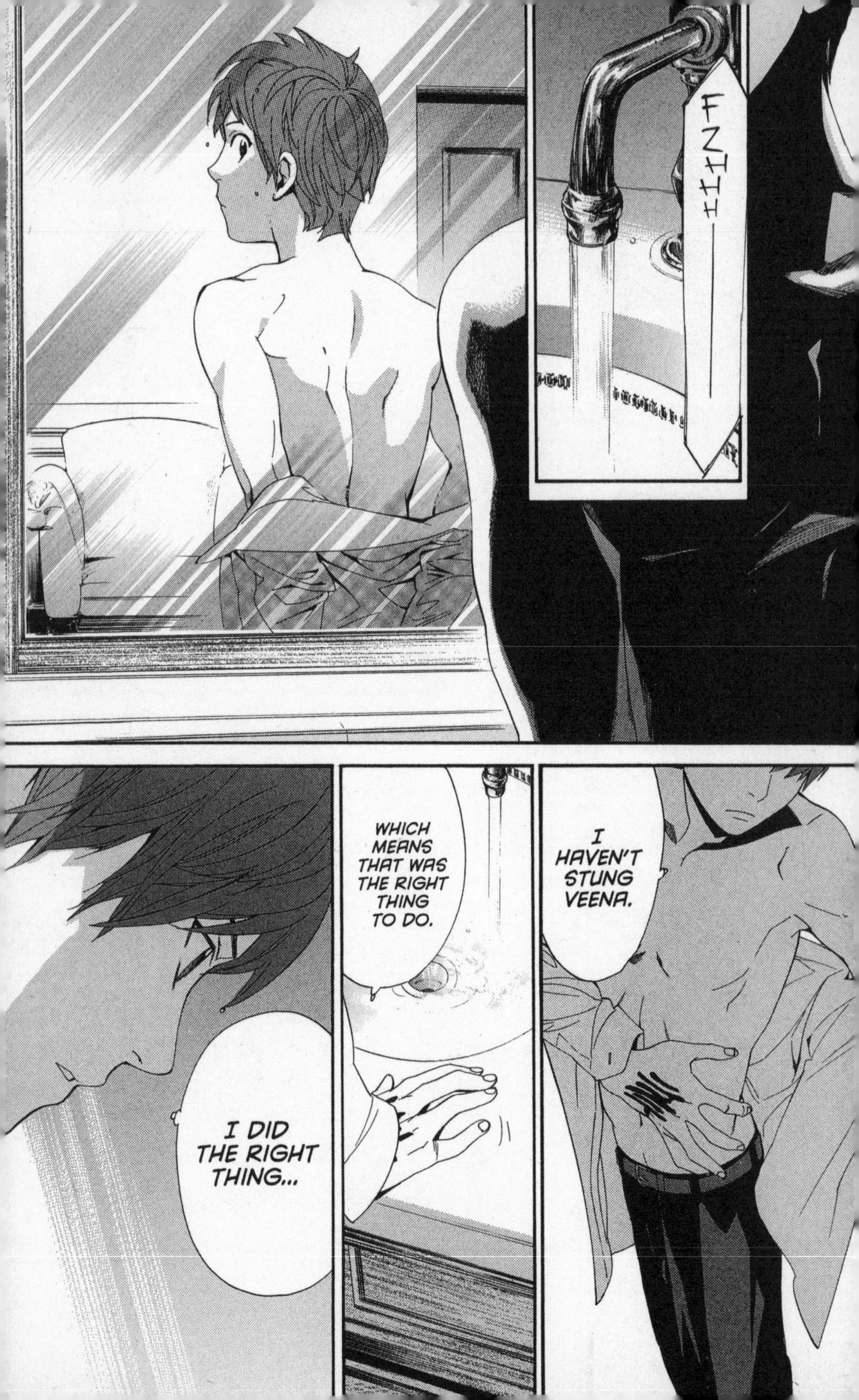
FZHHH—
I HAVEN'T STUNG VEENA.
WHICH MEANS THAT WAS THE RIGHT THING TO DO.
I DID THE RIGHT THING...

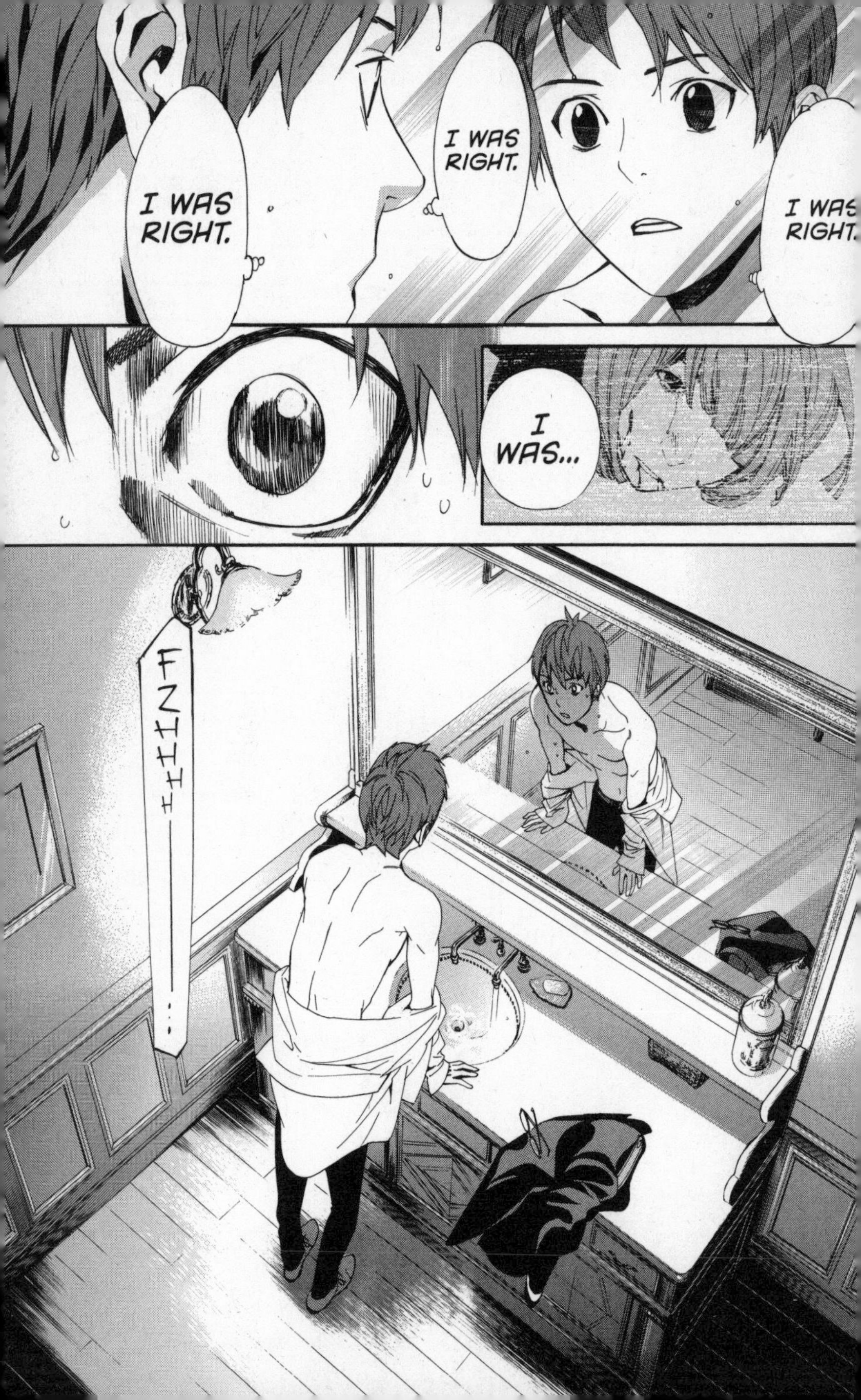
I WAS RIGHT.
I WAS RIGHT.
I WAS RIGHT.
I WAS...
FZHHHH...

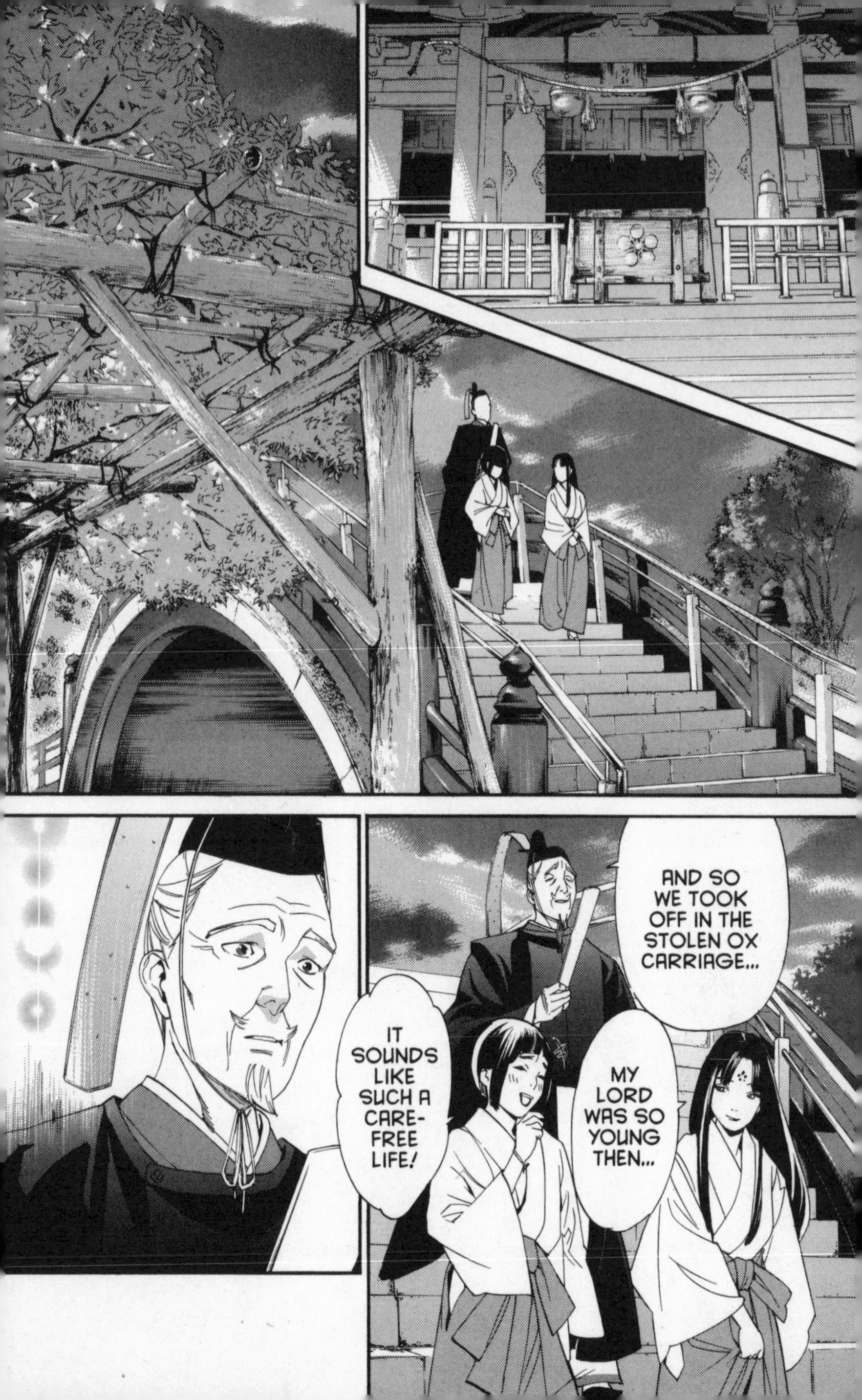
AND SO WE TOOK OFF IN THE STOLEN OX CARRIAGE...
MY LORD WAS SO YOUNG THEN...
IT SOUNDS LIKE SUCH A CARE-FREE LIFE!

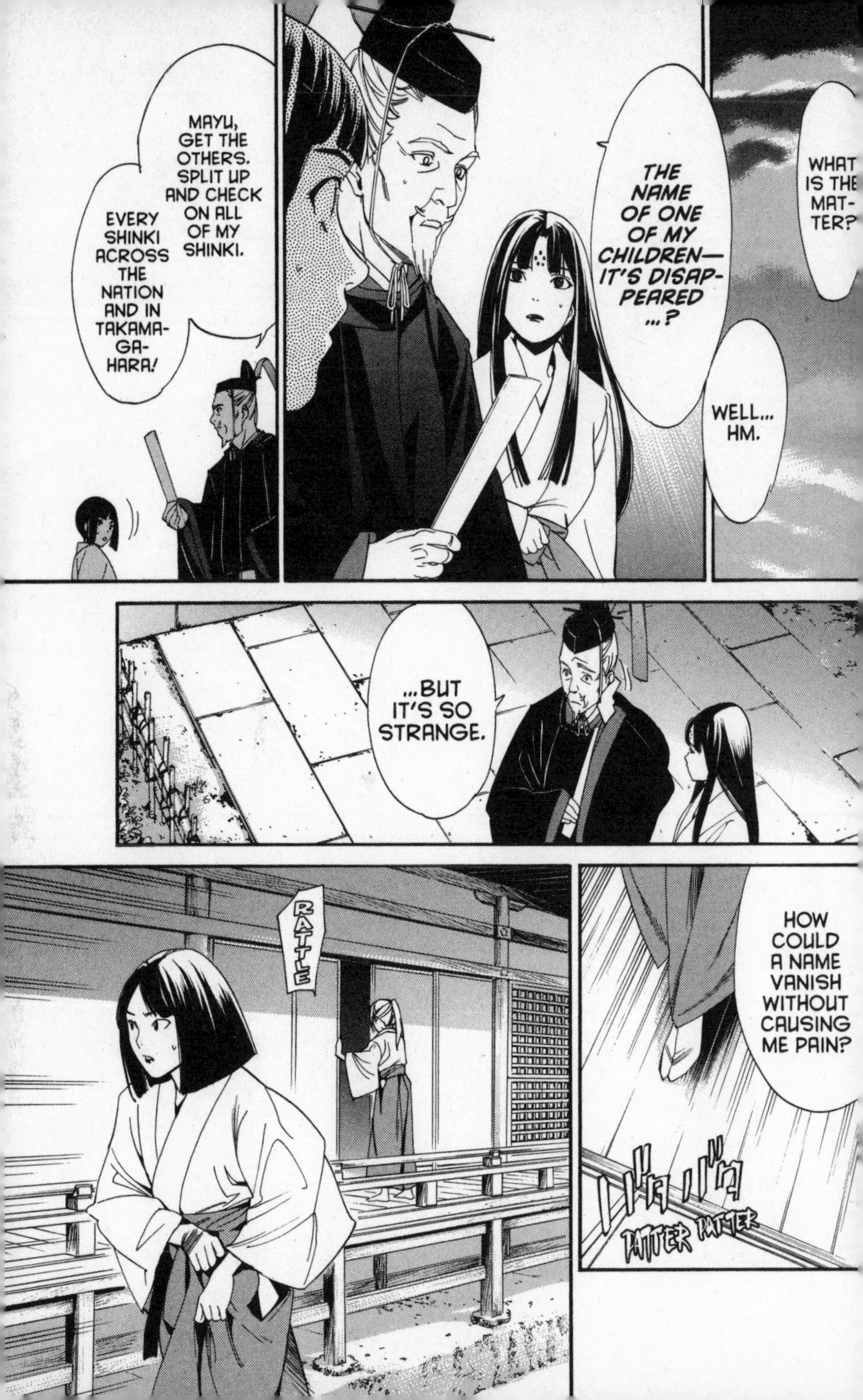
WHAT IS THE MATTER?
WELL... HM.
THE NAME OF ONE OF MY CHILDREN—IT'S DISAPPEARED ...?
MAYU, GET THE OTHERS. SPLIT UP AND CHECK ON ALL OF MY SHINKI.
EVERY SHINKI ACROSS THE NATION AND IN TAKAMAGAHARA!
...BUT IT'S SO STRANGE.
HOW COULD A NAME VANISH WITHOUT CAUSING ME PAIN?
PATTER PATTER
RATTLE

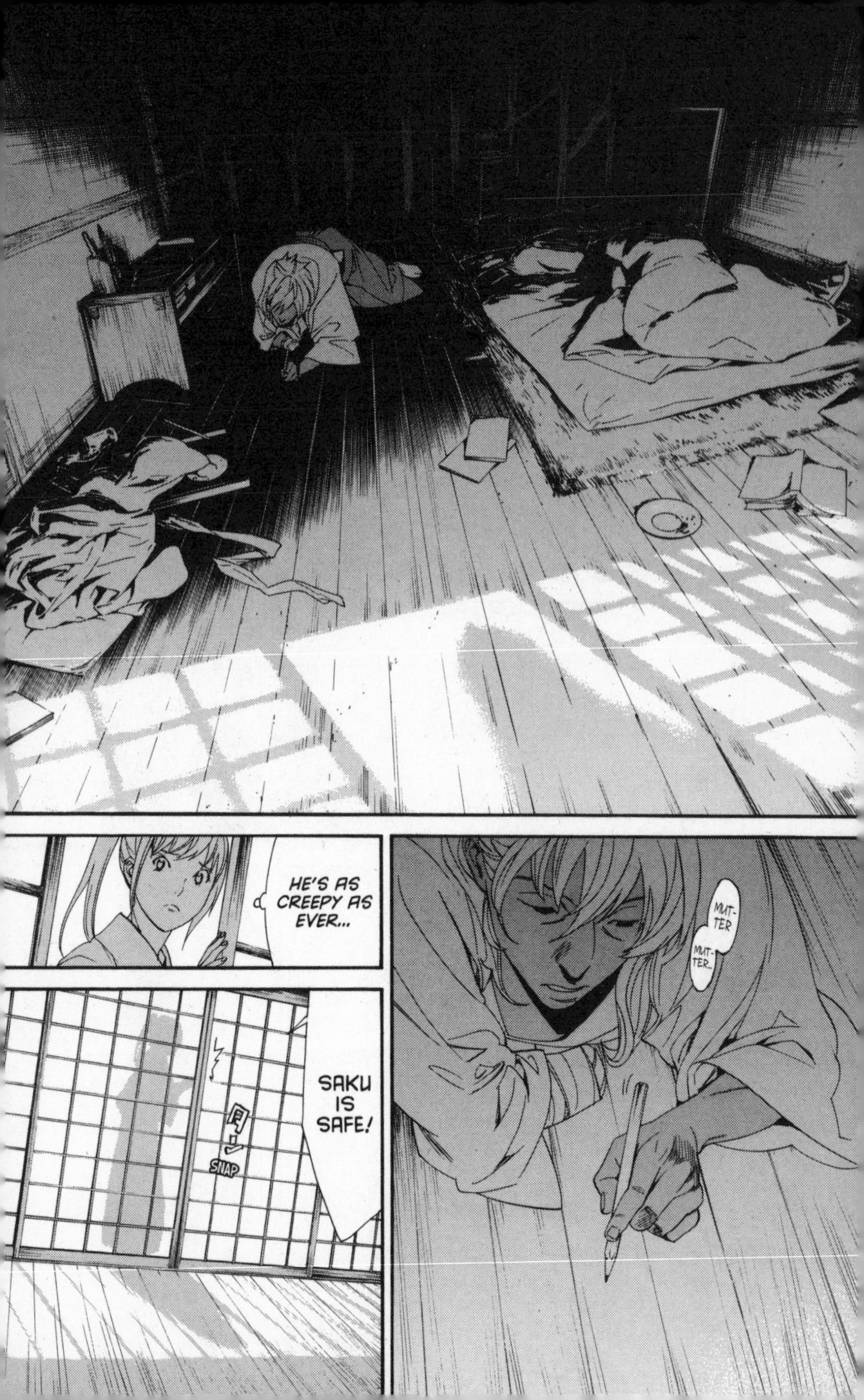
MUTTER
MUTTER...
HE'S AS CREEPY AS EVER...
SAKU IS SAFE!
SNAP

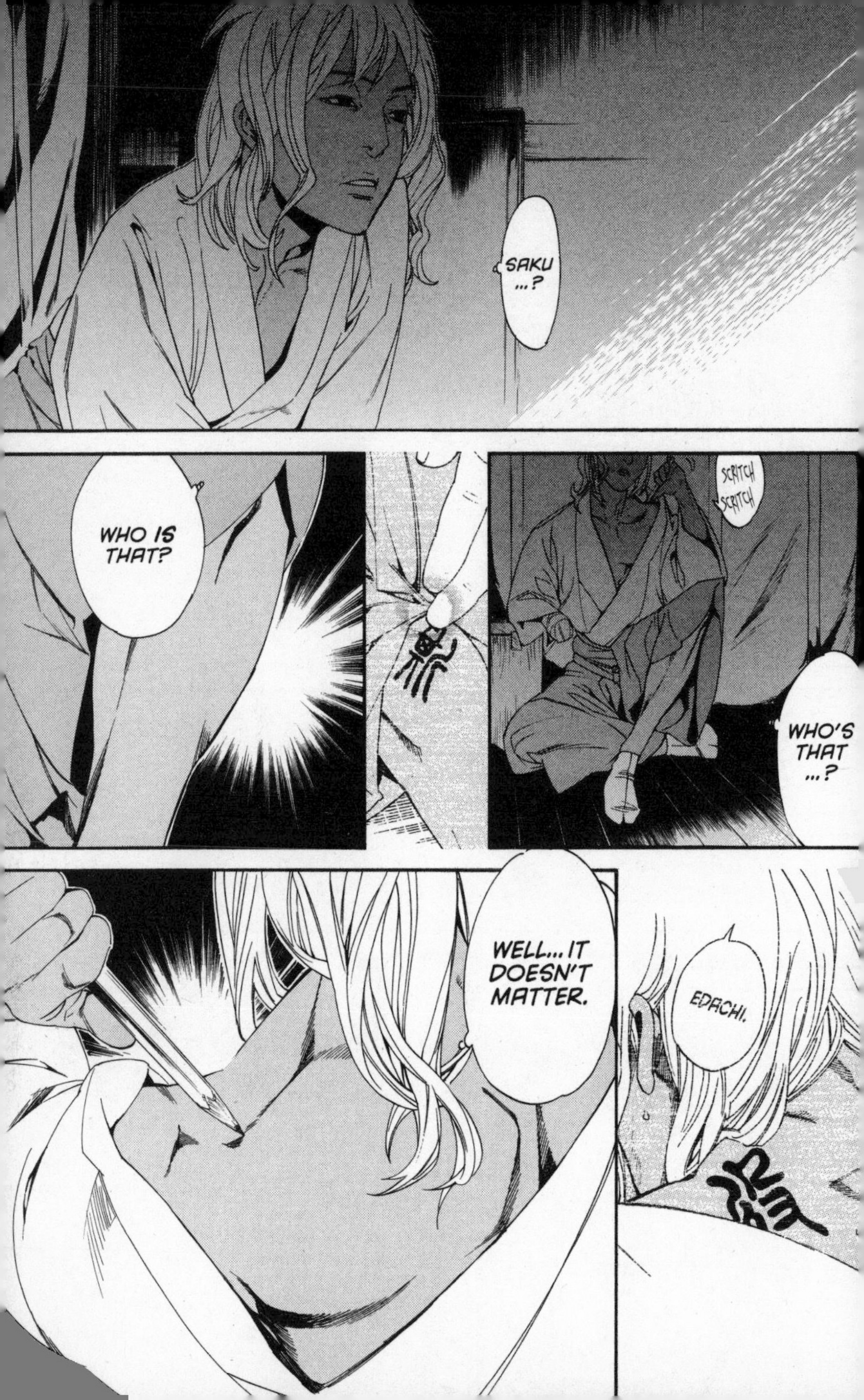
SAKU ...?
SCRITCH SCRITCH
WHO'S THAT ...?
WHO IS THAT?
EDACHI.
WELL... IT DOESN'T MATTER.

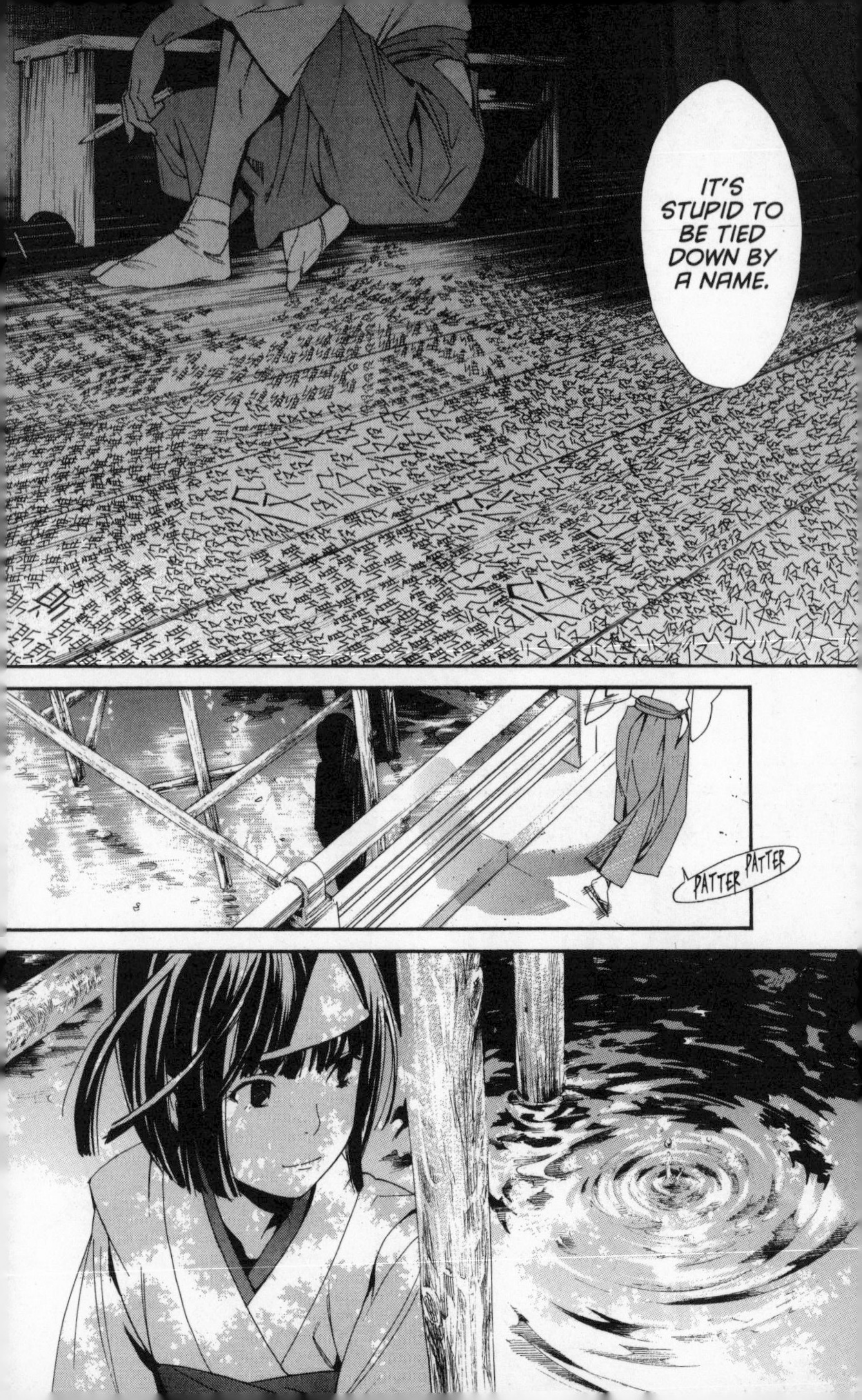
IT'S STUPID TO BE TIED DOWN BY A NAME.
PATTER PATTER

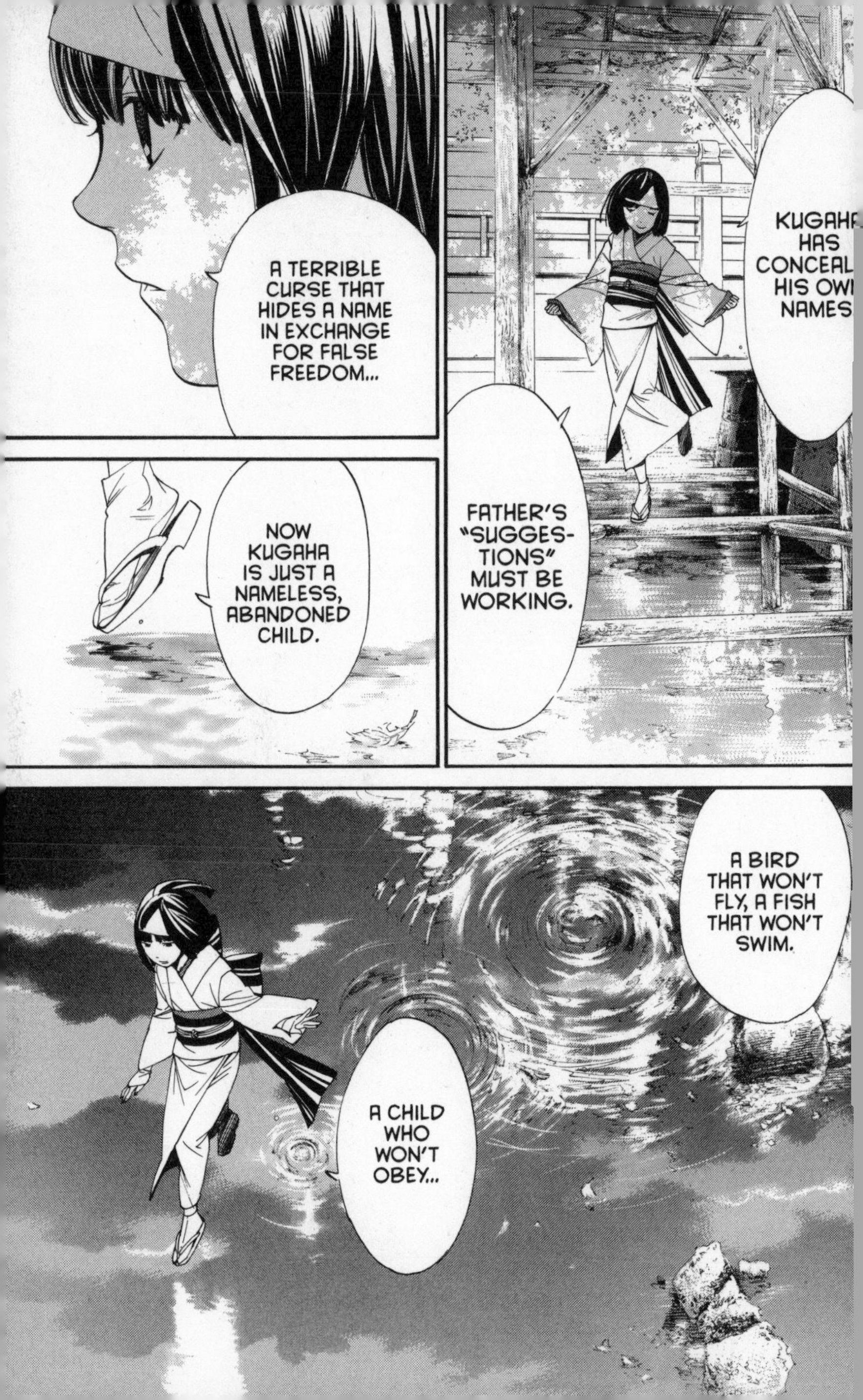
KUGAHA HAS CONCEAL HIS OWN NAMES
FATHER'S "SUGGESTIONS" MUST BE WORKING.
A TERRIBLE CURSE THAT HIDES A NAME IN EXCHANGE FOR FALSE FREEDOM...
NOW KUGAHA IS JUST A NAMELESS, ABANDONED CHILD.
A BIRD THAT WON'T FLY, A FISH THAT WON'T SWIM.
A CHILD WHO WON'T OBEY...

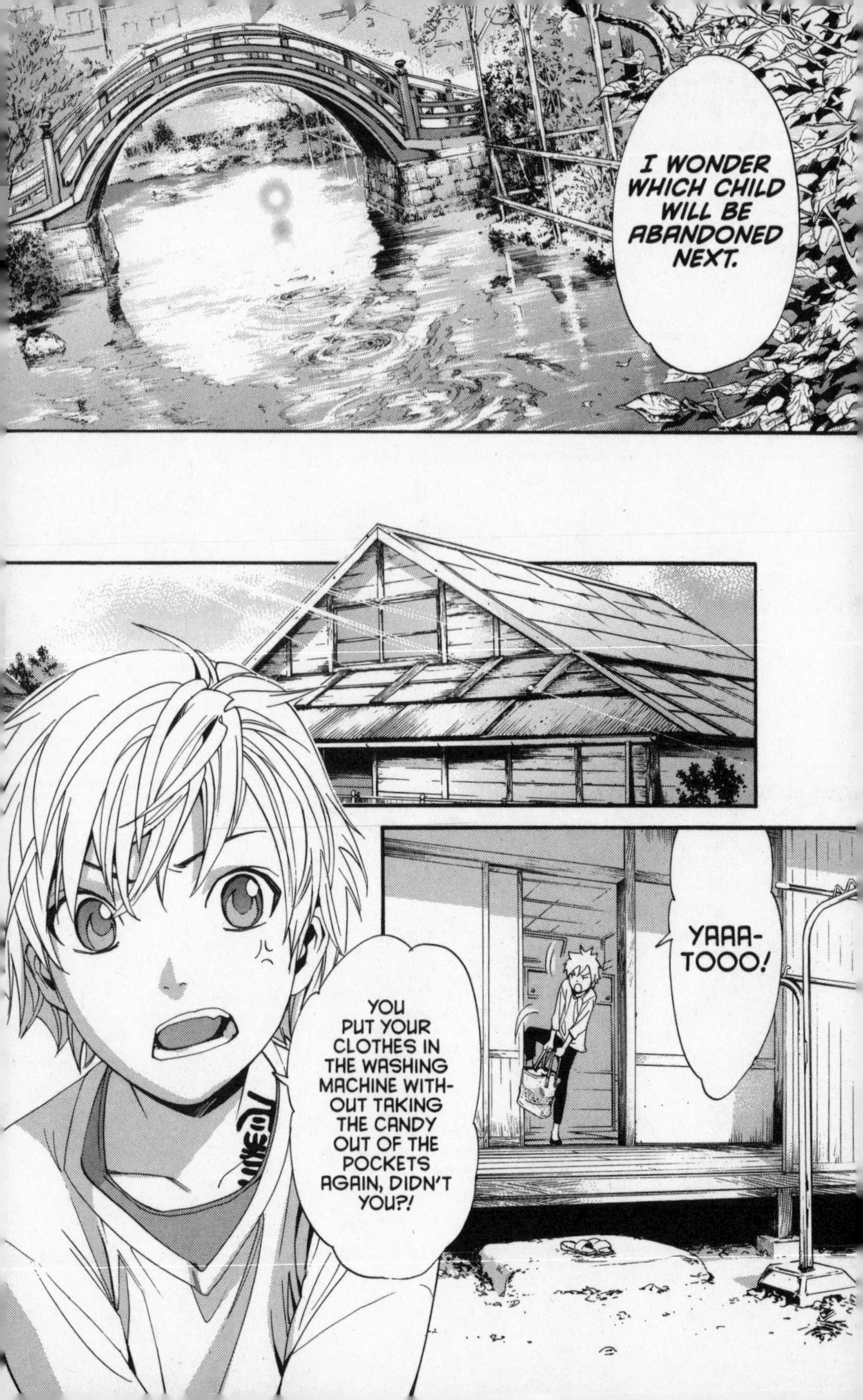
I WONDER WHICH CHILD WILL BE ABANDONED NEXT.
YAAA-TOOO!
YOU PUT YOUR CLOTHES IN THE WASHING MACHINE WITH-OUT TAKING THE CANDY OUT OF THE POCKETS AGAIN, DIDN'T YOU?!

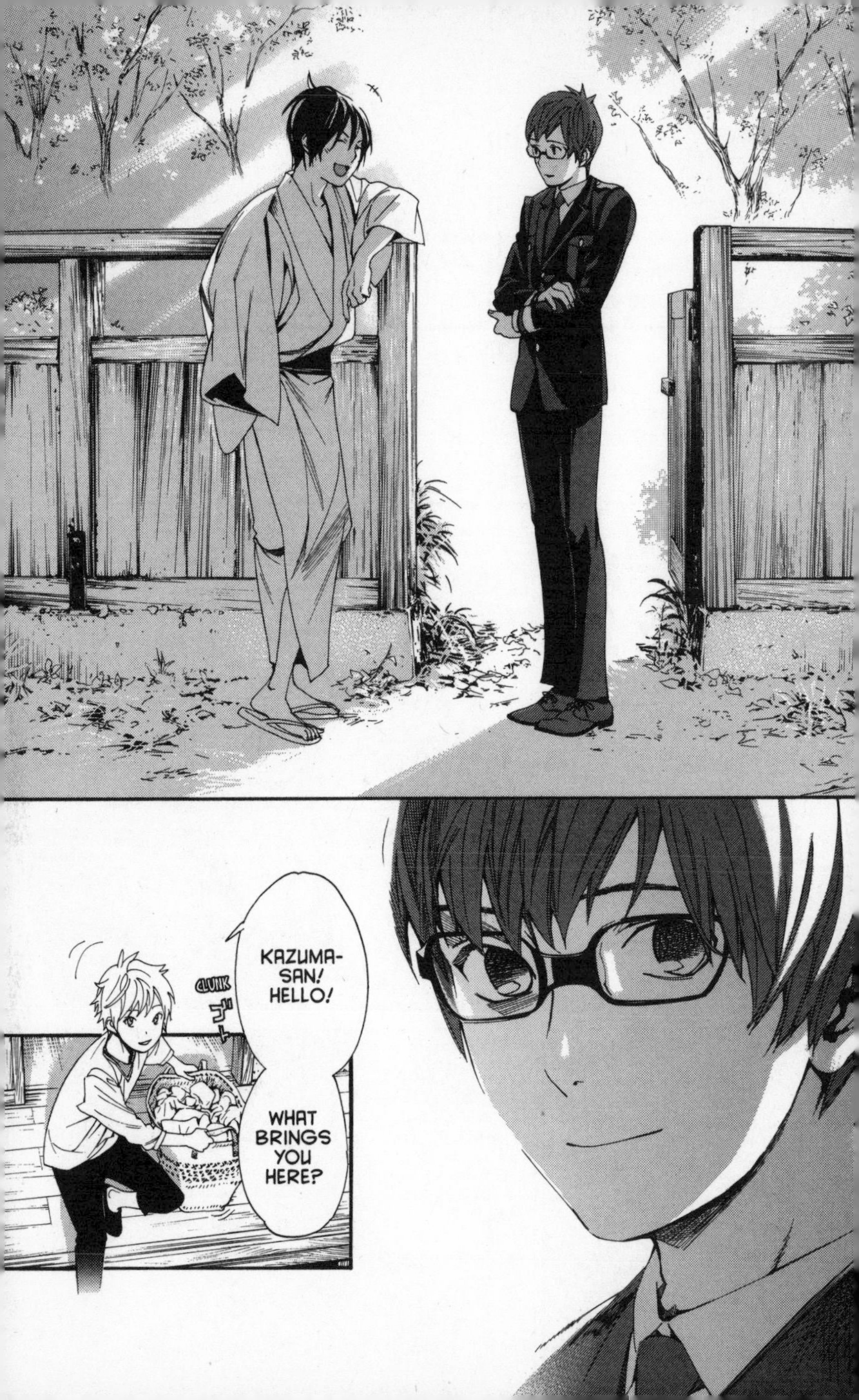
KAZUMA-SAN! HELLO!
WHAT BRINGS YOU HERE?
CLUNK
ゴト

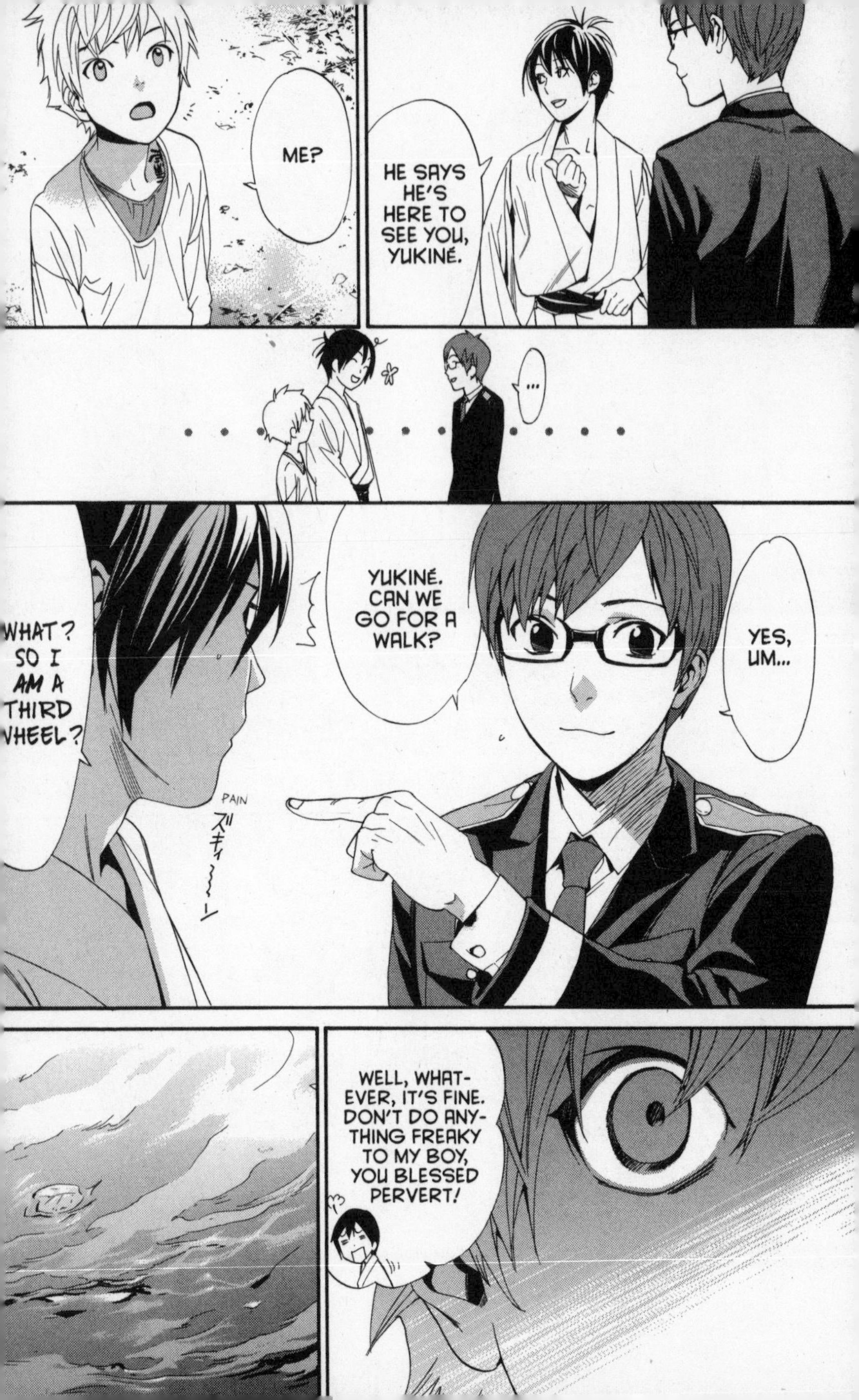
HE SAYS HE'S HERE TO SEE YOU, YUKINÉ.
ME?
...
YES, UM...
YUKINÉ. CAN WE GO FOR A WALK?
WHAT? SO I AM A THIRD WHEEL?
PAIN
ズキィ〜〜ン
WELL, WHAT-EVER, IT'S FINE. DON'T DO ANY-THING FREAKY TO MY BOY, YOU BLESSED PERVERT!

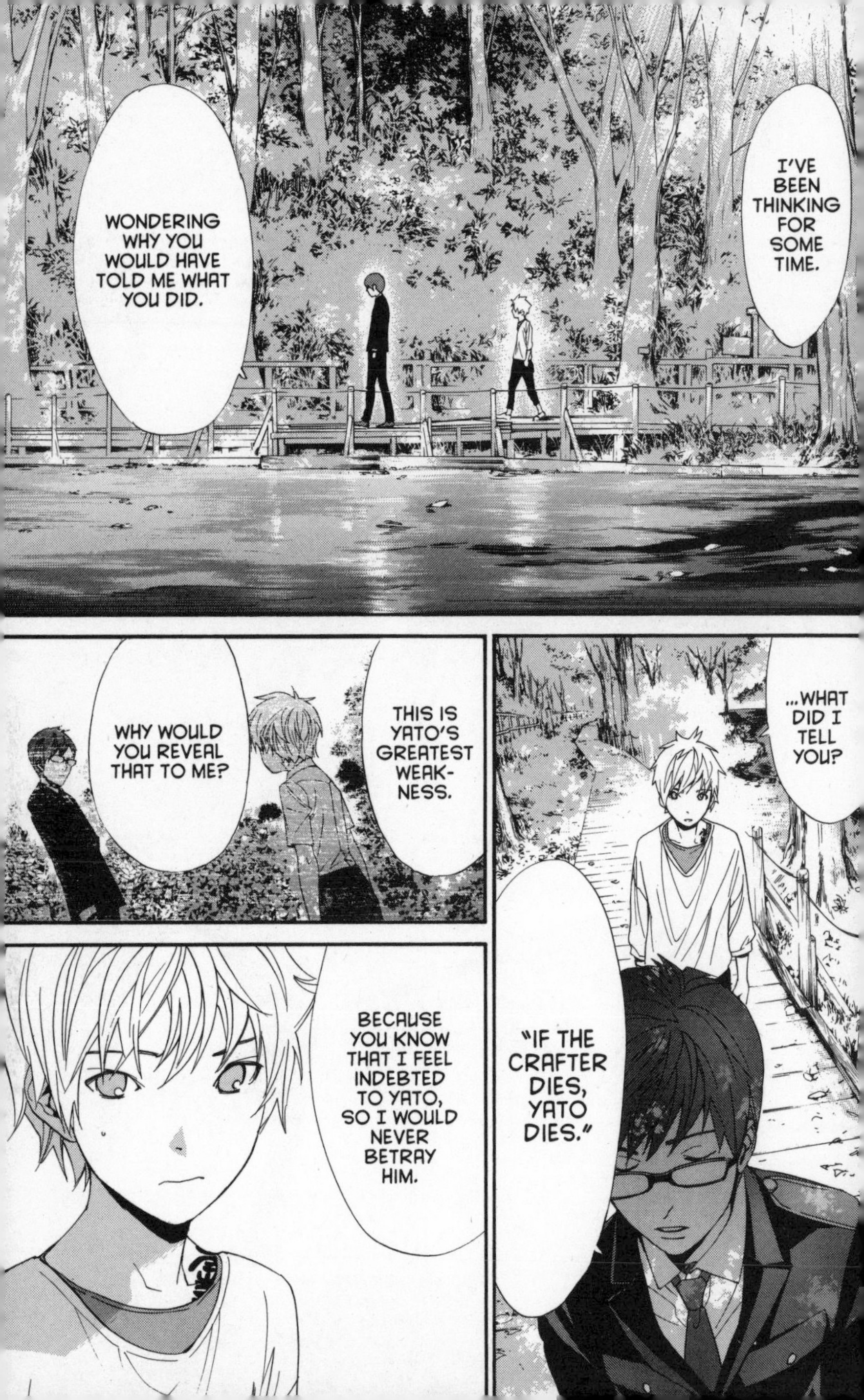
I'VE BEEN THINKING FOR SOME TIME.
WONDERING WHY YOU WOULD HAVE TOLD ME WHAT YOU DID.
...WHAT DID I TELL YOU?
"IF THE CRAFTER DIES, YATO DIES."
THIS IS YATO'S GREATEST WEAK-NESS.
WHY WOULD YOU REVEAL THAT TO ME?
BECAUSE YOU KNOW THAT I FEEL INDEBTED TO YATO, SO I WOULD NEVER BETRAY HIM.

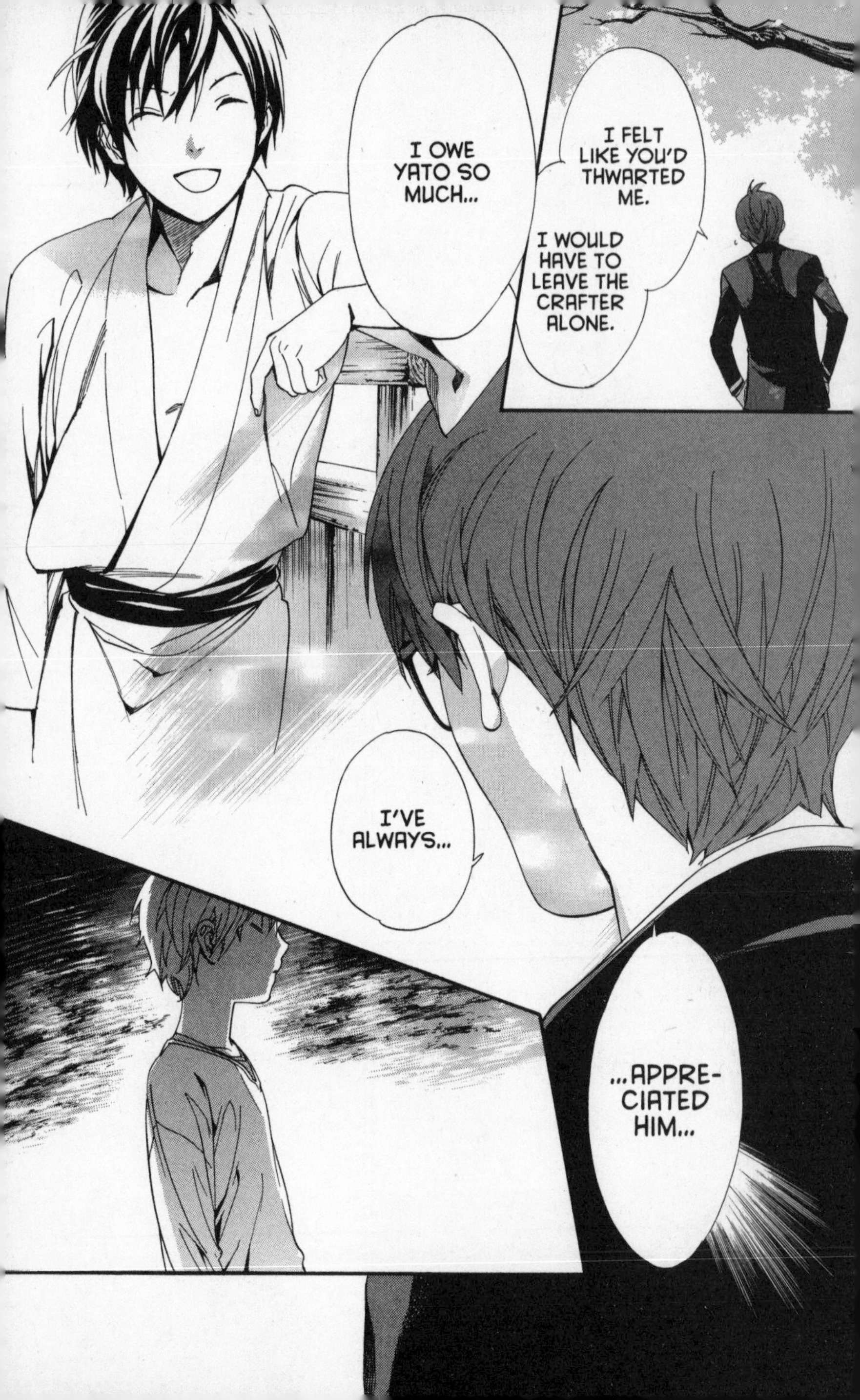
I FELT LIKE YOU'D THWARTED ME.
I WOULD HAVE TO LEAVE THE CRAFTER ALONE.
I OWE YATO SO MUCH...
I'VE ALWAYS...
...APPRE-CIATED HIM...

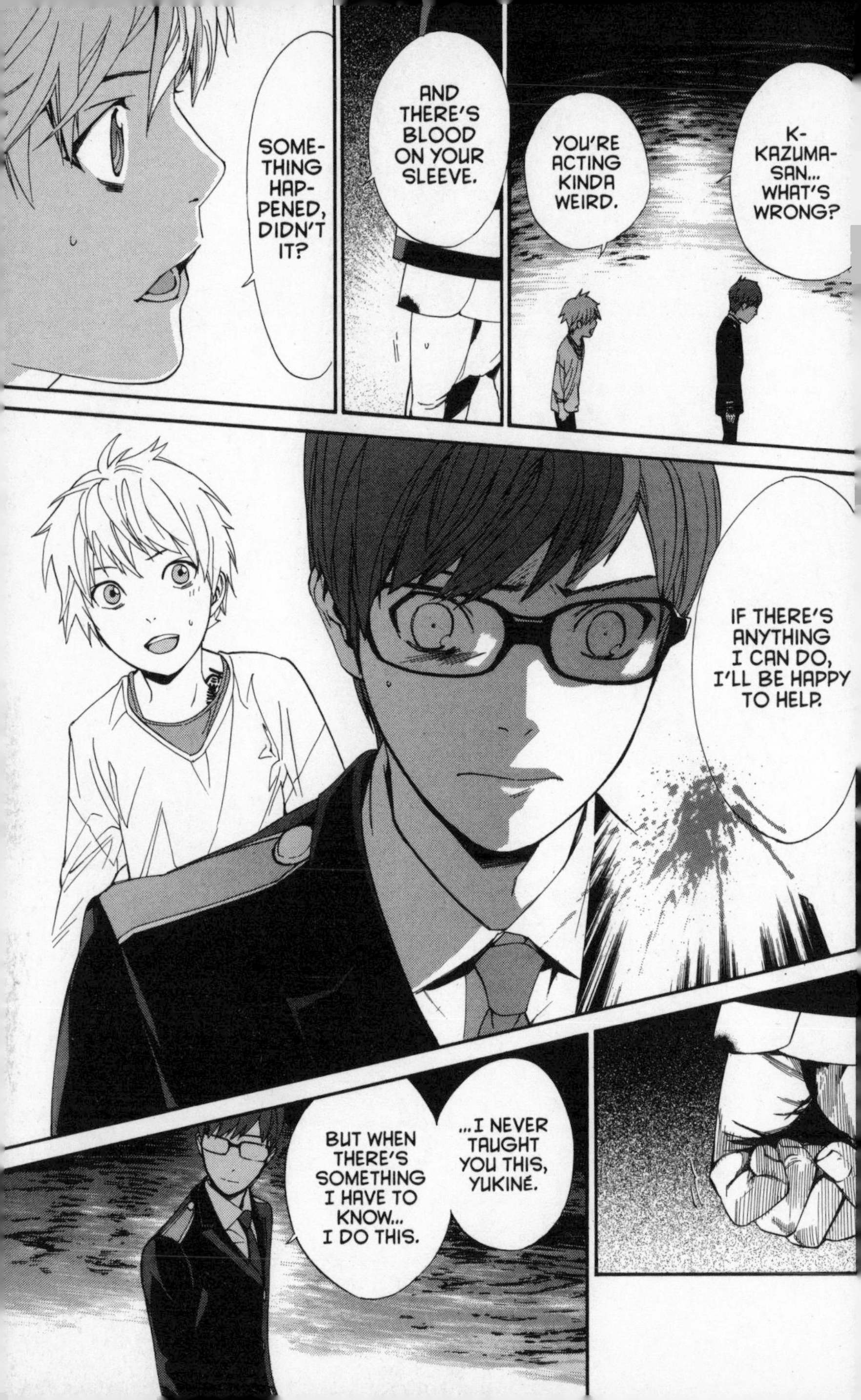
K-KAZUMA-SAN... WHAT'S WRONG?
YOU'RE ACTING KINDA WEIRD.
AND THERE'S BLOOD ON YOUR SLEEVE.
SOME-THING HAP-PENED, DIDN'T IT?
IF THERE'S ANYTHING I CAN DO, I'LL BE HAPPY TO HELP.
...I NEVER TAUGHT YOU THIS, YUKINÉ.
BUT WHEN THERE'S SOMETHING I HAVE TO KNOW... I DO THIS.

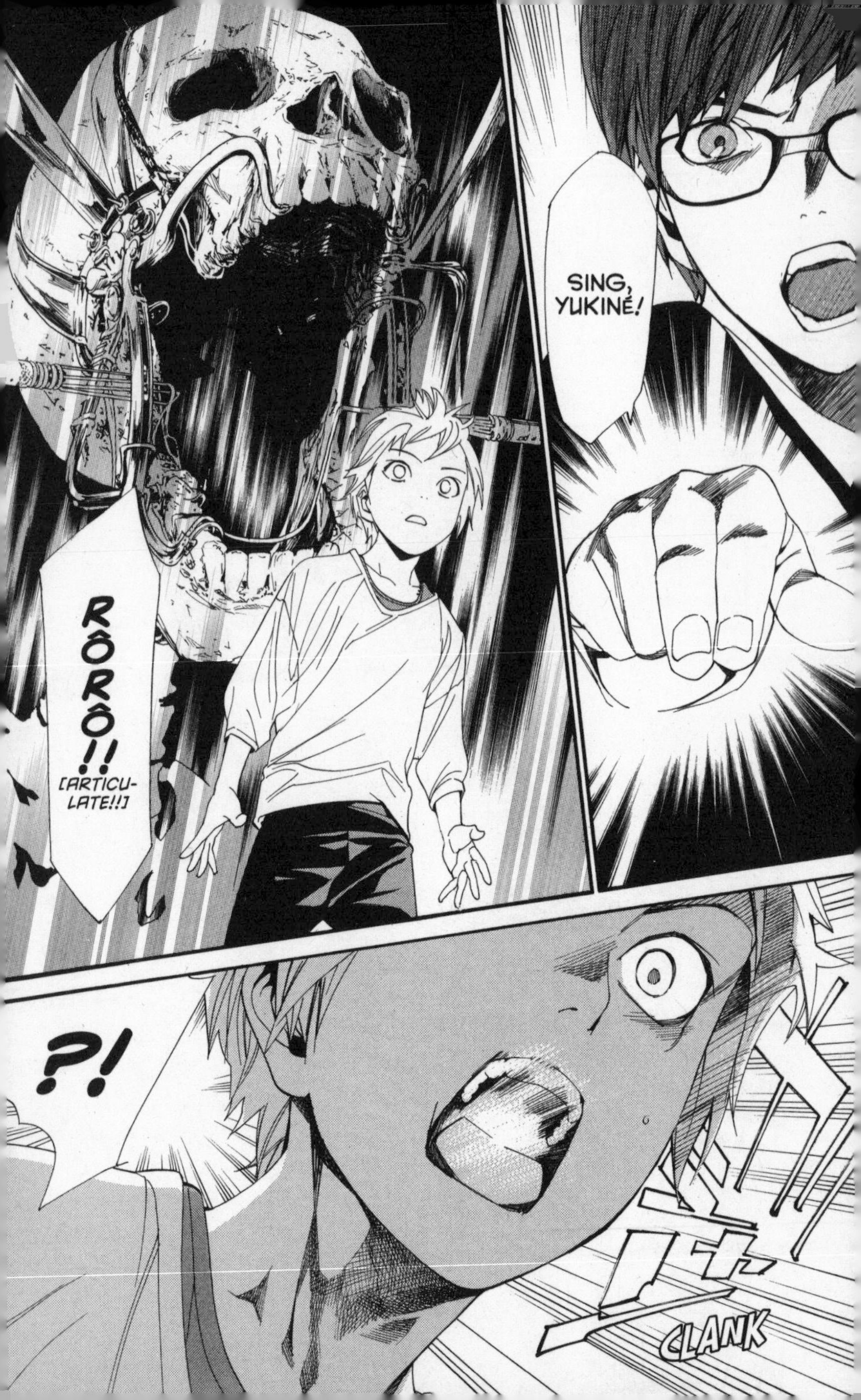
SING, YUKINÉ!
RÔRÔ!! [ARTICU-LATE!!]
?!
CLANK

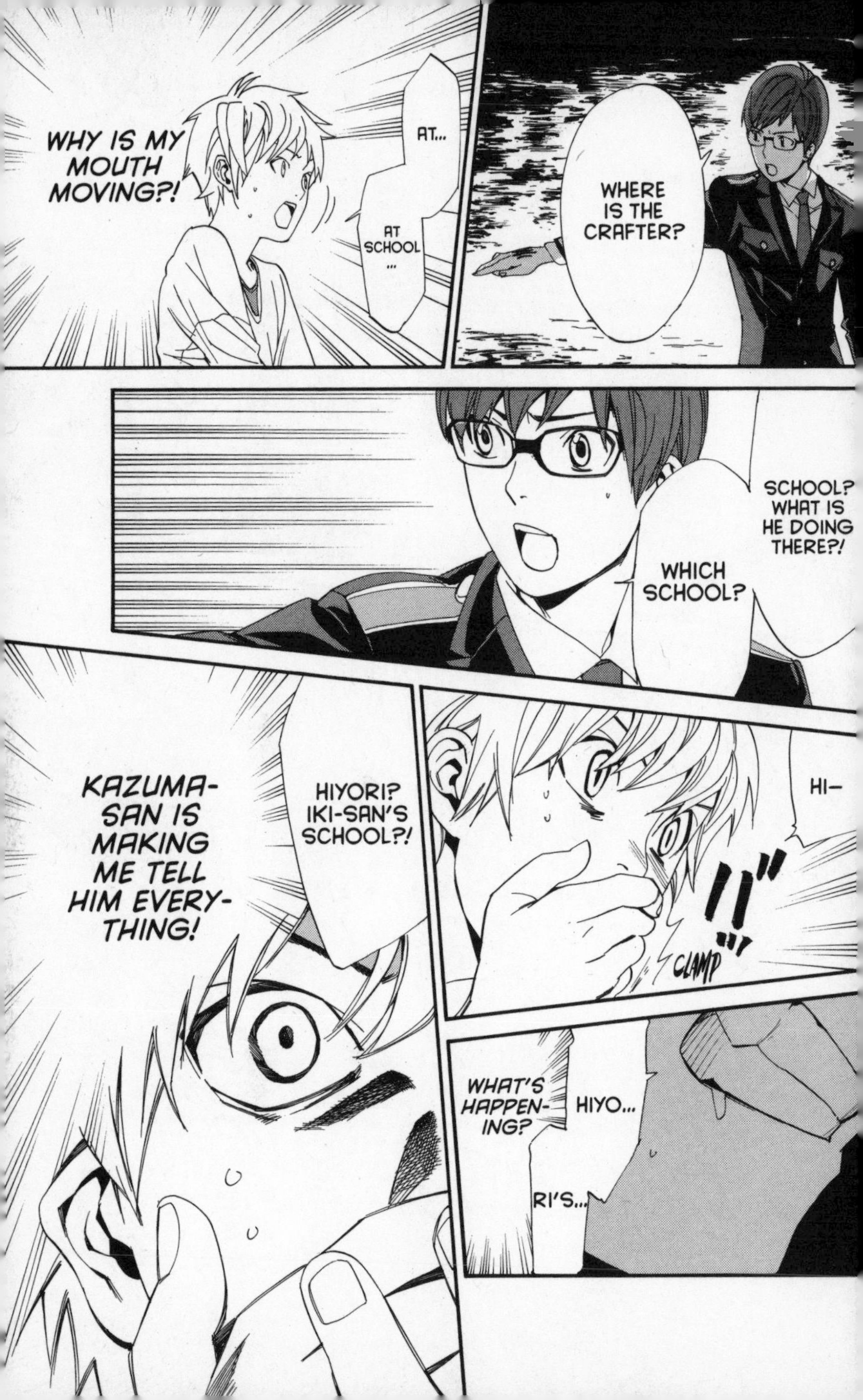
WHERE IS THE CRAFTER?
AT...
AT SCHOOL ...
WHY IS MY MOUTH MOVING?!
SCHOOL? WHAT IS HE DOING THERE?!
WHICH SCHOOL?
HI–
CLAMP
HIYO...
RI'S...
WHAT'S HAPPENING?
HIYORI? IKI-SAN'S SCHOOL?!
KAZUMA-SAN IS MAKING ME TELL HIM EVERYTHING!

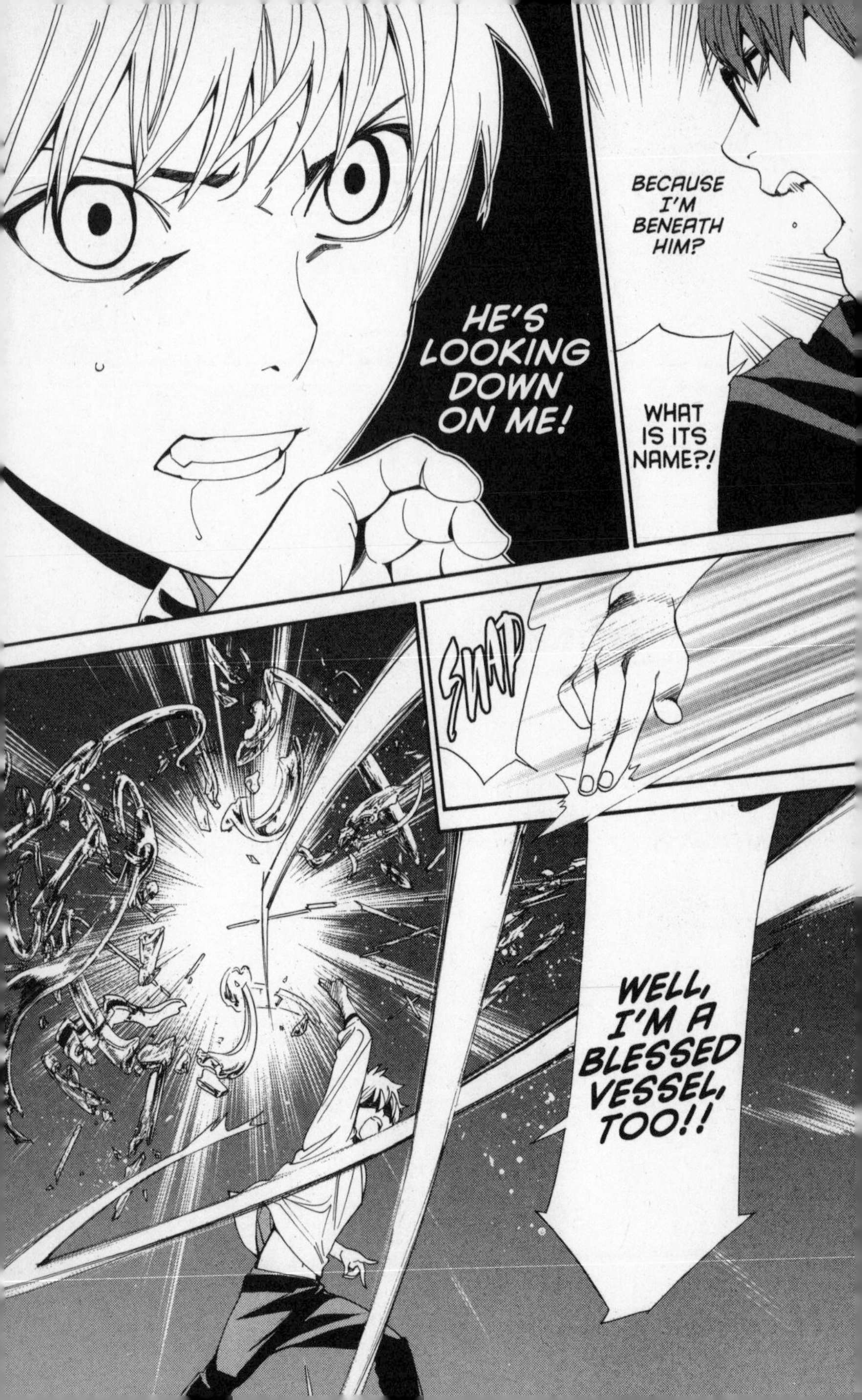
BECAUSE I'M BENEATH HIM?
WHAT IS ITS NAME?!
HE'S LOOKING DOWN ON ME!
SNAP
WELL, I'M A BLESSED VESSEL, TOO!!

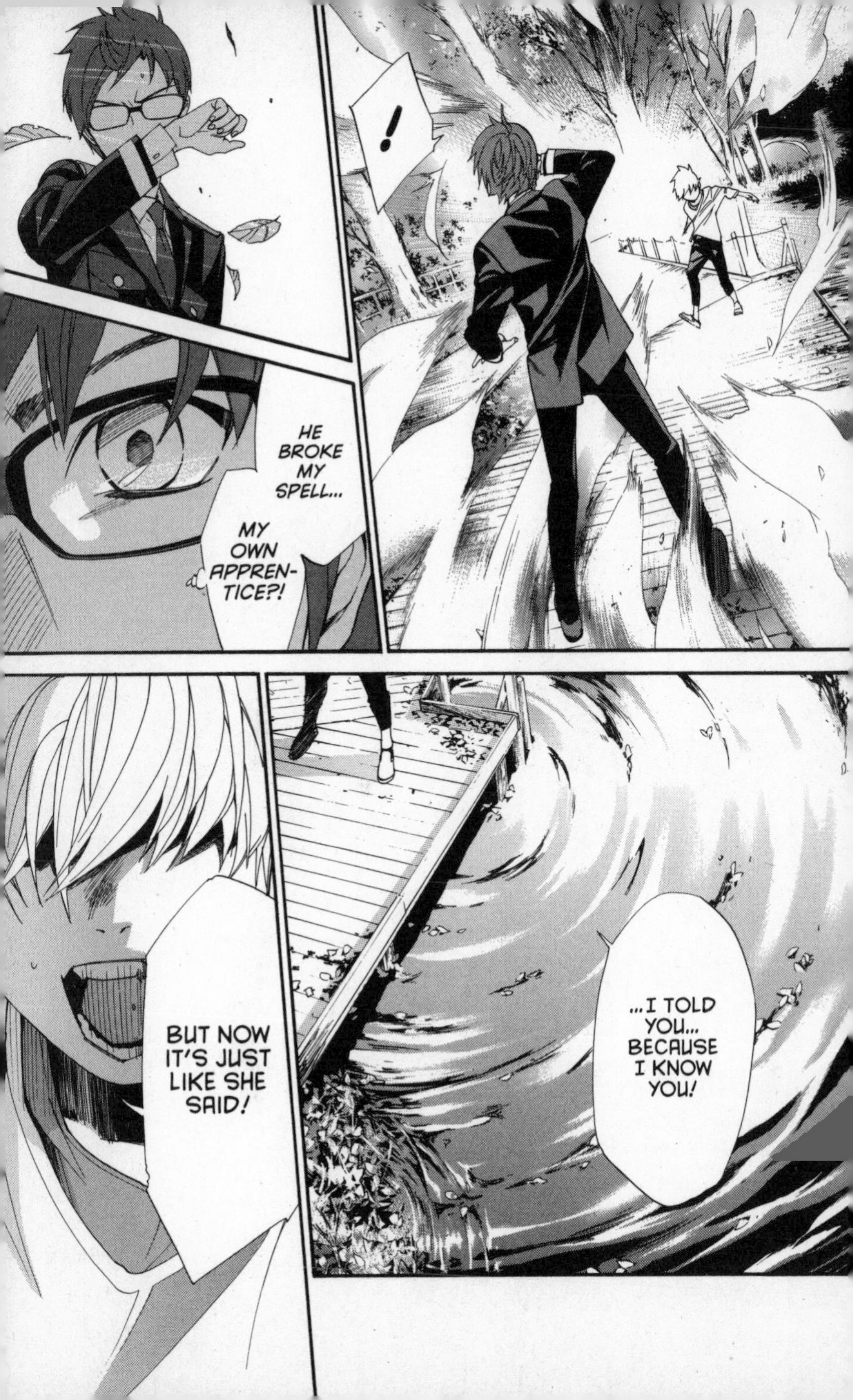
!
HE BROKE MY SPELL...
MY OWN APPRENTICE?!
...I TOLD YOU... BECAUSE I KNOW YOU!
BUT NOW IT'S JUST LIKE SHE SAID!

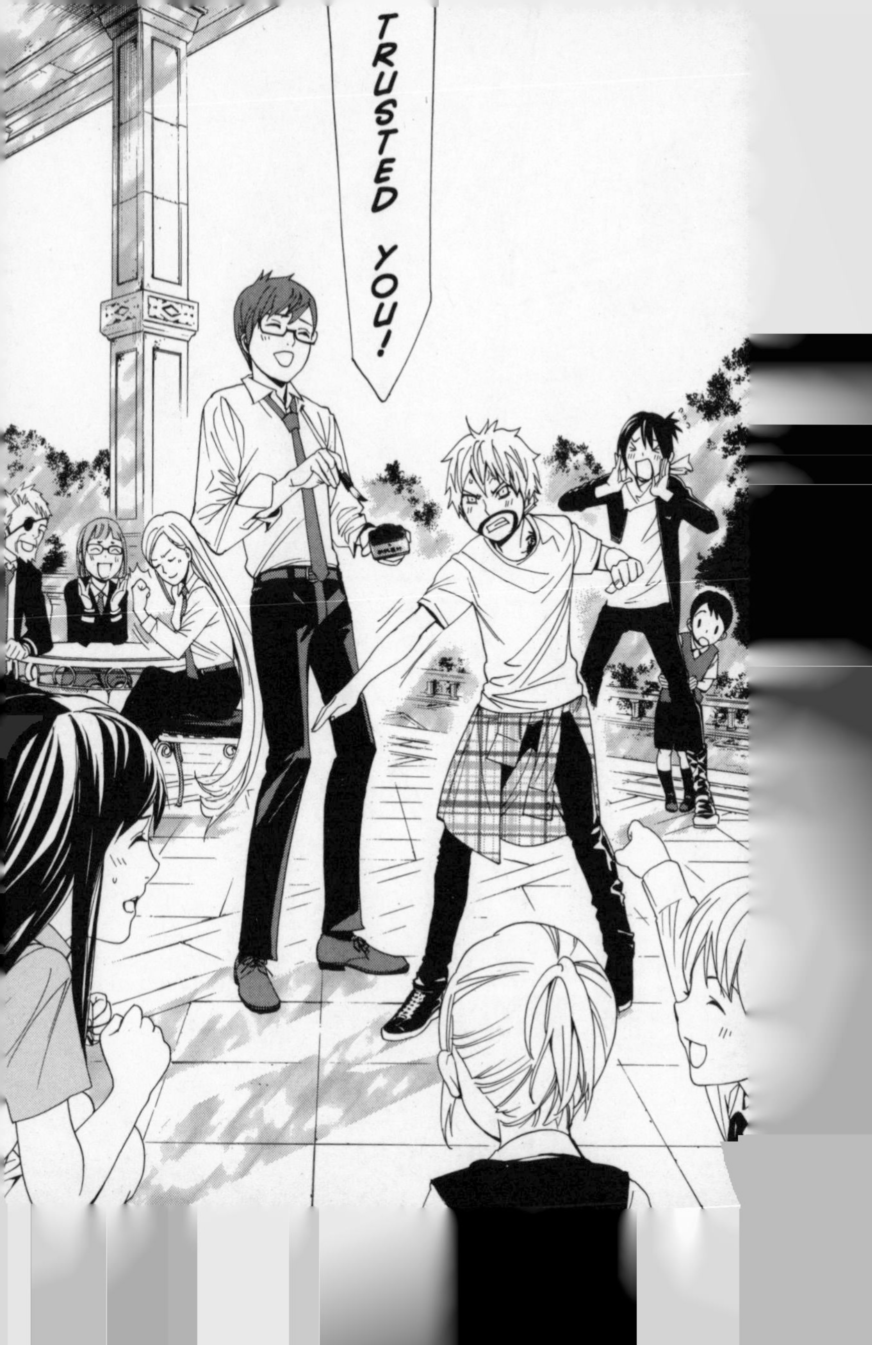
TRUSTED YOU!

野

兑

神

ATROCIOUS MANGA

BESTOWERS OF NAMES

ザ・ゴッドファーザー

—THE GODFATHERS—

DON OF THE NORAGAMI FAMILY
KANKÔ* AKA TENJIN
*ANOTHER NAME FOR SUGAWARA NO MICHIZANE
HIS AMBITION IS INSATIABLE! HIS POLITICAL ENEMIES ARE SENT INTO EXILE!
HIS GOAL: DON OF THE ENTIRE POLITICAL WORLD!!
MY LORD. SURELY YOU DO NOT INTEND TO ONE DAY BECOME PRIME MINISTER?
OF COURSE NOT. I WANT NOTHING OF THE SORT.
I WANT TO BE... REGENT.
MY LORD, YOU'RE IN THE WRONG ERA.

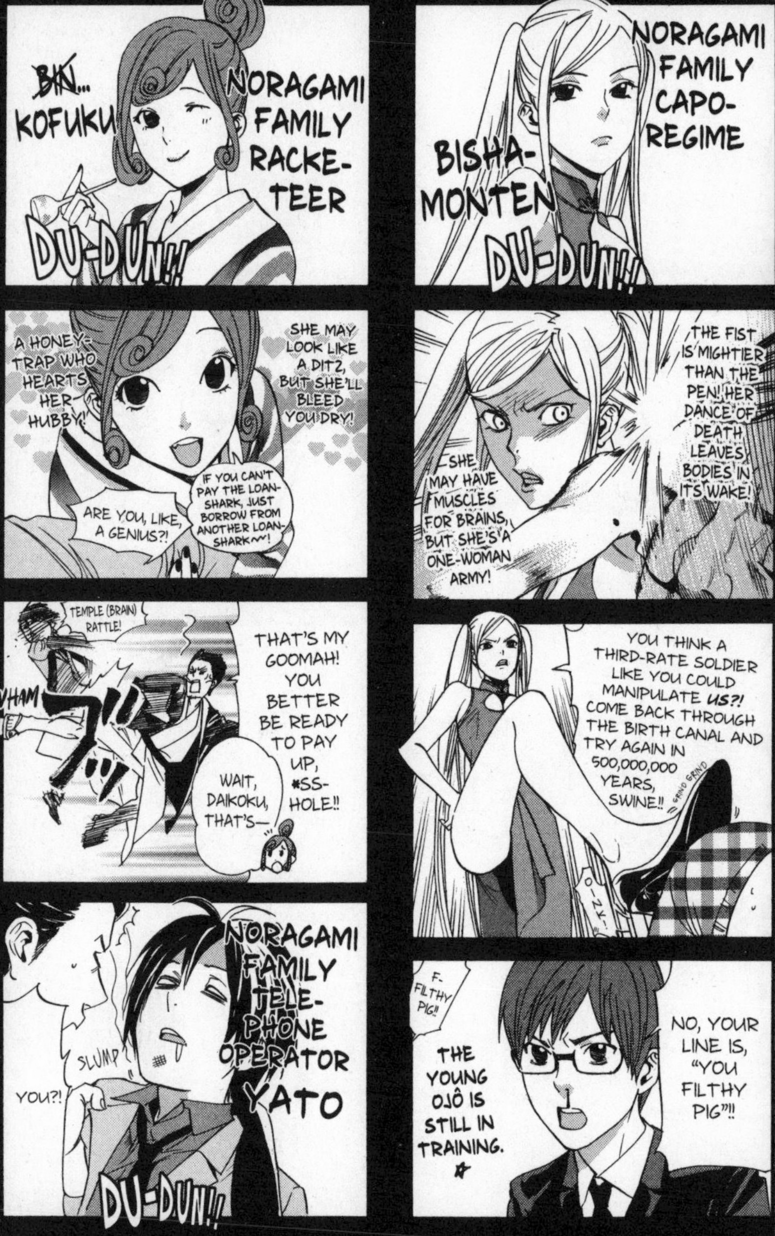
NORAGAMI FAMILY CAPO-REGIME
BISHA-MONTEN
DU-DUN!!
THE FIST IS MIGHTIER THAN THE PEN! HER DANCE OF DEATH LEAVES BODIES IN ITS WAKE!
SHE MAY HAVE MUSCLES FOR BRAINS, BUT SHE'S A ONE-WOMAN ARMY!
YOU THINK A THIRD-RATE SOLDIER LIKE YOU COULD MANIPULATE US?! COME BACK THROUGH THE BIRTH CANAL AND TRY AGAIN IN 500,000,000 YEARS, SWINE!!
GRIND GRIND
NO, YOUR LINE IS, "YOU FILTHY PIG"!!
F-FILTHY PIG!!
THE YOUNG OJÔ IS STILL IN TRAINING.
NORAGAMI FAMILY RACKETEER
BIN... KOFUKU
DU-DUN!!
SHE MAY LOOK LIKE A DITZ, BUT SHE'LL BLEED YOU DRY!
A HONEY-TRAP WHO HEARTS HER HUBBY!
IF YOU CAN'T PAY THE LOAN-SHARK, JUST BORROW FROM ANOTHER LOAN-SHARK~~!
ARE YOU, LIKE, A GENIUS?!
THAT'S MY GOOMAH! YOU BETTER BE READY TO PAY UP, *SS-HOLE!!
TEMPLE (BRAIN) RATTLE!
WHAM
WAIT, DAIKOKU, THAT'S—
NORAGAMI FAMILY TELE-PHONE OPERATOR YATO
SLUMP
YOU?!
DU-DUN!!

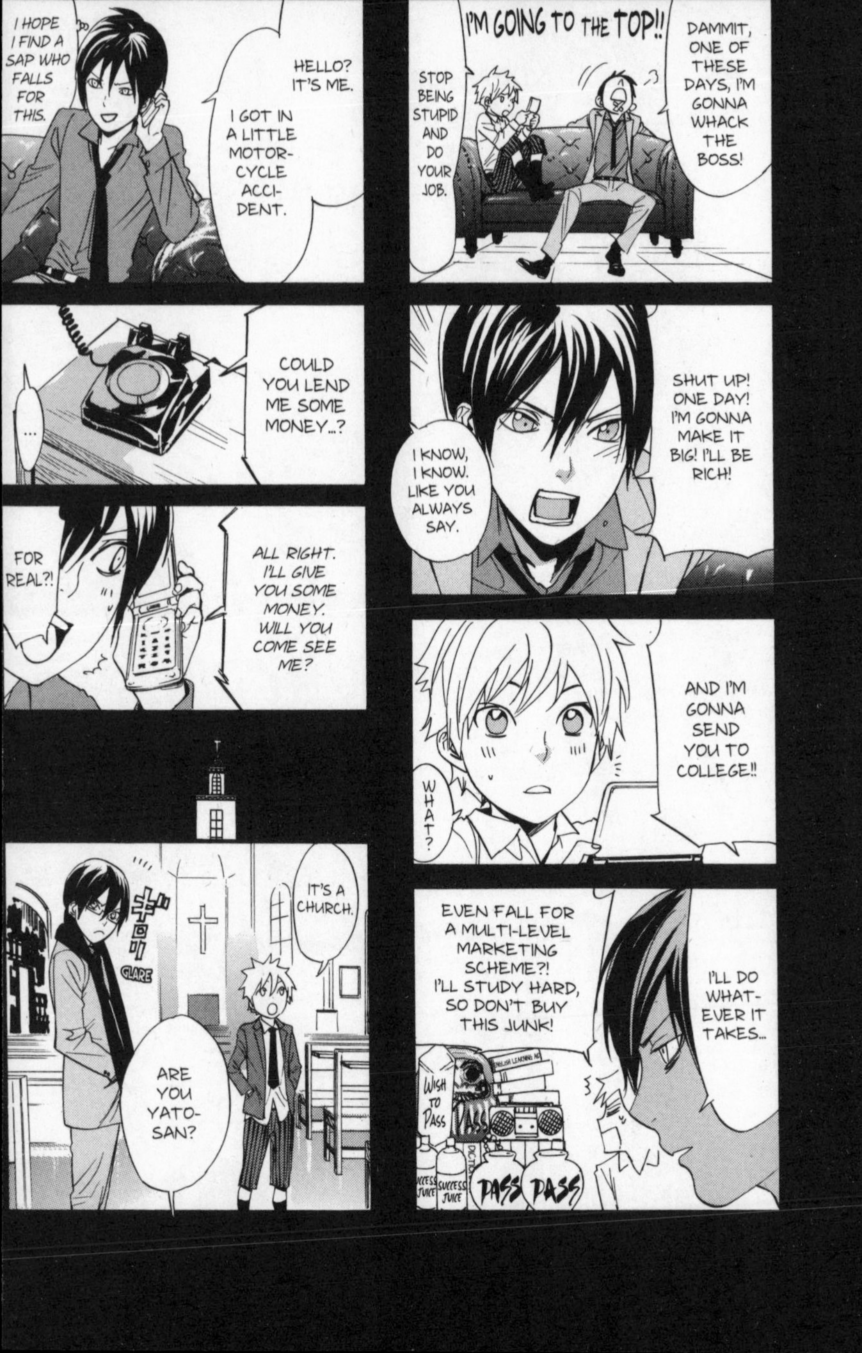
I'M GOING TO THE TOP!!
DAMMIT, ONE OF THESE DAYS, I'M GONNA WHACK THE BOSS!
STOP BEING STUPID AND DO YOUR JOB.
SHUT UP! ONE DAY! I'M GONNA MAKE IT BIG! I'LL BE RICH!
I KNOW, I KNOW. LIKE YOU ALWAYS SAY.
AND I'M GONNA SEND YOU TO COLLEGE!!
WHAT?
I'LL DO WHATEVER IT TAKES...
EVEN FALL FOR A MULTI-LEVEL MARKETING SCHEME?! I'LL STUDY HARD, SO DON'T BUY THIS JUNK!
ENGLISH LEARNING
WISH TO PASS
SUCCESS JUICE
SUCCESS JUICE
PASS
PASS
HELLO? IT'S ME.
I GOT IN A LITTLE MOTORCYCLE ACCIDENT.
I HOPE I FIND A SAP WHO FALLS FOR THIS.
COULD YOU LEND ME SOME MONEY...?
...
ALL RIGHT. I'LL GIVE YOU SOME MONEY. WILL YOU COME SEE ME?
FOR REAL?!
IT'S A CHURCH.
GLARE
ARE YOU YATO-SAN?

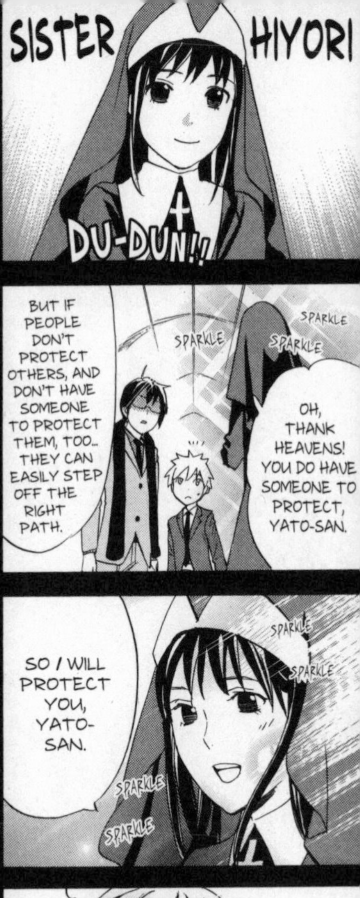
SISTER HIYORI
DU-DUN!!
SPARKLE
SPARKLE
SPARKLE
OH, THANK HEAVENS! YOU DO HAVE SOMEONE TO PROTECT, YATO-SAN.
BUT IF PEOPLE DON'T PROTECT OTHERS, AND DON'T HAVE SOMEONE TO PROTECT THEM, TOO... THEY CAN EASILY STEP OFF THE RIGHT PATH.
SPARKLE
SPARKLE
SO I WILL PROTECT YOU, YATO-SAN.
SPARKLE
SPARKLE
YATO IS CONVERTED!
I'M GOING LEGIT...
...ALL'S WELL THAT ENDS WELL?!
THAT WAS EASY.

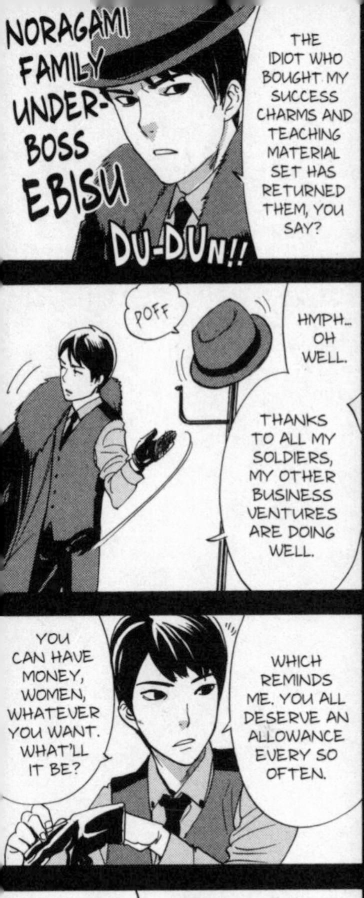
NORAGAMI FAMILY UNDER-BOSS EBISU
THE IDIOT WHO BOUGHT MY SUCCESS CHARMS AND TEACHING MATERIAL SET HAS RETURNED THEM, YOU SAY?
DU-DUN!!
HMPH... OH WELL.
THANKS TO ALL MY SOLDIERS, MY OTHER BUSINESS VENTURES ARE DOING WELL.
POFF
WHICH REMINDS ME. YOU ALL DESERVE AN ALLOWANCE EVERY SO OFTEN.
YOU CAN HAVE MONEY, WOMEN, WHATEVER YOU WANT. WHAT'LL IT BE?
TWIRL TWIRL!
WE WANT HUMAN RIGHTS.
WAIT, WAIT, KUNIMI. SAVE THE CANDLE SPIN UNTIL AFTER I'VE CHANGED CLOTHES.

[illegible]

[illegible]

師

TRANSLATION NOTES

Japanese is a tricky language for most Westerners, and translation is often more art than science. For your edification and reading pleasure, here are notes on some of the places where we could have gone in a different direction in our translation of the work, or where a Japanese cultural reference is used.

Crinkled old crazy, page 13

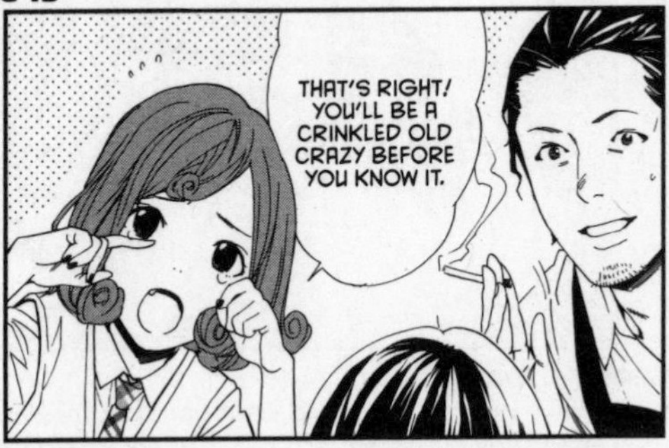
THAT'S RIGHT! YOU'LL BE A CRINKLED OLD CRAZY BEFORE YOU KNOW IT.

The expression used in the original Japanese is *shio-shio no paa*, which comes from a children's television show from the 1960's called *Kaijū Booska* (Monster Booska). The show featured a creature named Booska, who had his own nonsense-words to express various emotions. *Shio-shio no paa* was Booska's expression of disappointment, dejection, etc., and it may have come from a real Japanese phrase, *aona ni shio* (salt on greens), which is used to describe someone who has lost all their energy, like a vegetable that has wilted after being sprinkled with salt. Booska's phrase also happens to sound like *shiwa-shiwa no baa*, which means "wrinkled old lady." Kofuku may or may not have gotten the expressions confused.

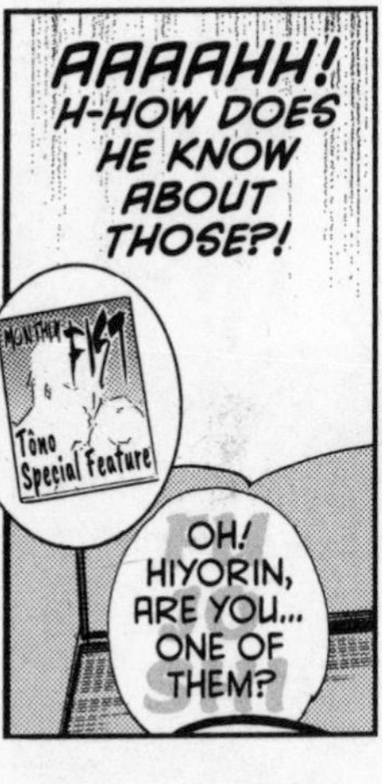
AAAAHH! H-HOW DOES HE KNOW ABOUT THOSE?!
Tōno Special Feature
OH! HIYORIN, ARE YOU... ONE OF THEM?

Fujoshi, page 14

Originally a respectful term meaning "woman," the word *fujoshi* has had its first *kanji* character swapped out for one meaning "rotten," thus turning *fujoshi* into a term which translates to "rotten woman." Certain fangirls use it to identify themselves as women who like to read or watch a different sort of naked guy-on-guy action than the wrestling that Hiyori enjoys.

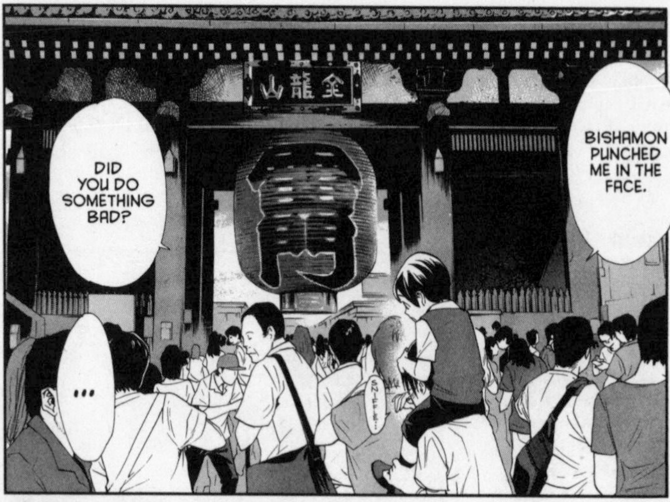

BISHAMON PUNCHED ME IN THE FACE.
DID YOU DO SOMETHING BAD?
...
SNIFF...

Sensô-ji, page 33

It has come to the translators' attention that they have failed to write a note for a single one of the many Shinto shrines and Buddhist temples that have appeared throughout Noragami. All but Yato's shrine are real places, most of which can be found in the Tokyo area. Sensô-ji, located in Asakusa, Tokyo, is known for the famous Kaminarimon, or Thunder Gate, pictured above.

Monk's staff, page 75

Specifically, Chiki takes the form of a Buddhist monk's staff known in Sanskrit as a *khakkhara* (sounding staff), or *shakujô* (tin staff) in Japanese. Because Buddhism forbids killing, the staffs were designed with rings that would rattle to warn small creatures (such as insects) to get out of the approaching monk's path so as not to be stepped on. The rattling also served to inform believers in the area that a monk in need of alms was present. Chiki has six rings, which could either represent the Six Perfections of Buddhism, or the six domains—hell, the preta domain, the animal domain, the asura domain, the human domain, and heaven. In Japan, monks were well trained in using these staffs as effective weapons.

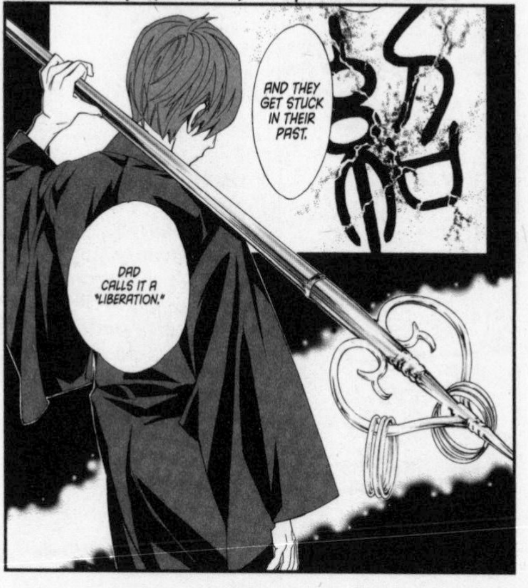

AND THEY GET STUCK IN THEIR PAST.
DAD CALLS IT A "LIBERATION."

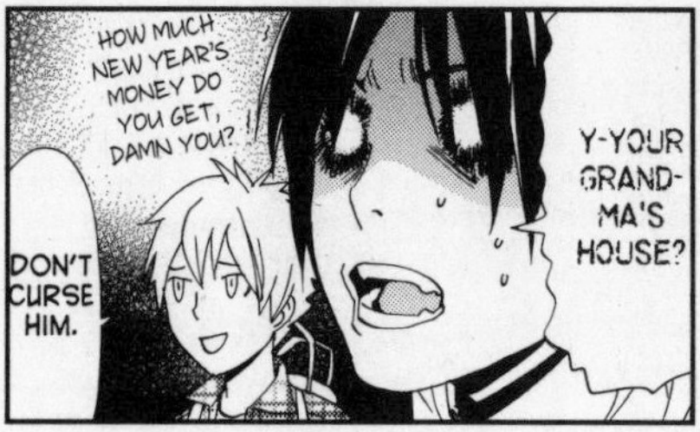
Y-YOUR GRAND-MA'S HOUSE?
HOW MUCH NEW YEAR'S MONEY DO YOU GET, DAMN YOU?
DON'T CURSE HIM.

New Year's money, page 103

It is tradition in Japan for parents and/or grandparents to give their children (or grandchildren) a gift of money on New Year's. It's not uncommon for the amount of money to be quite large, and it stands to reason that children with wealthy parents and grandparents would receive a larger gift.

Onii-chan versus Onii-sama, page 104

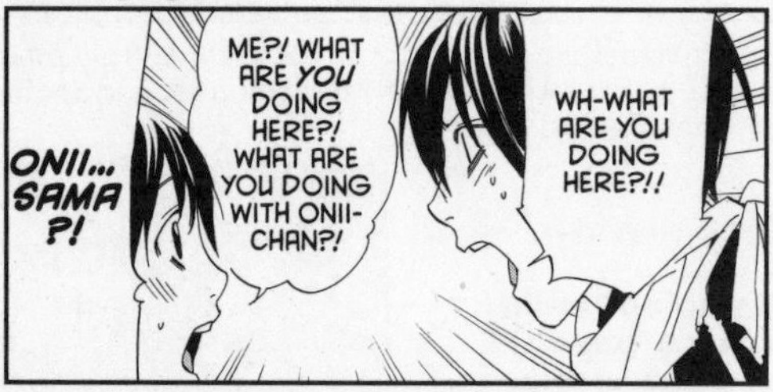
WH-WHAT ARE YOU DOING HERE?!!
ME?! WHAT ARE *YOU* DOING HERE?! WHAT ARE YOU DOING WITH ONII-CHAN?!
ONII... SAMA?!

Although we can't know for certain, there is likely some significance in Yato's choice to refer to Hiyori's brother as "Onii-sama." It is customary to address one's in-laws (or potential future in-laws) as if they were part of one's family. If a suitor has not yet won the family's favor, he or she may wish to get into their good graces by raising the level of respect. So, while Hiyori addresses her brother as "Onii-chan," Yato shows him the utmost respect (at least when addressing him) by calling him "Onii-sama" instead. Masaomi's reaction to the title indicates that he picked up on Yato's subtle declaration of intent.

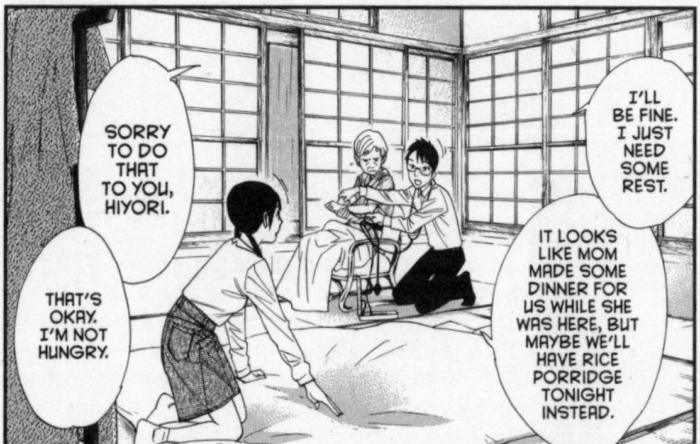
I'LL BE FINE. I JUST NEED SOME REST.
IT LOOKS LIKE MOM MADE SOME DINNER FOR US WHILE SHE WAS HERE, BUT MAYBE WE'LL HAVE RICE PORRIDGE TONIGHT INSTEAD.
SORRY TO DO THAT TO YOU, HIYORI.
THAT'S OKAY. I'M NOT HUNGRY.

Rice porridge, page 115

Rice porridge, or *okayu*, is a common dish served to people who are ill, because it is so easy to digest. It is made of mostly rice and water, possibly with toppings such as green onions or ginger to add flavor.

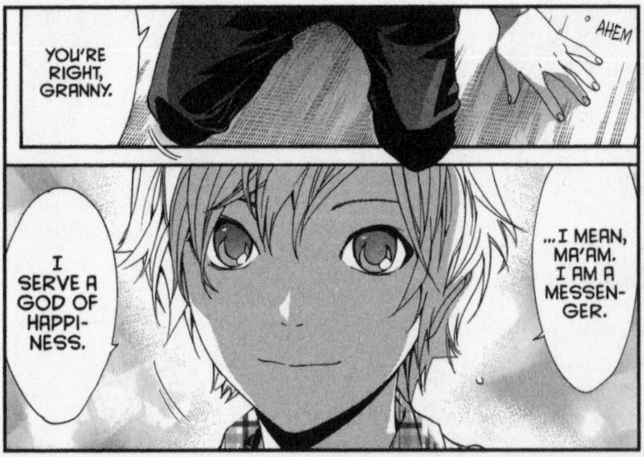
AHEM
YOU'RE RIGHT, GRANNY.
...I MEAN, MA'AM. I AM A MESSENGER.
I SERVE A GOD OF HAPPINESS.

Granny versus ma'am, page 129
The translators did a little bit of adapting here. What really happened is that Yukiné referred to himself as *ore*, an informal way of saying "I." Then, realizing that that's not the most polite way to address his elders, he switches to the more humble *boku*. Because we only have one first-person pronoun in English, it would sound a little odd to translate it literally: "I...I mean, I." So the translators found another way to express Yukiné's remembered manners.

Kameido Tenjin Shrine, page 170
Some readers may recognize this shrine from Volume 11, when Yato helped an old woman return a bracelet to its previous owner. This is the Kameido Tenjin Shrine in Tokyo, one of many shrines in the Tenman Group, and it is famous for its many wisteria blossoms.

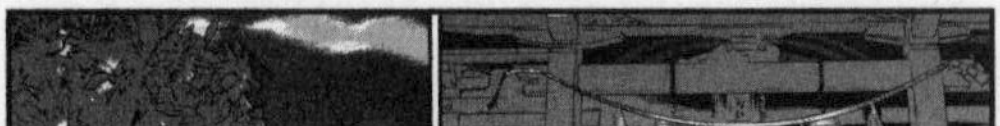

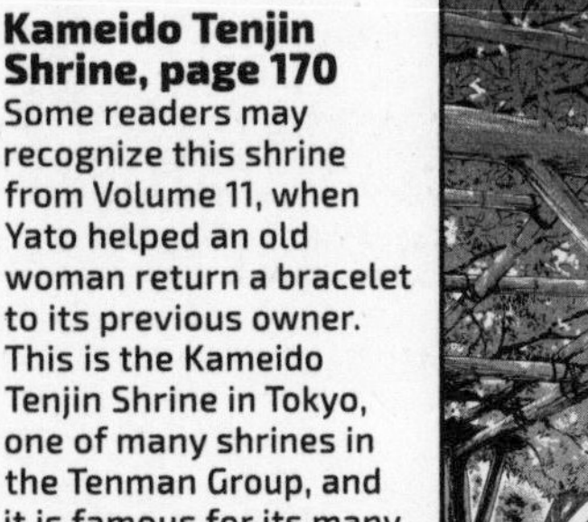
AND SO WE TOOK OFF IN THE STOLEN OX CARRIAGE...
MY LORD WAS SO YOUNG THEN...
IT SOUNDS LIKE SUCH A CAREFREE LIFE!

The stolen ox carriage, page 170
Back in Sugawara no Michizane's day, the ox carriage was a common mode of travel for the upper classes. Like expensive cars today, they were used as a means of showing off one's wealth, and were not necessarily the most practical way to get around.

Edachi & Saku, page 174
To help the readers understand the full extent of this shinki's floor art, the translators asked the letterer to provide this beautiful diagram. The shaded sections of the floor are where he has written the name Edachi, and the unshaded sections are where he has written Saku.

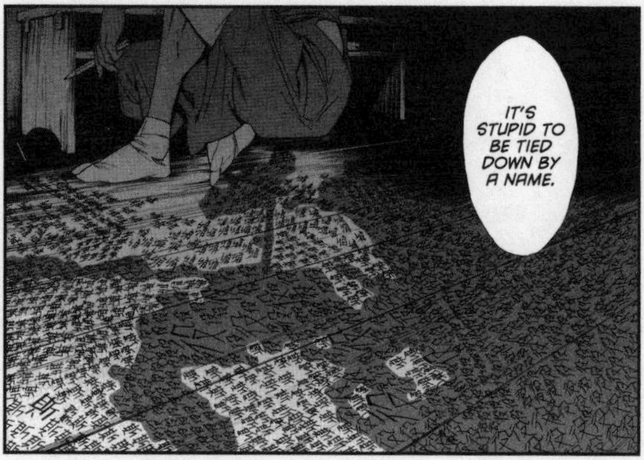
IT'S STUPID TO BE TIED DOWN BY A NAME.

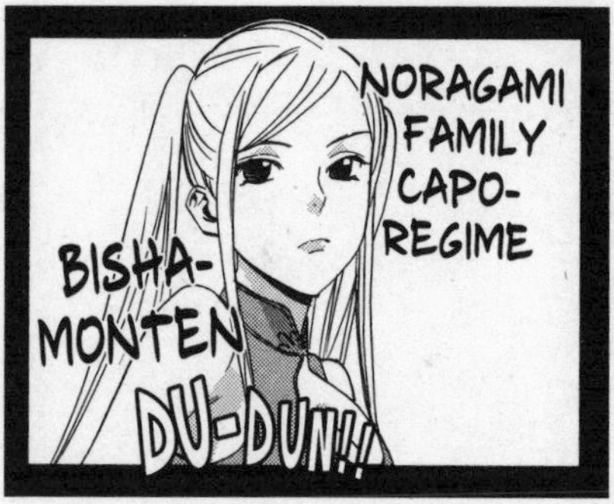
NORAGAMI FAMILY CAPO-REGIME
BISHA-MONTEN
DU-DUN!!

The Noragami Family Caporegime, page 189
Technically, Bishamonten is the leader of the Noragami Family's *kirikomi* squad, which is basically the hit squad, specifically dispatched to kill other *yakuza*.

Blesseditos and rubber signature stamp, page 197
In the Japanese language, often the main way to determine that a word is plural is to figure it out based on context. For example, the plural of shinki is shinki. That being the case, in modern times, sometimes a group of the same thing will be pluralized the English way—by adding an "s" to the end. So to get the "cool" name for a couple of blessed vessels, or *hafuri no utsuwa*, we add an "s" to it to get "*Hafuris*." The translators felt that merely adding an "s" to "blessed" wouldn't convey the fun of combining the word with a foreign language, so they chose to give the word a bit of a Spanish flavor.

As for the rubber stamp, in Japan it is common practice to use a *hanko*, or signature seal, to stamp one's name on official documents, package delivery forms, etc., in lieu of signing one's name. Adachitoka most likely took an eraser or some rubber designed for stamp-carving and carved the character for "blessed" on it to make a signature stamp for the Blesseditos. The font used is called *tensho*, or seal script, and, fittingly, is the same style of character that appears on a shinki's body when he or she receives a name from a god. The *kanji* character also means "celebrate," which makes it appropriate for many different special occasions.

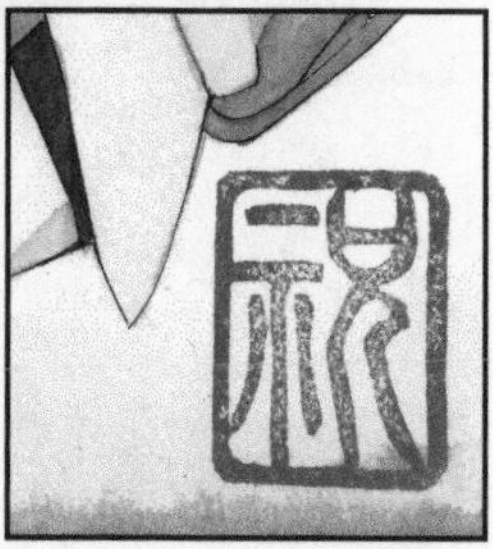

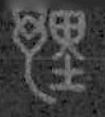

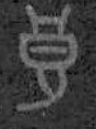

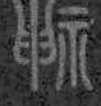

N
O
R
×
A
G
A
M
I

For the first time ever, this volume's cover features the Blessed Vessel Duo, the Blesseditos. I also made a Blessed rubber signature seal. It would be a shame to only use it the once, so I think I might use it on New Year's cards or something.

Adachitoka

A Kodansha Comics Trade Paperback Original.

Noragami: Stray God volume 14 copyright © 2015 Adachitoka
English translation copyright © 2016 Adachitoka

Published in the United States by Kodansha Comics, an imprint of Kodansha USA Publishing, LLC, New York.

Publication rights for this English edition arranged through Kodansha Ltd., Tokyo.

First published in Japan in 2015 by Kodansha Ltd., Tokyo.

ISBN 978-1-63236-255-1

Printed in the United States of America.

www.kodanshacomics.com

9 8 7 6 5 4 3 2 1

Translation: Alethea Nibley & Athena Nibley
Lettering: Lys Blakeslee
Editing: Lauren Scanlan
Kodansha Comics edition cover design: Phil Balsman